THE MAKING AND BREAKING OF MINDS

How social interactions shape the human mind

Isabella Sarto-Jackson, PhD

Konrad Lorenz Institute for Evolution and Cognition Research

Klosterneuburg / Vienna, Austria

Cognitive Science and Psychology

VERNON PRESS

www.vernonpress.com

In the Americas:
Vernon Press
1000 N West Street, Suite 1200
Wilmington, Delaware, 19801
United States

In the rest of the world:
Vernon Press
C/Sancti Espiritu 17,
Malaga, 29006
Spain

Cognitive Science and Psychology

Library of Congress Control Number: 2021947186

ISBN: 978-1-64889-465-7

Also available: 978-1-62273-331-6 [Hardback]; 978-1-64889-402-2 [PDF, E-Book]

Cover design by Vernon Press. Image by Gerd Altmann from Pixabay.

For
Kaylee and John

Table of Contents

List of Figures

Acknowledgments

This book would not have been written without the dedication of many Cognitive Science students from the University of Vienna and the Comenius University in Bratislava. My thanks go to all those excellent students who have contributed to the content of the book by working with great motivation on their frequently challenging projects, as well as spending months on evaluating and scrutinizing neuroscientific and cognitive science literature.

I owe deep gratitude to experts who introduced me to and taught me about social pedagogy, psychoeducation, and integrative pedagogy, especially Peter Sarto, Hermann Schügerl, and Stefan Sarto, respectively. Their professional expertise was invaluable for developing and framing the concept of the book. Equally essential for the book was Eva Lackner's critical view, which made sure that the content of the book was not only accessible to professionals, but also to the interested, non-professional public.

Three more scholars who need to be mentioned in relation to the interdisciplinary nature of the book are the unequaled philosopher, the late Werner Callebaut; the great scientist and polymath Ladislav Kovac; and the brilliant anthropologist Daniel O. Larson. Their sharp intellect and analytical thinking opened up novel paths of conceptualizing cognition, not least by including an evolutionary, developmental, and social context—all of which I drew from. I am also very grateful to the Konrad Lorenz Institute for Evolution and Cognition Research (KLI), in particular Gerd B. Müller, Guido Caniglia, and the Board of Directors of the KLI for contributing to provide an intellectually stimulating atmosphere and enabling interdisciplinary discourse that nurtures the growth of novel ideas and theories. The KLI distinguishes itself as a powerful incubator for these types of scientific advancements. I am glad to be part of this environment.

Some parts of the book have been presented in seminars and workshops. I am very grateful to all seminar and workshop participants for their thoughtful feedback that improved the clarity of several chapters. In addition, I am particularly grateful to have had the opportunity to discuss many aspects of the book in interdisciplinary symposia, most noteworthy those organized by Silke Gahleitner and colleagues. Above all, these interdisciplinary exchanges shaped the last chapters of the book.

Kayla Henley was essential to the process of structuring the chapters and for putting the last finishing touches to the book. I cannot thank her enough for being a wonderfully supportive, articulate, and at the same time meticulous editor.

Last but not least, I count myself extraordinarily lucky to have many special people in my life who have always been an inspiration and source of happiness while writing this book: my beloved Kaylee, John, Marlene, Quinn, Elena, Julia-Marie, Robert, Peter, Stefan, Monika, Elke, Sandra, and Shane in Austria, as well as Karin, Claire, Christian, Byron, Darcey, Rachel, Andrew, River, and Herbie in the U.K. For life would not be complete without an amazing family.

Introduction

Close to the historical city center of Vienna, there is an imposing building, opened first in 1862 by the Austrian pathologist, politician, and philosopher Carl von Rokitansky. The time-honored walls have served as the pathological-anatomical institution for more than a century. Visitors, students, and staff who enter the historic halls are welcomed by an epigraph at the pediment that still bears witness to its original dedication and reads *Indagandis sedibus et causis morborum*, which best translates to "Investigating the seat and causes of diseases." Today, the premises host the Center for Brain Research, a renowned research institution that is devoted to the investigation of brain functions in health and disease. Usually, the facilities of the center are not open to the public, but for one week every year, hundreds of teenagers between the ages of fifteen and eighteen flock into the venerable halls that are steeped in history. Once a year in March, the institute opens its doors for Brain Awareness Week, a global campaign to foster public enthusiasm and support for brain science.

In March 2014, about eighty teenagers, teachers, and a few other visitors crammed into the lecture hall of the Center for Brain Research. I gave a talk on the "Social Brain," discussing how social interactions shape the human mind. I was particularly interested in this topic, as I had previously changed my focus of research from molecular neuroscience to cognitive science and moved from the wet lab and microscopic studies of brain cells to a more theoretical approach, giving me a bird's eye view on the brain. My inspiring collaborations with philosopher and evolutionary biologist Werner Callebaut and anthropologist Daniel O. Larson particularly challenged a lot of assumptions and conceptual reasoning I had been trained in for almost two decades. Assumptions such as: it's the genetic makeup that determines our cognitive development. Or: all psychopathologies are a consequence of either a biological disease or a severe head injury. And last but not least: human cognition is the sole product of biological evolution, it's survival of the fittest, stupid!

The atmosphere in the lecture hall was exuberant, most likely due to the students' excitement of being out of their usual school setting and getting a whiff of the scientific world of brain research. The plenary discussion that followed the talk was vivid, and I tried my best to answer varied questions about brain processes, questions that usually derived from students' and teachers' own experiences and introspection. At the end of the event, I spotted my brother Peter, who was also in the audience. He approached me, coming to the front desk. Peter is a social education worker and was also teaching at the College of Social Vienna at that time.

Standing amidst a group of young students, he said, "I wish that many more people would learn about how our social environment shapes cognitive development. It would open our eyes to the importance of nurturing relationships, especially for children and teenagers."

"Social relationships are your domain," I responded with a smile, not fully understanding what he was trying to suggest. Scientists are usually more interested in elucidating theoretical causes of phenomena observed under very strict control of study parameters in experimental settings. When it comes to situations in daily life, scientists often have little to say—or prefer not to say much—about how research findings translate into real-life scenarios. Peter insisted that there was a lack of discourse between brain research and pedagogy, in particular social pedagogy. And this lack was to the detriment of all parties concerned.

He had a point. I remembered a conference I attended two years earlier that was organized by the Institute for Advanced Study in Delmenhorst, Germany. The conference was aimed at an interdisciplinary exchange between teachers and educators of biology and educational scientists. During one of the event dinners, I had the pleasure of sitting next to the keynote speaker of the conference, a professor of psychology and an expert in teaching-learning research. Throughout dinner, she repeatedly expressed her conviction that contemporary neuroscience could hardly contribute anything meaningful to psychology or help understanding how to educate children. By the end of the dinner, there was no feather left in the cap of a putative interdisciplinary endeavor between neuroscience and education. Her disdain for neuroscience was not directed at me or any of the other brain researchers present, in fact, one of her close collaboration partners was a neuropsychologist who specialized in neuroimaging of children during learning tasks. Her dismissal of the field was largely due to the fact that neuroscience, how she saw it, was a laboratory science that had nothing to contribute to real-life situations. While brain scientists sat in their professional ivory tower, educators and child psychologists were out there in the "wild" trying their best to fit day-to-day observations into traditional psychological theories. If anything, neuroscience may become relevant in a distant future when its methodology becomes applicable to genuine issues of everyday life. Until then, teachers, child care workers, and other experts working with children and teenagers had to rely on their real life, professional training, intuition, and historical, pedagogical knowledge. That's at least how my neighbor at the table saw it.

Remembering this incident at the conference dinner in Germany, I knew Peter's argument was right. Neuroscientists do not interact much with educators. There are of course some occasions of interdisciplinary exchange of individual researchers, but very often the fields remain separate, exposing a scarily vast explanatory gap that none of the disciplines is willing to tackle. And there are good reasons for hesitation. The human brain is complex; trying to understand it requires the joint effort of many subdisciplines, and we are still decades, if not centuries, away from having a solid picture of how any brain, let alone the human brain, works. In 2013, the European Union funded the Human Brain Project that employed scientists from more than a hundred partner institutions. A staggering one billion Euros were pumped into this flagship project with the aim of elucidating the mechanisms that underlie cognition, learning, and memory formation. Despite impressive advancements produced in the course of this huge, international endeavor, a comprehensive explanation of how the brain gives rise to the aforementioned cognitive processes still seems as far as ever.

I tried to dodge Peter's complaint. Researchers see it as a virtue to keep a low profile rather than offering speculations that are not fully substantiated by empirical data. I, like so many other scientists, had subscribed to this conviction for a long time. Much more research on cognition is required before we can connect the interdisciplinary threads of all data available. I was convinced that with this cautious stance, I voiced the opinion of the scientific community, not just my humble opinion. It's bold, if not irresponsible to make scientific claims without having all evidence necessary for a conclusion.

"Do you think it is more responsible to wait until scientists have gained a more complete understanding of the workings of the human brain while some people still accept it as a fact that their childhood experiences have little to do with their cognitive development frequently ensuing struggles later in life?" Peter challenged my reluctance.

That evening, I went home pondering how basic research often seems detached from what is going on around us. That is actually considered to be a good thing. As a researcher, you want to be objective—unaffected by anecdotal evidence or spurious cases. The more you accept a certain theory or follow a certain concept, the less open you are to critique, disproof, and counterfactuals. In a nutshell, as a researcher, you need to stay detached. Or not? The more I discussed and exchanged with philosophers of science, the more I became aware of how untenable the belief of objectivity in science really is. While many scientists may still argue that scientific claims are objectively describing facts about the world, it has been shown for a plethora of situations, including scientific work, that individuals' experiences vary greatly with personal situations, idiosyncrasies, the methodology and instruments available, as well as language, gender, and culture. In fact, psychologists have long emphasized an important distinction between sensation and perception to account for how aspects and phenomena from "out there" in the world are processed within our brains—be it the brain of a scientist or any other person. Thus, true objectivity in science is a naïve idea. Thomas Kuhn's and others' analyses have convincingly shown that scientists always view research problems through the lens of a paradigm that is bounded by axioms, methodological presuppositions, state-of-the-art techniques and concepts, and so forth. History and philosophy of science can open our eyes to how science has been and still is riveted by its academic zeitgeist and carve out conceptual shortcomings as inevitable consequences of our bounded rationality as humans. Perhaps it was time to look at brain development and cognition through the lens of social pedagogy? Maybe it was time to set the focus on cognitive development in children growing up in impoverished environments and under socio-economic hardship?

Fast forward a few years. The idea that social interactions have an immense impact on infant brain development has gained momentum in brain research. More and more scientists have started to look into how nature and nurture are intertwined. Researchers have designed ingenious studies—sometimes lasting over many years—that elucidate how stress, trauma, and deprivation influence the human brain. Such empirical observations and experiments pertain to an individual's development as well as transgenerational phenomena. The importance of social interactions for cognitive development—especially during infancy, childhood, and puberty—has become an undeniable factor in the scientific quest of understanding cognition. Yet how much of these findings have reached a destination where experts from neighboring disciplines or other fields can use these novel insights? There is still much to be done to bridge the interdisciplinary gaps and foster collaboration.

After the discussion I had with my brother in 2014, I have more and more closely worked with experts from various fields, including social workers, developmental psychologists, and child psychoanalysts. Many of the insights provided in the book are based on long discussions that familiarized me with puzzling discoveries or observations from fields of expertise separate from my own. Frequently, I was challenged to rethink previous, and often too simple, technical suppositions that followed ceteris paribus assumptions (i.e., all other things being equal or held constant). Sometimes, my conclusions were turned topsy-turvy, especially when I met children, teenagers, and adults whose personal history challenged findings from laboratory settings. In all cases, the people I had the pleasure and honor to work with were a constant inspiration to me and my work.

Some of the most important issues on the influence of social environment on human cognition that came out of these interdisciplinary interactions with a multitude of people shall be discussed in this book, a book that is the culmination of work and insights from numerous individuals—I just have the privilege of putting them into writing.

Chapter 1

Shedding New Light on the Nature-versus-Nurture Debate

When the male semen is enclosed in a hermetically sealed vessel for forty days and "putrified" in venter equinum, a moderately warm water bath that is supplied by the fermentation heat of horse dung, a human-like being will be generated from itself, but one that is transparent and without a body. By nurturing this being with the "arcanum sanguinis humani" – human blood – for 40 weeks, a quite vivid human child is created similar to one born by a woman, but much smaller. The former we call homunculus.

— Paracelsus. De generatione rerum naturalum (In: De Natura Rerum)

This excerpt of a recipe of how to generate a human-like creature—a so-called homunculus—without the need of a female womb can be found in Paracelsus' book *De Natura Rerum* that was published in 1584 and exerted its influence over centuries. Paracelsus, the medieval scholar, healer, and alchemist, provides herein a practical guide for the creation of life by mixing organic ingredients like semen and blood.[1] Nonsense. Superstition. Nobody would believe such unscientific babble anymore... yes, of course. But historically entrenched ideas resist abrupt disposal and often remain in our cultural knowledge for a long time. They might even change their appearance and get disguised in new, more reputable theories. The idea of human creation is such an example of how old, mythic notions strongly contributed to the intellectual framework of later scientific concepts. Paracelsus' homunculus constituted the foundation of how natural scientists of the seventeenth century thought about human procreation.

In 1677, Johan Ham discovered tiny particles in male semen and established the basis for the so-called preformation theory that prevailed until modern times. The Dutch astronomer and naturalist Nicolas Hartsoeker speculated in his work, published in 1694, that these tiny particles observed by Ham each

---

[1] Paracelsus, *De Natura Rerum*.

contain a microscopically small copy of an adult human.[2] Therefore, man must be preconstructed and development is simply a process of growth that allows the prebuilt organism to reach its mature, intended state. In the seventeenth and eighteenth century, Hartsoeker's illustration of the crouched man in a sperm cell (Figure 1.1) became an iconic representation of the process of procreation.

Until the nineteenth century, the scientific understanding of how human organisms develop was based on the idea that a miniature version existed within each male[3] human. Just like matryoshkas—the Russian nesting dolls— it only required the unfolding, or rather unwrapping, of the tiny person during development. In fact, the German word for development *Entwicklung* is synonymous with "unwrapping."

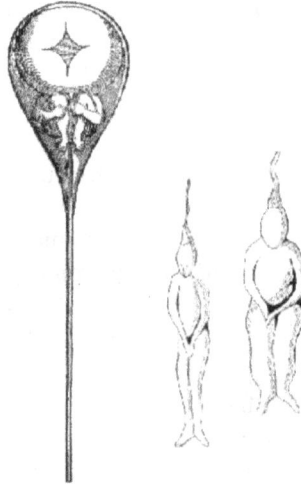

Figure 1.1: N. Hartsoeker's homunculus derived from a sperm cell. Lawrence, Cera R., "Hartsoeker's Homunculus Sketch from Essai de Dioptrique," *Embryo Project Encyclopedia (2008-08-14).*

With these major biological discoveries in the twentieth century, the dogma of preformed miniature humans increasingly lost supporters and was replaced

---

[2] Lawrence, "Hartsoeker's Homunculus Sketch from Essai De Dioptrique."

[3] The spermists, such as Hartsoeker, assumed that females only contributed to the nurturing of the developing being by providing egg cells as nutritional basis. This was in opposition to the ovists like Malpighi, Swannerdam, Vallisneri, who subscribed to similar ideas about the developmental process, but assumed that it was the female eggs rather than sperm cells that contained the miniature organism.

by concepts of modern biology. Modern biology owes its success to many mothers and fathers, one of them being Charles Darwin. One of the ground-breaking conceptual shifts was his publication *On the Origin of Species* in 1859 and the theory of evolution by natural selection set forth therein. As originally formulated by Charles Darwin and Albert Russel Wallace, the theory of evolution asserts that the environment puts selective pressure on organisms, resulting in the survival of those who are well adapted to the environment and further reproduction to generate the highest number of offspring.[4] Of course, Darwin did not know anything about the molecular mechanisms of inheritance. The discovery of genes and DNA as a carrier of the genetic information came much later, at the turn of the nineteenth to the twentieth century, and increasingly more biochemical details were discovered in the first half of the twentieth century. This makes Darwin's insights into the processes of inheritance and the formulation of his evolutionary theory all the more impressive.

Not all aspects of Darwin's original ideas have survived; some have been replaced, others proven wrong, and some have undergone a revival due to unexpected and more recent scientific findings. Originally, Darwin proposed in his pangenesis theory that minute particles, so-called gemmules, resided anywhere in the body and could be modified by the environment. These particles aggregated in the reproductive organs and were then transmitted from parents to offspring. Thus, Darwin believed in the inheritance of acquired characteristics—something that nowadays is usually associated with Lamarckism, a school of thought that fell in strong disfavor. With increasing empirical evidence from germplasm theory and the chromosomal theories of inheritance, the notion of gemmules was replaced with that of genes. The idea that the environment could modify heritable units and thereby transmit environmentally acquired information was wholly rejected. Only at a much later time, at the end of the twentieth century, the role of the environment in evolution has regained interest in the research field of epigenetics (see Chapter 4). The theory of evolution has undergone several scientific adjustments, yet the conceptual framework of natural selection appears as valid as when it was first published. It is, however, important to be aware that how we understand evolutionary theory today is not fully based on Darwin's original ideas, but draws from numerous findings from decades of scientific research and is owed to many ingenious minds. For the longest time in the twentieth century, the resulting prevailing theoretical framework of evolution was the Modern Synthesis. This largely mathematical approach reconciled Darwin's theory of evolution and Gregor Mendel's laws of inheritance (the laws were

---

[4] Darwin, *On the Origin of Species*.

independently rediscovered by the botanists Hugo DeVries, Carl Correns, and Erich von Tschermak-Seyseneggr thirty-five years after Mendel first published the observations of his plant breeding experiments, but received no attention during his time).

Today, school children already learn that genetic information is encoded in the double-helical strings of DNA (deoxyribonucleic acid) that are packed into chromosomes and are found in all our bodily cells. With this knowledge, we no longer believe in Paracelsus' recipe and magical powers emanating from horse manure, but rather rely on scientists in well-equipped laboratories to generate organisms by molecular or synthetic biological techniques. Understanding how an organism emerges from a relatively simple macromolecule like the DNA was also one of the many underlying motivations of researchers who aimed at deciphering the human genome. If one could decode the human genome and those of other animals, we would not only be able to understand the complete construction set of how to generate humans, we could also figure out what makes us the idiosyncratic individuals we are. What makes some of us susceptible to certain diseases? What makes us tall, strong, handsome, or intelligent? We could also find out what discriminates us from our next relatives, such as chimpanzees or bonobos and ultimately pinpoint what makes us human. Spurred by such high expectations, the two research groups, the "International Human Genome Sequencing Consortium" and Celera Genomics, competed for being the first in decoding the complete human DNA sequence before the turn of the millennium. In 2000, both groups published the first results of the complete human genome. The front page of the *New York Times* of June 27, 2000, read, "Genetic Code of Human Life Is Cracked by Scientists." Dr. Francis S. Collins, director of the National Human Genome Research Institute and leading scientist of the consortium said that "[w]e have caught the first glimpses of our instruction book, previously known only to God."[5] With the beginning of the new millennium, scientists have decoded the secret of life and human nature! But did they really? Do genes hold the precise instructions to create a being with all its capacities? Is the DNA a blueprint that exactly predicts each developmental step leading to a fully mature, predetermined creature? Before nodding our heads in awe, let us glance into the past and shed some historical light onto these questions.

Let us begin with a retrospective look at the 1930s and the economic depression that transpired. The genetic world sensation of that time happened in the form of quintuples of the Dionne family. In 1934, five baby girls were born in a Canadian village. It was a medical sensation that all five children survived, each of them only nine inches long at birth and together weighing less than

---

[5] Wade, "Genetic Code of Human Life Is Cracked by Scientists."

fifteen pounds. Yet the real scorcher for the rest of the world was the fact that the Canadian multiples—Annette, Cecile, Emilie, Marie, and Yvonne—were monozygotic. The girls looked like peas in the pod, five identical ones to be precise (Figure 1.2). At one point, this amazing similarity caused them to become a bigger tourist attraction than Niagara Falls.

Figure 1.2: Ontario Premier Mitchell Hepburn with the Dionne babies in 1934. From the Library and Archives Canada, "Mitchell Hepburn with Dionne Quintuplets," reproduction reference number C-019533.

Being removed from their parents and other siblings, the Dionne girls grew up on a newly constructed farm that was built in order to provide an environment where the kids could be closely observed as well as exhibited to the public. The farm was dubbed *Quintland* and in no time changed into a leisure park to become an immensely popular tourist destination. More than 6,000 daily visitors wanted to stand on the observation decks of the farm and watch the famous children through the one-way mirror. Inspired by the touristic success of this "fivefold subject matter," media and PR companies soon also wanted to capitalize on them. Contracts were signed on behalf of the children and plenty of money flowed into the coffers of the local government of Ontario, who held the guardianship of the children at that time. The infants could be marveled at in TV commercials, ads in papers and public spaces, and they even appeared in Hollywood films. Almost as a side effect, media talked their viewers into believing that the Dionne girls were not only genetically identical, but also loved the exact same things: be it their favorite food, clothes, or toothpaste. The subtle message conveyed was: same genes, same personality (Figure 1.3).

Figure 1.3: Dionne quintuplets (at the age of 13) in 1947 with their parents and a priest in the background. From the Library and Archives Canada, reproduction reference number PA-155518.

The message perfectly met the trend for biological determinism of the time. By the middle of the last century, gene centrism became the guiding principle in biology, its message spilling over to the general public. It carried forward the dictum: everything that makes us unique—our appearance, character, behavior, and so on—is predetermined at the moment of conception by the genetic program stored in our cells.

How does this credo hold up to newer scientific findings? Is everything we need to predict a person's traits, from eye color to intelligence, precisely encoded in the double helix? Indeed, the genetic information that is encoded in the double-helical DNA provides the necessary instructions to create the molecular building blocks of an organism, but does this mean that the DNA also contains the exact plan of how to assemble the building blocks? How to build a living being out of an exhaustive set of macromolecules? Preformationism sensu Hartsoeker and coevals has been proven wrong; geneticists and molecular biologists have expelled the imaginary manikins. The errant concept of the preformed homunculus has been replaced by the enlightened concept of a genetic construction kit. Rather than accepting the idea of a nested miniature man, we now accept that all living beings steadfastly develop by following an encrypted molecular blueprint.

Is this really all there is to the story of organismal development? The brilliant American biologist and evolutionary theorist Richard Lewontin was one of the harshest critics of this gene determinism. He called this way of gene deterministic thinking a modern form of preformationism. According to him, with the advent of gene centrism, the homunculus was simply replaced by the DNA molecule! The double-helical DNA has become the new iconoclastic symbol of organismal development (Figure 1.4). In lieu of an obligatory unwrapping of tiny Russian dolls, the compelling force is now attributed to genes. Genes are believed to execute a precise program that allows the generation of a complete organism by just uncoiling the double helix and reading letter after letter encoded in the DNA molecule.

Figure 1.4: The iconoclastic symbol of today, the DNA double helix
Public Domain Picture, Ref. 17902 from Pixabay.

Increasingly, more scientists have voiced strong doubts about this strict gene deterministic view. Especially when studying the (human) brain and cognitive processes, such a simplified, deterministic approach seems particularly unhelpful. This dissent leads us again back into history, to the nature–nurture debate that has its roots in the seventeenth century. In those days, philosophers René Descartes argued that humans possessed innate ideas (at that time, it was of course assumed that innate ideas were not based on biological-cognitive substrates, but emerged as God-given epiphanies). In opposition to this view, John Locke contended that the mind was a "blank slate" (the idea of the *tabula rasa* can be traced back to Aristotle, who first mentions that the human soul is an "unscribed tablet")[6]. Over the centuries, many scientists have grappled with the question of what is innate and what is based on learning and experience. Of all lines of research, probably the most spectacular ones—and closly followed by the general public—were twin studies, like the Dionne girls. Having mentioned the role of twin studies in biomedical science, a word of caution is warranted here. Over the course of the last century, many twin studies were performed under ethically questionable and inhumane conditions and misused for ideological reasons. It will fill several books to elaborate on those black marks on science, but I won't follow up on this topic here. Instead, my main concerns address aspects of the nature–nurture divide in those studies,[7] particularly studies that adhered to ethical principles. At the very outset, let me emphasize that despite decades of twin studies, there is still a massive disagreement about which conclusions can be drawn from the studies. Have we come any further in the nature–nurture debate since Descartes' and Locke's dispute? Given the success of genetics, can we assume that the decision was made in favor of genes, and thus innateness?

Perhaps the Dionne quintuples can contribute to this question. At *Quintland*, the five genetically identical children grew up thoroughly separated from the rest of the world and closed off from any human contact other than interactions with their physician, Allan Roy Dafoe, and a few nurses who took care of the daily routines of the children. This unnatural setting made the children ideal objects of studies, similar to lab rats. Retrospectively, it is evident that in the eye of the general public, only the infants' similarities were commercialized. The differences among the quintuples, their individualities, were not a big selling point and thus intentionally ignored. But were there physical, psychological, or cognitive differences between the five? Remarkably, in spite of their identical genetic outfit, the five Dionne children were quite different with respect to their health. Already at a young age, Emilie developed epilepsy and eventually died from suffocation during an epileptic seizure when she was only twenty years

---

[6] Locke, *An Abridgment of Mr. Locke's Essay Concerning Human Understanding.*

[7] I aim to refer mainly to retrospective studies, i.e., of primary importance was the fate of the children. Decisions were made in the interest of the children's welfare (or what was then considered best for them). Subsequent studies were done only after the lawful decision took place. Those studies predominantly applied statistical methods and investigated monozygotic versus dizygotic twins or, in much rarer cases, on monozygotic twins who grew up in separate families and domestic environments.

old.[8] Marie, the smallest of the five, suffered in her first two childhood years from a hemangioma, a benign tumor that was treated several times with radon tubes. As an adult, she had alcohol problems and was hospitalized for nervous depression. Marie died of a blood clot in the brain at the age of thirty-six. The other three sisters outlived Emilie and Marie for decades. Yvonne died of cancer when she was sixty-seven. The other two women, Annette and Cecile, are still alive today (as of 2021). Doctor Roy Allan Defoe, who spent most of his time with them during their childhood years, also documented other physical differences of the monozygotic quintuplets, such as different body heights and eyesight. As for the latter, Yvonne, Annette, and Cecile were far-sighted, but had otherwise normal vision. Emelie had little astigmatism in both eyes, and Marie had some incoordination of the eye muscle and did not always use both eyes equally. Despite their identical genetic inheritance (also reflected in their disease susceptibility[9]), the lives of the Dionne quintuplets turned out quite differently. Three of them—Marie, Annette, and Cecile—married and had children. Marie, who had severe psychological problems, placed her two daughters in foster care. Marie was the artistic one of the five and worked as a librarian. Emilie, the one who died young, went to a convent to become a nun.

The quintuplets' gaping life paths prompt us to ask: How much of a person's development and trajectory can be reliably predicted by peeking into one's genetic information? Are we creative, intelligent, happy, and successful because we had the right parents and our inherited gene combinations turned out to be in our favor? Or the opposite: are the simple-minded, less intelligent, unhappy, and unsuccessful individuals simply those who drew the short straw from the gene pool? If we go by this assumption, we contend that the intellectually limited and unsuccessful people amongst us may just be victims of a random and disadvantageous combination of genetic variations. Nothing we can do about their misfortune! At this point, I believe many of you may have become increasingly uncomfortable subscribing to a universal doctrine of genetic determinants for every aspect of our life. And you might ask yourself which role the environment plays in this argumentation.

Perhaps the divergent life journeys of the Dionne girls reflect interindividual variations that can unequivocally be attributed to environmental factors experienced later in life? After all, the girls did not only share the exact same

---

[8] According to the British Columbia Epilepsy Society website, Yvonne, Cecile, and Annette also developed epilepsy as adults, yet there were no reports of their epileptic conditions anywhere else.

[9] It is important to mention that epilepsy is multi-causal and many environmental factors can contribute to it; amongst other risk factors, being born prematurely significantly increases the risk of developing epilepsy.

genes, they also spent nearly the entire first nine years of their lives in the same, hermetically sealed environment with almost no contact with the outside world. Whatever happened afterwards to them might have triggered these differences in health and personality. Unfortunately, it is not quite as easy to pin down which factors are causally involved in healthy development. Despite the apparent commonalities of their childhood experiences, each Dionne baby experienced different situations—some of them not immediately relevant. In addition, many factors were never measured or detected at all. For example, two sets of Dionne children developed in shared embryonic sacs while in their mother's womb. The fifth one is believed to have shared an embryonic sac with a miscarried sixth baby,[10] a circumstance that may have affected her development and growth in a different way to the other four. Also, the first days after their birth, the larger two of the newborns spent more time in a basket by their mother's bed while the smaller three stayed in an incubator. This was undoubtedly of paramount importance for their survival. Preemies with such a low birth weight have difficulties maintaining a steady body temperature due to having less intrauterine time to accumulate and store body fat. The developmental process of fat storage usually occurs during the last five weeks of gestation, a period when preterm babies are already living outside the womb. Babies have a large surface area-to-weight ratio and quickly lose temperature if not kept warm. It is hard work for the preemies' little bodies to keep themselves at the proper temperature. They use a great amount of energy and oxygen to stay warm; ten percent more oxygen is needed for every one degree of colder skin temperature, to be precise. This energy and oxygen ideally should be used to help the baby grow and develop. It was therefore crucial for the survival of the quintuplets that an incubator was available to keep them warm. However, today, we know that babies benefit from having skin-to-skin contact with their mother. The so-called kangaroo mother care (KMC)—the practice of holding the baby on the bare chest with a blanket draped over the baby's back— has been proven to give premature and low birth-weight infants better chances of thriving later in life. In the case of the Dionne babies, the three smaller girls were physically separated from their mother longer than the other two. This may have had adverse effects for the more fragile ones of the five. In addition, one of the girls suffered from another devastating incident; a short note written three days after birth reports that the most delicate of the five experienced an episode in which her heart almost stopped beating and her whole body turned

---

[10] The mother suffered two hours of severe cramping and reportedly expelled a small, black egg-sized piece of tissue, which possible could have been Cecile's twin.
Rosack, "The Dionne Quintuplets: Perinatal Care à La 1930s Style," 348–355.

blue from lack of oxygen. Luckily, the baby was resuscitated by the nurse, who gave her a bit of rum as a stimulant.

Taken together, in spite of their shared environment, each girl was most likely also exposed to unique situations (we are aware of only a tiny fraction of them). Some of these experiences might have been subconsciously life threatening or traumatizing and could have had a lasting impact on them.

What are the chances of disentangling these factors and answering the question about what is inborn versus what is acquired? The more complex a trait (personality, psychological capacities, or cognitive abilities, etc.), the more uncharted territory we enter. Many biologists have long acknowledged the importance of environmental factors on gene expression, and thus development. Yet the gene deterministic view is still influential amongst scientists and non-scientists alike. It is still standard to read about genes *for* cancer, genes *for* autism, genes *for* language skills, etc. Moreover, discussions about genetic explanations for all sorts of physical and behavioral traits are no longer the topic of a few privileged researchers but attract public interest everywhere, via books, media, classrooms, private homes, and the public sphere. The impact of biology on our daily life is ubiquitous and already deeply entrenched in common parlance. Think of phrases like "You are just like your mother;" "You are your father's spitting image;" "A chip off the old block;" "Like father, like son;" "She has her mother's eyes." Such statements implicitly assume that we all agree on the predominance of biological (genetic) factors. Such a gene deterministic view has far-reaching consequences, especially for social or ethnic fringe groups. If traits, including cognitive abilities, are nothing more than manifestations of a genetic lottery, then nurturing environments won't be seen as effective measures. This assumption justifies arguments against positive social intervention against attempts to eradicate poverty, and against discrimination of marginal groups. Interventions may be seen as wasted effort as one tries to combat an inevitable, biological, and hereditary load. These contrary stances have developed a particularly antagonistic relationship in the fields of intelligence research.

In the field of intelligence research, genetic determinism became tragically famous by means of misguided psychometrics. Ironically, psychometrics started off as a well-intentioned approach to support socially deprived children. At the end of the nineteenth century, French psychologist Alfred Binet developed a test—the first IQ test in history—to investigate the cognitive performance of children of different age groups. He noticed that socioeconomically underprivileged children on average did worse on his tests than children of the same age. By providing special education, Binet aimed at helping these socioeconomically deprived children to cognitively catch up with their peers. The reliability of these early psychometric tests was remarkable. So remarkable that American psychologist Henry H. Goddard, who was quite skeptical toward psychometric studies at first, became quickly convinced of their accuracy. While Goddard used the test for assessing mentally disabled children at the beginning of his career, he later adopted it to routinely examine the intelligence of immigrants. His test results made big waves: Goddard discovered that eighty percent of the immigrants he tested turned out to be "feeble-minded."[11] This result pertained to immigrants from Hungary, Italy, Russia, and Jewish people. Shortly after these unexpected findings, Goddard published the results of his psychometric analyses of U.S. soldiers who fought in World War I. Again, he reported that different ethnicities exhibited marked differences in intelligence. Based on these findings, he came to the conclusion that certain communities and ethnic groups were born cognitively inferior. Much later in his life, Goddard conceded that his research had suffered from flaws. However, by then his publications were already deeply embedded in the public awareness and continued to haunt researchers as well as laypeople for a long time. This deep entrenchment within the general public's opinion was most likely due to the fact that his data exhibited socially and politically explosive force. One hundred years later, we have not yet broken free of the resulting prejudices. Some groups still face discrimination based on prejudices concerning their ostensible lower, inborn intelligence. Not so long ago, in 1994, political scientist Charles Murray and professor of psychology at Harvard, Richard Herrnstein, argued in over eight hundred pages in their book *The Bell Curve: Intelligence and Class Structure in American Life* that they found a strong correlation between socio-economic class and intelligence. According to these authors, it is fifteen times more likely for people of the lowest economic class to have IQ values in the bottom five percent range. Afro-Americans of the lower class in the U.S. exhibit an IQ that is on average about fifteen points lower than that of Caucasians.[12] This data prompted Murray and Herrnstein to claim that people born to Afro-American families or to families with low income are quite simply born with relatively low cognitive abilities. The most obvious alternative explanation, namely that poverty and belonging to certain ethnic groups may result in fewer chances to fully develop one's cognitive capabilities, is bluntly denied by the authors. Consequently, Murray and Herrnstein recommend that any social policies fostering underprivileged children will show little effect on individual intelligence. On the contrary, they conjure up a scenario in which educational and social subsidy programs will lead to an overall decrease of the nation's intelligence due to stupid people being encouraged to produce increasingly more descendants. Such mistaken social interventions will

[11] Dennert, "The Embryo Project Encyclopedia."
[12] Herrnstein and Murray, *The Bell Curve.*

generate a downwards spiral of stupidity, so they claim. More recently, similar arguments were entertained by Thilo Sarrazin in his best-selling, polemic book *Deutschland schafft sich ab* that was published in 2010.[13] The arguments given in these and similar publications are based on the central assumption that complex psychobiological traits such as intelligence are genetically determined. But has this conjecture about the innateness of intelligence been scientifically proven?

Sixty years after Goddard's large-scale testing of immigrants, researchers Seymour B. Sarason and John Doris have re-evaluated the same psychometric tests.[14] More precisely, they looked into the questionnaires, which were used about one hundred years ago to test Italo-American immigrants. They indeed confirmed Goddard's results: the then-tested immigrants apparently exhibited an IQ of only 87,[15] which is clearly below average (the average IQ within a given population is always 100 *per definitionem*). But a follow-up study revealed something staggering. Much to everybody's surprise, a significant change has happened in the heads of the immigrants' descendants. The grandchildren of Italo-American immigrants when tested psychometrically displayed IQ values that were significantly higher than average! These are of course comforting results for a group of people previously considered to be cognitively challenged, though the crucial point is: how can such a successful pursuit race that culminated in a catch-up and even in the outperformance of the average population be explained? Can genetic variation and natural selection be held responsible for such a staggering increase in intelligence that took place over the duration of only two generations? Certainly not. Genetic variations and mutations within a population followed by natural selection are relatively slow processes that cannot lead to such a significant jump in the evolution of cognitive traits. Clearly, this argues against the postulate that intelligence is solely based on innate factors.

Political scientist James R. Flynn has demonstrated that IQ values of the population of fourteen different industrial nations have increased between five and twenty-five points over the last decades. In his book, published in 2012, *Are We Getting Smarter?* Flynn shows an annual increase of 0.35 IQ points in Germany's population and an increase that is almost twice as high in Brazil and

---

[13] Sarrazin, *Deutschland Schafft Sich Ab Wie Wir Unser Land Aufs Spiel Setzen.*

[14] Sarason and Doris, *Educational Handicap.*

[15] At the same time, Sarason and Doris demonstrated that many of the immigrants who were tested performed so poorly because they did not understand a lot of English words and phrases used in the questionnaires. It thus remains to be shown what the main reason for the bad test results were: low cognitive abilities or poor English language skills.

Turkey's population.[16] Such massive increases cannot simply be ascribed to genetic variation and "betterment" of the population's gene pool.

What does this tell us about genetic inheritance of intelligence? Surely, there are differences between individuals due to genetic differences, but the myth that people are being born less intelligent because of their ethnicity or social class is scientifically untenable. Population-wide or nationwide increases in intelligence[17] at such a fast pace can only be explained by taking social factors into account. Consequently, support, nurture, education, improved living conditions, and many more factors clearly contribute to children's intelligence.

Evolutionary biologist Richard C. Lewontin said it best:

> Take two handfuls of seed from the same sack and plant them in separate plots, the first rich and the second deficient in nutrients. The plants in the first plot will grow tall and those in the second will be stunted. The average difference between the two groups of plants will be due entirely to environmental factors (nutrients), because the seeds come from the same sack and are therefore genetically the same. But the variability within each plot will be due entirely to genetic factors, because the environment is identical for all seeds within the same plot. In other words, heritability is 100% within each group, but the average difference between the two groups is due entirely to environmental factors.[18]

Thus, according to Lewontin, the concept of heredity of their difference is meaningless when comparing two populations. Yet a gene deterministic view talks us into believing that genes are *the* omnipotent controlling authority, which leaves little leeway for environmental influences on the organism. We must be aware that such a blinded line of thinking will inevitably guide us into a cul-de-sac.

It has become increasingly clear that there is no program that precisely determines each developmental step of an organism. This holds even more true for the brain. It is uncontested among scientists that there is no blueprint that exactly tells an organism how to precisely wire a brain. In fact, brain researchers have long shown that above all, it is the interactions with the environment as well as between individuals that are indispensable for the healthy development of a neonate's brain into an adult's brain. This emphasis

---

[16] Flynn, *Are We Getting Smarter?*

[17] There is still an ongoing debate about whether and to which extent intelligence can be measured by means of psychometric tests.

[18] Colman, "Race Differences in IQ," 182–189.

on the crosstalk between organisms and environment ascribes a more versatile role to the world we live in, a role that is different from just being reduced to the force of natural selection. Here, the physical and social environment actively contribute to shaping the organism rather than only exerting selective pressure and thereby "weeding out" maladapted individuals. Scientists have long acknowledged that the environment can act as "trigger" to switch on certain developmental processes. The underlying molecular account goes as follows: based on their genetic makeup, organisms possess predetermined potentials and risks that are slumbering latently. Critical environmental factors can trigger the expression of distinct programs in the organism that in turn result in certain behaviors or symptoms. Many biological studies have confirmed this assumption. In the biomedical sciences, the capability to trigger an adverse program and thereby put a genetically predetermined risk into effect is called genetic susceptibility, or predisposition. Examples range from somatic illnesses such as cancer, diabetes, or cardiovascular disease to various psychopathologies. Moreover, differences between individuals result in different susceptibilities. Due to the genetic basis of predispositions, such hereditary risks run in families and kinship-based populations.

Let me illustrate the concept of genetic susceptibility in more detail by using myopia as an example. Myopia (i.e., shortsightedness) runs in families, indicating a congenital mechanism. Yet myopia cannot simply be reduced to genetic causes. It is highly unlikely that our ancestors in the Pleistocene suffered from considerable shortsightedness. Strongly impaired vision would have caused a drastic disadvantage for survival of the afflicted individuals. Imagine a primeval environment in which it was vital to identify dangerous animals or enemies from afar. Our purblind forefathers and mothers would have quickly become a delicacy for primeval predators. Thus, having had a gene variant that caused shortsightedness would have resulted in a significant selective disadvantage for the affected individuals. It is therefore highly unlikely that such an adverse allele would have prevailed over millennia in a population. Why is there such a high percentage of people suffering from myopia then? Perhaps myopia is due to a spontaneous genetic mutation that occurred very recently, e.g., a few generations ago? The assumption of a spontaneous mutation causing myopia was refuted on the grounds that within the last century, shortsightedness rapidly increased in many populations in various different countries roughly around the same time. Another argument against myopia resulting from a recent spontaneous mutation in the human lineage is the fact that this condition can also be found in various species of domesticated animals. Importantly, animals of the same species living in the wild usually do not suffer from nearsightedness. This indicates that despite exhibiting a high familial incidence, environmental factors must crucially contribute to the manifestation of nearsightedness.

At the end of the 1960s, Roy Box and Curtis Johnson were instrumental in elucidating the gene–environment crosstalk leading to myopia. Box and Johnson's field studies took them to Utquiagvik (Ukpiagvik) in Alaska. This Alaskan village is one of the northernmost public communities in the world and the northernmost city in the U.S. According to the indigenous inhabitants, the Iñupiats, the village's name means "a place where snow owls are hunted," underscoring its remote location. In the 1960s, the Iñupiats of Utquiagvik had little contact with Western civilization. Nonlocal food, necessities, and other convenience goods had to be brought in by small planes from Fairbanks that is about 660 miles away. Electricity was available, but most homes were still equipped with kerosene or oil lamps rather than using electric light. Box and Johnson were particularly interested in the effects of the artificial light and the shortage of natural light. People living at the "place where snow owls are hunted" spend more than four-and-a-half months not seeing daylight for over eighteen hours per day. Moreover, from November 18 to January 23, Iñupiats don't see any daylight at all. Box and Johnson wanted to find out whether the lack of natural light and making do with artificial light caused myopia in the local population. Surprisingly, this seemed not to be the case. Despite having lived in Utquiagvik and using kerosene or oil lamps all their lives, the two researchers could not find a single Iñupiats over the age of fifty-eight who suffered from shortsightedness. Yet at the same time, almost half of the younger Iñupiats who were less than forty years of age suffered from myopia. This percentage was unexpectedly high, much higher than the rest of the North American population at the time. Was this medical condition[19] due to a very recent spontaneous mutation? This was unlikely, because symptoms of myopia did not occur at random, but developed at the same time in many Iñupiat families, and there was a high correlation between Iñupiat siblings suffering from it (yet all their parents had normal eyesight). It seemed a mystery that neither genetics nor lack of natural light and exposure to artificial light could explain the condition. The explanation was finally found in the social environment of the Iñupiats. In 1890, the U.S. Office of Education built a school in Utquiagvik. However, in the first decades after its opening, the local inhabitants sent their children only irregularly to school. After the Bureau of Indian Affairs took over and expanded the building, more and more children of the indigenous population attended school.

When Box and Johnson performed their studies, many young Iñupiats had good reading and writing skills, much better than their parents who attended school only infrequently during their childhood. These findings tipped the

---

[19] There is an ongoing debate what actually counts as an illness, disease, or medical condition. See C. Boorse (1997) for a bio-statistical definition of malfunction and disease.

researchers off about which factors to take into account. Firstly, there was obviously a genetic component at work. Secondly, the prevailing lack of daylight did not seem to be the chief culprit (though we will come back to that point, later). Over the course of evolution, the Iñupiats' ancestors had enough time to adapt to being in the dark for a significant proportion of their lives without deterioration of their eyesight. And artificial light on its own also did not seem to matter much, as proven by the older generation that did not suffer from myopia. Thirdly, activities that required working in the proximate field of vision, such as reading and writing, seemed to have a strong impact. Evolutionarily speaking, these activities were cultural novelties and there was not yet enough time for the organisms to adapt to these new, man-made environmental conditions. Fourthly, a developmental time window needed to be considered. It was the youngest generation, those who started to learn to read and write young, that was most affected by myopia. To this day, it is not yet fully elucidated what causes myopia. But Box and Johnson's studies were the starting point of many studies to follow that grappled with the interaction between genetics and environment (i.e., GxE interactions) with respect to eye development and its effect on emmetropia (i.e., normal vision). More recent studies have found that myopia is due to an elongated growth of the eyeball, i.e., the eye grows too long from front to back. As a consequence, images are not focused on the retina—the light-sensitive tissue in the back of the eye—but rather the image focus falls in front of the retina. This refractive error is comparable to a wrongly adjusted telescope or camera providing only blurred pictures. Normally, the focal length of the eye's optics ensures that images of objects fall on the retina rather than in front or behind it. How is the growth of the eye regulated to ensure correct focus? It is real-life vision that guides the growth of the eye, particularly, visual processing of objects that are most commonly encountered in the organism's environment. Indeed, shortsighted people have a good near vision but poor distance vision. This looks like a maladaptation trait given our typical human environment. But it actually represents a successful adaptation for an individual whose eyes are predominantly exposed to objects in the proximate field of vision. It has long been recommended by ophthalmologists and optometrists to cut down on excessive work on computers and extensive reading under artificial light in favor of spending time outside. This recommendation draws from findings that show natural light of over ten thousand lux blocks excess growth of eyeballs. Daylight stimulates the release of dopamine in the retina, and this neurotransmitter blocks the elongation of the eye during development. But it is not just lack of daylight, as we have learned from the Iñupiats from Utquiagvik, but activities that predominantly employ the proximate field of vision. Contrarily, the natural environment offers many more opportunities to expose one's eyes to distant, objects thereby avoiding an unbalanced visual load.

As we can see from this example, there are multiple environmental factors that contribute to myopia. The extensive studies of myopia represent only one example of a plethora of studies investigating gene–environment interactions. This example should make clear that many organismal functions are not predetermined by a strict genetic program but adapt depending on the environmental conditions the individual encounters. But what about the underlying genetic factors? What progress has been made in elucidating the congenital mechanisms of shortsightedness? So far, more than 160 genetic risk factors have been identified that seem to be causally involved in myopia. Humans have about thirty thousand genes in their genomes (the exact number of how many genes humans have is controversial depending on how scientists define what a gene is. The figure of thirty thousand refers to noncoding RNA genes and protein-coding genes, including splice variants, but not pseudogenes). This begs the question of at what point is it appropriate to stop and speak of a genetic disposition for a certain condition: when two hundred, one thousand, or maybe ten thousand genetic factors are involved? This debate is still pending. Moreover, the example of myopia should convince us that it is often counterproductive to search only for genetic causes or just deleterious environmental influences. There is a tight intertwinement between genes and environment that represent two sides of the same coin. Why do we then still tenaciously stick to the idea that many human traits are predominantly determined by our genome? This persistence is particularly mystifying since gene deterministic accounts do not even seem to hold true for somatic conditions like myopia,[20] as we have seen. It can be assumed that it will hold even less true for character and psychological traits or complex cognitive capacities such as intelligence.

But we should not stop here when discussing gene–environment interactions. The examples so far still focus on the primacy of one's genetic endowment. If you are lucky enough to possess a beneficial combination of alleles (an allele denotes a certain variation of a gene) and you grow up in a nurturing environment, you should be able to reach your full potential—less so if you grow up in deprived surroundings irrespective of having a favorable genetic makeup. On the other hand, if you are unlucky and have a predisposition for a certain adverse trait, a detrimental environment will have a significant negative impact on your course

---

[20] There are, however, a few genetic disorders that are the result of only a single or a few mutated genes. These diseases are quite rare, and it is important to note that even monogenic disorders such as sickle cell anemia have different pathophysiologies, depending on the individual affected and the environment he/she lives in.

of life (e.g., causing a disease or a suboptimal cognitive, behavioral, or psychological condition).

Notwithstanding the importance of susceptibility, this concept only captures a limited part of the overall picture. There is increasing evidence for the environment being much more intertwined with organismal development rather than just having an influence on the genetic makeup. This intertwinement goes far beyond what I have described previously. In a nutshell, many traits are neither predetermined by a strict genetic program nor simply the outcome elicited by specific environmental triggers. Instead, organisms themselves influence their own development. Individuals not only continuously adjust to environmental circumstances and specific living conditions they find themselves in, but also modify their surroundings. Notably, this view of organism–environment interaction is quite different from a view that only sees the latter as a trigger, which unmasks latent genetic disposition. Here, individuals are not just passive entities harried by external forces, but change their environment, sometimes to a very significant extent and within an extremely short time period (with respect to evolutionary times). Just like the Iñupiats who spent more and more time reading and writing in conditions of artificial light and thereby having their biological propensities effected by this cultural shift, which ultimately led to a steep increase of myopia in the population. Taken together, the nature–nurture intertwinement is characterized by reciprocity that does not *a priori* separate causes from effects. This means, it is not just the environment that provides causal factors (e.g., triggers, pressure of natural selection) and the organism that suffers the effects; instead, there is an interchangeability of cause and effect. Rather than passively succumbing to the pressure of the environment, organisms actively change their surroundings, thereby modifying the effect it has. Thus, organisms and environment are tied through reciprocal processes continuously influencing each other. This reciprocal causality is reminiscent of the picture of the "painting hands" (Figure 1.5, inspired by M.C. Escher's lithograph "Drawing Hands") in which the components of the picture complement each other in an interactive loop thereby simultaneously completing this artwork.

In biology, this causal reciprocity has been coined niche construction.[21] Many animals undergo niche construction and modify their environment in their species-typical way: beavers build dams, ants carry out "farming," earthworms generate modified ecological conditions by burrowing, digestion, and excretion.[22] Of all organisms, we humans are certainly the most

---

[21] Odling-Smee et al., *Niche Construction the Neglected Process in Evolution.*

[22] The process of niche construction has first been described by Charles Darwin (although he did not use this term) when referring to how earthworms modify their habitat. As a result of the accumulated effects of previous generations of earthworm

paradigmatic species of niche constructors, as we have brought about completely new habitats: we have created ecological, cultural, social, technological, and even virtual spaces.

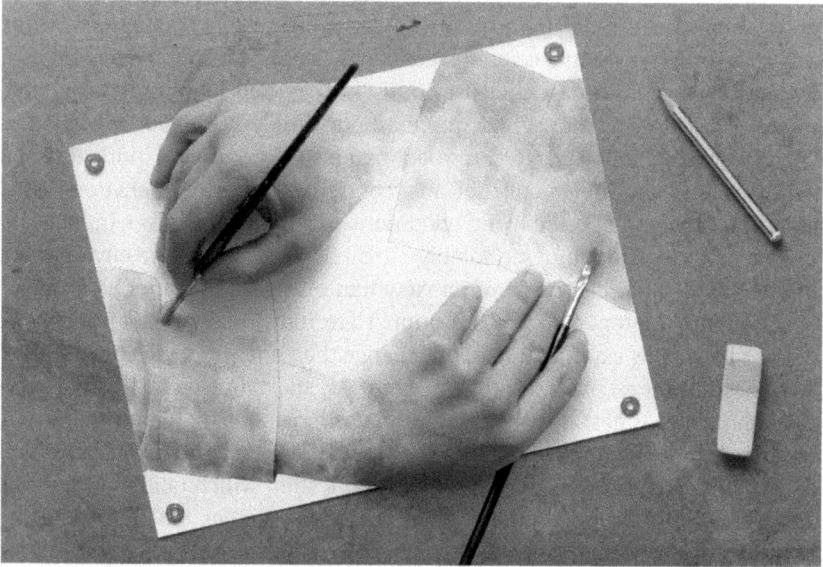

Figure 1.5: "Painting hands" photo-manipulation inspired by the artwork of M.C. Escher "Drawing hands" (@AdobeStock_215491054).

Let us return to the well-studied example of myopia. We have seen that genetic as well environmental factors are involved in developing this condition. Now, consider that because of better education, children become more proficient readers than their parents. Some kids will change their environment in order to spend increasingly more time inside the house for reading (or nowadays in front of computer and cell phone screens), thereby contributing to their worsening eyesight. The more proficient they become and the more they enjoy reading, the more their myopia will get aggravated. At the same time, distance vision becomes increasingly neglected the more time they spend inside. Humans of the twentieth century have created an unbalanced visual load due to lack of exposure to distant objects in the natural environment in favor of proximal objects in our artificially constructed environment. In other words, processes of cultural evolution have caused a worsening of a biological

---

niche construction, subsequent generations of earthworms live in radically altered ecological environments with starkly modified selection pressures.

trait (i.e., emmetropia) within a few generations. This is possible, because niche construction processes typically operate faster than natural selection.

Cultural processes that precipitate niche construction have entailed important consequences in the evolution of human traits, particularly of psychological and mental capacities. Importantly, humans do not only modify their ecological but also social environment. As a consequence, we create an ever-increasing disequilibrium between evolved traits and environment, thereby enlivening an upward spiral. This cranked-up effect can explain some extreme behavior and exceptional cognitive traits such as risk taking, creativity, or extraordinary intelligence. On the other hand, it can also cause psychopathologies by exaggerations of adaptive traits. Anxiety, depression, and narcissistic personality disorders may be such "adaptive behavior gone wild" in our modern social environment. Take for example Marie, the physically most delicate of the Dionne babies. Because of her frailty, she probably spent the longest time in the incubator away from any skin-to-skin contact with her mother or nurse. Marie was also the one who nearly died a few days after birth. She was one of the two sets of Dionne children who developed in shared embryonic sacs. Her twin with whom she shared the embryonic sac was Emilie, to whom she was also closest. Emilie died at the age of twenty. Although we are now in the realm of pure speculation, it is not difficult to imagine that all these incidents likely contributed to the development of her depression and her drinking problem. It can be assumed that her alcohol problem aggravated the episodes of depression. In addition, she had two daughters who she gave into foster care. This emotional and highly charged decision may have contributed to the worsening of her psychopathological condition. Eventually, she died from a blood clot in her mid-thirties. Marie's death may have been completely unrelated to her psychopathologies, but some studies have reported correlations between psychosocial stress and stroke in other patients. We don't know enough about Marie's case, but all in all, we would make a grave mistake looking solely at isolated factors, be it genetic or environmental, for explaining her medical history.

The take home message is that the dynamic reciprocity of gene–environment interactions such as niche construction processes makes a nature–nurture distinction meaningless. Just like in the picture of the "painting hands" (Figure 1.5), none of the two hands has primacy over the other, they simultaneously create each other.

Further chapters will be exploring this concept of environmental feedback in more detail. We will see how neuroplasticity (Chapter 2) and gene expression (Chapter 4) are a direct consequence of the environment impinging on our biological endowments. Later chapters will also discuss how our brain constantly undergoes learning and adaptive processes due to socioenvironmental experiences that cause cognitive changes that go way beyond what can be predicted from just looking at genes (Chapter 5). Based on the aforementioned insights of how nature and nurture are inextricably linked, it will be expounded how human infants vitally depend on cooperative interactions with their caregivers, ensuring that they develop into resilient adolescents and healthy, mature adults. But rather than confining our exploration to typical trajectories of brain development, this book will critically examine what happens when crucial social interactions are missing or go awry. The subsequent chapters take a critical look at brain development and cognitive maturation when children and adolescents are exposed to negative environmental conditions like stress and traumatic experiences (Chapter 6), social neglect (Chapter 7), and maltreatment (Chapter 8). Since biological inventory and environment constantly feed off each other, adversities encountered in the environment have a severe impact on learning, memory, and emotional development. These cognitive developmental deviations in turn beget lifelong challenges with respect to emotional attachment, interpersonal relationships, and social behavior.

Chapter 2

Brain Development and Plasticity

[C]onsider the possibility that any man could, if he were so inclined, be the sculptor of his own brain, and that even the least gifted may, like the poorest land that has been well cultivated and fertilized, produce an abundant harvest.

— Santiago Ramón y Cajal. Advice for a Young Investigator

In August 1995, at the Jersey Shore of Cape May, a little girl's life changed forever. Christina Santhouse was seven when she contracted a rare, non-infectious childhood illness called Rasmussen's Encephalitis. This condition is a brain disorder caused by an autoimmune defect. In a healthy person, the immune system serves to protect the body by destroying pathogens, such as bacteria, viruses, or other germs. In an autoimmune disease, the system goes awry and immune cells start destroying healthy cells in the body. In Rasmussen's Encephalitis, lymphocytes (i.e., a type of white blood cells) of the errant immune system rapidly infiltrate the cerebral cortex, leading to a widespread inflammation and destruction of the cortex. The disease progression is accompanied by worsening seizures and gradual neurological deficits. Christina, who was a standout soccer player, popular student, and halfway to a green belt in karate, started to suffer from twitches, first in her ankle, then in her legs. The twitches got worse, and within six months violent seizures shook her body more than a hundred times a day and forced her into a wheelchair. Drug treatment quickly became ineffective and left her parents with only a few drastic choices. Rather than chemotherapy or steroid treatments, doctors at Johns Hopkins' Children's Center in Baltimore recommended hemispherectomy due to the severity of the illness. In this procedure, the right half of Christina's brain was to be removed to stop Rasmussen's encephalitis from paralyzing and then killing her. She would be the fifty-ninth child who ever underwent this kind of last-resort surgery. When her parents were faced with the doctors' medical advice, they could not believe their ears. Lynne Catarro, Christina's mother, was shocked when told that the only potential cure was the removal of half her daughter's brain. Lynne recalled, "I had never heard of surgery like that before. It seemed very barbaric."[1]

The surgery was high risk, nobody could predict the long-term outcomes. The doctors didn't set high expectations. On February 13, 1996, Christina's right half of the brain where the inflammation had taken root was completely removed in a surgical procedure that took about fourteen hours. The operation saved her life—the seizures stopped.

But what sort of life can one expect to lead with only half a brain? It has been known for a long time that when a hemisphere of the brain is removed, the contralateral side of the body (i.e., the side of the body that is opposite to the respective brain half) becomes paralyzed. This is because the somatosensory and motor cortical maps of the paralyzed side of the body that are located in the opposite hemisphere are missing. The immediate outcome of Christina's operation was no surprise. After the hemispherectomy, Christina's left arm and left leg were left mostly paralyzed and she lost peripheral vision in one eye. Luckily, she kept her ability to speak. As in most right-handed people, Broca's area and Wernicke's area (i.e., the brain regions involved in speech production and language comprehension, respectively) were located in Christina's healthy, left hemisphere. Being young, the doctors hoped that the girl's remaining side of the brain could compensate for some of the functions lost due to the missing hemisphere. Neurological studies have shown that the cerebral cortex is not fixed in structure and function, but highly dynamic, a phenomenon that is referred to as neuroplasticity. Neuroplasticity denotes the brain's ability to reorganize neural connections, a process that is crucial in childhood and adolescent brain development, as well as for recovery from neurotrauma. Neuroplasticity plays an important role in life-long memory and learning, not only in young people, but also in adults.

Children in general have a greater capacity for neuroplasticity. Just think of how much faster than most adults they acquire new skills, such as learning languages or playing an instrument. Thus, there was hope that Christina's motor and sensory functions would be at least partially transferred to the motor and sensory cortex in the remaining hemisphere. If this were the case, she could regain the ability to walk and move her left hand and arm again. However, a transfer of function to the remaining healthy cortex that would result in taking over the tasks of the missing side is neither automatic nor guaranteed. And some skills, such as the fine motor control of the contralateral side, would most likely remain impaired for the whole life. Christina's case was no exception to the medical prospects.

---

[1] Boccella, "20 Years after Surgery, a Full Life with Half a Brain."

Still, Christina Santhouse has succeeded beyond anyone's expectations. Painstakingly and persistently, she re-learned most routine activities. Thanks to intense therapy and the help of a leg brace, she managed to walk again. She went back to school and worked hard, much harder than ever before. Doing homework assignments and studying for tests took her twice as long as before her operation. But eventually, she graduated from high school. Being no longer able to play soccer because of the dangerous physical contact, she rose to a new challenge. She took up bowling and soon excelled on the high school bowling team of which she became captain in her senior year. At the age of seventeen, she got her driver's license and is now one of three people who have undergone hemispherectomy and are able to drive. Christina pushed herself through college and on to a graduate degree. According to the Hemispherectomy Foundation that tracks about two hundred children worldwide who have undergone this drastic surgery, only a handful of patients manage to go on to college. Christina earned her undergraduate and master's degrees in speech-language pathology from Misericordia University within five years. Now, she is in her early thirties, has a job with the Bucks County Intermediate Unit as a speech therapist, lives in a ranch house in Yardley, and is married. She gives interviews on TV shows, for newspapers and magazines, and speaks at schools and professional conferences. An impressive life journey of a young woman, especially one with only half a brain.

Christina is one of the figureheads of patients who have undergone radical brain surgery and managed to thrive in their lives. Her story gives hope to parents of children suffering from severe neurological diseases and is an inspiration to these young people. And for neuroscientists, she is an emboldening, real-life testimony of how malleable the human brain is.

Christina's is not an isolated event of neuroplastic changes occurring after severe brain damage or neurosurgical intervention, but her case is certainly one of the most remarkable ones. Putting neurological diseases aside, why is Christina's case of any relevance for healthy children and adolescents? The answer is perfectly simple: we all own a brain that is highly plastic.

These intriguing, neuroplastic outcomes should not be taken as self-evident. Indeed, for the longest time during the nineteenth and twentieth century, scientists agreed that brain connections are "hardwired." The conviction that brain connections are essentially static can be backtracked to mechanical philosophy and metaphors that described the body's organs as clockwork, or a machine. In the seventeenth century, Thomas Hobbes sought to trace the physical basis for ideas and associations to mechanical motions in the head.[2]

---

[2] Hobbes, *De Homine*.

His ultimate aim was to turn the study of human knowledge into a branch of physics, explicable through classical mechanics.[3] This mechanical philosophy constituted the breeding ground for subsequent theories about the human mind and gave rise to new fields of natural sciences. A highly popular one in the first half of the nineteenth century was phrenology. Phrenology—nowadays regarded as obsolete and pseudoscientific—was developed by German physician and neuroanatomist Franz Joseph Gall. Gall and his fellow phrenologists claimed to be able to "read" a person's character by measuring bumps on his or her skull. What seems blatantly absurd today was not completely made up out of thin air; Gall was a first-rate neuroanatomist and meticulously examined brains for many years before turning to phrenology. He performed neuroanatomical studies and depicted the brain's cortical surface in accurate drawings. At some point, he became aware that the contours of the brain surface were unique and differed from person to person. He termed those seemingly distinct areas of the anatomical landscape of the cortex "mental organs." He postulated that the relative size of any particular mental organ is indicative of the power or strength of that organ. The observed interindividual differences were believed to not only hold true for contours of the cortical surface, but also for the overlying skull. Based on these interindividual anatomical peculiarities, he concluded that human character traits were localized in the mental organs of the brain surface, which in turn were reflected as bumps on the skull surface. According to Gall, the formation of these idiosyncratic shapes took place during infant development when the skull ossifies over the brain. Consequentially, the external skull form could be used to diagnose the mental organs and by extrapolation also the internal states of the mental characters. Gall believed that he had established a scientifically accurate relationship between aspects of character, which he called "faculties," with distinct mental organs in the brain. Although phrenologists of disparate camps never managed to agree on a number of the most basic mental organs—anything between twenty-seven and more than forty were purported—they were never at loss for naming pivotal personality traits (Figure 2.1). There were bumps for destructiveness, amativeness (i.e., an indicator of keen sexual appetite), veneration, sublimity, and many more.

Phrenology also became increasingly popular amongst laypeople. Despite being scientifically questionable, Gall's theory was cited in plentiful pamphlets, as well as in anthropological and natural philosophical publications that were most widely read at that time. Scientific lectures were held for public entertainment that further promoted the ideas of phrenology. This strong interest took hold among the middle and working classes, which became

---

[3] Schwartz and Daugman, "Brain Metaphor and Brain Theory," 9–18.

increasingly aware of the role of natural sciences in society and began regarding scientific knowledge as important and an indication of sophistication and modernity. Yet phrenology was not just an amusing pastime of the bourgeoisie and proletarians; it pervaded the highest circles. Even Queen Victoria and Prince Albert invited the Scottish phrenologist George Combe to read the heads of the royal offspring.

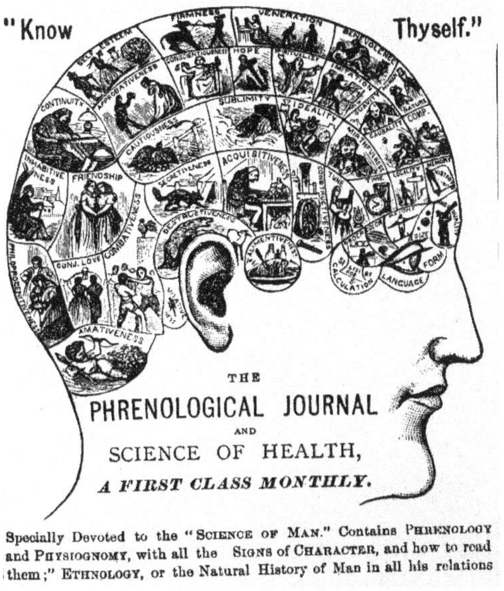

Figure 2.1: A phrenology chart of 1883
Credit: Phrenology: Chart. Credit: Wellcome Collection.
Attribution 4.0 International (CC BY 4.0). Chart from 'The Phrenological Journal' ("Know Thyself"), print from Dr. E. Clark.

Phrenology turned out to be a powerful tool for cementing ideologies. It provided a rationale for the categorization of people. Members of the upper class used the topology of their own skulls to justify their superiority. Rather than acknowledging their economical or sociological inheritance of class position, they accredited their status to a superiorly developed brain. Thus, phrenology gave a seemingly scientific explanation of why some people were less privileged than others. It was convenient that a person's misfortune was nobody's fault, but a consequence of his or her own brain's topology. One particularly illuminating text section referring to an example of phrenological specimen described by German physician and phrenologist Johann Gaspar Spurzheim reads as follows:

No. 29 – A very short miserable forehead, unfit for the manifestations of superior intellect; with the organs of Acquisitiveness, Cautiousness, Reverence, Marvellousness, and Secretiveness, large, while those of Combativeness, Self-Esteem, Hope, and Benevolence, are small.[4]

It is easy to see how phrenology came to be an attractive "scientific method" for racist endeavors in justifying the superiority of one ethnic group over others. By means of comparison of skulls, Caucasians were deemed to be the most beautiful race. On the other end of the spectrum, there were Australian Aborigines and Maoris who were facing the phrenologist verdict of never becoming civilized since they had no cerebral organ for great arts.

Unsurprisingly, phrenologists were also quick at hand with explanations that fueled gender stereotyping. Female skull topologies were claimed to be indicative of underdeveloped mental organs, making women incapable of artistic or scientific achievements. Other typically female skull topologies revealed larger mental organs that allegedly were necessary for the care of children and religion. Phrenology provided an explanation for social inequality by resorting to the natural, anatomical inequality of people's brains and head shapes.

But not everybody employed phrenology like gambling with a loaded dice in order to secure supremacy. Despite providing scientific evidence of inequality, people of the middle or lower classes still accepted phrenological practice, because it offered hope. Phrenology showed ways to improve oneself and better one's social status. Notwithstanding the central postulate that each brain was composed of clear-cut cerebral organs, phrenologists did not assume that these organs had an immutable and static nature. Very few people were deemed to have a naturally perfect balance between organs. It was rather believed that one could achieve a better balance by rigorously exercising beneficial organs and repressing deleterious ones. Consequently, phrenologists suggested that "lesser" people could improve through proper education. Most remarkably, phrenologist Félix Voisin ran a reform school. His curriculum aimed at correcting the minds of children who had suffered hardship, such as neglect or abuse. His school also accepted children who were at high risk of inheriting mental disorders. He hoped that reorganizing children's disorganized brains would bring about positive changes.

In retrospect, it is uncontested that phrenology extrapolated well beyond empirical findings and departed far from science. Nonetheless, Gall's doctrinal principles were pioneering neuroanatomic interpretations and neuroscientific

---

[4] "Article XIV: Sixty Phreonological Speciment," 285–288.

hypotheses in the decades to follow. One assertion that was taken over by other scientists was the notion that the brain is not a homogenous unity, but an aggregate of mental organs with specific characteristics. Admittedly, after phrenology fell in disfavor, scientists no longer spoke of mental organs, but the neuroanatomic concept of specific brain areas being associated with certain character traits or behavioral traits was still reminiscent of earlier phrenological talk. A second highly influential assertion was that the cerebral organs are topographically precisely circumscribed within the brain. Many scientists followed the idea that there was a one-to-one mapping of brain areas and functional traits, including character traits, and this relation could be described in an objective and generalizing way. Brain atlases bespeak this localizationist thinking that is deeply entrenched in contemporary neuroscience. Thus, despite being highly controversial from the very beginning and later regarded as an erroneous amalgamation of primitive neuroanatomy with moral philosophy, phrenology invigorated localizationist thinking, especially in neuroanatomists and psychiatrist of that time. Moreover, Gall's hypotheses that character, thoughts, and emotions are located in specific parts of the brain can be considered an important historical advance toward neuropsychology.

Besides phrenology, localizationism had its roots in many philosophical and scientific schools and was endorsed by influential researchers all over Europe. These scholars ardently advocated the theory that the brain is composed of distinct parts, each with its sovereign function. According to localizationists, each mental function can be attributed to a distinct, single physical area of the brain, envisioning a comprehensive map thereof. Such a map was believed to solve a multitude of medical puzzles, including the etiology and physical basis of epilepsy, aphasia, brain tumors, stroke, syphilis, and tuberculosis.

This conjecture was not just guesswork and far-fetched speculations; in fact, there was ample evidence that cognitive functions were localized in distinct brain areas. These findings had nothing to do with phrenology, but relied on much more credible empirical research. One of the most famous proponents of the localization theory was French anatomist Paul Broca. In 1861 in Bicêtre Hospital, Paul Broca examined a patient named Louis Victor Leborgne.[5] Leborgne suffered from a progressive loss of speech ability, and by the time he was admitted to Broca's ward, the only syllable he was capable of uttering was "tan." Scientific literature usually refers to Broca's famous patient as "Monsieur Tan," a nickname the hospital staff gave him because of his linguistic oddity. Most noteworthy, Monsieur Tan had no problem understanding the questions he was asked despite his aphasia. Thus, he did not have any disfunctions in language perception or other cognitive tasks. Broca predicted that Monsieur

---

[5] Konnikova, "The Man Who Couldn't Speak."

Tan's impaired speech production was due to a lesion in a specific area of his brain. Although Broca was not the first one who suggested a causal relationship between speech disfunction and a certain brain region, he was the first to provide convincing evidence for it. A few days after his neurological examination at the Bicêtre Hospital, Monsieur Tan died. Broca performed a superficial autopsy of Leborgne's brain that confirmed the anatomist's assumption. He identified a lesion in the frontal lobe of the left hemisphere, more precisely a softening of the brain in the third frontal convolution. Broca published this result and concluded with the famous statement "la lesion du lobe frontal a été la cause de la perte de la parole," meaning "the lesion located in the frontal lobe was the reason of the loss of speech" (see Figure 2.2). This statement reverberated through the minds of many physicians and psychologists until today.[6] In the following years, Broca found more autopsy evidence in favor of his hypothesis that language articulation is distinctly correlated with an area at the frontal lobe of the left hemisphere. His findings strongly supported other localizationist claims and triggered a spiking interest in the localization of various other functions in the cerebral hemispheres.

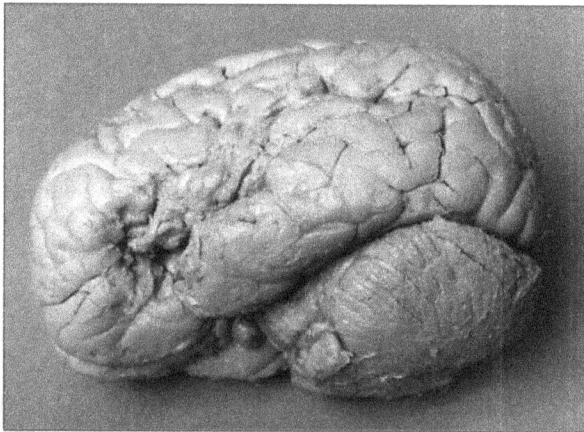

Figure 2.2: Brain of Mr. Leborgne alias Tan. From Dronkers et al., 2007, p. 1436. Original at Musée Dupuytren, Paris.

Broca's discoveries had wide implications for natural sciences, and for brain research in particular. At that time, language was viewed as a God-given ability in humans and considered part of the soul. Thus, attributing language to a material component in the brain was a considerable shift toward materialism. And of course, these findings significantly strengthened the localizationist agenda.

---

[6] Rutten, *BROCA-WERNICKE DOCTRINE*.

Around the same time in England, another advocate of localizationism, David Ferrier, undertook physiological experiments on monkeys. He used an experimental strategy of impairing distinct brain areas and observing the functional consequences. The underlying logic was what his colleague, the English neurologist John Hughlings Jackson, called *natural* experiments of disease with respect to human patients. Jackson recognized that focal necrosis, cerebral tumors, or lesions in human brains were causally related to pathological processes of focal epilepsy. From this, he established a consistent scientific method based on the systematic analysis of anatomy, pathology, and physiology. He tried to link softening, discoloration, or erosion of areas of the brain with loss or disturbance of functions. Medical experimenters like Ferrier exploited Jackson's meticulous studies of human postmortem brains to apply this information to animal experiments. Ferrier surgically inflicted lesions in monkeys that were located in comparable regions to the focal lesions which Jackson found in his epilepsy patients. However, the animal studies often did not give unequivocal conclusions. Ferrier had problems to tell exactly which functions had been impaired by the surgical lesions. Was the paralysis caused by the cerebral mutilation or was it a shock reaction from the operation itself? Some brain regions proved to be more fruitful for investigation than others. The motor cortex was such an example. Jackson's patients who suffered from partial seizures showed an intriguing pattern of sequential progression of myoclonic jerks. The seizures seemed to start in one hand and then systematically move up the ipsilateral side of the body toward the face. Jackson's thesis was that initially a tumor or lesion had destroyed parts of the motor cortex. Subsequently, the tumor would trigger what he called "discharging" properties that animated muscles and led to seizures. In partial epilepsy, abnormal discharging electrical activity occurred in distinct areas of the cortex and caused an abnormal movement that progressed through the body. Based on these clinical observations, Jackson hypothesized that different areas in the cortex might be responsible for the movement of specific parts of the body. Jackson's clinical work and his hypothesis were taken as a support of the localization movement, although Jackson himself was never a localizationist.[7] Meanwhile in Germany, two physicians—Gustav Fritsch and Eduard Hitzig— confirmed Jackson's hypothesis in dogs by demonstrating that the motor cortex could be electrically stimulated. The German physicians applied electrodes to the exposed brain of dogs and observed the dog's muscle movements on a galvanometer. They then claimed that the movements were caused by the part

---

[7] Engelhardt, "John Hughlings Jackson and the Mind-Body Relation," 137–151.
"I am neither a universaliser nor a localiser.... In consequence I have been attacked as a universaliser and also as a localiser."

of the brain that was stimulated. Localizationist like Ferrier in England quickly seized the potential of the electrical brain stimulation. The use of electricity in medicine was common during this period, so Ferrier could successfully adapt Fritsch and Hitzig's research method. In a short time, Ferrier's electrical work on the brain became very detailed. He surgically opened the animals' skull and applied electrodes to exceedingly small areas of the cortex. Based on his precise measurements, he generated detailed functional maps of the brains of various animals. But animal experiments were just a stepping stone for localizationists in order to prove that all regions of the human body were represented in discrete parts of the nervous system. The ultimate goal was to transfer localizationist discoveries to the living human brain and incorporate them into clinical practice. Localizationism reached its apex in the middle of the twentieth century, thanks to neurosurgery. Especially the ground-breaking work of American-Canadian neurosurgeon Wilder Penfield, who contributed largely to the localizationist agenda. Penfield wanted to specify regions that were responsible for memory, epilepsy, and personality. Penfield was an exceptional surgeon who invented a special procedure to treat patients with severe epilepsy. He ablated distinct regions in the brain where the seizures originated. So far, this was standard practice in neurosurgery. But in order to avoid destroying other cortical regions that were essential for the patient's well-being, he stimulated the brain with electrical probes before the operation. Thus, his patients could report immediately what they experienced while having their cortex electrically stimulated. Patients undergoing this procedure were only under local anesthesia and thus conscious and awake. This may sound cruel prima facie, but once the skull is open, the procedure is pain-free because there are no pain receptors in the brain. To make sure that Penfield accurately targeted the areas responsible for the seizures and spared other regions, he requested his patients to talk, write, count, and read during the electrical stimulation. By observing their responses, he could effectively reduce the risk of removing brain tissue during the surgery that was essential for other cognitive functions. For the sake of exactitude, he labeled each position of the cortex where he applied electrical currents with tiny numbered slips of paper. These slips represented the different functions observed in the patient upon electrical stimulation that he believed to correlate with certain brain areas. For example, the patient's verbal responses were analyzed to map the speech area of the brain and thereby avoid excision of this region during operation. From these results, Penfield came up with his famous somatosensoric and motor cortical map (Figure 2.3) that showed how the brain mirrors the body from an inside perspective.

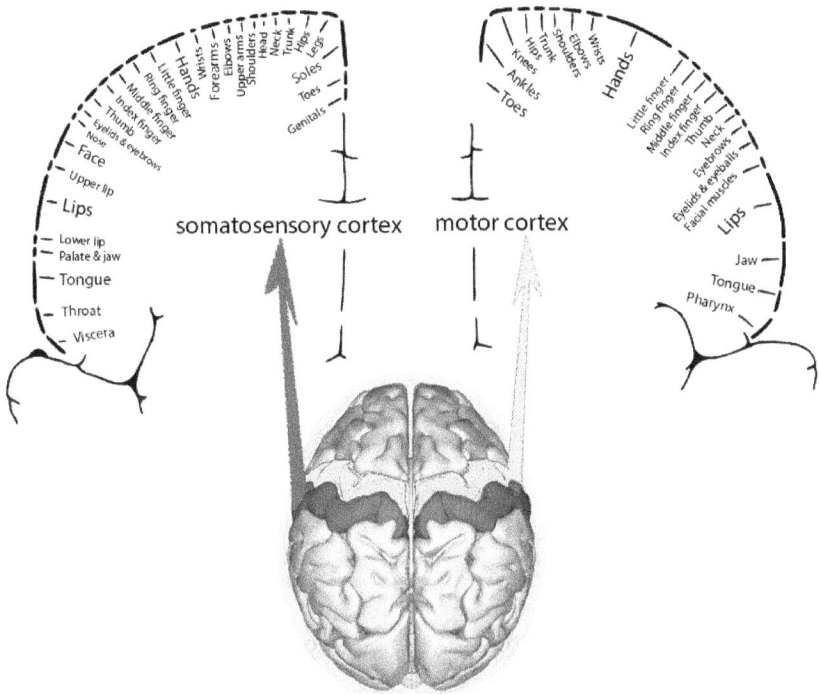

Figure 2.3: Sensomotoric cortex, after Penfield and Rasmussen (1950). Image modified.

Penfield's map of somatotopic organization applied to both sensory and motor systems. His functional maps of the brain are still in use for the diagnosis and treatment of head wounds and brain tumors. They are also used as a working model for many speech and behavioral disorders. But could the findings be generalized to other functions, emotions, and even character traits? Penfield's mapping of the brain did not reveal that epileptic fits or electrical stimulation of brain surface elicited emotional reactions in humans. Nonetheless, localizationist research paved the way for psychosurgery. In one of his publications, Penfield described the relief of psychiatric symptomatology after the resection of tumors, abscesses, and other brain lesions.[8] At the 1935 International Congress of Neurology in London, Penfield reported this observation. The conference gathered neurologists, neurosurgeons, neuroanatomists, psychologists, and physiologists all exploring the functions of the human brain. At the same congress, Yale physiologists John F. Fulton and

---

[8] Penfield and Evans, "The Frontal Lobe in Man," 115–133.

Carlyle Jacobson presented a paper on chimpanzee brain experiments. The Yale scientists reported that they could change chimps' temperaments by means of surgery. By partial ablation of the frontal cortex, the animals became aggressive and would "shake and kick the box, pull their hair, and sometimes urinate and defecate, throwing their excreta."[9] On the other hand, if the scientists performed a complete resection of the anterior frontal association cortex, the animals became calm and docile. From these studies, Fulton and Jacobson alluded that the frontal cortex was associated with emotions and temperaments. Leading medical experts of the human brain who attended this conference connected the dots from Penfield's and Fulton and Jacobson's studies. One of the attendees was the Portuguese neurologist Antonio Egas Moniz who, much to the surprise of the audience, suggested that the same intervention may be used in humans with psychiatric diseases. In fact, Moniz had already long planned such a procedure and the presentations heard at the congress may just have given scientific justification to his ideas. After his return to the Medical School of the University Lisbon, Moniz enlisted a long-time staff member and neurosurgeon to develop an operation that became known as leucotomy. They tested the procedure on twenty patients with schizophrenia, anxiety, and depression. Technically speaking, Moniz did not aim at excising matter from the patients' brains, but to create a barrier between the frontal lobes and other major brain centers. To this end, the surgeon drilled holes in the patient's skull and injected ethanol into the subcortical white matter of the prefrontal area in order to disrupt the tracts of neuronal fibers connecting the prefrontal cortex and thalamus. Since the operating doctors did not achieve favorable results on several occasions, they changed the method. From the ninth patient onward, the neurosurgeon used a cannula, an instrument they called leucotome, to cut circular lesions in the white matter of the frontal lobe. Shortly after, this practice that was enthusiastically taken up by surgeons in other countries and performed with various methodological modifications until the 1970s.

Notwithstanding that psychosurgery has always been a controversial medical field, the practice of psychosurgery grew. One of the central ideas of psychosurgery was to heal patients by removing the cerebral sites of aggression and antisocial behavior.[10] Donald Hebb later critically stated that the psychosurgical agenda of that time concerning the frontal cortex followed the dictum that a "bad brain is worse than no brain at all."

In the United States, Walter Freeman fervently followed his mentor and idol Egas Moniz. Freeman was a neurologist and neuropathologist first at St.

---

[9] Shutts, *Lobotomy: Resort to the Knife.*
[10] Gaylin et al., "Psychosurgery and Brain Stimulation in Historical Perspective," 24–72.

Elizabeth's Hospital, Washington D.C., and then at George Washington University. He adopted Moniz's practice, modified the procedure, and renamed it transorbital lobotomy. Freeman dispensed with the leucotome and sterile clothing and utilized an icepick he scooped up from his kitchen drawer. More a showman than a surgeon, he operated without gloves or mask. In fact, Freeman never had formal neurosurgical training. But he compensated his lack of expert qualification by performing theatrical antics. As for the procedure, he inserted icepicks into the corner of patients' eye-sockets and hammered them through the bone with a mallet. By moving the crude instruments back and forth, he severed the connections to the prefrontal cortex of the brain. During his time as a psychosurgeon, Freeman performed over 3,500 lobotomies. About fifteen percent of his patients died from the procedure, while others were left severely brain-damaged. Many patients had to be retaught how to eat and use the bathroom. Of the approximate 3,500 patients, nineteen were minors, including a four-year-old child. One of his youngest patients was Howard Dully.

Howard Dully was four when his mother died of cancer. She had just given birth to Howard's second brother. After the tragic death, Howard's father, Rodney Lloyd Dully, relocated for professional reasons and took his two older sons with him. Howard was deeply affected by his mother's passing. He remembered her as a loving and indulgent woman and could not understand why she "left" the family. Nobody told him about the circumstances of her death, so for a long time, he felt guilty and became severely troubled by fears of abandonment. Howard's father, who was scarred by the economic crisis and overseas military duty during World War II, was no comfort to the child's troubled soul, being emotionally distant and physically brutal. He used to beat his son with wooden battens, which the boy had to choose himself. Not only was Rodney Dully violent and emotionally abusive to his oldest son, he also spent long hours away from home in order to make a living for his family.

Supporting the widower, some women of the neighborhood helped by sewing or doing the laundry for the Dullys. One of the neighbors named Lucille "Lou" Cox, who had two children of her own, eventually became Howard's stepmother. Howard remembered his stepmother Lou being a cold and demanding woman who found her new stepson's behavior impossible to control. She would spank the children for anything she deemed inappropriate. His stepbrother later confirmed that for a long time Howard was spanked on a daily basis. His body was always full of bruises. Within a few years, Howard became a troublemaker. When he got restless or bored, he started to misbehave. He stole, lied, smoked, broke rules, and was constantly in trouble at school. But often he was also punished when he did not do anything wrong, or he was blamed for things his stepbrothers did. The relation between Lou and Howard deteriorated badly. Besides the regular beatings, he suffered from emotional abuse and casual neglect. He was often forced to eat meals on his own as punishment for having piggish table manners. On occasion, his stepmother starved him, did not allow him to use the front door of the house, and locked him in his room while his brothers and friends were having a birthday party.

When Howard turned ten, Lou attended nursing training at the local college. There, she picked up the idea that her stepson might suffer from mental illness. Her first idea was that he had an extra chromosome that caused some sort of mental disease and made him rebellious. Although she soon abandoned her idea about the chromosome abnormality, she got increasingly convinced that there was something emotionally wrong with the boy. She consulted psychiatrists and mental health experts requesting medical attestation of her presumption. By the age of eleven, Howard had been examined by six different psychiatrists, but all of them attested that he was "normal" and four of them said that the problem laid with her, not the child. Eventually, Howard was referred to Walter Freeman, who by that time had been disowned by the medical community and ran a private practice in Los Altos near San Francisco. Lou's description of Howard's symptoms did not convince Freeman at first. She complained that her stepson did not play with toys but used them as weapons or was destructive with them. She also reported that he cried more easily than anybody and seemed afraid of everything. Finally, she pointed out that Howard would occasionally defecate in his pants although he had mastered the toilet many years ago. In a handwritten note, worded in a dispassionate style, Lou reported to Freeman:

[Howard] has monkey-like gestures and mannerisms—i.e., scratching head and body. Tires easily. Needs more sleep. Falls asleep easily in chair. Eyes bloodshot when tired. [...] Won't move when told time is short. Doesn't use good judgment. Comprehension not good. Seems useless to convey reasons. Won't do homework.[11]

Neither Rodney Dully nor Howard's weekend caretaker confirmed the symptoms described by Lou. In fact, the weekend caretaker insisted that it was Howard´s environment that was deleterious for the child's mental stability. Freeman met Howard four times and could not find anything wrong with him. Only after Lou claimed that she feared for herself and for her family's safety, Freeman diagnosed Howard with childhood schizophrenia. At that point, the psychosurgeon eventually suggested to change the boy's personality by means of transorbital lobotomy. It was Howard's twelfth birthday when Lou and

---

[11] Dully and Fleming, *My Lobotomy*, 134–135.

Freeman agreed on the child's lobotomy. The last note Freeman took before Howard was admitted to Doctors General Hospital, a private institution on the outskirts of San Jose, reads as follows:

> I asked Howard about his recollections of his own mother and he was able to give me a few rather objective details but he didn't go into any discussion of his attitude toward her and his desperation at losing her. He says that he recently had the experience of hearing somebody in his room rather angrily talk at him; he turned on the light and nobody was there. He doesn't remember the words but he was very alarmed. In regard to talking to himself he says he just talks to himself; he doesn't answer any spirit voice. He has a certain fascination with license plate numbers and also with words like "spring" that have a number of different meanings.[12]

On December 15, 1960, when Howard was just over twelve years old, Freeman performed his transorbital lobotomy. Howard was not told about the procedure before or after the operation. He had no idea what happened to him and only remembered that he woke up in a fog. The fog was a typical symptom of patients undergoing Freeman's intervention. Even today, Howard still wonders what transpired during those ten minutes with Freeman and his ice pick. By some miracle, the procedure did not turn him into a "vegetable" or kill him. But Howard's life took a sharp turn. Where he was previously interested in fixing mechanical things, he no longer had the passion or the energy to repair anything. Although things seemed to change for the better after the operation, Howard soon had a relapse. His stepmother described his relapse as him contributing to nothing at home and unwilling to bathe. After the alleged relapse, Howard was put into custodial care. First placed into juvenile penitentiary, then transferred into an asylum, he ended up in a boarding school for the mentally ill. As an adolescent and young adult, he was in and out of jails and halfway houses. In between these phases, he was homeless, drug-addicted, an alcoholic, and a small-time criminal. Eventually, Howard took control of his life. He became a responsible father of two sons, married Barbara, and started working as a bus driver. In 2005, Howard Dully's life story was broadcasted on national public radio. It created a firestorm and drew more listener response than any other program that had ever aired there. Two years later, Dully's memoir, co-authored by Charles Fleming, was published under the title *My Lobotomy*. Readers couldn't help but wonder how Howard's life might have turned out had he not undergone the brute surgical treatment. At the same

---

[12] Ibid.

time, given the imprecision of the procedure, Howard is luckier than most lobotomy survivors. Apart from his tear ducts possibly being damaged by the procedure and having sinus problems due to the intervention, he claims that his thinking processes work normally for the most part. The fact that he did not end up crippled for life or reduced to living in a persistent vegetative state made Howard one of the very few lobotomy patients who recovered well enough to tell his story—a story that warns us of scientific border transgression, and a story that presumably gives an account of an adolescent brain that could at least partially compensate for the damage that was done to it by undergoing neuroplastic events.

In the 1960s, the use of large-scale psychosurgery declined, but psychosurgery on a smaller scale survived. In many countries, stereotactic methods to remove or destroy a small piece of the brain are still in use today. These interventions are used to treat depression, obsessive-compulsive disorder, and schizophrenia. About a third of patients show significant improvement in their symptoms after operation. More recently, psychosurgeons increasingly avert from ablative psychosurgery in favor of deep brain stimulation. To this end, electrodes are implanted into distinct brain areas for local electrical stimulation. While Wilder Penfield did not succeed in eliciting emotional reactions in the process of mapping the human brain, deep brain stimulation showed more encouraging results. Contrasting Penfield's studies in which just surface areas of the cerebral cortex underwent electrical stimulation, deep brain stimulation targets subcortical brain nuclei. A surgically implanted neurostimulator sends electrical pulses to the brain interfering with neural activity at the target site. The implanted device is then calibrated by a neurologist to optimize symptom suppression and control side effects. The advantage of this psychosurgical practice is that it allows change in brain activity in a seemingly controlled manner. And, in contrast to lesion techniques, its effects are reversible. A number of target sites have been used for treatment of depression and obsessive compulsory disorder, most notably the nucleus accumbens that is known to play an important role in the processing of reward and reinforcement experiences. For the treatment of schizophrenia, implantation of electrodes into the septal nuclei have been used. The septal nuclei also seem to play a role in reward and reinforcement, at least what is known from animal studies.

Today, the most encouraging results in favor of deep brain stimulation come from patients suffering from Parkinson's disease and a number of otherwise intractable disorders, including essential tremor and dystonia. Deep brain stimulation can alleviate the symptoms in these patients; however, the efficacy of the treatment is dependent on a set of parameters, including the neurophysiological properties of the targeted brain area. For Parkinson's disease, a few sites in the brain can be targeted, but the two most common ones are the subthalamic nucleus and the globus pallidus interna. Particularly in the past five years, new insights into the underlying neural mechanisms of deep brain stimulation have been gained. It has become evident that the treatment causes neuroplastic changes in the activity and functional connectivity of the neuronal networks. The changes observed affect short- and long-range connections and can occur directly or through a network of cortical and subcortical regions.

These findings are instructive for two reasons. Firstly, they are indicative of a plastic nature of the brain. Secondly, they show that plasticity seems to continue well into adulthood. One huge problem localizationists—be it neurosurgeons, psychosurgeons, or neuropathologists—faced was explaining how damage to a certain brain area did not always produce the same outcome. In fact, despite his clear localizationist agenda, Wilder Penfield's results were by no means clear cut. Rather than being restricted to areas with exact borders, he found considerable overlap between brain regions. For example, a distinct area of the motor cortex seemed to control muscles of the hand but also the upper arm and shoulder on occasion. Penfield attributed this functional overshoot to interindividual variations in brain size and thus localization. Other studies have confirmed such interindividual differences. Additionally, there are other explanations as to why brain areas are much more diffuse than localizationists envisioned (see also Chapter 5). One of these explanations is based on the development of an individual, his or her ontogenesis. Based on clinical studies from children who suffered impairment in their language ability (e.g., due to an injury in the cortical Broca's area), Penfield showed that these young patients redeveloped normal language skills. Thus, some individuals must be able to forgo Broca's area and reorganize neural connections, thereby shifting the speech production area to a noncanonical language region of the brain. This observation held true for children with brain lesions that occurred before puberty. On the other hand, adults who suffered from similar lesions rarely fully recovered and often did not regain verbal abilities beyond the point they reached five months after impairment. These empirical results provide convincing evidence that adult brains are less malleable than younger ones.

In any case, Penfield's observation of children fully recovering after severe damage to Broca's area argued against a conventional, strict localizationism. It strongly indicated that neuroplastic events occurred. How was the observation of a critical period during which the brain is plastic brought in line with localizationism? Localizational purists assumed that each mental function could be attributed to a distinct, single physical area. These areas were generalizable and justified neuroanatomical, cartographical endeavors. This school of thought is still pervading many biological and psychological disciplines. In fact, in the 1980s and '90s, the theory of brain modularity found more zealous defenders. The idea that the brain is regionally parceled out and functionally specialized has led to the formulation of the massive modularity hypothesis, which became especially popular among evolutionary psychologists. This hypothesis postulates that the entire mind divides into highly specialized modules, much like a Swiss Army Knife. Accordingly, the mind can be viewed as an assembly of specialized tools, each designed for a particular purpose. Curiously, some aspects of phrenology seem to have undergone a revival in the massive modularity hypothesis of modern evolutionary psychology.

An orthodox localizationism could not easily be reconciled with a concept of neuroplasticity. But proponents of localizationism as well as those championing the massive modularity hypothesis had to concede the occurrence of neuroplastic events. Also, based on his own findings, Penfield accepted that the human brain was plastic to a certain extent, but he believed that plasticity was limited to a critical period.[13] He assumed that puberty marked a turning point when the brain lost plasticity and became rigid and fixed. The accepted doctrine then was that the brain's ability for adaptation and reorganization is lost after childhood. According to this view, plasticity is synonymous with natural brain development, and only in exceptional cases, e.g., brain injuries, tumors, etc. did neuroplastic processes cause deviation from predetermined developmental trajectories. Localizationist thinking thus expounds that the brain's topology is not yet fixed during early childhood. But in the course of the normal brain maturation process, a precise cerebral map emerges, and that map consists of innate cognitive modules whose inherent functions are prespecified.

There is an intriguing parallel between this localizationist thinking and the gene-centric view discussed in Chapter 1. In fact, evolutionary psychologists explicitly claim that the neonate brain harbors innate cognitive modules whose contents are specified in one's genetic makeup. Yet, as I have already described in detail in Chapter 1, there is no genetic blueprint that holds the master control and orchestrates a defined program to be executed. Rather, ontogenesis is a process that relies on gene–environment interactions. Individuals having the same genotype (e.g., twins) respond to environmental variations in different ways. Such effects may be even more pronounced when comparing individuals with different genotypes. This corollary pertains to most if not all organismal subsystems (e.g., from the molecular to the tissue and organismal level; from the behavioral to the psychological level). As discussed in Chapter 1, the interplay between biology and environment seems to be particularly relevant

---

[13] Penfield and Roberts, *Speech and Brain Mechanisms.*

for human brain development; here, nature and nurture constantly work together in a reciprocal manner to shape the human brain. As ingeniously argued by Gerald Edelman, the brain is not an instructional, but a selectional system. This means there is no construction plan of how to exactly connect the roughly eighty-six billion neurons of the human brain with each other. In fact, we would not nearly have enough genes to provide instructions for a precisely hardwired neuronal circuitry. Neither is the circuitry simply attributable to incoming environmental signals that trigger a certain wiring. On the contrary, our brain operates like a selectional system. There is a vast abundance of neuronal connections in early childhood, many more than will survive during one's lifetime. These connections (i.e., synapses that mediate the communication between neurons) are the product of genes that work in concert with non-genetic factors, like maternal factors. But there is also a good deal of randomness involved (e.g., based solely on the vicinity of neurons). Rather than following a general and pre-programmed plan, our overall neuronal connections have a unique, individualistic nature to begin with. Thus, genes may dictate that we will have a human kind of brain with roughly the same kind of macromolecular circuits, but random individual differences exist right from the beginning. These differences increase steadily due to the effects of neuroplasticity. On a cellular level, neuroplasticity can be defined as the ability of the brain to form or eliminate synaptic junctions between neurons. Selection operates on the abundant synaptic connections by strengthening or weakening of certain synapses based on the experiences a person makes. Because each person's life history and experiences are different, different patterns of connectivity are selected. In this way, distinct synaptic activities get amplified and a unique brain is shaped. This view is diametrically opposed to strict localizationist and modularity thinking.

To reiterate, connections that are used more often are strengthened, leading to the consolidation of synaptic connectivities. On the other hand, connections that are not or hardly ever used are weakened or eliminated. The latter is called synaptic pruning and results in the removal of synapses. In other words, synaptic changes in response to environmental stimuli follow the use-it-or-lose-it principle: more stimulation causes stronger synaptic connections, while a lack of stimulation causes a loss of synapses. Synaptic consolidation, pruning, and synaptogenesis are considered to be important mechanisms underlying learning and memory formation. These processes are particularly prominent during distinct stages of children's brain development that have been associated with critical periods—periods of high receptiveness to environmental stimuli—mentioned previously.[14] Thus, the idea that cognition,

---

[14] Ibid.

personality, and behavior are wholly innate or hardwired at birth is strongly contested by neuroscientific research. During ontogeny, the human brain is constantly changing due to experience, social interactions, emotional development, and self-reflection.

One of the most prominent scholars who made the case for neuroplasticity was the Spanish neuroanatomist and Nobel Prize awardee Santiago Ramón y Cajal. More than a century ago, Ramón y Cajal accumulated a wealth of supporting empirical evidence for plasticity of the brain and championed this idea in his earlier writings. He discovered neurons to possess an amoeboid-like structure at the end of the axon of developing nerve cells. He termed this axonal ending growth cone and hypothesized that it was guided toward its target tissue by chemical substances—findings that were later confirmed using more sophisticated staining and imaging techniques. He assumed that chemical substances were being secreted by other cells that lined the growth cone's path. Reacting to these chemicals, neurons expand their processes and branch out. Importantly, he observed that fetuses, newborns, and babies of a few months only had short and unbranched protrusions. He speculated that these cellular protrusions elongated and became more complex in the course of developing into an adult. But Ramón y Cajal did not stop there. He extrapolated his empirical findings and envisioned human intelligence is manifested by the plasticity of neurons. Let's enjoy how the ingenious neuroanatomist Ramón y Cajal described his ground-breaking hypothesis in his own words:

Les faits d'observation que nous venons d'exposer sommairement, et qui sont d'une portee si considerable en soi, nous ont suggere une hypothese susceptible de faire comprendre mieux que toutes les autres, soit l'intelligence acquise a la suite d'une education mentale bien dirigee, soit l'intelligence hereditaire, soit les adaptations cerebrales professionnelles, soit encore la creation de certaines aptitudes artistiques.

La gymnastique cerebrale n'est pas susceptible d'ameliorer l'organisation du cerveau en augmentant le nombre de cellules, car, on le sait, les elements nerveux ont perdu depuis l'epoque embryonnaire la propriety de proliferer; mais on peut admettre comme une chose tres vraisemblable que l'exercice mental suscite dans les regions cerebrales plus sollicitees un plus grand developpment de l'appareil protoplasmique et du systeme des collaterales nerveuses. He la soite, des associations deja creees entre certains groupes de cellules se renforceraient notablement au moyen de la multiplication des ramilles terminales des appendices protoplasmiques et des collaterals nerveuses; mais, en outre, des connexions intercellulaires tout a fait nouvelles pourraient s'etablir grace a la neoformation de collaterales et d'expansions protoplasmiques.[15]

The translation is as follows:

The facts of observation which we have just briefly explained, and which are of a scope so considerable in itself, have suggested to us a hypothesis that is better than all the others in making us understand, be it the intelligence acquired from a well-directed mental education, be it hereditary intelligence, be it professional adaptations of the brain, or be it the creation of certain artistic skills.

Cerebral gymnastics is not likely to improve the organization of the brain by increasing the number of cells, for, as we know, the nervous elements have lost the property of proliferating during the embryonic period; but it may be admitted as a very probable thing that mental exercise arouses a greater development of the protoplasmic apparatus and the system of nervous collaterals in the cerebral regions. In his case, associations already created between certain groups of cells would be considerably reinforced by means of the multiplication of the terminal branches of protoplasmic protrusions and nerve collaterals; and, in addition, new intercellular connections could be established by the novel formation of collaterals and protoplasmic expansions.

Ramón y Cajal's statement about neural plasticity, particularly about the underlying cellular and subcellular processes as well as its cognitive consequences for the individual, were truly visionary. However, in his later writings, he accepted the then-dominant opinion that "nerve paths are something fixed, ended, immutable"[16] in describing the mature nervous system. This firm belief in a static, mature brain influenced neuroscientific thinking for over fifty years and encouraged a view of fixed neuronal circuits that link disparate brain regions. Especially any changes that occurred in an adult brain were thought to represent events of neurodegeneration rather than generative, neuroplastic processes. Consequently, any damage that caused a loss of function was assumed to be permanent. Or as Ramón y Cajal formulated it, "[e]verything may die, nothing may be regenerated."[17]

---

[15] Ramón y Cajal, "The Croonian Lecture," 444–468.
[16] Ramón y Cajal et al., *Cajal's Degeneration and Regeneration of the Nervous System.*
[17] Colucci-D'Amato, et al., "The End of the Central Dogma of Neurobiology," 266–270.

Today, it is uncontested that human brains are highly plastic. Our brains have the physiological, neural, and cognitive capacity to reorganize themselves. Neuroplasticity enables an organism not only to compensate for brain lesions or defects, but also provides the basis for all learning processes and memory formation. This malleability allows the brain to flexibly respond to an ever-changing natural and social environment. In fact, the first one who came up with a theoretical concept that brain plasticity underlies learning processes was the American psychologist William James. In 1890, he formulated a hypothesis that the brain and its functions are plastic with regards to habits and learning.[18] Assuming that the brain was critically involved in habits and that actions were based on brain processes, he concluded that habits developed through frequent usage of certain neural pathways. Learning or unlearning habits occurred by strengthening or weakening these pathways, respectively. He thus concluded that the brain was not hardwired, but plastic. And this plasticity continued throughout adulthood, since new habits can also be learned well after childhood.

Nonetheless, the concept of neuroplasticity was only accepted around the 1970s, when more and more incontrovertible evidence for it became available.[19] This reluctance to acknowledge the importance of neuroplasticity by the scientific community was partly because the term itself is ill-defined and often used as an umbrella term. Depending on the field of study, different aspects of neuroplasticity are examined, and the term varies in its meaning. Broadly speaking, neuroplasticity refers to the occurrence of non-pathological changes in the brain and its functions. Plastic rearrangement may appear on different scales, for example, on the synaptic, subsynaptic, cellular, or circuitry level, or on whole brain scale. Furthermore, changes may occur only for a short time or for moderate to long intervals (e.g., from minutes to day or years). Neuroplastic events cause an adaptive reorganization of brain circuitry in response to the organism's social and cultural environment, as well as the individual's experience. Thus, the environment does not only exert its effects by influencing gene expression (as discussed in Chapter 1), but also crucially contributes to shaping brain anatomy. As a consequence, neuroplastic events together with gene–environment interactions constitute one's individual behavior and cognitive skills.

What does this tell us with respect to brain development in children? As argued in Chapter 1, we humans are the prime example of niche constructors and are in constant reciprocal interaction with the environment. This is particularly noteworthy since human babies spend an extended period of their

---

[18] James, *The Principles of Psychology*.
[19] Rosenzweig, "Aspects of the Search for Neural Mechanisms of Memory," 1–32.

brain maturation outside the womb. The charismatic paleontologist and evolutionary biologist Stephen Jay Gould contended that humans are essentially *extrauterine fetuses* for the first year of their lives. If we were to follow a comparatively long intrauterine development as our ape relatives, the actual gestation of humans should be twenty-one months, yet human babies are born naturally prematurely. Only when a baby is about one year old does it reach a comparable state of brain and body development as an ape baby at its birth. Moreover, human brains grow postnatally at a similar rate as ape brains before birth. Because of their helplessness and being constantly cared for in the first years after birth, infants' developing brains are not tied up with learning how to quickly become independent and survive on their own. Rather, the toddler's brain development is unfettered to process a plethora of stimuli from the environment. This enables extensive and ardent learning processes unprecedented in the animal kingdom. Anthropologists believe that especially prosocial child-rearing practices have crucially contributed to the massive increase in brain size in human evolution. In fact, the increase in brain size and complexity during human infancy is exceptional amongst all primates. The volume of the brain grows fourfold in the first six years of life ending up as about ninety percent of the adult brain size.[20, 21] This increase is paralleled by prolonged maturation times with distinctly orchestrated sequences of sculpting grey matter densities and enlargement of white matter. The latter is due to an increase in the numbers of axonal fibers, thickening of axons, and hierarchical myelination processes. Enlargement of white matter contributes to the speed and complexity of connections in the brain. White matter stops increasing around the fourth decade of life. The maturation processes of the grey matter, on the other hand, proceed from the evolutionarily "old" parts of the brain, like diencephalon and hindbrain to the cerebellum and pons, to the evolutionarily "recent" parts like the primary and higher areas of the cortex. This increase in grey matter volume may be partly due to the formation of new neurons (i.e., neurogenesis), but is mainly attributable to an exponential increase in synaptic connections in various cortical regions. This exuberant process occurs during childhood and peaks in late childhood, followed by a substantial decline in synaptic density during adolescence. Non-invasive imaging techniques have shown that some brain regions lose about seventeen percent grey matter in adolescence. This synaptic loss represents an important neurodevelopmental process during which the maturing brain is molded and refined. The decline in grey matter is due to experiential selection as described earlier. Thus, the period of neural development necessarily involves enormous

---

[20] Blakemore, *Inventing Ourselves: the Secret Life of the Teenage Brain*, 122.
[21] Blos, *The Adolescent Passage: Developmental Issues.*

structural changes in the brain, including the birth, differentiation, and migration of new neurons followed by elaboration of their dendritic structure and the formation of synapses.

In a nutshell, neuroplastic processes are particularly far-reaching and effective during childhood and adolescence. Unfortunately, this remarkable capacity of brain malleability is not always a blessing. Sometimes it can turn into a curse, as it leaves children and adolescents in particular vulnerable to negative environmental and social factors. Physiological or psychological traumas (e.g., physical traumas stemming from head injuries and concussions or psychological traumas from abusive and neglecting social environments, respectively) strongly interfere with the adaptive shaping of "normal" neural pathways. Patterns that have been learned during childhood are the most formative ones, for it is at this time period neuroplasticity is greatest. Neural pathways that were strengthened in infancy are the ones we most easily draw from, even though the behavior elicited may be harmful in a given situation. On the contrary, rarely used behavioral patterns or behavioral patterns elicited by experiences encountered later in life are less effective because they rely on neural pathways that are weaker due to synaptic pruning. Thus, when trauma victims re-experience responses from developmentally traumatic events in the past—very often without being able to remember the actual situation of their personal history—they fall back into a reactive state of self-protection and survival behavior learned early in life. Even situations that appear normal to other people, such as a crying baby, a minor argument, etc., can trigger an overreaction in a developmentally traumatized person. The traumatized person feels unable to cope with the situation and re-experiences an adverse childhood situation in which a similar state was aroused. This state of fear and helplessness is nonconsciously experienced as a threat to well-being and triggers a developmentally early reactive survival behavior. An adult who grew up in a nurturing environment has an extended potential of self-regulation. Contrarily, developmentally traumatized persons when emotionally overwhelmed cannot make use of mature potentials of self-control and fall back into other behavioral patterns that were acquired during childhood.

Importantly, not only the first few years of life, but also adolescence is a critical period of neuroanatomical changes. Until the second half of the twentieth century, scientists had assumed that the human brain does not change much after childhood. Huttenlocher's studies of post-mortem brains of different regions of the human brain indicated drastic neuroplastic changes that started right after birth and only leveled off at early adolescence. For the first time, these findings suggested that parts of the brain do not stop developing in childhood, but instead continue to develop throughout adolescence. This explained earlier findings that certain cognitive capacities such as some aspects of creativity are higher in adolescence than at other times of life. Also, memories from adolescence and early adulthood are more vivid and long-lasting than memories from any other time in our lives, a phenomenon that is called the "reminiscence bump." Sarah-Jayne Blakemore, the British cognitive neuroscientist who studies adolescents' brains by non-invasive imaging techniques emphasizes that that adolescents' brains are physically different from younger children's brains and from adults' brains. According to Blakemore, adolescence is a distinct stage in terms of brain development. At this phase, individuals are most susceptible to influences from their social environment. She reasons that because of this high malleability along with a pronounced receptiveness of social influence, people are "re-inventing" themselves during adolescence. This is in perfect agreement with previous findings from other scholars who have characterized adolescence as a "second individualization process" and a "second chance" to resolve infantile conflicts that are revived at puberty.[22] Thus, early psychological assessments of adolescence being a distinct psycho-social phase is corroborated by neuroscientific evidence, indicating that sweeping neuroplastic processes happen during this stage of life. Having said that, neuroanatomical and functional changes do not only occur during critical periods in the first two decades of life but happen throughout the whole life (albeit to a lesser extent when getting older). We will return to this important issue in Chapter 5.

---

[22] Eissler, "Notes on Problems of Technique," 223–254.

Chapter 3

Normalcy in the Light of Plasticity

The judges of normality are present everywhere. We are in the society of the teacher-judge, the doctor-judge, the educator-judge, the social worker-judge; it is on them that the universal reign of the normative is based; and each individual, wherever he may find himself, subjects to it his body, his gestures, his behavior, his aptitudes, his achievements.

— Michel Foucault. Discipline and Punish: The Birth of the Prison

A healthy human body is often referred to as running like a perfect machine. The machine analogy goes back to the English anatomist and physician William Harvey, who was the first to describe the systemic circulation of blood in the body by reducing the process to its elements and explaining it in detailed, mechanistic terms. His work inspired French philosopher, mathematician, and scientist René Descartes. Descartes claimed all organisms to be mindless, mechanistic automatons. This, so he asserted, would also hold true for humans, at least as far as the body and the brain as an organ are concerned. In contrast to animals, however, Descartes believed that humans, being the apex of creation, possess a brain that is connected to the soul.[1] The soul, not the brain, was deemed to confer thinking. This mechanistic vista inspired scientists for centuries to come. They imagined a healthy body, including a healthy brain, to function like a well-made clock or power plant. Fritz Kahn, a German gynecologist and popular science writer of the last century, most imaginatively illustrated the inner workings of the human body using metaphors of industrial life in tune with the most innovative inventions of the time. He depicted parts of the human body with spectacular, man–machine analogies, e.g., muscles were depicted as gear wheels; the digestive system as being equipped with conveyor belts; and the brain as a complex factory with distributing centers, secretaries, and cameras. Kahn's works became immensely popular because he succeeded in making complex principles of nature understandable to lay people through his technological metaphors and fanciful illustrations (Figure 3.1). His series *Das Leben des Menschen* (Human Life) soon became an international best-seller and further

---

[1] Lokhorst, "Descartes and the Pineal Gland."

entrenched mechanistic thinking. Mechanistic and optimized—this is how the healthy human body became to be perceived by the general public.

Throughout the last decades, mechanistic analogies speak to us directly out of popular writings and pictures. Kahn's books served as an idea generator for the 1966 classic science fiction film *Fantastic Voyage* by Richard Fleischer. The film portrayed a team of medical experts that were shrunk together with their ship to the size of a microbe and injected into a man's body to rescue him from dying of a cerebral venous thrombosis. A few decades later, a remake named *Innerspace* was produced by Steven Spielberg that made the theme even more famous to an international audience. In one famous scene, the main character, renegade Navy test pilot Tuck Pendleton, grins into the mirror, slaps himself, and exults "The Tuck Pendleton machine—zero defects!" The message conveyed by Tuck Pendleton in the movie, like in many popular books, is simple: the parts of his body equal cogs in a well-oiled machine. And a healthy body must operate machine-like and error-free. Irrespective of the impoverishment of such a metaphor, the machine analogy remained an important symbolic representation not only in the public view but also in the biological and biomedical sciences. And it has indeed served well and provided a number of insights. But at the same time, the success of the mechanistic approach often led to cognitive shortcuts and left researchers grappling with the aftermath of simplification. When we assign machine-like attributes to the body, we may talk ourselves into believing that we are some sort of specimen of a general production series—passive and fixable. In fact, biomedicine has become dominated by a mechanistic overconfidence that takes engineered solutions to ill health as the favorite way forward. Today, most physicians and biomedical researchers subscribe to the medical model of disease that is based on a causal-mechanistic view. Central to the medical model is the assumption that there is something like a "normal" realization of a biological process. Abnormality, on the other hand, is characterized by a significant deviation from normal physiological functioning. Such abnormality is expressed as outwardly detectable symptoms that can be objectively measured and then appropriately treated. This rationale goes for somatic (i.e., bodily) diseases as well as psychopathologies. The latter means that the cause of any mental disorder is believed to lie in biological (i.e., biochemical, molecular, cellular, neurophysiological) abnormalities within the affected brain.

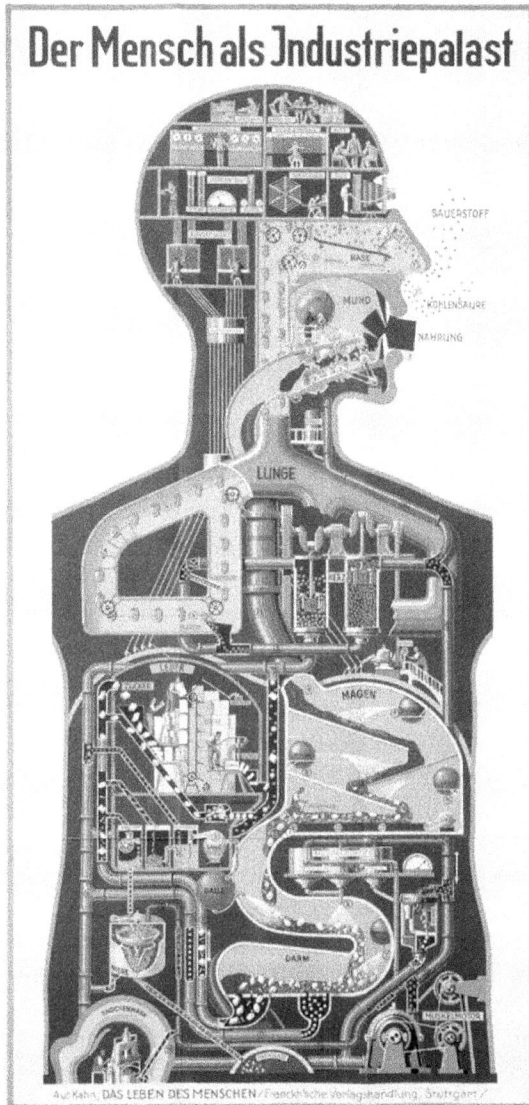

Figure 3.1: Fritz Kahn (1926) Der Mensch als Industriepalast. In: Das Leben des Menschen, Band 3. Stuttgart: Kosmos Gesellschaft der Naturfreunde, Franckh'sche Verlagshandlung.[2, 3]

---

[2] Kühne, "Der Mensch Als Industriepalast."
[3] "Incredible Man-Machine Analogies."

By succumbing to the medical model and the resulting corollary that the human body functions like a machine, we are importing serious conceptual problems. Firstly, how shall we define the standard of being healthy or functioning "normally"? While it is relatively easy to figure out when a machine is broken, defining average functioning in humans usually requires a reference group. In addition, we chiefly focus on the individual, thereby ignoring the environment. The assumption is that if you are ill, you are ill regardless of which part of the world you live in—Europe, Asia, the U.S., or anywhere else. Moreover, we contend that "normal" development does not influence the trajectory of a disease. Of course, development is important for the timing and onset of the disease, but development itself is understood to proceed in the same manner in all individuals. We, thus, tend to disregard idiosyncrasies and life histories. And eventually, we heuristically assume that treatment of a disease equals the turning of a few cogs. After all, the mechanistic goal is to restore a state that is considered normal. In order to achieve this, we must bring the sick person into line with the respective reference group.

Let us first look at how we define what is normal and what is not with respect to brain functioning. Many psychopathologies have undergone re-definitions over the course of time. What was considered an illness a century ago may no longer be seen as desirable to be treated. The fact that some human behavior was considered an illness may even fill us with terror and awe today. This already indicates that what is classified as disease is not as clear-cut as one might naïvely assume. But no more than we can classify a disease can we define what a reference group is. What can be considered "normal" and what not often seems ambiguous. For instance, until 1973, homosexuality was classified to be a disease in the Diagnostic and Statistical Manual of Mental Disorders-II (DSM-II). Along with diagnosing homosexuality as a disease, a set of therapeutic interventions, so-called conversion or reparative therapy aiming at changing an individual's sexual orientation, were applied. Such techniques included ice-pick lobotomies (the pseudoscientific treatment Howard Dully was submitted to); chemical castration; the application of electric shock to genitals; and nausea-inducing drugs that were administered simultaneously with the presentation of homoerotic stimuli. Needless to say that all these pseudoscientific practices turned out to be ineffective and in many cases harmful. Thankfully, most Western countries have, already several decades ago, abandoned the pathologization of sexual orientations and the ensuing cruel treatments.

Another conjectural mental illness was drapetomania. In 1851, American physician Samuel A. Cartwright named and described this alleged disease.

Drapetomania referred to a slave's desire to flee captivity.[4] Appealing to the authority of the bible, Cartwright argued that slaves are born to be submissive to their master and *normally* have no desire to run away. In fact, he discussed in detail that if the master is kind and takes care of the enslaved person's physical needs, the slave is spellbound and cannot run away. To ensure subservience, it would suffice to keep slaves in a submissive state and treat them like children. If a slave nonetheless shows the desire to escape the master's control, it must be a mental disorder. Cartwright suspected that the malady was a consequence of a master being too friendly and treating slaves as equals. If warning signs of imminent flight occurred, such as encountering the slave as being sulky and dissatisfied without reason, Cartwright recommended whipping as a therapy. If this remained ineffective, it was advised to surgically remove both big toes to make it physically impossible for the slave to run away.

What may sound like an inhumane absurdity today was not just the abstruse opinion of a misguided few. After delivering a paper before the Medical Association of Louisiana, Cartwright's conjectural diagnosis and treatments were widely reprinted in the South of the United States. It indeed reflected the view of a majority of white people living in the South in the eighteenth and nineteenth century. This illustrates how movable borders between normalcy and disorder can be if it were to be determined by those who benefit from it. Even if there is a reference group that seems to largely confirm a classification scheme (e.g., most slaves did indeed not run away), it does not necessarily mean that the classification is biologically founded.

Harriet Ann Jacobs, an African-American slave who escaped slavery and later became a writer in her autobiography, *Incidents in the Life of a Slave Girl*, gave a rare insight into the distorted narratives concerning the slaves' behaviors and minds. Let us see what Jacobs said about a slave girl's desire to be free while hiding in a shed from her master's search party and bloodhounds:

> This continued darkness was oppressive. It seemed horrible to sit or lie in a cramped position day after day, without one gleam of light. Yet I would have chosen this, rather than my lot as a slave, though white people considered it an easy one; and it was so compared with the fate of others. I was never cruelly over-worked; I was never lacerated with the whip from head to foot; I was never so beaten and bruised that I could not turn from one side to the other; I never had my heel-strings cut to prevent my running away; I was never chained to a log and forced to drag it about, while I toiled in the fields from morning till night; I was never branded with hot iron, or torn by bloodhounds. On the contrary, I

---

[4] Cartwright, "Diseases and Peculiarities of the Negro Race."

had always been kindly treated, and tenderly cared for, until I came into the hands of Dr. Flint. I had never wished for freedom till then. But though my life in slavery was comparatively devoid of hardships, God pity the woman who is compelled to lead such a life![5]

Yet freedom was not unambiguously considered to be an appropriate treatment of endured plight of enslavement. Even in Germany in the 1920s, where slavery had not been an issue for a long time, psychiatrist Emil Kraepelin expressed reservations about the aftermaths of liberating African Americans from slavery. Since incidents of psychopathologies were much higher in the white population of the United States in the nineteenth century, it was argued that slavery had a protective effect on mental health. Kraepelin indeed deemed it mentally harmful for black people to be free. Drawing from William White (1903),[6] Kraepelin reported a sudden rise of mental illnesses in African Americans. While in 1870, only 367 African Americans per million displayed symptoms of mental disorders, in 1880, 912 per million showed mental illness sysmptoms, and in 1890, 980 per million were mentally ill. Also, in the North of the United States, the percentage of mental illnesses in the African American population became highly alarming. While white Americans in the South had a ratio of healthy people to mentally ill of 1:456, Black Americans had a "much healthier" ratio of 1:1,277. On the other hand, Black and white people of the North were equally more troubled. The ratio of healthy to mentally ill people was 1:520 for white Americans, and even 1:452 for African Americans.

These figures seemed to absurdly justify an interpretation that slavery and forced labor was in the best interest of the tormented. And it supported the misguided idea that within certain populations, freedom was a pathological desire. It required a long process of advocacy for human rights of African Americans to set the picture straight. Drapetomania as a medical term for a mental disorder could still be found in Thomas Lathrop Stedman's *Practical Medical Dictionary* as late as 1914, where it was defined as vagabondage or dromomania, an uncontrollable or insane impulsion to wander.[7] And in the 1920s, the highly influential German psychiatrist Kraepelin continued to quote White's diagnosis of drapetomania, as mentioned earlier. Eventually, by the middle of the twentieth century, drapetomania was no longer considered a disease. In Europe in general, drapetomania was not a widely debated issue since slavery was no longer legal on that side of the Atlantic. But another "disease" termed fugue, poriomania, or dromomania (i.e., roaming urge or

[5] Jacobs, *Incidents in the Life of a Slave Girl: Seven Years Concealed.*
[6] White, "The Geographical Distribution of Insanity in the United States," 257–279.
[7] Stedman, "A Practical Medical Dictionary."

impulsive vagabondage) plagued the inhabitants of the old world. Fugue or dromomania became well known in the medical and psychiatric literature, first occurring in France and Italy, and later spreading to Germany and Russia. Interestingly, fugue, i.e., the act of running away sometimes in delirious states, has been known forever but only in 1887, it became a specific, diagnosable type of insanity.[8] Once the medical profession turned its attention to this phenomenon, more detailed etiological diagnoses ensued. Unlike drapetomania in the States, dromomania was not seen as a disorder in its own right but as a morbid episode of variable causation. Psychiatrists of the late nineteenth century defined impulsive vagabondage as a symptom of mental illnesses like epilepsy or hysteria. In addition, a new class of psychopathology was identified that was tagged with the label of neurasthenia, a condition characterized by physical and mental fatigue. The latter did not involve symptoms of amnesia while wandering around, but it became a social indicator and included the stigmata of degeneracy. From there, it was just a small step toward associating the malady of fugitive behavior with low-class migrant laborers and "gypsies." In Germany and Austria, dromomania became known under the name *Wandertrieb* and was soon to be attributed to homeless people in general. From the end of the nineteenth to the beginning of the twentieth century, being homeless and displaying symptoms of Wandertrieb equaled a personality trait disorder. This diagnosis also included children and adolescents who were believed to exhibited poriomania as a consequence of various psychopathologies. Still in the early 1950s,[9] poriomania was argued to be caused by endogenous mental disorders that seemed to be sex-linked and hereditary. Emil Kraepelin[10] described vagabonding people as mentally—and frequently also physically—inferior and possessing full-fledged psychopathologies.

In 1926, child psychiatrist August Homburger[11] described case studies of children and adolescents who suffered from the urge to run away. Although he conceded that a large group of these young vagabonds came from abusive families where they experienced neglect and unkindness, he also identified a significant amount of the children and adolescents who expressed symptoms of compulsive wandering due to pathological mania or imbecility. Let me cite here Homburger's case study of Ludwig E. whom he diagnosed with inborn vagabondage and childhood deviousness (translated from German):

---

[8] Hacking, *Mad Travelers: Reflections on the Reality of Transient Mental Illnesses*.
[9] Trott, "*Und dann bin ich abgehauen*," 25.
[10] Jablensky, "The Diagnostic Concept of Schizophrenia: Its History, Evolution, and Future Prospects."
[11] Homburger, *Vorlesungen über Psychopathologie des Kindesalters*, 512–513.

Ludwig was the 12 year old son of a cemetery caretaker. [...] Ludwig started school at the appropriate age, but disliked attending school, and constantly received bad marks. Right from the beginning, he was irritable, angry, and did not get along with his siblings. From the age of 8 years onwards, he ran away, skipped school. He stayed away from home overnight for the first time when he was 9 years old. When he was 11, this had happened ten times. Because his parents could no longer afford the police fines imposed, they took the child to a medical examination after the possibility of a pathological cause had been brought to their attention. The parents reported that the boy frequently complained about having a head ache and being tired and that he still had wetted the bed when he was 6 years old. They did, however, not report any other physical conditions or symptoms, especially none that was indicative of epilepsy.

On the other hand, the boy has developed an unfavorable character. He was lying and fond of sweet things and had already borrowed money in the name of his parents when he was 10. He was slightly moronic and also lazy. He avoided homework, ran away, visited other kids, stayed away for longer than agreed, and was then afraid to go back home. Instead, he repeatedly stayed outdoors at the cemetery and slept there overnight. Once he stayed away from home for 3 days and was eventually found in a hedge of the graveyard where he – according to him – had slept; he looked dirty and starved.

As the usual motif for running away, he stated to be afraid of punishment, especially being hit when not knowing anything in school.

According to Homburger, the most striking attribute was Ludwig's lack of fear of the cemetery. The child psychiatrist marveled that the boy did not spend the night at the cemetery because of sentimental feelings; instead—and that was most surprising to Homburger—Ludwig hid there without fear, creeps, timidity, or veneration. The boy seemed not to mind making a sleeping place out of sacks and straw mats at the graveyard whenever he was afraid of going home. Homburger concluded from this medical examination that the main reason of the child's vagabondage was fear of—what Homburger called "justified"—punishment. At the same time, Homburger found the child to be "moronic" and incapable of meeting the demands placed on him; Homburger assumed that not even diligence would spare the boy from humiliation and punishment. The child psychiatrist questioned whether Ludwig could accomplish his homework because of a presumable lack of the necessary intellectual preconditions. In addition, Homburger observed that Ludwig did not fit in at school because of being frequently angry, irritable, and litigious. Homburger also reported that the boy became increasingly less influenceable over the years. Eventually, he developed a strange and, for a child, atypical emotional hebetude. Consequently, Homburger predicted that such a combination of inborn traits did not only cause the propensity for vagabondage and other childhood deviousness but would also drive various antisocial behavior when the boy matured.

Some authors believe that pathologizing of abscondence and seeing it as a— at least partially—congenital personality deficit rubbed off on how we perceived and still perceive homeless people.[12] Biologizing homelessness shirks policy makers from a socioeconomic responsibility and assigns blame to the genetic roulette, a strategy that had already worked "well" for individual school achievements and educational issues (see Chapter 1 concerning the intelligence debate). How devastating this may be for the individual can be exemplified by Ian Hacking's concept of "looping effects."[13] Hacking studied such looping effects in the realms of psychopathologies and demonstrated that the verbal discourse about certain psychopathological or psychological phenomena has a fundamental impact on how this very phenomenon is framed, theorized, experienced, and treated. Hacking has meticulously described how people are affected by what we call them and, even more, by classification. Consequently, these pathologizations can become self-fulfilling prophecies. According to this concept, classification provides a framework within which people can express their own actions and make constrained choices. Thus, people shape their behavior, experience, and self-understanding in response to the possibilities society acknowledges and expects. In fact, Hacking reports looping effects for conditions like dromomania, hysteria, ADHD, and many more. He offers an interactive concept of classifications that can influence the people classified who in turn influence what is classified and thereby modify or replace the classification itself. Contrary to the general assumption that classification relies on definite properties, Hacking claims that these properties are moving targets because we interact with them through investigation and thereby change them. Consequently, the people investigated also change. Take again dromomania as an example. On one hand, parents whose child was diagnosed with this disorder were absolved from their full parental responsibility like in the aforementioned case of Ludwig E. After all, parental care was believed to be of little avail against a child's biological fate. On the other hand, dromomania became a welcome diagnosis that exculpated adults who did something wrong, like leaving one's family during a stressful

---

[12] Ibid.
[13] Hacking, *The Social Construction of What*.

period, going on a fugue with the employer's money, or deserting from the army. This is not to say that the person did not suffer from a mental disorder or experience a temporary mental breakdown, but the way it was expressed, e.g., by wandering off for an extended period of time, was afforded by the classification that was prevalent at that time. In France during the late-nineteenth and early-twentieth-century, the prototypical patient suffering from fugue (i.e., dromomania) was a working-class man who had a home that he was driven to flee from. Contrarily, in Germany, the classification of dromomania mainly targeted homeless and was associated with degeneracy. In other countries like the United States or the British Islands, dromomania was virtually unknown. Hacking explains this by arguing that expressing symptoms require a certain niche in which patients can "thrive" and in which certain symptoms are socially accepted. What is the evidence for Hacking's hypothesis of social niches providing the required environment for certain pathological behaviors?

Over the last fifty years, in addition to models based on biological inheritance, other explanatory models of disorders gained more and more importance. In the 1960s, the focus shifted to a psychological-pedagogical approach. This approach no longer tried to exclusively look at the individual (e.g., the child who ran away), but also included his or her social environment. Rather than being a strict biological abnormality, dromomania became a symptom of lack of adaptation to certain family environments and was believed to be caused by a child's poor upbringing and neglect. Running away was seen as a regressive defense mechanism triggered by antisocial feelings, low frustration tolerance, and defiance. Thus, dromomania was still considered symptomatic for certain psychopathologies, but in addition to biological causes, psychological factors and parenting were now given more emphasis. People suffering from it were still assumed to belong to the underclass and have low intelligence. In spite of taking the social environment into account, wandering off was nonetheless considered a maladaptive reaction based on poor upbringing of the individual concerned. Such vista entailed other "therapeutic" interventions like police measures or institutional care combined with strict surveillance and control. Of course, these provisions did little to ameliorate the stressful situation a person experienced during the urge of running away, as it neither addressed the initial cause nor the child's need for safety.

Let me illustrate this by giving an example of a traumatized child whose symptoms were dealt with but causing the symptoms to subsequently manifest themselves in a different form. At a recent workshop, I learned of a highly traumatized, eloping young boy who was placed in a juridical care facility. The social workers there who often had to deal with runaways made sure to lock the entrance door in the evenings so that the institutionalized children did not get themselves into dangerous situations by running away in the middle of the night. For the first few weeks after his admission to the institution, the young boy suffered from panic attacks and insomnia. These symptoms appeared much worse than before when he was still with his family. The therapist soon discovered that the symptoms were due to physical abuse the boy experienced at home. At home, however, when he could not cope with situations of extreme stress anymore, he ran away and spent extended periods of time away from his family. In the new surroundings of the institution, the causal factor—the abusive perpetrator—was no longer present, but the change of environment still caused a high level of stress in the child. Yet his usual means of stress relief by absconding was no longer available to him. This led to a build-up of emotions that spiraled into aggravated anxiety symptoms. Eventually, the boy managed to find new ways of handling the stress and became mentally more stable. Much to the surprise of the social workers of the group, they found the child's sneakers hidden under his pillow. The sneakers seemed to provide a highly comforting feeling for him. The immediate availability of his running shoes conveyed the subjective impression that he could leave whenever he wanted, which ameliorated his symptoms. Under the supervision of the therapist, the boy's overall mental condition improved and he eventually agreed to remove the sneakers from under his pillow to the floor as long as they remained within reach. This arrangement between the child and the therapist ensured the active employment of a positive coping mechanism rather than running the risk that a lack of alternative, effective coping strategies may manifest as even more severe psychopathological symptoms.

This example highlights that looping effects may play out in completely unexpected ways by expressing symptoms in ways that are acceptable or "adaptive" in a given environment. This is especially true for children and adolescents whose brains readily undergo extensive neuroplasticity in order to adjust to the particular social environment they face. It can easily be envisioned how looping effects may open an avenue to channeling symptoms in more beneficial ways for the person affected by taking advantage of the malleability of young brains. Experienced child therapists could provide appropriate guidance here. The important issue is that looping effects have to be understood in relation to the underlying causes. Even if a runaway child no longer absconds from home or foster care and seems to have "improved," the traumatizing cause that triggered the symptom in the first place may not have been addressed at all. Looping effects probably play a paramount role in how contemporary virtual technology is used—by children and adolescents as much as adults. At this point, it must be emphasized that looping effects are reciprocal processes that can undergo changes as well as reinforcement. In other words, we again encounter a strong nature–nurture intertwinement, similar to what was discussed in Chapter 1. Special attention should thus be given to self-reinforcement that may prove detrimental for the child. "Optimizing" adaptation to a given niche may have long-lasting negative effects when the person is confronted with other social environments that pose challenges to the behavior previously developed.

Over the last decades, the psychological-pedagogical approach that merely focused on the person and encouraged an apportionment of blame to the individual was increasingly criticized. In the 1970s, a new approach based on socialization theory took root. The focus was now shifted to the social environment and the person's social history. Problems were investigated in the context of relationships that occurred within the system. Accordingly, symptoms like dromomania were considered constructive problem-solving strategies as a reaction to a toxic environment be it a family, educational, or institutional environment. Within this framework, interventions targeted the broader system rather than in the individual alone.[14] It moved the thinking away from linear to circular causality and aimed at changing the family dynamics, expecting to change individual personality and identity along with it. Additionally, symptoms of psychopathologies such as dromomania were no longer considered to be limited to only low-income families. A distinction was made between deficit families and conflict families. The former described family systems that suffered from a lack of material and non-material resources and usually were found in the lower class. The assumption was that socioeconomic disadvantages favored family structures that enabled dissocial behavior and personality disorders. These symptoms could not be counteracted against by educational measures available within the family system due to poor education of the family members and lack of financial means. Consequently, measurements taken frequently included placement with foster care. Conflict families, on the other hand, referred to families from middle and higher classes that experienced severe conflict situations leading to traumatization of the child. These families usually have the financial and non-material resources to negotiate imminent stress situations but use their resources to conceal problems and hide them from the public gaze rather than addressing the causes. The attenuation of the conflict potential can then lead to an aggravation of the overall complex of problems, more severe traumatization, and triggering psychopathological symptoms in the persons concerned. Most commonly, interventions tackling conflict families rely on social work and family therapy that draw from systems theory.[15] Systems theory in social work closely looks at the interrelationships of all family members and its dynamics, including developmental lifecycle challenges. One of the core

---

[14] Burnham, *Family Therapy: First Steps towards a Systemic Approach.*
[15] Forder, "Social Work and System Theory," 23–42.

insights of systems thinking in family therapy is that there is no "normal" family structure or organization, but that all interactive family processes are highly dynamic.

This brings us back to the beginning of our discourse of the mechanistic world view of psychopathologies and how to define normal with respect to an individual or a system such as a family. The endeavor to biologize and search for biological or, more precisely, for genetic foundations for any deviant behavior, cognitive trait, or idiosyncratic personality has rarely proven fruitful (as we have seen in the nature-nurture debate concerning intelligence in Chapter 1).

Notwithstanding the increasing acknowledgment of psychological-pedagogical and socialization theories, the medical model and its underlying mechanistic world view still prevail in debates about cognitive and personality traits. This is due to the assertion that more than any other theory, the medical model seems to successfully employ criteria of objectivity. It provides an account of biological normalcy based on statistical measurements of quantifiable, physiological parameters. In today's world of scholarly work, quantifiability and statistical normality convey objectivity, rigor, and scientific soundness. Thus, while the medical model allegedly provides a gold standard using objective, controlled, and reproducible methods, other theories are often considered to draw from "soft" sciences because they rely on qualitative approaches. Normalcy and quantifiability serve as established and well-proven key determinants in scientific discourses. The definition of normalcy in the context of health and disease was first worded by Christopher Boorse in his biostatistical theory[16] and was widely discussed thereafter. According to Boorse, all disorders can be described as no more than a biological dysfunction that in turn can be defined in terms of statistical normality. Hence, a disorder is anything that deviates significantly from an average value of a certain parameter found in a reference group. A reference group means a standard population that is representative for certain parameters when evaluating somebody's behavior and cognitive capacities. Consequentially, the aim is to draw a line between what is "normal" in a reference population and what is not. Following Boorse, being "normal" can be fully defined in biological terms. Here, we move away from dubious diagnoses like drapetomania and turn to children displaying severe behavioral problems and mental "abnormalities." Many such behaviors and alleged disorders have been defined in biological terms, and some deviant behaviors and illnesses are still ascribed to congenital factors

---

[16] Boorse, "Health as a Theoretical Concept," 542–573.

today. In this vein, the biostatistical account has been the standard view held by most medical professionals as well as scientists throughout the last century.

To exemplify this thoroughly physical account of psychopathologies and the perceived superiority of nature over environment, let me give you three short excerpts of medical diagnoses made by certified psychologists or psychiatrists whose job was to assess the physical and mental health as well as the personalities of children institutionalized at castle Wilhelminenberg in Vienna, Austria. What was not known, or at least not overtly acknowledged, by the child psychologists and psychiatrists and certainly never scrutinized was that the children of castle Wilhelminenberg suffered from severe maltreatment and were psychologically and physically victimized by staffers and external perpetrators. About forty to fifty years later, the Vienna city authorities conducted an investigation that upturned massive and systematic cases of child abuse, including widespread beatings, systematic rape, and even murder. With this caveat in mind, let us turn to the individual psychological assessments of three different children. The case reports are excerpts from the final report published in 2013 by the Vienna city authorities and are translated from German.

Case 1: Psychological report of a ten-and-a-half-year-old girl who was admitted to castle Wilhelminenberg in 1961 due to a pending risk of "squalidness."

> The girl examined had been sexually abused by her foster father at the age of 7 (?). She currently lives with her mother and stepfather and has already been taken to child counselling once before (in 1960). At that time, she had caused troubles at home, probably triggered by her neurotic "background." Dr. P., who then examined the minor, suggested to send her to castle Wilhelminenberg for observation. But the parents could not bring themselves to do so. In the meantime, however, the child's behavior worsened. E. forges signatures, steals, especially sweets – probably aiming at gaining pleasure – lies, and has damaged plants and furniture several times. During the examination, the girl appeared inhibited, seemed embarrassed, and when her wrongdoings were mentioned, she pretended not to know why she misbehaved. From her weak hints, it emerged that she felt alienated and emotionally neglected. Real evidence that would support this claim could of course not be found.[17]

---

[17] Helige et al., *Endbericht der Kommission Wilhelminenberg*.

Case 2: Psychological report of a seven-year-old girl who had been institutionalized at castle Wilhelminenberg in 1966.

Reason for visit: masturbation, self-imposed shackling, peculiar behavior.

Currently, the minor gets attention due to her hysteric tendencies, which are expressed by screaming for hours, working herself up into emotional states until turning blue, coquettish posturing, abnormal suggestibility, and sensation mongering. For example, she put herself in shackles to impress her fellows with a mendacious story and to take center stage. Masturbation is self-taught but is doubtlessly supported by an abetting character and physical foundations.[18]

Case 3: Psychological report of a nine-year-old boy who had been institutionalized at castle Wilhelminenberg in 1959.

Background: Born out of wedlock, the minor was put into foster care with his maternal grandparents straight after birth. He was quite pampered and soon displayed education difficulties. Following the death of the grandfather, the mother took the boy back but could not dedicate much time to him due to her job. Being unattended, he loitered around. He committed several thefts, did not cooperate at school, and stood out because of his readiness for mischievous behavior. Occasional abuse-like corporal punishment failed to achieve the success the mother hoped for. After hesitating for a long time, she agreed to his transfer and observation to castle Wilhelminenberg as suggested in the primary assessment of 23.06.1958.

The psychologist who examined the boy came to a devastating conclusion, suggesting that the child's inborn personality deficits were beyond repair and only were aggravated by his grandparents' tender and nurturing environment.

Assessment: K., who is relatively tall for his age, exhibits a defective physique. The pasty, saggy skin, the poor, limp posture, the slightly protuberant eyes (also a series of signs of degeneration) give him an unfresh and old appearance. Rather shy at the beginning, he soon shows a lack of distance: he becomes importunate, takes one's hand, wants to know, see, and touch everything. His motoric calmness is striking.

---

[18] Ibid.

According to his stupid, simple-minded behavior and also partially to his school performance, one can consider him moronic. However, the results of the psychological assessment and his teachers' assessments only partially coincide. K. shows an average intelligence quotient with significant variation. His best results are in the domain of graphic cognitive processes, his worst in the domain of logic processes. Reduced critical abilities, playfully-dallied (infantile), and relatively slow pace of work clearly show that his potentially available capacities rarely come to light – if at all only when a problem affects one of his scarce personal interests. His personality is of little value. He is selfish, craves for recognition, and does everything to be recognized as important. To this end, he finks on his fellows, lies, plots and schemes, but plays innocent and unfairly persecuted whenever he gets caught (and this happens almost all the time because of his ineptitude). He is too primitive to realize that he virtually provokes rejection by his fellows. Trying to arouse his ambitions for reasons of guidance only brings fleeting success: 1. because his relationships with educators are not durable and 2. because he does not have a proper will of his own and has no stamina. All he proffers are evasions and excuses. If one approaches him more vigorously on occasions, he completely shuns, displays a mask outwardly and transfers his activities to the subsurface. Notwithstanding that these behavioral patterns are rooted in inherited predispositions, we will have to understand them eventually also by taking living conditions into account that contributed a lot to his special status. It is no coincidence that K. – in spite of having always been problematic – became particularly bad after being transferred [from his grandparents] to his mother. Having been pampered in the family of the grandmother, sometimes being the pivotal center point, he then faced a totally different world. He had to share the role with his brother and, in contrast to the grandmother, the mother reacted to lack of discipline with severe punishment. So, his preexisting squalor got enhanced by another neurotic nuance. Further institutionalization will superbly serve his education. Without it, there is the risk of repeating school classes anew or maybe even admission to a special school for retarded children. Recovering from his squalor and achieving proper social adjustment cannot be expected, but rather just an acquisition of greater daily routine.

Conclusion: Depraved boy with low value of intellect and character. Change of environment and caregivers caused an increase in problems.[19]

These case reports indicate the psychologists' strong conviction of the biological basis of "abnormal" behavior and character traits. Despite the occasional concession to potential influences from the social environment, the cause of the abnormalities is deemed to lie with the children, with their biological make-up and innate cognitive capacities. After all, the average child does not show such deviant behaviors. This corollary also became more entrenched in the mind of the general public, who echoed those experts' assumption and thereby contributed to the propagation of biological normalcy. In fact, residents living in the neighborhood of castle Wilhelminenberg reported that they were told as children to avoid interacting with the institutionalized children of the castle because of the inmates' defective characters and low intelligence. The institutionalized girls were stigmatized as sexually depraved or morally impaired, and the institutionalized boys as prowlers with criminal energy. One neighbor remembers that he was told as a child that "the girls there were difficult, troublesome, and loopy."

At all times, people have had ideas ready at hand about what can be considered normal and what not. But as discussed previously, the notion of normalcy has changed many times over the last decades. What was considered a mental illness—such as homosexuality, drapetomania, or dromomania—are no longer regarded to be pathological. Today, many cases that show deviations from the average and range outside a reference group no longer fulfil the "criteria" of biological abnormality. With the gain of influence of socialization theory, a child's upbringing in relation to his or her family and social system came increasingly to the fore. The cognitive and personality development of the child is soon seen as processes of growth and adjustment to society. The various social groups to which a child belongs to, such as family and peers, presumably provide a variety of different social situations for the young person to learn techniques of behavior and cognitive processing to adjust to new modes and challenges of life. After all, that's what children's and adolescents' neuroplastic brains do best, adjusting to their social environment.

Yet, as already discussed in Chapter 1, recent research shows that causality is not unidirectional and forces the individual to passively succumb to the pressure of the (social) environment. Niche construction theory tells us that organisms actively change their surroundings and, to a certain extent, adjust it to their needs and requirements. Still, the notion of subjection of the organism

[19] Ibid.

to the environment pervades our minds. This subjection is captured by the dictum of the "survival of the fittest" that memorably sums up the traditional adaptationist program, which emerged toward the end of the nineteenth century and still prevails, albeit in a weaker form. This pan-adaptationism holds that all organismal traits have evolved into a state of optimum with respect to their environment.[20] Thus, the general assumption is that only individuals who are best adapted (i.e., fittest) will survive to produce offspring, whereas less adapted ones will be weeded out by natural selection. However, the pan-adaptationist program has been heavily criticized over the previous decades.[21] One of the most important points that have sparked the debate concerns the erroneous assumption that physical and psychological traits show a nearly perfect fit to nature. This fit is considered to be achieved by the environment posing "problems," which the successful organism "solves" and eventually reaches optimal or nearly optimal solutions. This way of thinking neglects the fact that the environment does not remain stable but changes continuously. This means that a system is not merely maintained by a consistency in conditions that allows it to always return to a particular—optimized—state (i.e., homeostasis), but instead, biological systems are highly dynamic and continuously alter and develop along multiple possible trajectories.[22] Thus, many traits, especially those involved in human cognition and personality, are not fixed and do not follow a predetermined, optimal trajectory that is stably buffered against any environmental perturbation as some evolutionary psychologists[23] would have us believe. On the contrary, rather than being encoded for optimal fit, most traits change, develop, and mature owing to a reciprocal interaction between the organism and its environment that allows for context-specific plasticity. In addition, biological structures are usually not produced from scratch, but built from preexisting structures, like layers upon layers of history. This way, organs, molecular structures, physiological pathways, etc. are tinkered, and such tinkered features are far from optimal. Ergo, biological systems do not develop following a blueprint for perfection, but draw from a developmental repertoire that provides affordances—how the organism can experience the environment and interact with it in multiple ways.[24] This reciprocity shapes traits that are not optimal but rather just "good enough" to survive and reproduce in dynamic

---

[20] Gould and Lewontin, "The Spandrels of San Marco," 581–598. The latter bestowed natural selection with a near omnipotence "in forging organic design and fashioning the best among possible worlds."

[21] Ibid.

[22] Waddington, *The Strategy of the Genes.*

[23] Cosmides and Tooby, "Origins of Domain Specificity," 84–116.

[24] Karmiloff-Smith, "Ontogeny, Genetics, and Evolution," 44–51.

surroundings.[25] Populations that exhibit traits that allow for a significant degree of plasticity depending on the habitat show an appreciable advantage over those whose traits are maximally optimized to fit a given environment. Populations displaying flexibility avoid running into blind alleys of evolution if changes in the environment occur. In any case, such a fatal situation can nonetheless occur in face of abrupt environmental changes to which a population cannot react rapidly enough due to an unavailability of appropriate biological responses.

Humans display an impressive range of plasticity to adjust to their environment. This phenomenon holds true for many organismal characteristics, but seems to be particularly significant for cognitive traits. Neuroplasticity, as discussed in Chapter 2, allows an abundance of modifications in the organization of the neural anatomy and function during the entire lifespan of an individual in response to environmental variability. Ensuing the richness of social and cultural influences that our ancestors historically have faced and that we continue to face, neuroplasticity has enabled us to cognitively forge ahead to break new ground. For instance, plasticity and radical environmental changes have facilitated exaptations. Exaptations are processes that cause features that were evolutionarily selected for a particular function (adaptations) to be later co-opted for a new use. Or alternatively, some features may not have been the product of natural selection (non-adaptations) but still can be co-opted for current use. Such exaptations are believed to be of particular importance for the evolution of human cognition and culture. After all, there are many traits related to human cognition that appear to have become of paramount importance because of selective forces based on cultural evolution and human-specific niche construction. Paleontologists and evolutionary biologists Stephen J. Gould and Elizabeth Vrba have pointed out that "[m]ost of what the brain now does to enhance our survival lies in the domain of exaptation."[26] Paradigmatic examples of exaptations are our cognitive capacities for processing symbols for reading and performing arithmetic. Reading and arithmetic are relatively new inventions of human culture. Given the relatively short time span, it is highly unlikely that cognitive traits for these culturally new achievements have evolved by natural selection. Instead, it is much more plausible that our ancestors already possessed specialized cognitive networks that were involved in pattern recognition and in the processing of visual, visuospatial, and

---

[25] Gailer et al., "Morphology Is Not Destiny," 369–383.
[26] Gould and Vrba, "Exaptation—a Missing Term in the Science of Form," 4–15.

linguistic representations.[27, 28, 29] These brain networks have then been diverted from their original uses to perform new functions for culturally new tasks, often by connecting to brain areas with other functions.[30]

Remarkably, processes of cultural evolution typically operate faster than processes of biological evolution by natural selection.[31] Cultural and technological evolution happened in the blink of an eye, evolutionarily speaking. Niche construction considers exactly such circumstances under which cultural transmission can overwhelm natural selection.[32] This happens because niche construction modifies selection pressure and amplifies the impact of individuals on their environments through reinforcing feedback loops. As a consequence of human niche construction, an ever-increasing disequilibrium between evolved traits and environment is created, shifting the process of nature-nurture reciprocity toward the latter. A special process is *social* niche construction in which organisms modify their own social environment and influence the conditions of their own social evolution.[33] Social evolution is driven by social competition[34] and cooperation and may explain some extreme behavior and exceptional cognitive traits.

Individuals themselves play a crucial role in the generation of their surroundings and habitats. Man-made social niches foster certain cognitive or behavioral traits, while attenuating others. Hence, certain social niches favor specific neuroplastic processes in individuals, who in turn ensure the maintenance of this very niche to which their brains are well adapted. This process can be transmitted over generations, as children usually inherit their parents' and grandparents' ecological, cultural, and social niches. Many behavioral and cognitive traits that result from such reinforced feedback loops within social niches are highly adaptive, like social learning and teaching behaviors, prosocial child-rearing practices, and pair bonding. Others may start off as beneficial for the majority of group members, but due to social competition, become detrimental for the survival of some group members at a later time point. Take child care and child-rearing as an example. When our ancestors lived as hunter-gatherers, their lifestyle was characterized by low-fat

[27] McCloskey et al., "Cognitive Mechanisms in Number Processing and Calculation," 171–196.

[28] Dehaene and Cohen, "Cerebral Pathways for Calculation," 219–250.

[29] Dehaene et al., "Sources of Mathematical Thinking," 970–974.

[30] Barry, "Perception and Visual Communication Theory," 91–106.

[31] Perreault, "The Pace of Cultural Evolution."

[32] Laland et al., "Cultural Niche Construction and Human Evolution," 22–23.

[33] Laland et al., "An Introduction to Niche Construction Theory," 191–202.

[34] West-Eberhard, "Sexual Selection, Social Competition, and Speciation," 155–183.

diets, high mobility, low birth rates with relatively long intervals (four years) between births, exclusive breastfeeding for the first two years, low population density, and living in small (twenty-five to fifty people), kin-based social groups.[35] With the onset of agriculture and the abandonment of nomadic lives, modern humans changed their diets, started to live in larger communities, and reduced the intervals between births, with a resulting increase in birth rates.[36] Increasing birth rates, shorter intervals between childbirth, and shortened breastfeeding periods required an intensification of prosocial activities of group members. An increasingly important role in child rearing was therefore devolved to kin as well as non-kin group members, which was further spurred by a rise in economic prosperity due to changes in lifestyle. The wealthier, more influential, or more dominant a person, the easier it was for her to afford parenting aides or cajole other group members into support. With the onset of agriculture and animal husbandry, property rights co-evolved[37] as an important effect of social competition. Such rights secured claims to the products of one's labor. In foraging cultures, property rights were of lower relevance because most of hunter-gatherers' mobile and dispersed resources could not cost-effectively be demarcated and defended. Agriculturalists, though, came to acknowledge the possession of wealth—like crops, dwellings, and animals—to be highly advantageous.

At some point, property rights entailed inheritance rights that lead to further cementing disparity due to social competition. While prehistorical inheritance systems are unknown, researchers know a good deal about millennia-old historical regulations of inheritance due to written historical records of different cultures. Further insight has been gained by anthropological and sociological studies of contemporary societies and cultures. Based on these lines of research, it seems that intergenerational wealth transmission among agriculturalists tends to be rather unequal and mostly patrilineal (i.e., only male children can inherit), but most importantly for our argument of social niche construction is the fact that the enactment of hereditary rules of physical property coincided with the inheritance of a social niche. In addition, non-egalitarian inheritance systems causing discrimination based on gender and birth order further incited social competition, leading to a multiplication and diversification of social niches. Interestingly, property rights went beyond chattel, land, dwellings, and livestock, and included also human beings. As a

---

[35] Dunbar, "Coevolution of Neocortical Size, Group Size and Language in Humans," 681–694.

[36] Bocquet-Appel and Bar-Yosef, *The Neolithic Demographic Transition and Its Consequences*, 35–55.

[37] Bowles and Choi, "Coevolution of Farming," 8830–8835.

consequence, a social niche emerged that was occupied by slaves, women, and children who were considered legal properties in many societies. They were seen as assets that contributed to the prosperity of persons of high status. As a result, social niche construction ensured not only the transmission but also the transgenerational accumulation of affluence.

The settlement history of American colonies provides one of many historical examples of social niche construction through socioeconomic power. At that time, children were crucial as colonial labor force. More than half of all people who came to the colonies south of New England were indentured servants. The majority of them being minors on average between fourteen and sixteen, and the youngest being only six years old.[38] Many of these children were orphans or were born out of wedlock and then routinely separated from their mothers upon weaning and bound out to a master. Or they were slave children, who were sold away from their parents by their masters. Others were brought from Europe as indentured servants without parents, such as the London street children. These "street urchins" were coerced by the City of London to be transported to the colonies where they were employed like adult workers. These children were important economic producers who ensured the maintenance of the landowners' social niches. Therefore, the right to exert control over them was a matter of local court regulations and legislations adopted by those in charge. In doing so, social niches could be conserved. This course of action pursued in the New World followed a long historical tradition that was practiced on the other side of the Atlantic Ocean. It allowed the re-construction of a social niche for deprived children that had already "proved itself" in the Old World. Mary Ann Mason, professor emerita at the School of Social Welfare at UC Berkeley writes in her book *From Father's Property to Children's Rights* about the legal aspects of children who were considered properties under American law:

> The harsh manner in which colonialists treated children reflected the English tradition. Colonial family law and employment law were still firmly tied to their English origins. Common law relating to indenture contracts for children, custody following divorce or the death of a parent, and the disposition of orphans and bastards traversed the ocean virtually unchanged. Sometimes these laws were modified in practice by the colonialists. For the most part, however, these laws were well suited to the New World experience, where the demand for labor exceeded the

---

[38] Mason, *From Father's Property to Children's Rights*.

available supply of adult workers. These laws did not formally change until the nineteenth century.[39]

The notion that children were an adult's property may not be particularly surprising from an extended historical perspective. What is most interesting, however, is the observation that property claims to children were not just based on biological parenthood, as could be expected. As far as some social niches were concerned, claims were based on the provision of sustenance, i.e., claims to a child could be asserted when providing the opportunity to live in an appropriate niche. The legality of such property claims was first reasoned by John Hobbes:

> The title to dominion over a child, proceedeth not from the generation, but from the preservation of it; and therefore in the estate of nature, the mother, in whose power it is to save or destroy it, hath right thereto. . . And if the mother shall think fit to abandon, or expose her child to death, whatsoever man or woman shall find the child so exposed, shall have the same right which the mother had before; and for this same reason, namely, for the power not of generating, but preserving.[40]

Notably, contemporary laws of many countries continue to treat children as property, either of their parents or the state. Legal paternity still exposes a rhetoric of ownership, possession, and exchange.[41] The fact that children were seen as property without rights over a long historical period facilitated parental behavior of child neglect, maltreatment, and even infanticide until today. Violence against children has pre-dated modern society by millennia but still prevails. Important clues to child protection in order to fight violence and abuse can be found in studying the law and culture of historical societies, particularly how they treated their bondsmen, slaves, and women.[42] Such studies give hints as to which social niches were available to the most helpless members of a society who often shared the same social niche. In societies that treated children as properties, atrocities often remained unpunished and were quickly swept under the rug. How children are treated is therefore tied to culture as well as a particular social niche and economic condition.

Child labor regulations usually protected the rights of the proprietors rather than those of the underage workers. Those regulations were still abundant

---

[39] Ibid.
[40] Hobbes and Molesworth, *The English Works of Thomas Hobbes of Malmesbury.*
[41] Maillard, "Rethinking Children as Property."
[42] *Slaughter of the Innocents: Child Abuse through the Ages and Today.*

during the time of the Industrial Revolution in the eighteenth and nineteenth century and partly also during the technical revolution (or second Industrial Revolution) at the end of the nineteenth and beginning of the twentieth century. With the onset of the scientific-technical revolution in the middle of the last century and the information and digital revolution happening now, a significant shift in the social environment occurred and new social structures emerged. Following economic changes, societal changes ensued and new social niches were created, including protected social niches for children. Today, increasingly more countries pass laws to protect children against cruelties and inhumane treatment. Partly accountable for these societal upheavals was a growing interest in human intellect and mental work that resulted from the most recent cultural revolutions, which slowly ousted the importance of physical work. This novel trend also seized the working class of the Western world, opened new avenues, and enabled working-class children to occupy social niches that were previously inaccessible to them.

In addition to social changes, the industrial revolution had far-reaching consequences from a biological point of view—not all of them positive for humans. Harvard paleontologist Daniel Lieberman argues that the Industrial Revolution had a significantly higher impact on human health and well-being than the agricultural revolution.[43] This is because the transition from agrarian to industrial economies took place in a breathtakingly short time, namely over a few hundreds of years. Industrialization occurred within less than a dozen (human) generations and profoundly altered everything from human population sizes, health, working, living conditions, diet, to almost any aspect of the ecological environment—think of the emergence of big cities, factories, overpopulation, traffic, and so on. At the same time, our bodies have not had enough time to evolve in order to cope with all the aspects of the new environment we inhabit. Due to the fast pace of human niche construction over the last few hundred years, humans are now confronted with a striking paradox. Despite more wealth, impressive advances in health care, sanitation, and education, our bodies face challenges that were virtually unknown a few generations ago. According to Lieberman, these challenges arise from an evolutionary distortion of biological traits that have evolved to be beneficial in one environment and were carried over into another environment where they ended up becoming maladaptive.[44] This phenomenon became known as evolutionary mismatch theory[45, 46] Examples of evolutionary mismatches

---

[43] Lieberman, *The Story of the Human Body.*
[44] Trevathan, et al., *Evolutionary Medicine.*
[45] Diggs, "Evolutionary Mismatch: Implications Far Beyond Diet and Exercise."
[46] Lloyd et al., "Evolutionary Mismatch And What To Do About It."

include Type 2 diabetes, heart disease, osteoporosis, eating disorders, and phobias like vertigo.

The Industrial Revolution as outlined by Lieberman was, however, only one of the incisive transitions that occurred over the last centuries. The subsequent scientific-technical as well as the information and digital revolutions that took place over the last eighty years were much more than just cultural transformations; they comprised economic and social changes that rapidly and radically altered the historical trajectories of humans, as well as the terrestrial and partially even extraterrestrial environment. The aforementioned cultural transformations went hand in hand with social evolution driven by processes of niche construction. Social evolution, however, has dramatically outpaced our biological evolution, leading to a mismatch between modern social environments and our psychological, cognitive, and personality traits. Such mismatches can appear as psychopathologies like social phobias, addictive behavior, and other mental disorders.

The notion that biological evolution failed to keep pace with the rapid progression of cultural evolution that caused the emergence of physiological and psychological illnesses, as postulated by the evolutionary mismatch hypothesis, stands in opposition to the medical model previously discussed. The medical model looks at causal-mechanistic explanations and seeks to give an ahistorical and purely physiological account of pathologies. On the contrary, drawing from niche construction and the evolutionary mismatch hypothesis, we can understand pathologies, especially psychopathologies in a very different way.

It should be noted beforehand that definitions of "normal" or "healthy" based on the evolutionary mismatch theory are not uncontroversially accepted. Critics deprecate that normalcy cannot merely have evolved as an adaptation to the environment for two reasons: First, some disorders have spread widely in populations despite a selective pressure against such dysfunctions. Second, not every trait that has evolved is useful or has a function. Accordingly, it cannot be possible for such traits to become dysfunctional. Let us reconsider these points of criticism. For one thing, biological traits—be it physiological, psychological, or cognitive—are far from optimal and display a wide variational spectrum within a population, as mentioned earlier. Consequently, it is by no means clear-cut how to define what is normal and what is not. Drawing a boundary between normal and abnormal seems to involve a certain degree of arbitrariness that is not unequivocally supported by the underlying biology. I have previously discussed the medical model and its mechanistic account by means of examples such as homosexuality, drapetomania, and dromomania. Following this line of thinking, we may reject the medical model of disease and readily agree with a normativist account. Normativists postulate that what we consider abnormal and classify as disorders is driven by social conventions. This means that a certain culture or society attributes a tag of abnormality to traits that may be seen as normal in other cultural or societal settings. Moreover, there may be a political agenda behind such "diagnoses." For instance, certain populations or subpopulations can be grouped together by allegedly diagnosing medical disorders that are actually based on practical utility, be it social or political. If that is the case, definitions based on utility would clearly take recourse to evaluative rather than medical judgments. In fact, my previous examples of drapetomania and dromomania can prima facie be explained by a normativist account.

Although several historical cases of diagnostic procedures and classifications of illnesses may not require any further explorations and could be fully explained by applying a normativist framework, this nonetheless won't give us the complete picture. Some people suffering from diseases show symptoms that clearly deviate from physiological or psychological responses of most other people. These people may severely suffer from strong symptoms irrespective of their subjective awareness or knowledge about having a particular disease or not. In fact, they might never have been diagnosed with a disease. Or they may have even been told to be perfectly healthy or normal because of missing diagnostic tools or lack of available physiological markers. Yet, these people may feel ill and their symptoms are considered pathological in any sociocultural context.

To further elucidate this point of view, let us look at the highly controversial issue of attention deficiency hyperactivity disorder (ADHD). According to the DSM-5, ADHD is characterized by poor attention, hyperactivity, and impulsivity.[47] Depending on the severeness (or genetic penetrance) of ADHD, symptoms might impair the child's functioning in daily life, like in school or when interaction with peers, parents, or teachers. In adulthood, most symptoms diminish but some still persist in an altered form. In line with a naturalistic explanation drawing from the medical model, ADHD is considered to be the result of a biological condition rather than poor parenting or early childhood adversities. Molecular genetic studies have supported a strong genetic contribution and heritability to ADHD. The disorder appears to be caused by a dysregulation of certain neurotransmitter systems, especially serotonin.

Normativists have reached the opposite conclusion. Cross-cultural and social health studies have shown that diagnoses for ADHD varied depending on ethnicity, social background, geographic region, and whether the child

---

[47] *Diagnostic and Statistical Manual of Mental Disorders: DSM-5.*

examined was covered by health insurance or not. The lack of consistency of diagnoses given by child health experts provided strong arguments against a naturalistic account of ADHD. Advocates of normativism therefore claimed that ADHD is purely socially constructed for the purpose of allowing parents or teachers to medicalize and pharmaceutically pacify those children who express inconvenient or annoying behavior. In this sense, treatment for ADHD is considered to be an assault of the children treated, and these infants are altered for the sake of punitive or authoritative judgments of the society they were born into.

So, where do we currently stand in the controversy between naturalists and normativists? A civil rights movement has emerged that propagates "neurodiversity." This movement draws from normative considerations but acknowledges the naturalist basis of human diversity. It originated in the 1990s as a challenge to the medical model of disease and its underlying naturalistic and causal-mechanistic vistas. Neurodiversity is understood as a natural part of our genetic inheritance and evolution of the human species. The biological factors that contribute to deviations from the cognitive norm are not seen as pathological, but rather as variations of the human genome leading to a neurological pluralism.[48] This pluralism has been highly advantageous for human society because it enabled evolution in the first place.

The neurodiversity movement has traditionally espoused autistic people, especially "high-functioning" individuals within the spectrum of autistic disorders. Despite their neurological idiosyncrasy, "high-functioning" autists have significantly contributed to contemporary computer technology and progress and should therefore be given appropriate opportunity to develop their ideas in a suitable setting. MacEachron's calls for a neurodiversity-tolerant and respectful society that supports interindividual, neurobiological differences, rather than antagonizing them. At this point, normative issues loom large. In short, the neurodiversity movement holds that it is the neurotypical-dominated (i.e., "normal") world that requests children (and adults) with different mental states or neurological conditions to fit into societal norms of the average reference group. Such normative arguments were made for autism, ADHD, developmental coordination disorder, developmental speech disorders, dyslexia, dyspraxia, dyscalculia, dysnomia (i.e., difficulty in remembering words, names, or numbers), and other mental health conditions such as bipolarity, schizophrenia, schizoaffective disorder, sociopathy, obsessive-compulsive disorder, and Tourette syndrome. Proponents of neurodiversity advocate for children and adults whose minds work differently

---

[48] Blume, "Autistics, Freed from Face-to-Face Encounters, Are Communicating in Cyberspace."

from "average" or "normal" persons to find their place in the world where they feel they can fit in. In other words, supporters of the neurodiversity movement propagate picking one's niche in the sense we have discussed earlier.

However, psychologist Devon MacEachron bemoans that there is too little positive reinforcement that enables people with neurologically different minds to flourish. While society is slowly recognizing and beginning to accept the benefits and advantages of diversity among people, with respect to gender, ethnicity, sexual orientation, and physical disabilities, neurological differences among people are still considered to be mental dysfunctions. Where are the niches in our world where neurodiverse individuals can fit in? This might be the most imminent problem the neurodiversity movement faces. It will mainly be neurotypical individuals who create and provide niches for neurodiverse individuals. Or perhaps not? Will it therefore lie at the discretion of the "normal," neurotypical individuals and their willingness to create space for those who do not conform with traditional psychological and behavioral norms? Rephrasing this on a meta-level, MacEachron's plea is a call for the construction of novel niches. In fact, niche construction seems to have already taken place and paid off for autists and people with social anxieties. Cultural transitions owing to the information and technical revolution have created virtual spaces for social interaction that have become a part of our "normal" life style. Many autistic people have found the internet to have improved their lives, because it offers them a unique way of communication that is socially accepted at the same time.[49]

However, the concept of neurodiversity is still quite controversial. Advocates of the medical model point out that the mental differences associated with these conditions nonetheless cause severe impairments in many areas of a person's life, something that is marginalized by defenders of neurodiversity. Jonathan Mitchell, a blogger and autist, is a strident opponent of the neurodiversity movement. He cautions against trivializing the disabling aspects of disorders for the sake of political correctness and wrongly attempted political and societal inclusion.

Let us return to the claim that neither the medical model nor normative accounts like the neurodiversity movement will give us the complete picture of how to define normalcy. What is then missing to complete our picture? Let us again invoke the image of the "painting hands" (Figure 1.5). Most likely, we visualize the picture how it has been reproduced from the original, e.g., like the figure depicted in Chapter 1. We probably entertain our sensations while perceiving the oeuvre either in its entity or in detail. What we usually leave aside

---

[49] Ibid.

is imagining the process of its formation, the intricacies that led to the emergence of the final work. In analogy, when we investigate a certain biological disorder or abnormality in a person, we first assess the status quo. To this end, we measure physiological parameters, watch for symptoms, and try to identify markers that tell us about the state of the patient. What is largely overlooked in the debate is the process of the disorder, its development. Yet as discussed previously, biological systems do not merely remain constant, returning to a state of homeostasis upon perturbations like diseases; instead, biological systems continuously change and develop. If a system is perturbed, it won't simply go back to its initial condition but will end up at a different point along one of the multiple trajectories. Thus, we are not dealing with a mechanism like a seesaw, as often depicted in medical reports about homeostasis and some physiological factors that are out of balance. Instead, we should be envisaging something quite different, more like a wildfire. We owe this analogy to the Russian-Belgian physical chemist and Nobel laureate Ilya Prigogine. In fact, Prigogine predicted that many processes in nature resemble phenomena like fire. Such processes are complex, transformative and most importantly, they are irreversible.

Remember that the "painting hands" (Figure 1.5) symbolized the reciprocal interactions between environment and the organism's genetic composition. What we left out of the picture was the role of development and organismal change. In the previous sections, we tackled questions about how well an organism fits into a given environment by focusing on adaptive versus non-adaptive traits. In doing so, we were actually looking at adaptedness rather than adaptation.[50] Adaptedness is a state of being—a state of how well a trait contributes to the organism meeting the exigencies to survive and reproduce in a certain environment. It has a finite quality range, is measurable, and can thus be compared to a given reference state. Our previous discussion about specifying parameters in order to define what can be considered normal versus abnormal falls into this category. For example, the human body temperature is a physiological adaptation to hot and cold climates. Although there are significant interindividual variations in body temperature, the average internal temperature is thirty-seven degrees Celsius. and a certain temperature range can be given to define normalcy and health in human population. However, body temperature is not a fixed parameter in an individual; the body continuously works through thermoregulation to remain in homeostasis. When this state is perturbed by external conditions, the body counteracts the challenges. To counteract cold, it can react through thermogenesis (e.g., muscle-induced shivering and metabolic non-shivering occurring in brown

---

[50] Reiss, *Not by Design: Retiring Darwin's Watchmaker.*

adipose tissue). On the other hand, to counteract heat, the human body reacts by sweat evaporation to cool down. Other external factors, such as infections by pathogens, can also be counteracted by an elevated body temperature or fever. Although fever temporarily perturbs the temperature homeostasis of the body, it is a highly adaptive process because it represents an efficient host defense strategy against pathogens. In any case, body temperature seems to be an exemplary case of adaptedness and homeostasis in which compensatory mechanisms preserve the relative constancy of a trait despite external perturbations (although there is accumulating evidence that the average body temperature as well as the capacity of thermoregulation changes with age).

In contrast to adaptedness, adaptation is better characterized as the property of a dynamic system to return to a trajectory rather than to a distinct state after perturbations. Consequently, an optimal reference state cannot be unequivocally pinpointed thereby making it difficult to stipulate general thresholds and limits for an organism. This is due to the fact that organismal development has many junctions and branch lines. This leads to the deliberation that (1) health and normalcy can only be defined in relation to a given environment; and (2) there is a continuous change of both the organism and the environment due to reciprocal feedback loops. This prompts us to assess and define (1) at multiple time points in different environmental (i.e., ecological and social) contexts.

With this mindset, let us now re-examine the question of normalcy in psychological and cognitive traits. Transient changes in behavior and attitude help individuals fine-tune their adjustment tactics to their particular niche and cope with everyday social life. This adjustment can be understood as the adaptedness of a behavioral or psychological trait. Homeostasis can be achieved by such transient changes. While positive attitudes increase fitness in situations of opportunity, negative attitudes cause a halt in investing in hopeless endeavors and encourage the quest for alternative strategies. As an example of the latter, children who were raised in neglecting or abusive social environments display responses of fear and sadness that help them cope with this adverse situation and may attract support by alloparents (i.e., adult caregivers other than biological parents). Now, consider that psychological processes of emotional regulation taking place along developmental trajectories. This means the child not only learns how to best respond in specific social situations, but also that these acquired behavioral patterns shape her further psychological and cognitive development through re-enforcing processes. Emotion regulation processes are crucially determined by the quality of attachment a child has to primary caregivers. Thus, human attachment theory[51] (as will be discussed in Chapter 7) can be interpreted from an evolutionary perspective of niche construction and neuroplasticity, allowing adaptation to a given niche. Accordingly, abnormal styles of attachment, specifically anxious attachment and ambivalent attachment, may in fact be adaptive in certain social situations.[52] Say, if a mother is disinclined to invest in her child, it would be less beneficial for the infant to display secure attachment falsely signaling her environment that nothing is amiss. On the contrary, anxious or avoidance attachment may help the child to attract the support of other adults of the social group or explore alternative strategies of self-calming. As a consequence, seemingly inappropriate behaviors—such as anxiety, isolation, aggression, or addictive personality traits—may indeed be adaptive in certain social contexts. Interestingly, some psychologists and psychiatrists have claimed that certain psychopathologies like social anxieties, depression, or narcissistic personality disorders that are exacerbated by our modern social environment are mere exaggerations of adaptive traits."[53]

Emotional and social neglect during childhood can lead to adaptive behavioral changes driven by neuroplastic events during these critical phases of development. However, these behavioral patterns that may have proven useful in adverse social environments will most likely be maladaptive in other social niches. This is due to the fact that niche construction generates opportunities as well as constraints. We human beings contribute to the creation of our niches by molding them to best fit our own needs. We get born into a certain social niche that other family members and society have constructed for us. The aforementioned historical example of child laborers without rights was an illustration of a social niche constructed for the benefit of some individuals at the expense of others due to social competition. As infants mature into adults, they aim at selecting new niches that are available to them, a process termed "niche picking."[54] In the animal kingdom, the selection of niches by organism is adaptive, as it brings the individual in contact with more favorable conditions. Niche picking does not simply mean making a choice of optimal conditions. What is seemingly optimal also depends on the state the organism is in and is a result of its previous exposures to certain environments.[55] In addition, different organismal processes and behaviors may have different requirements, thus the niche eventually selected may be a compromise between conflicting needs that would be most adequately met in

[51] Bowlby, "SEPARATION ANXIETY," 251–269.
[52] Chisholm, "The Evolutionary Ecology of Attachment Organization."
[53] Stevens and Price, *Evolutionary Psychiatry*, 94.
[54] Scarr and McCartney, "How People Make Their Own Environments," 424–435.
[55] Lewontin, *Dialectical Biologist*.

different places. In humans, these different needs are often best addressed by belonging to different social groups. In order to become a member of a given group, it is expected that "neophytes" adapt to the social niche in question by adhering to the group's constraints, i.e., its characteristic values and norms. These constraints are not immutable but molded by the group members. Each group comprises of people who have their goals, aspirations, and agendas but some of these constraints can be in direct conflict with the neophyte's own aspirations. As a result, some neophytes will not be able to adjust well to a particular social niche, especially when having experienced a contrasting social environment during childhood or adolescence, as discussed earlier. Amongst all primates, human relationships appear to reach unique depths of emotional, cognitive, and physical intensity. The ability to enter and commit to meaningful and high-quality relationships must be acquired early in life in the social niches provided and has implications for one's mental and physical health. If members of a social niche cannot provide appropriate scaffolding for the child to experience positive relationships, the child will acquire dysfunctional behavioral patterns that cause social mismatches and can manifest themselves in an array of maladaptive tendencies.[56, 57] Symptoms of maladaptation will then outcrop in adult relationships or when joining a foster family. Such maladaptive responses are experienced as stressful. To avoid stress reactions, individuals will seek out niches that match previously established behavioral patterns that were shaped in response to social experiences made in childhood and adolescence. This will usually be reflected in their adult relationships and may also affect their choices of niches, such as workplaces, professional associations, political and governmental affiliations, etc. This phenomenon of picking an adverse niche is not limited to humans but can also be found in animals. Mice will preferentially return to familiar places when experiencing states of high arousal. Familiar places are clearly given preference over unfamiliar ones, even if the animals experienced physical pain in the former and no punishment in the latter.[58] To avoid stress experienced due to maladaptation when finding themselves in environments that do not match their behavioral or cognitive patterns (poor niche picking), individuals manipulate their environment. This means they construct niches to make their environment match their acquired behavioral or cognitive patterns rather than modify their behaviors or cognition.[59] This process can help explain why when abused or neglected children become parents themselves, they once more create abusive or neglecting familial environments. This may initially seem

---

[56] Uchino, "Social Support and Health," 377–387.
[57] Reblin and Uchino, "Social and Emotional Support," 201–205.
[58] Mitchell et al., "Arousal and T-Maze Choice Behavior in Mice," 287–301.
[59] Wexler, *Brain and Culture Neurobiology, Ideology, and Social Change.*

surprising, given the findings that the human brain remains extremely malleable and plastic throughout life and is capable of producing different behavioral patterns. However, it is important to note that neuroplasticity decreases in the course of brain maturation. In the adult brain, neuroplastic events are still taking place in various areas of the neocortex but occur to a lesser extent in other brain regions. Once a developmental path is taken triggered by negative incidents, it guides the subsequent neural development along other trajectories than those that would have been available without these initial adverse experiences.

As described in detail in Chapter 2, human babies are not born with the extensively connected neuronal circuits characteristically found in adult brains. Brain development initially occurs with an overproduction of neurons *in utero*. After birth, neurons increase in size, and neuronal networks develop by first generating an early exuberance of synapses, a process of adaptive synaptogenesis that all humans undergo. Synaptic connections are then selectively adjusted or pruned in response to external, environmental stimuli. Concomitantly, some neurons undergo selective cell death (apoptosis). Net synapse elimination begins postnatally, accelerates at onset of puberty, and extends into adulthood. The synaptic strengthening is accompanied by an increase in myelination to hasten these connections. Myelination is an insulation process that encases the axons of neurons, thereby increasing neural connectivity and enhancing the communication speed along these neural pathways. As discussed in Chapter 2, the various neurobiological maturation and alteration phenomena are summed up under the umbrella term neuroplasticity. Organisms constantly learn and gather information about their environment and incorporate these details in the growing brain circuitry by representing features of the environment in idiosyncratic but distinct, activatable brain connections. Importantly, the long duration of brain maturation during extended human childhood and adolescents gives humans the possibility of progressively acquiring skills in physical, behavioral, cognitive, and emotional domains.

On the other hand, the extended time of human infancy and adolescence causes a parent–offspring conflict. This is due to the fact that the infant's need for resources reduces the fitness of the parents, an observation that was first described by Robert Trivers.[60] I will discuss this point in more detail in Chapter 8. For the moment, let us keep in mind that this intergenerational conflict is manifested in some opposing interests of parents and their offspring, especially if resources are scarce and when families are suffering economic hardship. In short, a fast development of the infant benefits parental fecundity,

---

[60] Campbell, "Parental Investment and Sexual Selection," 136–179.

while a slow development benefits offspring fecundity. This can also be modeled in terms of neuroplastic events. Computational models using an unsupervised algorithm called adaptive synaptogenesis indicated that larger rates of synaptogenesis and synaptic plasticity speed up the development of mature neuronal connections. Consequently, overall brain maturation proceeds faster but happens at the expense of adult performance and accuracy of neuronal networks. Thus, the time span allowing for synapse overproduction and synaptic modification leading to mature connectivity is balanced with subsequent neural performance—this neurobiological tug-of-war reflects the parent-offspring conflict. The outcome of the model, therefore, strongly argues for a compromise between speed and efficiency of neural development.[61]

Empirical studies in mice have shown that the generative neuroplastic processes like synaptogenesis occur in the neocortex of adult mice[62, 63] and is also ongoing in the primate neocortex throughout life.[64] At the same time, eliminative neuroplastic processes like synaptic pruning and synapse elimination are high in childhood and adolescence but drastically slow down in early adulthood. The maintenance of a relative constant synaptic density in adulthood is most likely due to a replacement of functionally immature synapses by mature ones. As a consequence, net synapse elimination is high in childhood and adolescence and evens out to no net change in the adult age of the organism. What is of particular importance for our argument is the total net reduction of active synapses in the developing brain. An exuberant number of cortical synapses present in childhood before the drastic rearrangement processes in adolescence may be able to compensates for various mental and cognitive dysfunctions due to a sheer excess in the number of synaptic connections. At that point, it seems as if homeostatic processes can balance out the impact of severe genetic or environmental perturbations. However, brain development proceeds in a highly dynamic yet constrained fashion that follows certain available trajectories rather than allowing all possible functional and anatomical outcomes. Thus, with the onset of massive pruning events and synapse rearrangements during adolescence, these dysfunctions can no longer be compensated, leading to the emergence of behavioral, psychological, and cognitive symptoms. This neurodevelopmental model is currently one of the

---

[61] Ju et al., "Limited Synapse Overproduction."

[62] Holtmaat et al., "Experience-Dependent and Cell-Type-Specific Spine Growth," 979–983.

[63] Knott et al., "Spine Growth Precedes Synapse Formation," 1117–1124.

[64] Stettler et al., "Axons and Synaptic Boutons Are Highly Dynamic," 877–887.

favored hypotheses for explaining psychopathologies like schizophrenia and autism.[65]

Since all humans start off with different genetic constitutions and experience different environmental cues in their respective social niches, we should now take a closer look at how we define normalcy. Taking the socio-cultural environment into account in which children and adolescents grow up, we may gain some hints concerning the availability of certain neurodevelopmental trajectories for an individual. Returning to the example of ADHD, we may now be able to bridge the opposing views of the naturalistic and normative accounts. Children vary in their genetic outfit, and due to complex interactions of the genetic and gene-regulatory levels, some individuals will display conspicuous behavior like poor attention, hyperactivity, and impulsivity early in life. Depending on the cultural niche in which the children live, these behavioral symptoms may be enhanced, suppressed, or redirected into different behavioral patterns. Reciprocal feedback loops can cause a severe manifestation of symptoms or the diversion of symptoms along alternative developmental routes, leading to high creativity and surgency.

It would, therefore, be more enlightening to embrace the idea of neuroplasticity spanning a continuum of events that includes structural and functional remodeling during development, life-long learning processes, as well as much of what we consider to be psychopathologies. Following this perspective, several (clearly not all) psychopathologies would then account for a subset of the natural continuum of brain plasticity. This aligns well with the neurodiversity movement that may be as crucial for humans as biodiversity is for life on Earth.[66] Hence, neurodevelopmental processes can explain a broad spectrum of "abnormalities" derived from the continuous interaction between the person, one's biological foundations, one's social niche, and the developmental paths that are accessible due to the constraints based on these multidimensional interactions. Most importantly, we can now see why the social niche is of such paramount importance to child development. Psychiatrist Bruce Wexler got to the heart of it when he wrote that "one person's nature is another person's nurture."[67] In addition to organismal challenges based on the individual biological foundations, our social surroundings can be the making or breaking point of how we develop.

---

[65] Blakemore, *Inventing Ourselves.*
[66] Armstrong, "The Myth of the Normal Brain: Embracing Neurodiversity," 348–352.
[67] Wexler, *Brain and Culture Neurobiology, Ideology, and Social Change,* 16.

Chapter 4

Gene Expression: Nurture Fueling Nature

It happened on an autumn day in 2006, when Penny Waldroup, accompanied by her female friend Leslie Susan Bradshaw, took her four children to Kimsey Mountain in Polk County near Greasy Creek, Tennessee. There, in a secluded trailer park, lived her estranged ex-husband and father of her kids, Davis Bradley Waldroup Jr. As soon as the two women left the car and approached him, Bradley Waldroup, who had been drinking all morning, picked a quarrel with them. The quarrel ended in a bloody clash in which Bradley Waldroup shot his ex-wife's friend Bradshaw eight times at point-blank range. He then went after his ex-wife, who had fled in panic, shot her in the back, severely mutilated her with a machete, and dragged her back into his trailer mobile. All this took place while their four children watched in horror, surrounded by splattered blood. Bradley icily ordered the terrified kids to say goodbye to their mother, telling them they wouldn't see her again. Penny Waldroup—paralysed by fear—bade a final farewell to each of her children, telling them that she loved them.

At that point, Bradley Waldroup decided that he wanted to have sexual intercourse with his ex-wife and pushed her into the bedroom. But he became upset because she was too messy. By pure luck, Penny Waldroup escaped from the trailer as a police officer drove up the access road. She hid in the police car and managed to survive her ex-husband's attacks. Leslie Bradshaw was less fortunate; when the policeman found her body, she was dead.

In 2009, Davis Bradley Waldroup Jr. was tried in Benton, Tennessee with the attempted murder of his ex-wife, Penny, and the felony murder of Leslie Susan Bradshaw. Bradley Waldroup confessed everything without remorse. And since he did not merely lose his temper on this October day in 2006, but cold-bloodedly walked through the crime even though his children were present, a death penalty jurisdiction was expected. Such a decision would have normally led straight to death row and, in Tennessee, to a lethal injection. However, Waldroup's defense attorney Wylie Richardson embarked on a strategy that later came to be known as the "genetic defense" strategy. The attorney consulted forensic psychiatrist William Bernet of Vanderbilt University for a psychiatric evaluation of the defendant. But Bernet came up with an "evidence" that was much better as a mitigating factor than the psychiatric assessment. The psychiatrist had Bradley Waldroup's DNA tested in the Vanderbilt University's Molecular Genetics Laboratory and hit the mark with his hunch.

Waldroup's DNA contained a certain allelic variant of the monoamine oxidase-A (MAO-A) gene. This gene is involved in the metabolism of the neurotransmitter serotonin. Serotonin is believed to play a crucial role as a "mood stabilizer." Having too much or too little serotonin can be critical. People like Waldroup who harbor a certain variant of the MAO-A gene apparently do not have enough of the neurotransmitter serotonin in the brain and are therefore assumed to be prone to heightened levels of aggression and outbreaks of violence. Psychiatrist Bernet cited scientific studies claiming that the combination of this particular gene variant and having experienced childhood abuse increased the risk of being convicted of a violent offense by more than four hundred percent. In the popular literature, the genetic variant that was identified in Waldroup's genome is often referred to as "murder gene" or—if one wants to give it a positive connotation—"warrior gene."

The defense attorney's strategy worked. The jury found that Waldroup had a genetic predisposition of going berserk. Rather than being sentenced to death for premeditated murder, the charge was reduced to manslaughter. The court handed down a relatively lenient sentence for voluntary manslaughter in the death of Leslie Bradshaw and attempted second-degree murder of his wife, Penny. Waldroup got away with a thirty-two-year prison sentence rather than a lethal injection.

One juror of the trial, Debbie Beatty, reported that it was the scientific evidence that convinced her. She reasoned that the defendant was not entirely in control of his actions. According to records, she said "[a] diagnosis is a diagnosis. You know, it's there. A bad gene is a bad gene."[1]

How did forensic psychiatrist William Bernet come up with the idea that allowed defense attorney Wylie Richardson to build a defense strategy for Bradley Waldroup based on the accused's genetic makeup? It was a smart move that drew from insights of cutting-edge research of the post-genomic era. Scientists had shown that laboratory mice with mutations in the MAO-A gene, which caused a lack of the MAO-A enzyme, displayed highly aggressive behavior.[2] Interestingly, however, it had already been demonstrated about thirty years earlier that this particular gene was linked to a predisposition for violent behavior.

The importance of the MAO-A gene in regulating human aggressive behavior appeared for the first time in a famous human case in the Netherlands. Han Brunner and his colleagues at the Nijmegen hospital studied a Dutch family in which several male members who had a deficient version of the MAO-A gene

---

[1] Hagerty, "Can Your Genes Make You Murder?"
[2] Scott et al., "Novel Monoamine Oxidase," 739–743.

were pathologically violent.[3] The initial clue came from a woman who walked into the University Hospital in Nijmegen in 1978 and sought medical advice. She told the clinical geneticists at the hospital that for five generations, the males in her family, including her own son, suffered from some sort of mental debility. During the genetic counseling sessions, more details about the condition of the male members of her family came to light. Based on the woman's report about her immediate family members, as well as information based on a family tree that the woman's grand-uncle had drawn in 1962, Brunner and co-workers identified a dozen males in the family all suffering from the same disorder. These men had relatively low IQs of around 85, a value that is considered to be on the border of mental retardation. In addition, the men exhibited severely violent behavior: one had tried to rape his sister; another tried to drive over his boss; another one had violently forced his sisters to undress.[4] Looking for biological factors that lie at the root of the violent behavior, the Dutch researchers guessed that the culprit was to be found on the X chromosome. This guess came from the observation that the condition only affected males of the family and the trait seemed to be heritable. Men are vulnerable to an X-linked gene defect because, in contrast to women, they only have one X chromosome. Women, on the other hand, have two X chromosomes. Thus, as long as females possess only one compromised X chromosome, they do not suffer from the condition, while men have to rely on the only X chromosome they carry. If there is a defect, then it will show. Females can act as carriers who may pass on this allelic variant to their male offspring. In 1988, Brunner and co-workers from the University Hospital started performing genetic linkage analysis, a technique that aimed to identify a certain stretch of DNA, a so-called marker, that is always inherited along with a pathological condition. In the case of the Dutch family, the researchers looked for a stretch on the X chromosome that was specific for all males who displayed the clinical condition in question, namely a low IQ as well as aggressive behavior. Over several years, the geneticists analyzed the X chromosomes of twenty-eight members of the Dutch family and finally found a genetic marker that was considered a good candidate. The DNA stretch identified was specific to all violent men of the family and some of the women of the family, the latter who presumably were carriers of the genetic defect. Contrarily, none of the nonviolent male family members examined by the researchers had this marker. The specific stretch of DNA identified contained hundreds of genes, but one gene was a particularly interesting candidate. The gene that the geneticists picked for further investigation was the MAO-A gene. As discussed, this gene

---

[3] Brunner et al., "Abnormal Behavior Associated with a Point Mutation," 578–580.
[4] Richardson, "A Violence in the Blood."

was known to encode for an enzyme that breaks down the neurotransmitters serotonin, dopamine, and norepinephrine. The latter was of specific interest to the researchers because this neurotransmitter is known to contribute to stimulating the sympathetic autonomic nervous system, resulting in raised blood pressure and increased alertness during the fight or flight response. The other two neurotransmitters, serotonin and dopamine, are also involved in regulating mood and alertness. Indeed, Brunner and his colleagues confirmed that the men of the Dutch family who possessed the genetic marker also had excess levels of neurotransmitters norepinephrine, serotonin, and dopamine in their bodies and in their urine. Until now, it was not clear how MAO-A deficiency and an excess of neurotransmitters resulted in lower IQ and aggressive behavior. Han Brunner pointed out that a genetic defect itself does not cause violent behavior, but seems to contribute to lowering the threshold for this type of behavior. The individual genetic makeup might act as a biochemical trigger that predisposes men with this genetic variant to violence when under stress. Supporting Brunner's argument of stress-triggered aggression, the Dutch family study revealed that two other male family members committed arson following the death of a close relative. About thirty years later, Waldroup's attorney built up his plea on a genetic foundation by arguing that his client's genetic variant of the MAO-A gene, together with bad childhood experiences, made him predisposed for becoming a "natural born killer" when exposed to situations of provocation.[5]

Let us go back to the last chapter in which I emphasized the conceptual advancements concerning the multiplicity of factors that contribute to human behavior and personality. With this in mind, was the court decision in the "Waldroup ruling" a step back toward biologism and gene determinism? What is the actual contribution of the MAO-A gene to unspeakable atrocities like the one committed by Bradley Waldroup? Can a certain allelic variant of a gene be synonymous with a class of neurotransmitters that skip out of balance and elicit barbaric symptoms and heinous acts by the gene carrier? What about other factors, such as upbringing, stressful experiences, family and social environment in general, etc.?

Although the attorney's plea drew strongly from genetic evidence, he actually presented a multilayered sociobiological phenomenon to the jury. The defendant was portrayed as a ticking time bomb that went off because the wrong factors coincided. This argument comprised much more than genetic determinism exploited in order to probe a loophole in the law. So, how can we

---

[5] McDermott et al., "Monoamine Oxidase A Gene," 2118–2123.

fathom this multifaceted causality of genetic, developmental, and past and current environmental influences driving a person's behavior and cognition?

In the case "State Tennessee v Davis Bradley Waldroup," the attorney's strategy of defense was based on the claim that a certain genetic variant caused a deficit of the neurotransmitter serotonin in the defendant's brain. This line of reasoning did not only prove to be successful as a mitigating factor in the aforementioned lawsuits but also essentially informs biomedicine and psychiatry (although it is not always agreed upon). Based on the medical model of diseases, many scientists as well as medical professionals deem an imbalance of certain neurotransmitters to be causally involved in triggering psychopathologies and psychoses. In fact, it is the long-held aim of psychopharmacology to target neurotransmitter systems that are out of equilibrium and administer psychiatric drugs for the purpose of reversing neurochemical imbalances. Pharmacotherapy is expected to restore normal brain homeostasis by clinically effective drugs, thereby shifting the mental state back to normalcy.

Yet in the previous chapter, I argued that homeostasis (e.g., levels of a neurotransmitter like serotonin) gives us only a snapshot of one's idiosyncratic biological physiology. So even if Waldroup's serotonin levels were lower than average as compared to somebody else's, and that was due to him possessing a certain allelic variant of the MAO-A gene, this does not say much about his overall physiology and psychology. In fact, many people have low levels of serotonin, such as people with severe depression, yet they don't run around chopping up people with machetes. Also, allelic variants of MAO-A gene connected with aggression are not rare. In fact, these variants are carried by approximately thirty-three percent of the population. This would indicate a lot of putative killers roaming around freely. In order to make a claim for Waldroup (whether justified or not), we need to take his personal life history into account as well as circumstances that led to the crime. Thus, to understand a being in its entirety, we must resort to the development that this particular individual undergoes while living in a particular social and environmental niche. Furthermore, behavioral patterns acquired in this particular niche must be mapped onto the current situation in which the organism finds itself.

A lack of concern toward developmental aspects and situational contexts has posed serious challenges to psychopathology research. Above all, scientists have not yet succeeded in coming up with a standard definition of neurotransmitter levels and composition in a healthy person. It is worth noting that neurotransmitter levels differ from individual to individual and can widely vary depending on the situation and life history of the individual. Thus, despite all efforts, no valid definition of normalcy with respect to neurotransmitter and neurohormones exists; in fact, it may never be possible to define a standard level that is strictly valid for everybody. For example, the levels of neurotransmitter serotonin in the blood may vary by up to four times between individuals, and there is a complex cross-talk between serotonin and other hormones and neurotransmitters (as discussed in Chapter 6). Serotonin levels not only depend on the biological make-up, but also on the social environment, thereby shaping a person's psychology and behavior through neuroplastic changes. The fact that complex interaction and regulation patterns of neurotransmitters such as serotonin are highly sensitive to developmental experiences lay bare the shortcomings of a mechanistic explanation of diseases: psychopathologies and personality disorders are not merely a derailment of brain homeostasis due to deviant biochemical and neurotransmitter balances. With a few exceptions, genetics cannot tell us much about psychopathologies without also considering one's idiosyncratic life history.

Coming back to the infamous killer gene, Waldroup's attorney, Wylie Richardson, argued along these lines of nature–nurture intertwinement: Waldroup's particular genetic predisposition based on a variant of the MAO-A gene together with his bad childhood experiences made the defendant a "natural born killer" when exposed to situations of provocation.[6] Yet amongst the different aspects of this versatile argument invoked by the defense, the one aspect that strongly hit a cord with the media was that concerning Waldroup's genetics; this simplified assertion of the gene as the culprit reverberated through various medial outputs, catching public attention. The general public read that science has come up with a causal explanation! Finally, scientists have identified a predictive marker for a person's rampant violence and hopefully provided a fulcrum for preventing similar atrocities in future!

Unfortunately, the real scientific message—the impact of the cross talk between genes and environment that facilitates the occurrence of aggression in high provocation situations—somehow got lost in translation. To summarize again, there is evidence that humans who possess a certain allelic variant of the MAO-A gene, leading to low levels of expression of this gene, seem to be at risk for developing antisocial behavior when previously having had experience of childhood maltreatment. In contrast, humans who harbor a different allelic variant, leading to high level expression of MAO-A, seem to be better adjusted to handling effects of childhood maltreatment.[7] Thus, despite allowing for discriminating and objectively measurable parameters, the genetic constitution of a person is only one of many components making up one's personhood. Most importantly, genes have different effects depending on at which time during

---

[6] Ibid.

[7] Caspi, "Role of Genotype in the Cycle of Violence in Maltreated Children," 851–854.

development they are active. Certain circumstances in an organism's life can cause genes to be expressed at lower levels or be silenced altogether. Such variation in gene activity can be due to control mechanisms that are not encoded in an individual's DNA sequence but due to chemical modifications (e.g., DNA-methylation, histone modifications) affecting the respective genes. These modifications act as control switches that can turn genes on or off depending on environmental factors such as one's diet, social interactions, sleep, exercise, aging, and, most notably, stress. This functional variation in gene expression due to environmental influences can either depend on a distinct DNA sequence or on mechanisms that are not encoded in the DNA. The former includes DNA segments that regulate transcription, RNA processing, RNA stability, translation, or protein activity of its own or a different gene product. The latter concerns control mechanisms of gene activity independent of the DNA sequence (such as paramutations, imprinting, gene silencing, and position effect that can be conferred via DNA methylation, histone modification, or non-coding RNAs) and is termed epigenetics. Thus, allelic variants of a gene may be important for one's genetic constitution and therefore one's neurotransmitter levels, but this tells us only one part of the story. The other part depends on mechanisms of gene expression that control the gene activity. Modifications that affect gene activity are caused by external factors and circumstances an individual encounters in his or her life. Hence, all gene effects need to be viewed in the context of idiosyncratic life histories. Consequently, rather than parroting deterministic simplifications about genetic predispositions for violence as propagated by the yellow press and pseudoscientific writings, let us look into the numerous ramifications of variations in gene expression to gain a more complete picture of what "makes or breaks" an individual.

All organisms face periods of environmental challenges as they grow and develop. To cope with these challenges, organisms possess a capacity for adaptive plasticity; that is, by undergoing changes they become better adapted to their habitats. Adaptive plasticity is often put into effect by mechanisms of gene regulation like those mentioned previously. Genes that are expressed at certain times and in response to certain environmental conditions provide organisms with the capacity of adaptive plasticity. This means, in spite of having the same genetic outfit, individuals can significantly differ in how they act, look, or function as a direct consequence of the environment they live in. When these changes improve the chances of survival, it is called adaptive plasticity. By these means, gene regulation underlying adaptive plasticity enhances survival rates in rapidly changing or constantly varying environments. Such behavioral, morphological, and physiological modifications in response to the environment may last throughout an individual's lifespan. One form of adaptive plasticity is neuroplasticity (Chapter 2), which concerns processes in the brain facilitating how organisms cope with environmental variation.

Studies of gene regulation have increasingly gained momentum complementing classical genetic studies. It seems that understanding gene regulation can provide an explanatory framework of how to link environmental factors to genetic factors. Elucidating the underlying biological processes of gene regulation made environmental influences measurable and quantifiable. This pertained to the external as much as the internal environment of an organism. The latter inquires how signals from surrounding cells and tissues affect their neighboring cells and tissues within an organism. Rethinking the molecular mechanisms and how the same DNA can be expressed differently depending on its environment led to a non-preformationist way of looking at how a complete organism can originate from a single cell. Rather than subscribing to pre-programmed instructions laid down in the fertilized egg, development is understood as intricately intertwined with cellular organization as well as other constraints, such as maternal factors.

For instance, consider a multicellular individual like a human whose body is composed of trillions of cells: each cell of an individual's body contains DNA molecules with the exact same genetic information, irrespective of it being a liver, brain, or heart cell, etc. But due to epigenetic processes, the expression and subsequently the function of the genes on the DNA are differently regulated. Signals from one tissue cell modify the DNA of neighboring tissue cells so that within the whole organism the expression of gene products in that one cell gets synchronized with gene expression in cells with the same cell fate and at the same time diverges from cells following other trajectories. By way of epigenetic modifications, the very same DNA can code for different cells like a liver, brain, or heart cell. By turning off some genes while keeping other genes active, cells can grow and develop into all sorts of different tissues and give rise to a fully functioning organism. This also explains why only about one to two percent of the three billion base pairs of human DNA code for proteins. This means that anywhere from ninety-eight to ninety-nine percent of the entire human genome has some other—often unknown—function. One important function of this non-coding DNA is the regulation of genes that code for proteins. Hence, there may be a huge part of the DNA that regulates rather than codes for proteins. The public research consortium "Encyclopedia of DNA Elements," or ENCODE[8] for short, expanded the aim of the Human Genome Project (Chapter 1) that set out to decode the complete human DNA sequence. Starting in 2003, ENCODE aimed at the functional characterization of the human DNA sequence by mapping functional elements, e.g., identifying DNA

---

[8] "The Encyclopedia of DNA Elements (ENCODE)."

sequences that bind proteins or are associated with chemical modifications. The ENCODE consortium found that about eighty percent of the bases in the genome, despite most of it not being involved in protein-coding, exerted some biochemical activity and could serve a regulatory role.

Scrutinizing gene regulatory effects led to a relativization of the alleged leverage of genetic "programs" in cloned organisms. Originally, the fact that the exact same DNA sequence is found in practically every cell of the body of an individual provided the rationale for generating cloned organisms.[9] This excitement culminated in the endeavor of cloning profitable livestock, deceased pets, and hitherto non-existent life forms like chimeras or organisms with completely novel traits. Yet many such efforts grossly failed. For over fifty years, scientists in laboratories all over the world have successfully optimized cloning techniques for the transfer of individual genes or relatively short DNA fragments from one species to another, even if the host and donor organisms stemmed from quite distantly related species. It actually proved almost impossible to transfer the whole genome of a donor into a recipient organism (i.e., cloning by somatic cell nuclear transfer, SCNT) of a distantly related lineage. Many of these endeavors in mammals foundered because cloned zygotes would not implant in the uterine lining of the recipient or cloned embryos would stop developing and growing at a very early stage. This may be due to various obstacles, some technical (e.g., the use of dye and ultraviolet light destroying the extracted donor DNA), others due to developmentally aberrant processes in the zygote (e.g., loss of key proteins involved in cell and chromosomal division, abnormal gene expression, and epigenetic modification in the donor DNA). Surprisingly, DNA taken from somatic cells.[10] and transferred into a fertilized egg cell of the same species proved to be a highly difficult and inefficient endeavor.

After recognizing these challenges, the first successfully SCNT cloned animal became an international celebrity. In 1996, the attention of the whole world was fixed on a newborn sheep named Dolly. Dolly was the first clone sheep (Figure 4.1) generated by using the DNA of a somatic cell of an adult white-faced sheep that was then transferred into an enucleated egg cell of a black-faced foster mother sheep. The resulting embryo that eventually grew into Dolly was

---

[9] A clone is an organism that has the identical genetic information as a parent organism from which it derived. The generation of a clone does not require the fertilization of an egg by a sperm cell, but can be achieved by using any cell of an individual. Thus, a clone usually has a single genetic parent.

[10] In contrast to germline cells (egg or sperm cells), somatic cells are cells of the body, like skin cells, liver cells, neurons, etc. that have developed into specialized cells (= differentiated) and were believed to have lost their ability to produce new individuals.

genetically identical to the white-faced donor mother. And most intriguingly, neither sperm nor egg cells were necessary for this procedure. Instead, Dolly was generated from an udder cell of the donor animal.

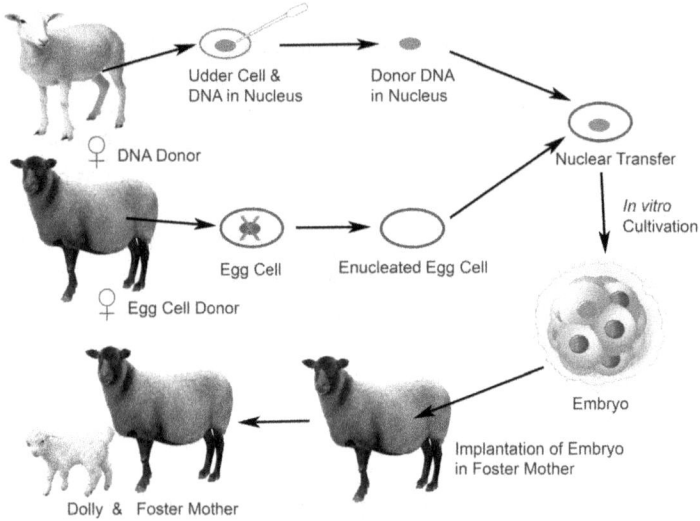

Figure 4.1: The cloning procedure of Dolly.
Source: Pawar, "Transgenic Animals: A Short Review." Image modified.

This success fueled the imagination of researchers and non-scientists alike, raising hope to create identical individuals by simply taking the DNA of any desired bodily cell.[11] The spectacular cloning experiment catapulted scientists into a new situation of being able to promise the production of organisms on demand. However, at the age of six-and-a-half, clone sheep Dolly had to be put down after developing lung disease. Usually, sheep can live to eleven or twelve years of age. Dolly was cloned using an adult udder cell from a healthy six-year-old sheep. The type of lung disease Dolly developed is most common in older sheep. In addition, Dolly also suffered from arthritis that developed prematurely. On the molecular level, it was found that Dolly had shorter telomeres than other animals of the same age. In fact, the lengths of Dolly's telomers resembled those of a sheep that would be six years older, like those of her donor mother. Telomeres are pieces of DNA that protect the ends of chromosomes. They get shorter with every cell division and are therefore

---

[11] The cloning procedure could presumably be undertaken for almost any somatic cell except those that have lost their nucleus and thus do not harbor any DNA, like red blood cells.

considered a measure of cell aging. Dolly is not the only cloned animal that died prematurely. Experiments of cloned mice revealed that these animals also suffered premature death. These findings indicate that somatic cells grow old by aging on a molecular level. Despite having the same DNA and thus the same genes in all bodily cells, somatic cells seem to undergo some modification during life time.[12]

I have referred to epigenetic changes that depend on influences from the environment. It is quite possible that epigenetic modifications such as methylation patterns on the DNA prevent the rejuvenation of DNA from an aged somatic cell. Thus, rather than the genome, it might be the epigenome that is the most significant driver of cell differentiation, maturing processes, aging, and interindividual differences. Epigenetic modifications affect the function of many different genes and can therefore be the cause of all sorts of changes throughout a person's life, including diseases. Luckily, such changes caused by epigenetics or variations in gene expression that lead to an increase in the susceptibility to diseases—somatic or psychopathological—cannot be passed on to the next generation. Or can they? While most adaptive changes based on variations of gene regulation do not get transmitted to the offspring, the story is different in some cases. There is good evidence that the effects of epigenetic regulation can penetrate subsequent generations. To study transgenerational epigenetic effects, researchers have generated animal models, most famously the so-called agouti mouse. Agouti mice are genetically identical but can look completely different in color and size depending on external factors, such as the mother's diet. For example, one mouse may be small with dark fur, its genetically identical twin may be obese with yellow fur, and another twin may be in the middle of the weight range and may have brown and yellowish mottled fur. Thus, despite their identical genomes, their appearances (i.e., their so-called phenotypes) strikingly differ. This is, as you may have guessed, due to differences in gene expression in these mice.[13] Upstream of the agouti gene, these mice have a retrotransposon insertion (i.e., a regulatory element that is inserted before the agouti gene locus). In normal, healthy mice, the agouti gene is expressed only for a short time during development. After this short period, the agouti gene is silenced for the remainder of the mouse's life by the attachment of methyl groups to the regulatory regions of the agouti gene. Methylation results in the DNA's compaction and prevents the transcription of the agouti gene. On the other

---

[12] This and subsequent experiments indicated that cloning was not as safe a technical procedure to generate identical organisms as initially assumed. In addition to DNA, there are many more factors that are essential for the development of an individual.

[13] Duhl et al., "Neomorphic Agouti Mutations in Obese Yellow Mice," 59–65.

hand, in yellow and/or obese mice, the regulatory regions of the agouti gene are not methylated. Hence, without methylation these genes are continuously active and "turned on" throughout the mouse's life. Mice whose agouti gene is constantly expressed are characterized by their yellow fur, obesity, and high risk of suffering from diabetes and cancer as adults.

The most striking insights concerning the agouti mice resulted from changing the expression of the agouti gene simply by changing the mothers' diet before and during pregnancy. Feeding the mothers vitamin B12, folic acid, choline, and betaine led to phenotypically altered offspring with brown coat color, slender physique, and significantly reduced disease susceptibility.[14] On the contrary, newborn control mice with the same genotype from mothers fed with regular diet were obese, had yellow fur, and were susceptible to various diseases.

These findings showed for the first time a causal mechanism that linked maternal nutrition to the development of diseases, a mode of inheritance termed "fetal programming hypothesis."[15] Appropriate nutrients can apparently silence the agouti gene by methylation of the upstream regulatory sequence without altering the regulatory or gene sequence. Rather than the genome, it is the epigenome that causes phenotypic differences in genetically identical individuals. This impressively demonstrates the power of gene regulation by external influences on a given DNA strand. Moreover, these experimental findings corroborated decade-long twin studies in humans such as behavioral, psychological, and etiological differences. A similar point was already made when discussing the different fates of the Dionne quintuplets (Chapter 1). Despite being identical twins and thus having the exact same genetic outfit, the Dionne sisters exhibited conspicuous idiosyncrasies. While three of the Dionne sisters were reported to be largely in good health, Emilie Dionne suffered from severe epileptic seizures from the dawn of infancy, and Marie Dionne struggled with mental health problems during most of her adult life. We don't know enough about the Dionne sisters' individual life experiences to correlate putative psychological harm or troubles with their health problems; however, as discussed earlier, right after birth three of the Dionne babies were separated from their mother and put in an incubator to stabilize their body temperature—for very good reasons, of course. Nonetheless, such an experience could have had long-lasting impacts on a child's psychological development. Furthermore, it can be assumed that the older the sisters grew, the more diverging paths they took upon their lives' journeys and the larger the ensuing differences in their social environment. Adding to this, small

---

[14] Waterland and Jirtle, "Transposable Elements," 5293–5300.
[15] Barker, "Fetal Origins of Coronary Heart Disease," 171–174.

interindividual differences can be significantly enhanced by the environment, as discussed earlier (Chapter 1) and epitomized by the "painting hands" (Figure 1.5). Such reciprocal interactions can generate feedback loops, thereby either strengthening beneficial developmental effects or aggravating adverse ones. Dynamic feedback loops occur throughout every child and adolescent's development. Such effects challenge naïve character attributions from folk psychology in which character traits are genetically given. Children are not born to become natural-born leaders, go-getters, self-starters, oddballs, team players, or outsiders. Early in life, we all assume social roles that continuously get reinforced or weakened depending on our particular social environment. Tellingly, Fred Davis, the official photographer of the infantine quintuplets who played an important role in the young girls' lives, confessed that he was above all fond of one of the quintuplets and favored her over the others. In an article featured in the *Globe & Mail*, he admitted "I supposed Yvonne is my favorite. She photographs well. She's the leader of the quints, too, and whatever she does the others do."[16] Interindividual differences of how each of the sisters coped with her social and physical environment and which psychological or bodily traumas either experienced may have contributed to differences in gene regulation. Changes in gene regulation then led to adaptive plasticity, including neuroplasticity, that in turn shaped behavior, psychology, and ultimately may have contributed to a broad range of somatic and psychological conditions. The Dionne quintuplets are not unique with respect to adaptive plasticity, but are unique in that they were naturally born "clones" whose idiosyncratic life stories tell us a lot about nature-nurture interrelationships.

More recently, the intimate intertwinement of gene regulation and environment has come to the fore in biomedical research in humans. Epigenetic studies focusing on DNA methylation in particular have gained momentum. Today, it is known that about forty percent of human DNA is methylated, which means about forty percent is differently regulated than non-methylated DNA. Usually, most methylated elements concern the de-activation of rogue DNA elements that lurk throughout the genome. These rogue DNA elements represent a disease risk if left non-methylated or aberrantly methylated. For example, changes in methylation patterns have been linked to various types of cancer and to congenital disorders such as Angelman syndrome and Beckwith-Weidemann syndrome.[17] In some cases, methylation can modulate the expression of regular DNA regions, causing surprising, long-lasting, and even cross-generational effects. Epigenetic research is a relatively new field of research, thus epigenetic studies in humans

---

[16] Noël and Bennett, *The Dionne Quintuplets and Their Entourage.*

[17] DeBaun et al., "Epigenetic Alterations of H19 and LIT1," 604–611.

are rare. Remarkably, one of the most prominent examples of epigenetic research came from some unexpected findings in humans. In an epidemiological study on the consequences of malnutrition experienced during the Dutch Famine (the "Hunger Winter" in World War II),[18] epigenetic processes were invoked for the first time to explain pathological phenomena in humans. The "Hunger Winter" of 1944–45 caused severe undernutrition of the Dutch population and had the most dramatic impacts on women who were pregnant. The study revealed that this period of maternal starvation not only had profound effects on the intrauterine growth of the fetuses, but also on the babies' states of health after birth and throughout their lives. In fact, the nutrient deprivation endured during the "Hunger Winter" has been identified as one of the major contributors to chronic diseases that people born at that time suffered from later in life. These findings are another example of the "fetal programming hypothesis." The mother's organism that is suffering from nutritional deficiencies signals the fetus that post-birth and long-term living conditions will be impoverished. In response, the development of the fetus takes an altered course, leading to changes in body size and an adjusted metabolism that prepares the organism for harsh conditions after birth. Hence, maternal undernutrition restricts intrauterine development and leads to lower birthweights in newborns. Subsequently, low-birthweight babies with changed metabolism are better adapted to a deficient environment than babies of mothers who were pregnant in an environment of abundance. Problematically, when the living conditions improve and the individuals find themselves in an environment of abundance rather than the anticipated dearth, the low-birthweight babies become maladapted. Later in life, such individuals are at a higher risk for diseases—obesity, diabetes, and cardiovascular—because their metabolism is adapted to an environment of shortage. Although not proven causally, only in correlation studies, it is highly likely that such developmentally plastic effects are attributable to epigenetic mechanisms.

Taken together, these findings from animal models as well as humans indicate that the development of the phenotype, including traits, characters, behavior, and appearance, is essentially determined by how genes are regulated. While mutations and allelic variants certainly play an important role in the variation of a given trait, regulatory mechanisms that influence these genes seem to be at least equally important. Yet the study of key regulators that can be influenced by environmental factors, such as one's diet and many other external influences, are largely understudied. One of the most prominent examples of how little is known about how environmental factors influence human health and disease has been captured by the so-called Glasgow effect.

---

[18] Heijmans et al., "Persistent Epigenetic Differences," 17046–17049.

The Glasgow effect refers to the poor health of Glaswegians leading to an appallingly low life expectancy—the lowest in the U.K. and among the lowest in all of Europe. In 2008, the World Health Organization reported that male life expectancy at birth in the Calton area of Glasgow at that time was just fifty-four years.[19] In 2016, premature mortality rates of both females and males were higher than anywhere else in Western Europe. Glaswegians' life expectancy at birth was reportedly almost seven years below the national average for men and over four years below the national average for women.[20] The most widely acknowledged factors associated with these highest mortality rates and lowest life expectancy in Western Europe seem to be the prevailing socio-economic deprivations in this geographic area. In fact, studies of mortality indicated that the Glasgow effect is a relatively recent phenomenon. Historical analysis of long-term trends in premature mortality indicated that in the 1920s, mortality rates in Glasgow were comparable to other big industrial cities in the U.K. such as Liverpool and Manchester. Yet at the start of the 1980s, the social-economic gap widened and was accompanied by poor life expectancies, a phenomenon that continued the following thirty-plus years.

Glasgow lies at the region's core of former industrial areas of West Central Scotland. This geographic region had a history of industrialization, especially of heavy industry and experienced politically-driven deindustrialization in the 1980s. Deindustrialization led to economic regression, followed by socio-economic deprivation by which Glasgow has been affected most significantly. Even in the more affluent Glaswegian neighborhoods, premature mortality rates are still fifteen percent higher in Glasgow than in similar districts of other big cities. Contrarily, citizens of Lenzie, an affluent town that is located about eleven kilometers northeast of Glasgow, could expect to live to eighty-two.

Despite these harrowing observations, some researchers disdain the term Glasgow effect because it suggests there may be a simple solution to a complex problem. The Glasgow effect most likely is the result of an interplay between a dozen or more factors. The blame may lie with the cold, rainy weather and lack of sunlight that causes chronic vitamin D deficiency, but also with alcohol, smoking, and drug abuse of the city's population. The causal key factor, though, where most strings run together seems to be poverty. Being poor results in an unhealthy diet, poor housing, and precarious community safety. Within the U.K., Glasgow is not alone in suffering from relatively high levels of income deprivation, resulting in poor health and high mortality rates across all ages. Two other cities in the U.K. whose citizens had experienced similar socio-economic hardship in the last forty to fifty years are Liverpool and Manchester.

---

[19] "Closing the Gap in a Generation: Health Equity through Action."
[20] Reid, "Excess Mortality in the Glasgow Conurbation."

Inhabitants of these two post-industrialized cities also face the lowest life expectancy compared to inhabitants of all other cities in England. As a result, poverty has unquestionably been acknowledged as a crucial determinant of health and a main driver of mortality, yet it does not provide a full causal explanation. The three cities in the U.K.—Liverpool, Manchester, and Glasgow—share similar histories of industrialization and deindustrialization associated with poverty and low well-being of inhabitants. Nonetheless, there is a striking difference in the case of Glasgow. While the distribution of income deprivation of the three cities' boroughs is almost identical, all cause premature mortality rates of people under sixty-five; although it is more than thirty percent higher in Glasgow than Liverpool and Manchester, especially in the age groups of fifteen to forty-four and forty-five to sixty-four years.[21] The stark difference in premature mortality of Glaswegians as compared to inhabitants of other low-income cities in the UK is attributable to the striking differences in the *causes* of death, as reported in several studies. Glaswegians relative to residents of Liverpool and Manchester were much more likely to die from lung cancer, alcohol-related causes, drug-related poisonings, and other external causes, as well as being almost seventy percent more likely to commit suicide.

Mortality is the highest in the most economically deprived decile of Glasgow. Most strikingly, however, is that mortality was also higher in Glaswegians of high socio-economic status, i.e., those citizens who were well off at the time of the study. This observation fueled the gainsayers' argument that poverty is not a strong driving force of ill health and premature death amongst Glaswegians. This indiscriminate denial is dangerously misguided because it only takes the population's current and most recent socio-economic status into consideration. Yet, as discussed before, the effects of poverty, economic hardship, and social stress are cross-generational. When babies are born into certain ecological and social niches, the environment they grow up in is largely preset. These niches are often similar to those inhabited by their parents and grandparents and channel a child's development along a given trajectory. Serendipitous upward social mobility later in life cannot fully compensate for the negative impact of the economic plight of their grandparents, parents, and maybe also during early childhood. Paul Shiels, a researcher at Glasgow University, explains that the pathological and moribund effects seen in Glaswegians can be tied to fetal programming by DNA methylation. Epigenetic modifications of the DNA, such as methylation levels, decline throughout everyone's life. This reflects a natural process of ageing and can be influenced by external factors such as diet (see the example of the agouti mice discussed earlier) as well as stress and adverse lifestyle. External factors that lead to epigenetic modifications exert a severe

---

[21] Walsh et al., "It's Not 'Just Deprivation,'" 487–495.

impact on the DNA of the developing embryo, even long before birth. Adverse external factors cause significantly lower levels of methylation in newborns whose mothers lived in more deprived areas of Glasgow and had experienced socio-economic hardship and distress during pregnancy. Thus, epigenetic modifications are already set before birth and exert their influence throughout life, even if socio-economic situations change. Moreover, there is increasing evidence that changes in methylation can be transmitted to children and grandchildren. Many Glaswegian middle-class people of today had very poor ancestors in their family tree several decades ago. Thus, Glaswegian parents or grandparents who were exposed to poor diet, low-quality housing, disadvantageous life circumstances, and high stressors in the past have a significant risk of passing on challenges to physical and mental well-being to their offspring via epigenetic effects. Given the transgenerational effects of epigenetics, it will take many decades to fix health inequities; although fixing them should indisputably be an ethical imperative, because ignoring such huge and remediable differences in health must be seen as social injustice that kills people on a grand scale.

What can we make of all this? In brief, our genes are just half of the story. The other half depends on prenatal experiences and even on experiences that were made by our mother and grandmother and effected gene regulation and modification on the DNA. Epigenetic changes induce the expression of adjusted physiological and morphological states in response to environmental conditions during critical periods in early fetal development. Once triggered, these plastic effects manifest in persistent, lifelong changes in the body structure and function. What is most noteworthy is that further studies have revealed a correlation between the nutritional status of pregnant women and the health of not only their children, but even their grandchildren. This indicates that some regulatory changes in gene expression not only influence an organism's physiology throughout life but also get passed on to subsequent generations.

This is not as surprising as it might sound. After all, you may remember from biology class in high school that primary oocytes are already formed by the fifth month of fetal life and remain dormant until puberty. In other words, the motherly DNA that deploys fifty percent of her child's genome is stored away in the germ cells while the mother is still in her mother's (i.e., the child's grandmother) womb. Imagine a woman who suffers from severe hardship or adversities while pregnant. Gene regulatory effects triggered by distress and privation will impact the DNA in the growing embryo's somatic cells (i.e., in her daughter or son) and may also impact the DNA in the embryo's germ cells (i.e., the same DNA that will be transmitted to the grandchild). These regular developmental processes make it biologically plausible for adverse effects to reverberate over three generations.

The observation that epigenetic effects can get transmitted to the offspring resonates with what psychologists have called transgenerational trauma. Transgenerational trauma asserts that the impact of traumatic events can be transferred from one generation to the next and explores how children and grandchildren of trauma survivors understand, cope with, and heal from trauma. This concept has been widely studied in descendants of concentration camp survivors. Similar transgenerational, psychological effects have been observed in children of abuse victims. But how can this vicious cycle be broken?

Maybe the most important message is that our genes, despite their formative power, are not deterministic. We are not prisoners to our genes or mere executors and stooges of a genetically engraved destiny. Our DNA is not an instruction book, and thus genetics will not be able to provide us with a complete set of answers. Genetics is a probabilistic science, giving much leeway to modulation from the social environment, for better or worse. Although some of us may have allelic variants in our DNA that increase susceptibility to certain somatic diseases, psychopathologies, or adverse behavioral traits, the same allels also represent genetic potential. What is devastating in one environment could be key regulators for success and growth in a healthy and nurturing environment.[22] Let us return to the horrific tragedy that shattered the life of the Waldroup family in October 2006 and view it in light of how transgenerational traumatic experience can be transformed into empowering victims of violence. Five and a half years after the horrible act of violence committed by Bradley Waldroup, filmmaker Doug Block photographed and directed a thirty-six-minute-long documentary entitled *The Children next Door* that gives an intimate look at the Waldroup family. Thanks to Block's cinematic work and the willingness of the Waldroup family to share the story about their trauma, we have the opportunity to gain a better understanding of how Penny Waldroup and her four children, Chelsea, Emily, Elijah, and Ashley coped with the impact of violence.

But before grappling with the family members' path to recovery, the film touches upon the question that is usually asked first: "Why does a woman stay with an abusive husband?" It becomes apparent that both Bradley as well as Penny Waldroup were raised in families fraught with domestic violence. Penny remembers her father being a severely ill alcoholic. Her parents, when drinking together, fought continuously. On some occasions, Penny's father brutally beat her mother and left her bruised. He even chased the family out of the house

---

[22] Boyce, *The Orchid and the Dandelion.*

with a gun on one occasion. Penny Waldroup's life with Bradley was remarkably similar to what she experienced in childhood. During their ten-year marriage, the abuse by her husband constantly swelled and eventually culminated in this one horrific incident.

For women in abusive relationships as well as children who have experienced domestic violence, it is difficult to free themselves from violent relationships. They have behaviorally and neuroplastically adapted to their abusive environment. Also later in life, they seek out similar social environments, a process I introduced earlier as niche picking (see Chapter 3). Adaptation to an abusive niche works particularly "well" if the abuser isolates his or her dependents by limiting or barring contacts to other social environments. In doing so, the abuser generates a deviant socio-cultural niche, separated from the outside world that leaves the family members maladapted to other, non-violent niches. Victims of domestic violence accept assaults and violence not only as part of their regular life, but believe that violent behavior reflects societal interactions in general. Chelsea Waldroup and her siblings learned to see violence as a normal part of their lives. In the documentary, Chelsea recalls that "even worse than all the violence against my mother was the fact that my siblings and I had begun to think this was normal. A simple conversation between the two would escalate into an argument, which in turn would lead to new bruises on my mother's body. At six years old, I believed this was how all families were."

Elijah says that his father exercised strict control over all family members and remembers being surprised that other families appeared non-violent. "You couldn't go anywhere or do anything without his say so. As soon as I went to my friend's house and I see how his family worked, I thought, my family is really strange."

Along with the acquired conviction that violence belongs to all social relationships, another devastating process takes root in the victims; victims of domestic violence lose their feeling of self-worth. This is due to the fact that the abuser exerts uncontested dominance over all other family members, allowing him or her to define a reality for the whole family solely at his or her discretion. Lacking the concession of one's own perception, victims cannot develop self-worth from within but become dependent on the abuser's fickle appraisal. Penny recollects that it took her a long time to realize her own worth. In response to the question why it is hard to leave an abusive relationship, she muses "[s]ometimes it is best to figure out you, before trying to figure out why. Have the confidence in holding your head high." The emotional scars fundamentally have altered Penny's as well as her children's self-concept, belief system, and how they look at their future. Living in a distorted reality created by their abusive father, they grew up with frequently repeated lies about their worth and who they would never be. It is extraordinarily hard to unlearn these feelings of humiliation and debasement that come with the lies that are repeatedly told by the abuser. These children were not only robbed of their childhood, but also of their self-perception and outlook on their own future. Unlearning the lies and reclaiming their life and future require that others share alternative perspectives that victims of domestic abuse are often unable to see for themselves. This is especially difficult when children are drawn into a conflict of loyalty, as was the case for Chelsea Waldroup. Despite witnessing her father's abusive and violent behavior, she still felt attached to him. From her childhood experience, she remembers that arguments "would start over the littlest thing... and then it would escalate into yelling and fighting... and then hitting... I felt like we had to keep it hidden. We knew it was wrong. We knew the violence was something my dad could get in trouble for, so we just chose not to tell—because we loved him." In fact, she recalls willingly adopting a submissive attitude and accepting his despotism "[w]e were all trying to find ways to make him happy. I felt like if I did more, if I cleaned, they would argue less." Years after the horrible incident, Chelsea is still trying to reconcile the picture she had of her father with his unfathomable actions. She says "[h]e was my hero. I loved him...and I hated my mom."

The members of the Waldroup family still carry devastating memories that are slow to fade. Elijah confirms "All I remember is...actually, I remember everything!" Not only the cruel October day in 2006, but also countless memories of other acts of violence by his father. "We hid back in the room. We would hear my mom say don't do that, don't, don't! You could hear him punching my mom in the face and stuff." The violence the family members experienced will continue to haunt them. It will be a long and difficult path of healing. Penny and her four children have moved to Georgetown, Tennessee. Penny is recovering from the attack, which has left her with a missing finger. Despite the pain they endured, the family members are an inspiration with their courage and perseverance in the face of daily struggles. Chelsea has graduated from high school and attends the University of Chattanooga. She is also advocating for increasing public awareness for domestic violence against children. Emily has started traveling, making new friends, and has completed middle school. Elijah strives to become a major player in his high school football team, determined to achieve his dreams. The documentary does not say much about Ashley, who is described as unique and unpredictable by her mother.

The Waldroup family must explore new, transformative cognitive and emotional territory that void the lies they learned when growing up with domestic violence. To emotionally heal, they have to break the cycle of violence, escape their abusive social niche, and value themselves. The recovery process will require a family effort that extends over at least two generations of children of domestic violence.

Chapter 5

Neurobiological Processes of Memory Formation

Memory... is the diary that we all carry about with us.

— Oscar Wilde. The Importance of Being Earnest

Henry Gustav Molaison was born on February 26, 1926, in Manchester, Connecticut. He grew into a young, sprightly boy with blond hair and bright blue eyes. He was the only child of a working-class couple who did not make much money, his father being an electrician and his mother a housekeeper. On top of their poor pay, they lost most of their little savings in the stock market crash of 1929. During his childhood, Henry's family had moved many times from tenement apartment to tenement apartment. When he was seven or eight years old, his family home was a second-floor walk-up apartment about a quarter-mile away from Colt Park in downtown Hartford, Connecticut. There, at the northern edge of the park, he crossed the road but didn't see the bicyclist who coasted down the hill. Henry was run over by the cyclist, landed on the left side of his head, and incurred a deep inch-long gash in his forehead just above his eyebrow.[1] He recovered quickly, but this head injury may have precipitated the malady he started suffering from a few years later. At the age of ten, Henry developed partial epileptic seizures. Despite his condition, Henry supported his family from his early adolescence onwards and took part-time jobs in a movie theater, in the shoe department of the G. Fox & Co. department store, and at a junkyard to supplement the family income. But the seizures continued to plague him almost every day over the following five years. Henry dropped out of school early and started learning a trade as a motor winder at Ace Electric Motors. At his fifteenth birthday, his condition worsened. His fits turned into generalized tonic-clonic seizures. He experienced his first tonic-clonic seizure when he was driving with his father and suddenly started convulsing and falling forward from the backseat. No longer able to control Henry's recurrent seizures, his family doctor referred the case to William Beecher Scoville, a neurosurgeon

---

[1] Dittrich, *Patient H.M.*

at Hartford Hospital. Scoville continued the medications, prescribing Dilantin, Phenobarbital, Tridione, and Mesantoin for indefinite treatment to be taken several times per day. Henry only showed little response. Soon, Henry had to give up his job at Ace Electric Motors and returned to high school. At the age of twenty-one, he eventually graduated from East Hartford High. But by that time, his epileptic episodes had become extraordinary severe, so severe and frequent that he was not given permission to collect his high school diploma on stage because of fear that he might have a seizure while everybody was watching. After his diploma, Henry began to work for Underwood Typewriter factory on a typewriter assembly line, yet his treatment refractory epileptic fits became more frequent, and he suffered from partial seizures and intermittent generalized seizures almost every day. To keep the seizures under control, Henry took increasingly high doses of anticonvulsant medication. By the age of twenty-seven, his epileptic attacks and the high medication dosage left him incapacitated for work and stopped him from leading a normal life altogether. Even when he was not seizing, Henry was mentally absent and withdrew from daily life, with the exception of occasionally listening to music on the radio or turning magazine pages.

In 1953, after Henry's generalized seizures had been progressing for a decade, his neurosurgeon Scoville suggested surgery, aiming at controlling the patient's epilepsy. Scoville subjected Henry to an electroencephalograph (EEG) to measure the faint electrical currents generated by the active neuronal networks in his brain. Coincidently, just while undergoing the procedure, Henry experienced a partial epileptic seizure. Nonetheless, the EEG did not reveal a discrete epileptogenic focus, i.e., a localized area in his brain where his epileptic fit originated. Due to the diffuse EEG results, Henry's operation was not an etiologically prompted targeted intervention. Rather, the anatomical target of the surgery (i.e., the medial temporal lobes) was chosen based on previous results of patients with severe mental disorders. However, these operations were usually restricted to one of the two brain hemispheres. Scoville, who reassured Henry's parents that his foremost aim was to improve their son's quality of life, suggested to surgically remove the young man's medial temporal lobes on both cerebral hemispheres. Unlike earlier operations that Scoville undertook on epilepsy patients in which he usually performed unilateral (either left or right) resection, Henry was the first epilepsy patient to undergo Scoville's "experimental" procedure of a bilateral temporal lobe resection. It must be remembered that Scoville's experimental operation happened during an era of medicine when large areas of the brain, its anatomy, and localized functions were still relatively uncharted. It was the same period of time when the misled American physician Walter Freeman performed his brutal, ice-pick lobotomy and when the exceptional American-Canadian neurosurgeon Wilder Penfield began to draft his ground-breaking anatomical–functional map of somatotopic organization of the brain.

In the summer of 1953, Scoville surgically removed Henry's inner parts of the temporal poles: large parts of both hippocampi and most of his amygdala and parahippocampal, perirhinal, and entorhinal cortices. Only small areas of about two centimeters at the back of the hippocampi and the entorhinal cortices were spared.

At first glance, the surgery appeared successful, as doctors were able to get control over Henry's seizures. The partial and generalized attacks occurred at a significantly reduced frequency postoperatively. But it soon became clear that this therapeutic success was a Phyrric victory. When examined by the medical team of the hospital, Henry described "his inner state as a constant feeling of having just emerged from a dream."[2] Much like the experience somebody would have when waking up after sleeping and finding oneself in a still confused state of reality. Only in Henry's case, the twilight feeling of gliding from dream to reality never abated.

What happened during the operation that caused Henry to find himself in a constant state of dazed feelings? Scoville was puzzled by the unexpected and unintended outcome of the operation. Did Henry's postsurgical condition give a hint to the function of the human medial temporal lobes? The surgery turned out to be devastating for Henry Molaison's cognitive functions. But as tragic as the intervention was for Henry Molaison as a patient, it opened up new horizons in memory research. His case still permeates the scientific and popular science literature. In fact, Henry Molaison became the most frequently mentioned and best-studied single patient in the history of neuroscience, better known as patient H.M.

Let's not forget that at that time the workings of the human brain were still largely a mystery in terms of how anatomy correlated with function.[3] Although the extraordinarily gifted neurosurgeon Wilder Penfield then had already become famous for establishing an anatomical–functional map of brain organization, his findings were taken up particularly by scientists investigating the sensory and motor systems or speech and behavioral disorders. Yet notwithstanding the triumphant progression of localizationism in the aforementioned research areas, the localizationist agenda seemed to have fallen short in the field of memory research.

---

[2] Ibid.

[3] Of course, contemporary scientists still face an exceptional challenge when investigating the functioning of the human brain. Nonetheless, impressive neurobiological insights have been gained, especially in the last fifty years that were unthinkable in Scoville's days.

In fact, despite the popularity of brain localization theories in many other neuroscientific fields, these theories seemed to be irrelevant for memory research. This critical view was fueled by researchers of the medical and scientific community who initially ridiculed the mapping efforts of localizationists as some sort of revival of phrenology. These critics were diffusionists who held the theory that the brain operated holistically and rejected a separation of parts or a pointillist division of labor in the brain. This theory was based on the influential work of the French physiologist Pierre Flourens, who had demonstrated that the cerebral hemispheres did not have areas associated with particular functions. His primary experimental animals had been pigeons, and he generalized these animal findings to human brains. He believed the hemispheres to be insensible to stimulation and to operate as indivisible wholes.[4] Following a distributionist agenda, memory researchers at that time subscribed to the view that there was no specific location in the brain where memories were stored. The conviction that memories are not specifically localized was largely owed to the American psychologist and behaviorist Karl Spencer Lashley. Inspired by the success of the European localizationists, Lashley was initially very interested in identifying the parts of the brain that were responsible for storing memory traces. Such memory traces were hypothetical structures that were termed engrams and were believed to represent specific units involved in memory storage in the brain. Since their exact mechanism and location were completely unknown in any organism, Lashley and his fellow researcher Shepherd Ivory Franz chose to perform their experiments on laboratory rats. They first trained rats to find food rewards in differently designed mazes. First, they observed that the animals improved their skills in navigating through these mazes and finding food after more and more training sessions. After the training, the scientists surgically lesioned multiple regions of the animals' brains and retested them to find out whether the animals then had trouble finding the food at the locations they were trained on before. If this were the case, the scientists would have had evidence that the targeted, lesioned brain area was involved in storing the location of a particular feeding ground in the maze. Despite lesioning multiple areas of the rats' cortices, Lashley and Franz could not discover any particular part of the brain that was clearly correlated with the incapability of finding the food or with the overall performance in the maze. At the same time, however, Lashley and Franz revealed that the amount of cortical tissue removed clearly had effects on the animals' knowledge retention. This led Lashley and Franz to the conclusion that memory traces are not stored in distinct and localized areas but are widely distributed across the whole cerebral landscape. Consequently, it seemed as if

---

[4] Walker, "The Development of the Concept of Cerebral Localization," 99–121.

multiple parts of the brain work together for memory and retention. This appeared in contrast to lesions in a small specific area that clearly interfered with the functioning of the animals' sensory or motor skills. Lashley also discovered if one part of the rat brain was damaged, other parts of the brain would compensate for the memory loss of this destructed part, a process that has already been described by Ramón y Cajal. American psychologists Edwin E. Ghiselli and Clarence W. Brown confirmed Lashley's empirical results by performing lesion experiments in various subcortical regions of rat brains and testing the animals in mazes. Following Lashley's studies and related experiments by several others, researchers came to agree that with respect to memory, the brain is essentially functioning as a whole unit rather than a modular assembly of different memory contents. These findings together with the seemingly distributed nature of memory traces culminated in Lashley's equipotentiality hypothesis that clearly went against localizationist theories of that time.

Against this backdrop of equipotentiality, Scoville's patient Henry Molaison shook the grounds of memory research. In January 1954, Scoville published a paper in the *Journal of Neurosurgery* entitled "The limbic lobe in man" in which he described the effects of the bilateral resection of the medial temporal lobes that he performed on Henry. In this publication, the neurosurgeon pointed out that the operation did not result in any marked physiological or behavioral changes with the one exception of a very grave, recent memory loss.[5] Initiated by widely renowned neurosurgeon Wilder Penfield, Scoville began a collaboration with Brenda Milner, a British-Canadian neuropsychologist who meticulously examined Henry's mental faculties. Milner and Scoville discovered that Henry had developed a dense anterograde amnesia and had become completely deprived of the ability to form new memories. Henry could no longer commit new events, names, or faces to his existing long-term memory and was completely unaware of any events that occurred prior to nineteen months preceding his operation. Henry's condition of amnesia did not improve. One and three-quarter years after the surgery, his memory was still so excruciatingly bad that Henry's mother complained that her son could not even be sent to the store alone for shopping. In fact, in the five and a half decades to come, Henry never recovered from his impaired ability to remember everyday encounters with people and events.

From a scientific point of view, Henry's tragic fate was a revelation. Milner's studies of Henry laid the foundations for modern memory science, providing evidence that there was indeed some sort of discrete seat of memory in the human brain. Importantly, many psychological and psychometric tests showed

---

[5] Scoville, "The Limbic Lobe in Man," 64–66.

that Henry's intellectual and perceptual faculties had remained intact. These findings again countered the notion of equipotentiality and the assumption that memory was intricately linked to intellectual and perceptual functions.

Milner's further studies of Henry unexpectedly revealed another extraordinary scientific insight. Surprisingly, Henry was able to learn and memorize processes that involved slightly sophisticated motor skills, such as drawing complex figures, performing mirror writing, and, later in life, using a walker. From this, memory researchers concluded that there must be a division between so-called procedural and declarative memory systems. Henry may have largely lost the latter, the declarative memory that is involved in recalling knowledge that is either learned as external facts or personally experienced. On the other hand, the former, his procedural memory, was still intact, allowing him to learn new action processes, hone them, and recall them accurately.

Partly triggered by the tragic case of Henry Molaison, memory science enjoyed an impressive upturn. Another key player in this research area was the Canadian psychologist Endel Tulving. He was the first to make a distinction between two types of declarative memory: episodic and semantic. Semantic memory refers to general knowledge about the world, such as facts, ideas, meaning, and concepts. It is often called factual memory and derives from what one has learned either through external sources such as reading or listening, or through personal experience. It is usually accepted as knowledge, without reference to its source. However, it should be noted that most scientists now agree that semantic memory is nonetheless tinted and influenced by our cultural environment and the social niches we live in. Above all, semantic memory is undated. It represents the knowledge that is not linked to a particular occasion on which it was acquired. According to Tulving, semantic memory is distinct from episodic memory. The latter is characterized as autobiographical memory and thus self-related. Episodic memory refers to the memory of experiences and specific events that happened during one's life but can usually be recalled at any given time point. This type of memory is always distinctly about the past and embedded in a temporal frame of reference, i.e., an event that has happened at a particular time in the past. All such autobiographic events derive from self-experience and have distinct self-relevance.

This is where the rubber hits the road—where the self is connected to mnemonic capacities. It is memories that make a person, particularly one's autobiographic memory. It is memories that form everything a person *is* by means of accumulated knowledge about everything she *was*. All the different scraps of memory are integrated into a whole to generate a complete picture of oneself. This insight about how memory forms selfhood is also owed to Henry Molaison, or rather his cognitive deficits. As mentioned earlier, when Scoville and Milner examined Henry, they found that their patient could no longer acquire new declarative (i.e., episodic and semantic) memories. When Milner worked with Henry for several hours, left the room for just a few minutes, and returned, Henry had already forgotten who she was. Milner had to reintroduce herself to her patient. Also, Henry would forget that he already had lunch and ended up having lunch twice within an hour or so.

However, episodic and semantic memories that Henry had acquired nineteen months prior to the operation seemed to be more or less intact. He remembered his parents, where he lived, where he went to school, and who his treating physician was. The unambiguous corollary was that Henry suffered from anterograde amnesia, but his retrograde memory was spared. Yet this latter conclusion turned out to be a grave error. Later, psychologist Suzanne Corkin demonstrated that virtually all of Henry's autobiographic memories that he had acquired before the surgery no longer existed or were completely inaccessible to him. Although he was aware of certain events that happened in his life, he could no longer connect them to himself. Rather than being able to string them together into an at least semi-coherent narrative, these events remained impersonal and unrelated pieces of information to him, like any factual knowledge. It no longer mattered whether he recalled a particular event of his own life or whether the event concerned somebody he read about in a news magazine. His episodic memory had become "semanticized"— none of his memories were personal anymore.

These unexpected findings fueled the scientific debate about how new information gets stored in the first place. Are there different mechanisms involved in storing semantic versus episodic memory contents? Contemporary neuroscience is still far away from being able to explain the details of memory storage and retrieval, yet the last fifty years of memory research has produced extraordinarily fruitful insights into how the (human) brain works. Everything we experience—be it objects, events, or places where they occur—are processed in separate sensory areas in the cerebral cortex. These topographic explanations strongly draw from Wilder Penfield's somatotopic mapping. After Penfield's pioneering studies, many other neuroanatomical, neurophysiological, neurosurgical, and psychology studies have shown that there are relatively distinct brain areas for vision, touch, hearing, and so forth. Despite this localizationist generalization, it is important to emphasize that Wilder Penfield's results, as well as many subsequent findings, were by no means clear cut. Today, most researchers agree that there is considerable overlap between brain regions rather than an anatomical pattern of distinctly delimited areas. For example, the motor areas that control muscles in the hand sometimes also control muscles in the upper arm and shoulder. Penfield attributed this functional border transgression to individual variation in brain size and localization. However, in the last decades, it has become increasingly clear that there is no simple localizationist brain topography that maps onto functions in a one-to-one manner. Notwithstanding the many amendments and adjustments localizationists had to undertake to fit their theory to empirical findings, the overall success of neuroanatomist in mapping brain areas for sensomotoric processes had a strong impact on memory research. Additionally, the wide range of experimental studies of short-term and long-term memory triggered by the first case studies of Henry Molaison inspired researchers to make assiduous efforts in trying to localize the seat of memory in more detail. A revived quest for memory traces (i.e., engrams) had begun. In fact, in the not too distant past, the most extreme localizationists held the hypothesis that an individual neuron represented an engram, which stored all relevant information about a given object or event. This hypothesis has often been referred to as the "hypothesis of the grandmother cells." A single grandmother cell was believed to get activated only under highly specific circumstances, like seeing a photo of one's grandmother.[6] If this one neuron got destroyed, one would completely forget Grandmother with one single blow. This hypothesis sounds quite absurd if we consider how many neurons die each day. Is it likely that one wakes up one morning and has forgotten all about Grandmother? Not surprisingly, this extreme localizationist interpretation of memory storage was heavily criticized. The major point of criticism was that it would not suffice to have one neuron dedicated to Grandmother, for one would require hundreds if not thousands of neurons to recognize Grandmother. Since the neuron in question may not get activated if grandmother wears different clothes, puts on a hat or glasses, and even if she just turns around and we see her profile instead of her directly facing us. According to the hypothesis of the grandmother cells, complex stimuli would need to be processed with one neuron per stimulus variation (e.g., grandmother with hat versus grandmother without hat, etc.), though the human brain would have nowhere near enough neurons to become activated by the amount of all possible cues of objects, people, places, or events. In agreement with this criticism of an extreme localizationist view, Lashley's experiments leading to the equipotentiality hypothesis sweepingly refuted the localizationist interpretation of memory and added grist to the mills of the diffusionists. Diffusionists argued that the brain worked as a functional whole with at best a few unspecific morphological substructures, and memory was equally distributed over multiple parts of the brain that work together to form memory content. For much of the last century,

---

[6] The idea of neurons storing memories in such a highly specific manner goes all the way back to William James, who conceived of "pontificial cells" to which human consciousness would attach.

these two camps (localizationists versus diffusionists) remained irreconcilable. Yet over the last decades, more and more memory researchers have found the dichotomy superfluous as theoretical demarcations between localizationism and diffusionism increasingly blurred. Recent studies using new powerful techniques of single-cell electrophysiology have revealed that there are indeed neurons in the visual system that fire selectively when the test person views pictures of certain celebrities but remain silent when pictures of other celebrities, places, or animals are viewed.[7] However, these findings are still a far cry from having discovered grandmother cells. In contrast to the hypothetical grandmother cell, the very neuron that gets activated when viewing a photo of a certain person also gets activated when reading that person's name or seeing another person closely related to the former one. Thus, rather than storing a single object, person, etc. as an engram or highly distinct memory trace, the neurons investigated seem to store abstract information or concepts about these objects, persons, etc. These neurons that respond in a remarkably selective and abstract manner to particular persons or objects were termed "concept cells."

The idea of neurons getting activated by abstract concepts rather than particular objects, people, places, or events is not as far-fetched as it may appear at first glance. Memories strongly rely on reconstructions of previous experiences of our external world. Our perception, in turn, is based on meanings we attribute to what we sense. Without having an appropriate concept or meaning, our perceptions remain serendipitous and scattered. Like in Henry Molaison's case, when he was examined in the 1990s to determine his general linguistic competence. Henry was shown a picture of a man rock climbing. Underfoot, just below the rock, the picture showed two other men, one of them pointing at the climber. The researcher asked Henry to describe the scene in one sentence and to use the words "fall" and "leg" in that sentence. She expected something like "One man tells the other that the climber may fall and break his leg." Yet, Henry could not come up with anything coherent or comprehensible in the interview.[8] Irrespective of his language competence, this and other examinations clearly indicated that Henry had severe problems in understanding concepts and meanings of events while perceiving them.

On the contrary, a "normal" person's perceptual apparatus extracts relevant features of the perceived event or object and thereby omits a large number of details. This attribution of meaning is highly subjective and involves abstraction. Consequently, our memory system by reconstructing previously perceived experiences also heavily relies on abstraction. The medial temporal

---

[7] Quiroga et al., "Sparse but Not 'Grandmother-Cell,'" 87–91.
[8] Dittrich, *Patient H.M.*

lobe (MTL) is crucial for this abstraction process underlying declarative memory. The MTL contains neuronal networks comprised of more or less specific concept cells. These concept cells get activated by more general cues than by idiosyncratic features of an individual person or object. Neurons in the MTL do not get selectively activated when observing Grandmother sitting, whereas another neuron gets activated when Grandmother is standing, wearing glasses, etc. Rather, concept cells fire at any instance related to Grandmother, including seeing her picture and reading or hearing her name. Such processes of cognitive abstraction allow neurons to be selective but makes them also prone to errors and noise. High specificity of MTL neurons is achieved by combining many concept cells. Thus, the distinct neuronal encoding (e.g., of a person, object, etc.) is then not just based on an individual neuron, but on its interconnectivity with other neurons and its partaking in specific neural assemblies. As a result, memory content is not stored as bits and pieces containing all possible, minute details and their variations distributed across millions or perhaps billions of neurons; instead, memories may be constituted by relatively few neurons, maybe a few thousands, that generate "sparse" networks[9] of encoding elements of abstract features. Establishing connections in sparse networks occurs quickly by linking groups of concept cells. In this way, memory elements of semantic facts can be linked to events of our lives. Connections of sparse networks of concept cells do not only "speak to themselves," forming circuits within the temporal area of the brain, but can also link to other brain regions—for example, to the cortical visual areas. Most importantly, networks of concept cells show high visual invariance, i.e., they get activated in response to a very specific individual or object (like one's grandmother), regardless of its size or viewing angle. This concept of sparseness of memory networks is in stark contrast to neurons of the cortical visual areas that do not abstract from complex stimuli but encode local details (e.g., the orientation of a line or silhouette). Connecting different circuits—e.g. say, the primary visual cortex, the fusiform face area (that is involved in processes of face recognition), and concept cells of the MTL, especially the hippocampus—is a way of linking perception to memory.[10] The MTL is not involved in perception *per se*, but concept cells fire explicitly to the conscious perception of a stimulus.[11] In other words, the concept cells are not necessary to recognize an individual object or person—say one's grandmother—but are rather crucial for creating new associations and memories. Establishing new associations by connecting sparse networks of concept cells enables us to

---

[9] Quiroga et al., "Sparse but Not 'Grandmother-Cell,'" 87–91.

[10] Suthana and Fried, "Percepts to Recollections," 427–436.

[11] Quiroga et al., "Human Single-Neuron Responses," 3599–3604.

remember at a later time point having seen Grandmother's picture. By way of associative connections, abstract and sparse representation of semantic knowledge is tied to episodic memories, thereby creating meaningful concepts that make up our subjective, individual worlds. In this way, meaning can be extracted and our memory thus encodes what is critical to be retained from our experiences. When we encounter objects and events in the world around us, our sensory pathways conduct sensory stimuli to cortical areas where information about the objects' and events' identity (color, shape, auditory and haptic information, etc.) are gathered. The sensory pathways then project to other areas in the cortex, the so-called multimodal cortical association areas, where many sensory details about perceived objects or events get co-processed. Other pathways that involve multiple areas of the cerebral cortex gather information about the location where events occur. These streams of information further signal to the medial temporal lobe (MTL). More precisely, the perirhinal cortex and the lateral entorhinal area of the MTL are involved in specific object processing and object familiarity (i.e., recognition specifics), whereas the parahippocampal cortex and the medial entorhinal area of the MTL process spatial contexts of the events. Eventually, these pathways converge at the hippocampus where integration of information occurs. The previously described concept cells that apparently extract meaning from experienced stimuli are localized in the hippocampus and other subregions of the MTL. In the tragic case of Henry Molaison, immediate perception was not impaired, but extracting a meaningful context of a situation was nonetheless almost impossible for him. In Henry's brain, the convergence of the anatomical pathways deriving from the cortex and subcortical regions were destroyed by the removal of large parts of the hippocampal tissue. Henry was unable to form new, cohesive memories of events within the context in which they occurred. This was clearly observed during the examination when he was shown a scene depicting a rock climber. Despite all efforts, he could not come up with a coherent sentence about the complexity of the scene. This incapability of perceptual coherence translates to memory formation. Without extracting meaning during perception, memory cannot be stored in any context but at best in snippets of unrelated content. For instance, Henry Molaison was able to reproduce a few, albeit very confused facts about John F. Kennedy's assassination, an event that happened ten years after his surgery. Yet any contextual association of this event was missing, and he mixed up facts related to JFK.'s death with various other unrelated names and places. Taken together, the MTL and especially the hippocampus seem to be essential for the contextual association of memory content.

These findings indicate that the hippocampus is strongly engaged in the consolidation period by forming associations of memory content. Memory consolidation (long-term memory storage) is a complex process that goes far beyond the simple storage of distinct, factual memories. Rather, memories do not remain isolated pieces of knowledge but get embedded into a larger framework of knowledge. Initially, memories are often connected to the history of one's experience into which they are incorporated and form an autobiographical context. Broadly speaking, memory can therefore be seen as an ever-growing network of interconnected content (with the aforementioned concept cells only being a small but significant part of it). This means that new information from the environment is incorporated into existing circuits, thereby constantly updating our knowledge. This process of associative linking ensures that our memory encodes essential meanings and concepts perceived and leaves aside countless unimportant details. Thus, memory formation is first and foremost selective and not indiscriminately accumulative.

But how does the selection of relevant memory content occur? So far, I have mainly described the gross-anatomical processes and brain areas that are crucial for memory. The brain regions as well as the pathways that connect these different regions are relatively stable and evolutionarily conserved amongst humans. Thus, it may be unclear how new memory contents can continuously get stored given the relative anatomical stability. It must be emphasized that the brain areas discussed generally comprise millions to billions of neurons, and the interconnecting neuronal pathways consist of many parallel bundles of axonal fibers of these neurons. Despite a gross-anatomical stability within the brain (with some exceptions following brain injuries or developmental compensation processes), many anatomical and functional changes in the brain occur on the micro and meso anatomical level, e.g., on the level of molecules, cells, and neuronal networks, respectively. Thus, to tackle how processes of learning and memory work, a multi-level perspective must be employed.

For example, studying spatial memory requires the investigation of mechanisms on multiple levels. In addition to its aforementioned role in episodic memory, the hippocampus is also involved in spatial memory. On the cellular level, individual neurons within the hippocampus get activated when the organism encounters new objects or events, similarly to the previously described concept cells. For example, specific neurons in the rodent hippocampus, so-called place cells, get selectively activated in response to specific locations in an environment. These cells also encode relevant objects and behavioral events at specific places within an environment.[12, 13] Most importantly, the same cells are associated with the formation as well as retrieval of memories of objects, events, and their spatial information. It has been

---

[12] Komorowski et al., "Robust Conjunctive Item-Place Coding," 9918–9929.
[13] Pastalkova et al., "Internally Generated Cell Assembly," 1322–1327.

suggested that the spatial representation by place cells in rodents is analogous to the representation of semantic memories in humans. Additionally, the activation pattern of place cells in response to a rat moving, anticipating, or memorizing a certain trajectory seems comparable to an episodic trace in humans.

But the hippocampus does not only comprise of concept cells and place cells that map the spatial context of an object or event, but also so-called "time cells" that map the temporal organization of experiences. These time cells are activated within neuronal networks at sequential moments in temporally ordered episodes.[14,15] Neuronal networks that integrate spatial as well as temporal information constitute the mechanism involved in memory formation that encodes and allows recall of the order of events in everyday experiences.[16] Yet importantly, objects and events are functionally distinguished on the level of the hippocampus. For the purpose of memory function, the human hippocampus can be separated into two areas: the posterior and the anterior hippocampus. Neuronal networks in the posterior hippocampus encode specific objects and related spatial information, whereas those in the anterior hippocampus link events within a context and strongly discriminate between different contexts. The formations of associations between different networks are involved in the creation of memories through contextual representation, thereby allowing distinct recollective experiences.[17, 18]

Place cells, concept cells, time cells, etc. are parts of overall tens of millions of neurons within the hippocampus (about 10^9 neurons in the MTL). When attributing an active role to the hippocampus with respect to a particular memory performance, researchers actually refer to a small fraction of neurons or networks of neurons rather than the activation of the whole brain region. Consequently, it has proven highly instructive to investigate brain activity during memory formation on the cellular (i.e., neuronal) level, as demonstrated by the earlier examples.

To further elucidate processes happening on the cellular level, one must look at a neuron's anatomy and physiology in more detail (Figure 5.1). Each neuron consists of a cell body with a nucleus. It is the nucleus where the DNA is located and where gene expression takes place (see Chapter 1 & Chapter 4).

---

14 MacDonald et al., "Hippocampal 'Time Cells' Bridge the Gap," 737–749.
15 Naya and Suzuki, "Integrating What and When," 773–776,
16 Eichenbaum, "Memory on Time," 81–88.
17 Eichenbaum et al., "The Medial Temporal Lobe and Recognition Memory," 123–152.
18 Squire et al., "Recognition Memory and the Medial Temporal Lobe," 872–883.

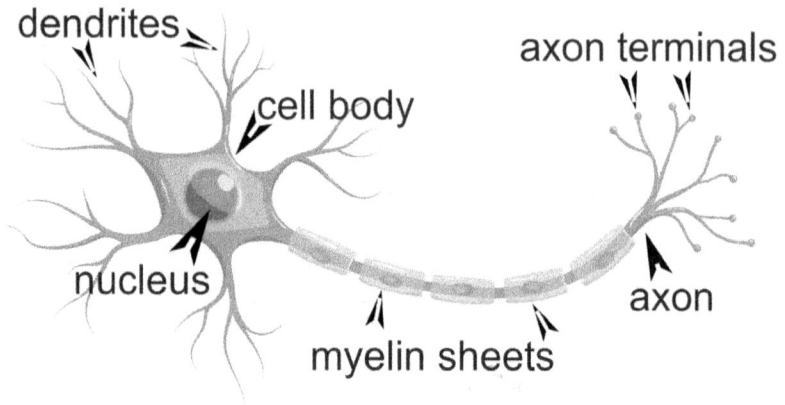

Figure 5.1: Schematic picture of a neuron; the DNA is located in the nucleus of the neuron (modified from @AdobeStock_290162954).

The DNA of every neuron is identical, and the same DNA is actually present in neurons as in any other cell of the body. The fact that a particular cell has developed into a neuron—rather than, say, a liver cell—is due to particular genes that were activated during a certain period in organismal development, starting with embryonic development. Also, the specific communication of a certain neuron with another neuron and the formation of long-term connections between these neurons largely rely on gene expression. At this point, it is important to emphasize again that genes do not get activated or silenced only during limited developmental windows (e.g., during embryonic development). Gene regulation (i.e., gene activation, silencing, or anything in between) in neurons continues throughout our whole life, albeit to a far lesser extent than in the embryonic stage. Each neuron communicates with its neighboring cells, such as other neurons, glia cells, or other cell types (e.g., epithelial cells, pericytes, and endothelia), thereby receiving a plethora of signals from its cellular surroundings. This communication frequently happens at cellular protrusions of neurons. These cellular protrusions are called axons and dendrites (Figure 5.1). Axons are the primary transmission route of information within the brain and from the brain to the periphery and back. On a physico-chemical level, what is referred to as information transmission are electrical impulses that rapidly travel along the axons of the neuron. The rapid transmission is ensured by myelin sheaths (i.e., modified glia cells) that wrap around the axon like insulation of an electric cable, thereby confining electrical impulse. Impulses are generated in the neuronal cell body, conducted along the axon, and terminate at points where one neuron contacts its target cell. The anatomical point where the axon of one neuron contacts a second (target) cell is characterized by the formation of a synapse. Frequently, such synapses are located on another type of neuronal protrusion, the so-called dendrites. Dendrites are usually shorter in length than axons, have a tapering shape, and receive input signals rather than transmitting them.

Dendrites (and also other areas of the neuron such as the cell body) receive a plethora of stimuli from other neurons and their cellular surroundings. These inputs can influence gene expression within a neuron. When specific patterns of genes are expressed in response to a stimulus, the neuron undergoes neuroplastic changes in its structure and function (i.e., neuroplasticity), a process that is required for long-term memory storage.[19] Neuroplasticity is an activity-dependent modulation of the function and structure and has been described earlier in this book (see Chapter 2). The particular case of rearrangements of synaptic connections is termed synaptic plasticity.

The idea of synaptic plasticity dates back to neuroanatomist Santiago Ramón y Cajal's cellular connectionist approach, which postulated that learning results from changes in the strength of the synapse,[20] as discussed in Chapter 2. Ramón y Cajal worked on the details of the brain for over fifty years, and he understood the working of the brain better than most. He observed the flexibility of neuron connections and speculated on how learning is manifested by the plasticity of neurons in the brain. He discovered that some neurons expand their processes to receive new inputs while others reduce them and assumed that this is due to a physiological attempt to maintain an overall equilibrium. Underlying learning processes, Ramón y Cajal envisioned plasticity of cortical neurons (see Chapter 2). This was in stark contradiction to the then-predominant reticular theory, which stated that the brain consisted of an extremely dense and intricate network of intertwined nerve cell branches. These branches derived from different cell layers of the brain and formed a continuous network (i.e., the reticulum) that was basically stable. According to the reticular theory, the brain was believed to be a network of continuous fibers; a reorganization and rearrangement of cells did not come into question. Ramón y Cajal disproved the reticular theory and experimentally demonstrated that cells of the brain were not continuous. He showed that brain cells are individual, contiguous units, connected in chains with gaps between the endings of the cell protrusions. The latter view of the brain consisting of individual brain cells was dubbed "neuron doctrine" and became the foundation of modern neuroscience. Individual neurons that interacted with each other over a distance and formed connections left much more notional

---

[19] Bacskai et al., "Spatially Resolved Dynamics," 222–226.
[20] Ramón y Cajal, "The Croonian Lecture," 444–468.

room for flexibility and paved the way for the connectionist approach that later provided the foundations for synaptic plasticity.

However, the time was not yet ripe for the victory march of neuroplastic explanations. Although Ramón y Cajal in his earlier writings[21] played with the idea that neurons are plastic and accumulated a wealth of supporting empirical evidence, he did not wholeheartedly follow through with it. On the contrary, later in life, he was subjected to the dominant orthodoxy that the mature human brain is static and immutable. This view of fixed neuronal circuits dominated the neuroscientific worldview for over fifty years. Since then, however, a paradigm shift has occurred in brain research. As described in more detail in Chapter 2, most contemporary neuroscientists agree that the human brain is plastic throughout a person's entire life. This means the brain has the physiological, neural, and cognitive capacity to reorganize itself. Neuroplasticity provides the basis for all learning processes and memory formation. This malleability allows the brain to flexibly respond to an ever-changing environment. Neuroplastic processes are particularly far-reaching and effective during childhood and adolescence. However, neuroanatomical and functional changes do not only occur during critical periods early in life but happen throughout the whole life (albeit to a lesser extent as we age). Neuroplastic events cause an adaptive reorganization of brain circuitry in response to the organism's environment as well as the individual's experience. Thus, the environment exerts its effects by influencing gene expression (see also Chapter 1) and thereby crucially contributes to neuronal and synaptic plasticity that underlie learning and memory. Whether certain memory contents will be stored for an extended period or not largely depends on the expression of specific patterns of genes.[22] Expression of these genes causes a change in the cellular components (e.g., the amounts of neurotransmitters, neurotransmitter receptors, ion channels, etc.) of the respective neuron. Such changes in the cellular components make a neuron more susceptible to become reactivated when similar circumstances in its cellular and physiological surroundings occur again. Following these molecular changes, a particular neuron will more readily fire again when stimulated. These physiological modulations can best be exemplified by scrutinizing neuronal activity during learning and memory processes, such as when recalling events, places, or objects. The place cells of the hippocampus are well-studied examples of pyramidal neurons that get specifically activated by appropriate triggers, namely by location-dependent stimuli. Place cells exhibit a spatially selective activity pattern and fire only when the animal is in a specific location

---

[21] Ibid.
[22] Kandel, "The Molecular Biology of Memory," 14.

in its environment. Generally speaking, each individual place cell becomes activated by a distinct trigger. This trigger (i.e., the spatial information) is different for each place cell (although some overlaps occur). When an organism enters a new environment, the animal quickly learns to navigate through the new location by activating respective place cells. The activation of place cells and the storage of spatial information according to this activation pattern occurs within a matter of minutes and can be stable for months. This long-term stability of patterns of place cells depends on the synthesis of new proteins. Importantly, while initial acquisition and early retention of memory seem to be independent of synthesis of new proteins, formation of long-term memories requires protein synthesis.[23] The molecular memory stored in an individual neuron is characterized by its specific gene expression pattern. Thus, on the level of brain cells, the physiology is determined by its cellular components that in turn is influenced by the expression of a certain set of genes.

Despite particular gene expression patterns and physicochemical properties, individual neurons are not highly exclusive but can get activated by mistake. To avoid misfiring, neural computations are performed by sets of neurons that work together (so-called population processing). Sets of neurons (also termed neuronal assemblies) must get activated together and fire at the same time. Co-activation of networks of neuronal population can average sporadic mistakes and filter out noise. Consequently, the system becomes highly selective, robust, and less prone to mistakes. Population coding therefore entails that neuronal populations perform better than single neurons with respect to signal-to-noise ratio.

The idea of neuronal populations, or cell assemblies, that undergo co-activation dates back to Canadian neuropsychologist Donald O. Hebb. In his classic monograph,[24] he argued that behavioral patterns like visual perception are built up gradually by increasingly connecting sets of neurons. Initially, rudimentary percepts or simple behaviors may be represented in specific and small sets of neurons of demarcated brain regions. Over time, more complex behaviors require the connection of larger cell assemblies, which he called phase sequences. The latter involves larger sets of cells from disparate brain regions. Hebb also claimed that such large assemblies inevitably harbor equipotentiality. If individual neurons get destroyed, alternative pathways ensure that behavioral tasks can still be carried out. Hebb's concept accommodated aspects of the localizationist as well as diffusionist vistas and became largely influential until today. Most importantly, his theoretical concept of cell assemblies also explained how learning can occur. He

---

[23] Agnihotri et al., "The Long-Term Stability of New Hippocampal," 3656–3661.
[24] Hebb, *The Organization of Behavior.*

contended that the constant stimulation of specific assemblies leads to structural changes in their connections. In his words: "When an axon of cell A is near enough to excite a cell B and repeatedly or persistently takes part in firing it, some growth process or metabolic change takes place in one or both cells such that A's efficiency, as one of the cells firing B, is increased."[25]

This principle has been termed Hebbian-learning and links functional changes with structural changes. There is now ample empirical evidence that if the firing of one neuron repeatedly assists in firing another neuron (i.e., neurons show a synchronized activation pattern), a strengthening of the synaptic connection between these neurons will ensue. The neurophysiological-neuroanatomical tenet first hypothesized by Hebb has since been condensed into the well-known dictum of "cells that fire together, wire together." Contrarily, if two neurons frequently fire out of phase, their synaptic connections weaken. It has been widely argued that this process of Hebbian synaptic plasticity underlies associative learning.

Thus, in addition to the aforementioned changes in single neurons (e.g., via gene expression), changes at individual synapses that connect neurons with each other are highly relevant for learning processes on the level of neuronal networks. Importantly, such synaptic changes will have an effect on the whole assembly. Following associative learning, more complex changes taking place at the synaptic connections of the neuronal assemblies will produce alterations in information flow through the respective neural circuit. Such alterations will cause changes in the behavior or perception of the organism.

On the functional level, the electric activity of neuronal assemblies can be measured. Modern electrophysiology has championed the parallel measurement of many dozens of individual neurons at the same time in response to various stimuli. But decades ago, Henry Molaison's brain network activities were also investigated thoroughly. At that time, the use of electroencephalograms (EEG) was the state-of-the-art technique to measure large assemblies of neurons. An EEG records weak electric currents by placing electrodes on the subject's scalp. This method has undergone technical development and refinement and is still in wide use today. In short, electric currents measured by EEG reflect a summation of excitatory and inhibitory postsynaptic potentials of neurons. Between the neurons are feedback connections that contribute to the synchronization of the firing patterns. These synchronized activities of large numbers of neurons derive from paced, rhythmic inhibitory activity and give rise to macroscopic oscillations that can be observed in an EEG. The brain generates spontaneous oscillatory activities that are characteristic for distinct

---

[25] Ibid., 62.

mental states. Different oscillation frequencies correlate with different brain states, e.g., states of relaxation or concentration, or states of deep sleep or REM sleep, etc. Thus, various brain activities display typical sequences of waveform types, which have characteristic durations and regular patterns. These different brain activities are reflected in spontaneous oscillatory rhythms. In addition, EEG can also be exploited to detect time-locked signals (i.e., stimulus-evoked potentials) that are associated with distinct events, such as stimulus processing or specific motor activity. Despite the long history of the EEG, the functional role of neural oscillations is still not fully elucidated and the putative encoding "language" of these neuronal assemblies are not well understood.

Human EEG studies have shown that synchronized activity of the hippocampus and the prefrontal cortex (PFC, the foremost part of the frontal lobe) can be detected in memory recall tasks. For instance, when test persons successfully recalled certain words, an enhanced synchronization between frontal and posterior brain areas (including parietal and temporal cortex) could be shown. This indicated that memory encoding involved an interaction between these two areas. Furthermore, depth recordings in epilepsy patients revealed synchronized oscillations between the medial temporal lobe and PFC during verbal recall tests. This suggested that encoding and retrieval of verbal memory is associated with the synchronized neural activity of PFC and the temporal lobe. In addition, different object-paired associative learning paradigms in monkeys showed different frequency bands within the hippocampus and PFC. Also, during working memory tasks, the simultaneous recordings in the hippocampus and PFC reveal synchronized activity of these brain regions.

Learning and memory formation seem to require synchronization processes on a network level mediated by neuroplastic processes on a synaptic and cellular level that are subject to neuromodulation (by dopamine and other neuromodulators). It is important to mention that elucidating how memory works does not only require an understanding of processes that underlie learning and encoding, but also of retrieval processes of previously encoded memory content. Returning once again to Henry Molaison, it has been clearly demonstrated that the hippocampus is crucial for associative learning and memory consolidation, as argued previously. At the same time, the hippocampus did not seem absolutely necessary for recalling long-term memories. Henry was capable of recalling pieces of semantic (factual) knowledge. These pieces of knowledge—long-term memories without any personal context—were stored in Henry's brain well before his operation took place. For example, he could remember some details about World War II, the attack of Pearl Harbor, Victory-in-Europe Day, and the German and the Japanese surrender.[26]

In being able to remember these events that occurred a long time ago, Henry must have had some parts of his brain intact that allowed him to access these historical facts. Due to the resection of most of the inner parts of his temporal poles, Henry lacked large parts of both hippocampi, amygdalae, as well as parahippocampal, perirhinal, and entorhinal cortices. Despite having barely any episodic memories, Henry still had access to some "semanticized" pieces of memory, like the important historic events mentioned previously. This clearly suggested that some information stored in Henry's long-term memory was relatively independent of the tissue that was removed during the operation. Consequently, researchers needed to take a closer look at other brain areas to find out which other parts may contribute to the storage and retrieval of long-term, semantic memories. And indeed, in the last few decades, memory researchers have accumulated increasing evidence that, in addition to the hippocampal area, the PFC appears equally essential for the encoding and retrieval of declarative memories. These two areas (the hippocampus and the PFC) communicate via robust neuronal pathways. More precisely, a part of the hippocampus (in humans it is the anterior part) projects to the medial and orbital prefrontal cortices. The anterior hippocampus is crucially involved in contextual representations, linking events within a context and discriminating between different contexts. The anterior hippocampus has direct (monosynaptic) outputs to the medial prefrontal cortex,[27] where information about the context of interrelated memories accumulates.[28] The role of the PFC in long-term memory has not been fully elucidated, but one of the key functions seems to be that it contributes to recalling memory content within other brain areas through strategic control over the retrieval process. This occurs via output pathways to other brain areas. The PFC has pathways back to the perirhinal and lateral entorhinal cortex of the MTL. The PFC may influence and bias the retrieval of specific object and event information via these pathways. Indeed, it seems that communication between these brain areas is essential for episodic memory processes.

Importantly, whether memory content can be retrieved or not is not solely defined by the age of the memory itself, but rather by how that memory relates to pre-existing knowledge and novel information encountered. Understanding how the hippocampus and the PFC contribute to memory therefore requires the disentanglement of how these brain regions support the encoding of new

---

[26] Dittrich, *Patient H.M.*
[27] Navawongse and Eichenbaum, "Distinct Pathways," 1002–1013.
[28] Preston and Eichenbaum, "Interplay of Hippocampus," R764–R773.

events with regard to the degree to which those events relate to prior knowledge.[29] During the learning process, the hippocampus links novel elements with those elements that are already stored in order to form new associations between the neocortex and those newly encountered elements. If these new associations are unrelated to previously stored elements, the hippocampus may foster linkages with neocortical information (feedback loops involving parts of the MTL) without necessarily engaging the prefrontal cortex. On the contrary, if newly learned elements overlap with pre-existing elements, the prefrontal cortex must be involved to form new associations. It is the role of the PFC to reconcile any putative conflicts in the association of novel and already existing elements. As time passes, long-term memory contents become gradually more generalized and overall contextualized. This neuroscientific explanation concerning the roles of the PFC and the hippocampal area toward memory is in agreement with the observations revealed by psychometric studies of Henry Molaison. Thus, memory consolidation comprises the transformation of a context-specific, episodic memory into a less detailed, more generic, semantic memory.[30] Analogously, the PFC also gets increasingly involved in memorizing public events, which may begin as episodic memories but rapidly evolve into semantic knowledge.[31] To emphasize again, memories that are not immediately integrated into a pre-existing knowledge framework do not require the involvement of the PFC initially. With the passage of time, these memories gradually become incorporated into the semantic memory circuit, requiring the engagement of the PFC. In short, lasting engagement of the hippocampus determines whether novel information remains active, e.g., as detailed episodic memories with autobiographical labels or as unique experience with rich multiple aspects. Contrarily, active engagement of the PFC is required for integrating new episodic memory into existing frameworks and contexts. The latter process is accompanied by a loss of episodic details and a "semanticization" of memory content. This is why the prefrontal cortex is often loosely referred to as the seat of the long-term, semantic knowledge. The PFC's involvement in long-term memory explains also why Henry Molaison was still able to recall some facts of the world before his operation, as his PFC was not significantly damaged.

In most humans under a certain age, retrieval failure is not a sign of pathology but is actually rather normal. Memory formation not only relies on learning and consolidation processes but also on processes of forgetting. Since humans use their memory system to optimize decision-making, the key lies in the

---

[29] Ibid.

[30] Winocur and Moscovitch, "Memory Transformation," 766–780.

[31] Smith and Squire, "Medial Temporal Lobe Activity," 930–938.

selection of relevant information rather than in the accumulation of complete information. Contemporary memory research therefore does not only focus on mechanisms of information storage (i.e., persistence) but also on mechanisms of forgetting (i.e., transience). The first clues about the natural occurrence of information loss during development came from child psychology. Humans do not simply accumulate memories from the very moment of one's birth. As already described in the late nineteenth century by Caroline Miles, adult humans usually cannot retrieve episodic memories of events that occurred at an early childhood age.[32] This phenomenon is known as childhood amnesia or infantile amnesia. Generally speaking, adults cannot remember events that occurred in the first two to three years of life. In addition to this phase of early infancy amnesia, there is a second phase in which adults recall only very few "spotty" memories from age three to seven years.[33] Childhood amnesia is, however, not an all-or-nothing phenomenon. Children do not experience an abrupt transition from "no memory" to "memory" at a specific point of time in their development. It is rather a gradual developmental transition in the ability to form enduring memories. Researchers have argued that this is due to infants not yet having either a concept of the past or a relevant concept of self.[34] But more recent research has shown that young infants are actually capable of creating memories; science seems to have grossly underestimated children's mnemonic competence. Preschoolers can create well-organized and accurate memories of stories and familiar events,[35] albeit less detailed than those of older children and adults. As early as nine months of age, children can also recall action sequences and scenarios. And such encoded memories have been found to be retrievable for up to two years.[36] Yet at some point, these memories seem to fade or get lost. Phrased in this way, childhood amnesia appears to counteract early learning processes. However, researchers have shown that forgetting is an indispensable feature of human memory at all ages. It may sound paradoxical, but forgetting improves mnemonic competence. People who can forget irrelevant events can better remember pertinent events, a phenomenon known as adaptive forgetting.[37] We only retain aspects about the world if this information is somehow useful and contributes to a coherent narrative. On the other hand, extraordinary mnemonic abilities that exceed those of average people by far are often characteristic for people with mental disabilities. One of the most remarkable examples of enhanced memory skills

---

[32] Buaer, "Oh Where, Oh Where Have Those Early Memories Gone?"
[33] Josselyn and Frankland, "Infantile Amnesia."
[34] Nelson, "Sociocultural Theories of Memory Development," 87–108.
[35] Siegler and Nelson, "How Young Children Represent Knowledge," 255–273.
[36] Nelson, "Quantitative and Qualitative Research," 263–272.
[37] Wimber et al., "Retrieval Induces Adaptive Forgetting," 582–589.

are those of so-called calendric savants (or "human calendars") who are able to accurately and rapidly recall memories from any given date. Persons diagnosed with savant syndrome usually excel in one specific memory skill like rapid calculation, artistic ability, map making, or musical ability.

For the workings of an average brain, it is healthy to filter out the relevant information of an event and the feelings associated with it rather than getting hung up on minute aspects of the event. The human memory system is, therefore, not devoted to encoding memory contents in full detail by storing identical mental or cognitive copies, but rather, memory is formed by linking particular and new memory content to related memories. The level of interconnection with other memory content is a good predictor of how well memory will be retained over time. Accordingly, things and events remembered best are those that have a direct relevance or importance for us and fit into already existing knowledge and narratives. Generating coherency and creating narratives is something our adult brain does really well—so well, we usually do not notice. Two of the first scientists to shed light on the importance of the brain's interconnectivity for creating coherent narratives were neuropsychologist Roger Sperry and his student Michael Gazzaniga.

In the 1960s, Sperry and Gazzaniga led pioneering studies examining patients who underwent split-brain surgery. These patients often suffered from generalized epilepsy and had to undergo a radical surgical procedure to reduce the amount of atonic seizures they experienced. During a split-brain surgery, the corpus callosum is severed, resulting in the partial or complete disconnection between the two hemispheres of the brain. The severance of the hemispheres causes each of the two halves of the patient's brain to generate its own separate perception, thoughts, and impulses to act. Sperry and Gazzaniga were the first ones to study these patients' perception and thought processes in detail. They set up an experiment in which they quickly flashed written words to either the patient's left or right field of vision. Surprisingly, patients who had a severed corpus callosum could only remember words they saw in their right field. Words shown to the left visual field seemed to have gone unnoticed by the subjects. But was it really the case that the brain did not process the stimulus in the left visual field? The left field of vision is controlled by the right brain hemisphere and vice versa. The patients who had their corpus callosum cut still had fully functional right brain hemispheres. It was only the main nerve tracks connecting the hemispheres that were disrupted. So why could the patients not recall what they saw in their left field of vision? In subsequent experiments, the scientists flashed images to either the left or the right viewing field of the subjects. Then, they asked the patients to draw or report what they saw. Results were unequivocal for all split-brain participants: they could only verbally report what they saw in the right visual field connecting to the left hemisphere, but were able to draw images of the objects that were presented to the left visual field connecting to the right hemisphere. From these observations, Sperry and Gazzaniga concluded that the left hemisphere of the brain (processing images of the right visual field) could analyze and produce language, while the right hemisphere (processing images of the left visual field) was "mute."

In 1981, Sperry was awarded the Nobel Prize for his groundbreaking discoveries. By the turn of the century, Gazzaniga had further pursued this line of research, turning his attention to another mystery about split-brain patients. Gazzaniga noted that despite their severed corpus callosum and the specialized functions of the two hemispheres, his patients always showed a unified sense of self. None of them reported feeling divided or fragmented. Gazzaniga set up another experiment in which he asked his patients to verbally explain, using the left hemisphere, an action that had been directed to and carried out only by the right hemisphere. He flashed an image of a snow scene to the patient's right hemisphere (activated by stimuli in the left visual field) and an image of a chicken foot to the left hemisphere (activated by stimuli in the right visual field). He then asked the patient to point to a set of cards lying in front of the subject that was visible to both hemispheres. The patient pointed with his left hand to a shovel (matching the image of the snow scene) and his right hand to the head of a chicken (matching the image of the chicken foot). Following the patient's choice, Gazzaniga asked the subject why he picked the card depicting a shovel. We want to recall that the image of the snow scene was shown to the patient's left visual field, activating the visual pathways of the right hemisphere that has to forgo language and verbal processing. The patient never mentioned the snow scene (flashed to the non-verbal right hemisphere), but instead made up a story and insisted that he chose the shovel because it is needed to clean out a chicken shed. Gazzaniga interpreted this experiment (and many similar ones that supported these initial findings) that the left hemisphere can make up post hoc answers that fit the situation. In other words, the left brain verbally interprets and rationalizes what we do. By engaging our left half of the brain, we seek explanations for events and construct narratives about incoming information (that were previously multi-modally processed via both hemispheres). In this way, our analytic, logical, and verbally competent half of the brain helps us to make sense of the world around us.

These findings corroborated previous claims about the profound asymmetry in the structural and functional organization of the cerebral hemispheres. Generally speaking, the left half of the brain is active when performing verbal tasks, including speaking and writing as well as when dealing with analytic, logical, and mathematical problems. On the other hand, the right half is active during visual, spatial, and tactual as well as emotional or intuitive tasks. This is of course only a very coarse-grained interpretation by reason of limitations inherent to the then-available methodology, but it can nonetheless serve as a rough functional attribution. Today, these earlier findings have largely been supported by novel imaging techniques, such as functional magnetic resonance imaging and others. That said, despite its lateralization, our brain does not have two independently working halves.[38] Although this cerebral specialization gives rise to seemingly separate cognitive functions, most tasks require the coordinated activation of many areas in both hemispheres. Thus, the idea of being a right-brained artist or left-brained scientist is a blatant myth that continues to haunt the popular science literature. In a nutshell, the connectivity between active brain regions is just as important as the operation of the distinct parts. This becomes particularly clear when trying to understand processes of learning, memory, and forgetting during the course of early brain development.

The human fetal brain develops in an asymmetric manner because of asymmetric hemispheric gene expression that starts in gestational week twelve.[39] Such anatomical asymmetries in the course of embryonic development were already observed more than a century ago. Neuroanatomists have found differences in size and structural patterns of the temporal lobes[40, 41] and the Sylvian fissure.[42, 43, 44] Furthermore, a large postmortem study reported an earlier appearance for the gyri and sulci (i.e., the folds and indentations, respectively, that give the brain its wrinkled appearance) of the right hemisphere.[45] This temporal difference in the development of the two brain halves is of particular importance for the subsequent argument.

Functional anatomic studies have demonstrated that in the majority of the human population, the right half of the brain does not engage in language production. Instead, it is active in non-verbal, often emotional expressions like crying, giggling, swearing, as well as mimicking, gesturing, singing, and dancing. The non-verbal right brain hemisphere is the first to develop in the fetus. After birth and in the first years of infancy, the right hemisphere continues to be developmentally dominant. Children communicate non-verbally through emotions, facial expressions, and body language. As argued in

---

[38] The two brain halves only work relatively independently when the corpus callosum, a think bundle of axons that allows communication and coordination between the two hemispheres, is severed.

[39] Sun, "Early Asymmetry of Gene Transcription," 1794–1798.

[40] Galaburda et al., "Planum Temporale Asymmetry," 853–868.

[41] Shapleske et al., "The Planum Temporale," 26–49.

[42] Eberstaller, "Das Stirnhirn," 371.

[43] Cunningham and Horsley, *Contribution to the Surface Anatomy*, xxi, 137.

[44] Retzius, *Das Menschenhirn*, 167.

[45] Chi et al., "Left-Right Asymmetries," 346–348.

Chapters 1 and 2, healthy brain development critically depends on inputs from the social environment rather than autarkicly following a program. This means that mother-infant communication during the early stages of childhood crucially shapes the child's brain development. Afterwards, once children start to understand language and learn how to speak, the left hemisphere catches up developmentally. The more active the child's left half of the cortex becomes, the stronger the child's language competence grows. Consequently, toddlers begin to name and compare things, understand their interrelations, and communicate their own subjective experiences owing to an increasingly linguistic proficiency.

Studies of hemispheric specialization are important for understanding memory formation in early childhood. Before children gain language competence, memories get stored and consolidated in a fundamentally different way than verbally explicable memories. It is the latter, the facts and vocabulary of events, which we consciously rely on later in life. Declarative memory becomes so prevalent that it seemingly upstages all other forms of memory. But in actual fact, our brain continues to store information unconsciously in implicit memory systems throughout life. In early childhood, this implicit memory is of particular importance. Before being able to use language to explain experiences and put them in order, memories are stored just as sound, touch, smell, and emotions they evoke. With increasing linguistic proficiency, the explicit memory system becomes more dominant. Nonetheless, based on stored, implicit memories, we automatically react to voices, facial features, gestures, and places experienced in the past. This is what we refer to when we speak of intuitive knowledge or gut feeling. We somehow "know" something without being able to word it. Due to the striking cognitive pre-eminence of our language capacity, we tend to verbally reinterpret implicit knowledge. We rationalize implicit memories and create narratives that seemingly fit our worldview. As shown in Gazzaniga's experiments with split-brain patients, the left half of the brain strongly contributes to generating such narratives. Thus, the left brain rationalizes, seeking explanations for every event we encounter, and generates broadly construed narratives. However, in early childhood, the left hemisphere is developmentally delayed compared to the right one. Research has largely focused on the investigation of explicit memory content, and most experiments testing childhood amnesia use a methodology that neglects the importance of implicit memory storage. Yet for pre-linguistic children, non-verbal cognition plays an eminent role that deserves much more attention from psychologists, neuroscientists, and pedagogues alike.

In general, processes of forgetting and retrieval failure are connected to neuroplasticity. In human infancy, the exponential increase in the growth of synaptic connections called "exuberant synaptogenesis" provides a fulsome substrate for subsequent experiential selection. After a period of drastic increase in synaptic connections, the child's brain undergoes a decline in synaptic density. In this phase of early childhood, synaptic connections that are frequently used get strengthened, whereas connections that are rarely used get pruned. The processes of continuous rearrangements of synapses due to synaptogenesis and pruning in response to environmental stimuli underlie learning and new memory formation (see also Chapter 2). These processes are highest in the first few years after birth. Yet synaptic pruning alone cannot account for the phenomenon of childhood amnesia. Studies have revealed that adults can retrieve far fewer memories of childhood events than would be predicted by simply extrapolating the adult forgetting curve.[46] There is another neuroplastic phenomenon, namely the process of neurogenesis, that causes the sweeping developmental amnesia in childhood. Neurogenesis terms the production of new neurons in the brain. It was previously assumed that neurogenesis in humans only occurred prenatally and ended after birth. More recent findings, however, have demonstrated significant postnatal production of neurons in the hippocampus. The cytoarchitecture of the hippocampus is formed at week twenty-four to twenty-five of gestation,[47, 48] and by the end of the second trimester, the embryonic and adult hippocampal formation display a striking structural resemblance.[49] Despite not undergoing any further anatomical differentiation, the hippocampus is not yet fully developed in young children but is nonetheless subject to neurogenesis. More precisely, new neurons continue to be added to the dentate gyrus layer of the hippocampus well after birth.[50, 51, 52]

The hippocampus is vital for stabilizing new memories and the transfer of memory content from short-term to long-term memory systems. When neurogenesis occurs, newly added neurons get integrated into neuronal networks that encode for already existing memory contents. This integration of new cells can disrupt existing circuits and increase memory loss that goes far beyond synaptic pruning. This is due to the competition between new and existing neurons, leading to a partial replacement of synaptic connections in given neuronal networks and memory circuits. This means that although the extent of learning and memory formation in infants seem to be comparable to

---

[46] Rubin, *Autobiographical Memory*, 191–201.
[47] Humphrey, "The Development of the Human Hippocampal Fissure," 655–676.
[48] Seress et al., "Cell Formation in the Human Hippocampal Formation," 831–843.
[49] Ábrahám et al., "Cell Formation in the Cortical Layers," 53–62.
[50] Eriksson et al., "Neurogenesis in the Adult Human Hippocampus," 1313–1317.
[51] Knoth et al., "Murine Features of Neurogenesis in the Human Hippocampus."
[52] Sierra et al., "Adult Human Neurogenesis," 47.

that of adults, the continued neurogenesis underlying normal brain maturation interferes with stabilization or consolidation of the memory traces. This causes an inability in children to form lasting memories. Scientists have argued that hippocampal neurogenesis contributes to the loss of existing memories and is, therefore, crucially involved in childhood amnesia. After childhood, neurogenesis drastically tapers off.[53] While there is significant neurogenesis in the dentate gyrus during prenatal brain development and in newborns (of about 1,600 young neurons per square millimeter of brain tissue at the time of birth), neurogenesis sharply declines during early infancy. In the first year of life, neurogenesis in the dentate gyrus decreases fivefold as compared to newborns. In the following six years of life, neurogenesis undergoes another twenty-threefold decline, and in the subsequent six years a further fivefold decline. In adolescence, neurogenesis becomes extremely low or may even stop. The decline of neurogenesis levels is paralleled by an increase in the ability to form stable long-term memories. Studies using animal models have supported these results and have demonstrated that an increase in neurogenesis enhanced forgetting,[54] whereas a decrease in neurogenesis mitigated forgetting.[55]

A consequence of forgetting is that not only "factual" (i.e., semantic) data but also emotional details become less accessible to conscious experience. This holds true for childhood experiences as much as for any experience throughout one's entire life. Fading episodic memories can prove highly advantageous in some instances. Forgetting helps coping with painful memories by reducing the intensity of the experience (traumatic experiences are remarkable exceptions; see Chapter 6). Contrarily, frequently recalled events—voluntarily or involuntarily, e.g., by indulging in happy memories or reliving traumatic episodes—can counteract forgetting and reinforce mnemonic engravement of these events.

There is good evidence that childhood memories do not simply get lost altogether. Instead, they might be "forgotten" in the sense that they are not accessible when one attempts to recall them actively and consciously. This is a significant difference because the latter type of forgetting indicates that we all may have a lot of intact, implicit memories to which we don't have conscious access. These memories are subconsciously stored, still available in principle, yet can only be recalled by evoking other interconnected, implicitly stored memories. For example, these forgotten childhood memories could be recalled when the right social or environmental context or appropriate stimuli are

[53] Ming and Song, "ADULT NEUROGENESIS," 223–250.
[54] Josselyn and Frankland, "Infantile Amnesia," 423–433.
[55] Akers et al., "Hippocampal Neurogenesis," 598–602.

given. These findings are particularly noteworthy in view of traumatic and abusive memories from early childhood that cannot be retrieved because of infantile amnesia.

Usually, adults can recall events from around the age of three and a half years, whereas some adults with a history of early abuse have memories starting only from the age of five to seven years. It has been argued that this mnemonic difference might be rooted in the asymmetric structural development of the human brain influenced by stressful experiences that interfere with memory encoding. Importantly, children can be primed and implicitly trained well before they can remember facts or autobiographical events. This strongly supports the previous statement that a wealth of non-explicable memories is formed before gaining linguistic competence. This observation is highly relevant when dealing with emotional trauma. Despite a lack of declarative memory, traumatized infants can form implicit memory in response to the abuse. This assumption has been supported by recent studies using functional magnetic resonance imaging. Brain scans of people with childhood abuse histories revealed that the subjects' right brain hemispheres were activated during flashbacks, while their left hemispheres were largely deactivated.[56] Traumatized people can experience flashbacks as if the traumatic event is happening in the present. In such a situation, the brain draws from implicit memory that causes strong emotional reactions, such as fury, terror, rage, shame, or numbness. At the same time, the analytic, verbal part of their brain and the explicit memory retrieval are not active, and thus remain unaware that the patient is re-experiencing and re-enacting the past. After the emotional uproar, the left hemisphere regains control, analytic-logic processing kicks in, and people try to rationalize what happened.

These findings are of paramount importance because they unveil a putative way toward understanding and perhaps also healing traumatic experiences. Psychiatrist and expert on post-traumatic stress disorder (PTSD) Bessel van der Kolk in his marvelous book *The Body Keeps the Score* highlights how trauma reshapes physiological and psychological functioning. He points to links between traumatic experiences and somatic illnesses (e.g., chronic pain, autoimmune diseases) as well as psychopathologies (e.g., depression, anxiety, OCD, and bipolar disorders). When traumatic events are stored as implicit memories, they find ways to manifest in the body as illness as well as in the mind as deviant behavior. Addressing implicit memory may open a path to deal with the trauma that cannot be explicitly remembered or verbalized. To this

---

[56] van der Kolk, *The Body Keeps the Score.*

end, van der Kolk has successfully explored somatic treatments including, yoga, drama, and sports to find new methods for recovery from PTSD.

Thus, studies from pre-linguistic childhood experiences as well as traumatic sensations clearly show the important role non-verbal cognition plays in memory storage. Notwithstanding the complexity of the aforementioned processes involved in memory generation, consolidation, and recall, they are further complicated by the integration of additional information pathways, including affective, motivational, and social information. This cross-talk is enabled by the association of long-term memory with other brain areas, including the amygdala, the nucleus accumbens, the ventral tegmental area, the thalamus, and hypothalamus, in addition to the hippocampal areas and the prefrontal cortex (PFC) discussed previously. Besides the already mentioned direct, mono-synaptic pathway that links the anterior hippocampus with the PFC, there are also indirect multi-synaptic pathways from the hippocampus to PFC that project through the nucleus accumbens, ventral tegmental area, the amygdala, and the thalamus. These complex multi-synaptic pathways are critically involved in emotional memory processing. The nucleus accumbens plays a key role in the cognitive processing of rewards, pleasurable experiences, motivational salience, and positive reinforcement. The aggregate of neurons of the nucleus accumbens receives convergent synaptic inputs from the PFC, the hippocampus, and the amygdala, forming a cortical-limbic circuit. In terms of memory function, this cortical-limbic network enables retrieval of hippocampus-dependent contextual information and amygdala-dependent emotional information via the PFC. Contextual and emotional information processed in the PFC allows the integration of old and new memories based on shared, overlapping features.

Another circuit that is of high importance for emotional processing of memory content involves the pathways from the PFC to the amygdala, that in turn projects to the hippocampus. The amygdala is located within the temporal lobe and has a primary role in emotion responses like fear, anxiety, and aggression to situations of stress or trauma. Since the amygdala has bidirectional projections with the hippocampus and the PFC, these reciprocal multi-synaptic networks via the amygdala enable episodic memory encoding and contextual retrieval related to emotional memory content.

Memory retrieval hugely relies on spatial as well as contextual information to understand the meaning of the memory content within a given context. Let me illustrate this point with an instructive example: context is of paramount importance when you find yourself in a putatively dangerous situation like encountering a wild animal—say, a shark. It makes a significant difference whether the animal is approaching you while you are swimming in the ocean or while you are observing it through the glass wall of an aquarium. But how does our brain derive contextual information and decode cues of the environment? Studies have shown that the process of contextual retrieval depends on both the hippocampus as well as the PFC and is highly adaptive. What makes contextual memory retrieval particularly adaptive is the fact that it is tightly linked to emotional regulation. This is largely due to the involvement of the amygdala. Since neuronal projections of the (anterior) hippocampus connect to the PFC as well as the amygdala, activity of these two latter brain areas can be coupled. This coupling enables the modulation of fear memory retrieval in a context-dependent manner. The reciprocal PFC-amygdala circuits gated via the hippocampus seem to be crucial for both contextual expression of fear as well as contextual inhibition of fear. Fear regulation is based on reliably discriminating between potential threats and absence of threats by rapidly resolving any ambiguity of cues perceived. In the course of our life, we have learned from experience that an animal behind a glass wall does not represent a threat. This learned information allows us to inhibit a spontaneous fear response. Thus, taking environmental contexts into consideration facilitates either emotional heightening or attenuation. The cortical-limbic circuit transmits contextual information of the salient stimulus from the hippocampus to the PFC that in turn generates context-appropriate behavioral response by interacting with the amygdala, resulting in aggressive/defensive or relaxed behavior.

However, our memory retrieval system is not "fail-proof." If emotional regulation is compromised, fear memories may become pathological and develop into anxiety disorders and PTSD. In these cases, fear memories become widely generalized across contexts rather than allowing a contextual discrimination between cues.

In summation, the subcortical route from the PFC via the amygdala to the hippocampus selects the specificity of memory retrieval. Interactions between the PFC and hippocampus accompanied by the engagement of the limbic system supports the ability to create contextual links between related memories and their emotional labeling. Involvement of the PFC allows the contextual retrieval of memories not only within a given context but also depending on a certain emotional state or circumstance. The different circuits described earlier are crucial for memory storage and retrieval. At this point, it must be emphasized again that our memory system is not devoted to encoding highly detailed memory contents as identical copies of experienced events or objects. Rather, information is recalled by means of communication between different parts of the brain, thereby actively reconstructing memory content rather than replaying an exact copy. This means that memory is by no means comparable to a cognitive library full of indexed filing cabinets. Instead, memory storage and recollection are highly dynamic processes. But despite these dynamics, human memory is by and large quite accurate with regard to key facts. On the other hand, it becomes unreliable and inconsistent over time with regard to specific details. Counteracting this unreliability, the more often an event or fact is recalled—or rather, reconstructed—the better it is remembered. Importantly, this feature of reconstruction is not an evolutionary "bug" but rather an extraordinarily important mechanism for learning. This cognitive flexibility enables updating of outdated or irrelevant information. Additionally, it suppresses distractions from other, previously stored memory content. For example, it enables humans to learn a new language, because it suppresses the activation of one's mother tongue and provides functional space for acquiring new grammar and vocabulary of the second language.

Interestingly, many contemporary cognitive scientists claim that the distinction between semantic and episodic memory is quite unhelpful or even misleading. They postulate that any knowledge, even the most impersonal facts like abstract school knowledge, lexical repertoire, vocabularies, any sorts of names, historical dates, and places are always acquired in a specific context and situation. What makes these "facts" semantic is that they have quickly lost their personal label, the connection to the learner, and any emotional tinting. Along this line of arguments, semantic and episodic memory may be encoded and stored in a similar manner, yet the difference between these memory systems occurs depending on whether personal or emotional labels remain associated with it.

For Henry Molaison, for instance, personal labels did not seem to play a role in anything he could recall consciously. There was no personal link to any of the events, people, or places he remembered. He knew the names of his parents and could recognize their faces but could not come up with anything that connected him to them on a personal or emotional level. According to award-winning journalist Luke Dittrich who tells Henry Molaison's fascinating and troubling story from a critical and ethical perspective, the befuddled patient once scribbled a note to himself on a scrap of paper. Henceforth, Henry carried the note with him in his shirt pocket to remind him about the current status of his relationship with his parents. The note read "Father's dead, mother's in a hospital, but she's well."[57]

Such an emotionally distant note probably seems odd to the average reader because we define ourselves not only in the way how we perceive ourselves, but also how we perceive ourselves in relation to others, e.g., we see ourselves as the spouse, child, parent, friend, etc. of someone. Generally speaking, there is a significant difference in the emotional quality between relations to people we

---

[57] Dittrich, *Patient H.M.*

know or know about and relations to strangers. In fact, it is the degree of emotion that is usually the defining feature of our relationships to others, be it in romantic relationships, friendships, family bonds, or even in our attitude toward public figures. If the emotional component is absent when remembering or referring to a close relative or friend, it is perceived as highly disturbing. This can be the case when patients suffer from Capgras syndrome. Capgras syndrome is a rare neurological disorder that renders patients delusional with the subjective feeling that a close family member or friend has been replaced by an impostor with identical looks. The renowned neuroscientist Vilayanur S. Ramachandran explains this rare syndrome as a loss of one's capacity to link episodic memories with subjective feelings toward a certain person.[58] When recognizing a person, we normally retrieve different memories concerning this person; we do not only remember "facts" (e.g., their looks, voice, postures, etc.) and internal concepts about the person (e.g., memories about their personalities and preferences), but we also recall our own feelings toward them. If the emotional information is damaged or inaccessible and can no longer be associated with related and, under normal circumstances, interconnected memory contents of the person in question, the patient experiences an unsettling inconsistency. The patient can no longer correlate outwardly perceived "facts" about the person with the inwardly processed perception; in short, the outside picture misaligns with the feelings toward the person. Consequently, the patient believes he is facing an impostor due to a betrayal by his own emotional memory. The Capgras syndrome is evidence of the crucial role that emotions play in creating autobiographic memories in a social context. Several decades before this interpretation about the relevance of emotions for selfhood, Henry's behavior toward his close family members certainly pointed to this conclusion. The lack of being able to create consistent memory contents for personal relationships was not surprising in Henry's case given that large parts of his limbic system (i.e., the system that is involved in one's emotional life) including his amygdalae and significant parts of his hippocampi had been removed. Coincidently, researchers working with Henry after his operation had described him as having a strikingly equanimous, tractable, and docile personality with a flat demeanor.

From these arguments, it seems clear that our memories are tightly intertwined with emotional experiences. It also clarifies why memories that have triggered strong emotions when experienced first are those remembered more readily and in more detail when recalled later. This seems to be particularly true for memories from adolescence. Adolescence is the stage in

---

[58] Ramachandran, "Consciousness and Body Image," 1851–1859.

human ontogeny that is characteristically accompanied by emotional upheavals due to developmental changes in the hormone system. Memories from that phase of life are more vivid and long-lasting than memories from any other time in our lives, a phenomenon that has been termed the "reminiscence bump," as discussed in Chapter 2.

Taken together, memory processes rely on the interconnected information transfer between different parts of the brain. But this interconnectedness that gives rise to memory formation does not only concern processual, factual, or autobiographic knowledge stored in the hippocampus and other regions of the neocortex, it also crucially depends on interrelations with the processing of emotions occurring in the limbic system. The limbic system, in particular the amygdala, when activated modulates neuroplasticity, thereby driving memory formation. On a psychological level, it is the emotional "labels" or "tags" that govern neuroplasticity and ensure certain events or facts to be better remembered. As discussed in Chapter 2, neuroplasticity is particularly marked in childhood and adolescence. During these developmental phases, the human brain undergoes large sculpturing and restructuring, yet because of its exceptional malleability, the developing brain also becomes highly vulnerable to negative impact from the surroundings, especially during these developmental periods, as will be discussed in the next chapters. Chapters 6, 7, and 8 will focus on how toxic stress, traumatic experiences, abusive or neglecting social environments, and severe poverty can afflict neural pathways and synaptic connections, thereby compromising cognitive development, emotional processing, and executive brain functions.

The Effects of Emotion, Stress, and Traumatic Experiences on Cognition

Unlike other forms of psychological disorders, the core issue in trauma is reality.

— Bessel van der Kolk. Traumatic Stress: The Effects of Overwhelming Experience on Mind, Body, and Society

Insights from neuroscientific studies, especially findings owed to Henry Molaison's tragic fate, have taught us that memories are neither fixed nor immutable as previously believed. There is now ample evidence that memory is not composed of engrams engraved in perpetuity. When remembering something, we make use of highly dynamic processes rather than harnessing memory traces that are distinctly encoded in specific neurons, dedicated to a particular memory content. Dynamic processes underlie learning, memory storage, and retrieval that all require the fluctuating, electrical co-activation of ramified neuronal networks. Thus, the dynamics of memory processes is owed to an active reconstruction of neuronal assemblies each time something is recalled. These reconstruction processes entail changes in content, associations, and emotional timbre. Due to the fluctuating neuronal activity modified by emotions, memories are not firmly codified but can be easily influenced, for example, through narratives, either provided by others or oneself. I have argued in the previous chapter that emotions play a significant role at various stages of memory formation, consolidation, and during the recall of experiences at a later date. In addition to their pivotal role in memory, emotions also determine how an individual perceives the world, makes important decisions, and constructs his or her identity. Hence, not only memory, but also a person's whole identity is hardly fixed, but constantly updated by integrating new knowledge and memories into an existing self-image goaded by emotions.

Remarkably, it is a relatively new take that emotions and memory, as well as cognition in general, are understood as being closely intertwined. For a long time, these mental faculties were strictly separated.

Despite some ground-breaking work on emotions at the end of the nineteenth century (e.g., by U.S. psychologist William James and Danish physiologist Carl Lange), for most of the subsequent century, brain research focused on rational and intellectual mechanisms of cognition, while ignoring the role of emotions by and large. A few decades ago, however, a conceptual shift set in. A new line of thought and scientific endeavor understood emotional and intellectual processes as working together and sustaining each other rather than being separated from each other. Following this novel conceptual approach, emotions are assumed to have global effects on virtually all aspects of cognition. As a consequence, it does not make much sense to try separating emotion research from memory research.

Today, there is ample evidence that emotions strongly influence episodic memory. We remember important moments of our lives particularly well due to going through a state of emotional arousal. From an evolutionary perspective, this makes a lot of sense. The human brain did not evolve to aloofly respond to purely "rational" manipulations of detached emotion. On the contrary, the brain—being the product of evolutionary pressures—has been selected to reliably use emotional information about pleasure and pain. Emotions signal which environmental incidents should be preferentially processed by our senses, guiding enhanced cognitive attention and thereby facilitating the quick detection of events of value. Such hedonic "tags" provide motivational significance for regulating attention, learning, arousal, and action.

The observation about the importance of emotional "tags" can be experimentally demonstrated using classic visual search tasks. In a visual search, increasing the number of irrelevant, distracting elements leads to an increase in time necessary to detect a specified target. This is, however, not true for emotional stimuli. In comparison to neutral stimuli, test subjects very rapidly detect spiders, snakes, and other putative threatening stimuli even when the visual search tasks are extensive. Additionally, even under conditions of limited attention, emotional stimuli show salience and are perceptually processed in a faster manner. It thus seems fair to conclude that emotions represent the principal currency in noticing and remembering what is of significant value in everyday life. This is quite uncontested for episodic memory, since events that evoke feelings of joy, sorrow, pleasure, and pain are clearly more effectively processed and recalled than mundane events. The semantic memory system also critically relies on emotions, as all facts and data are learned by passing through an emotional filter. Ask any progressive pedagogue and she will confirm that any study matter will be learned and remembered more effectively when accompanied by feelings of joy, pleasure, or surprise (or when accompanied by fear or disgust, unfortunately). Hence, emotions also play an important role in storing semantic knowledge. But in contrast to episodic memories, retrieved semantic knowledge is no longer associated with emotional labels. It has become genuinely semantic. How closely entangled episodic and semantic memory contents lie together was impressively demonstrated by psychologist Brenda Milner, who tested Henry Molaison. Henry had lost all memory traces of emotional relations to people, places, and events he had experienced before the hippocampi resection. Yet he could still recollect facts, such as who his parents were, where he lived, where he went to school, who his schoolmates were, and where he worked. Only, there was no longer any personal attachment to this information. Every part of his personal history, his episodic memory, had become completely "semanticized." Contrarily, in "normally" wired brains, emotions have a particularly strong impact on the explicit memory system. Emotionally charged memories become more strongly integrated in widely ramified neuronal networks. This process of synaptic strengthening and network integration makes memory content more easily accessible for conscious (i.e., explicit) retrieval.

As discussed earlier, emotions also modulate the implicit memory system, which in turn influences behavior without our awareness and stores memory content unconsciously. Implicit memory is of primary importance in early childhood before the onset of linguistic competence, but continues to operate in parallel to the explicit memory system throughout life. These two memory systems (i.e., explicit and implicit) mutually influence each other.[1]

More than a century ago, it was believed that brain processes involved in responding to emotional stimuli only occurred unconsciously. This assumption is owed to conditioning studies performed by Russian physiologist Ivan Petrovich Pavlov and the subsequent advent of behaviorism. Pavlov was awarded the Nobel Prize in 1904 for his work on classical conditioning. In probably the best-known conditioning paradigm of Pavlov, a laboratory dog receives a neutral conditioned stimulus, such as hearing the ringing of a bell. The conditioned stimulus is followed by an unconditioned stimulus, such as the presentation of food. Animals quickly learn to associate the sound of the bell with receiving food and eventually begin to salivate in response to the bell alone. Pavlov's work about conditioning became path-setting for various fields of psychology. Classical conditioning became hugely influential in behavioral studies, learning theories, and didactics. Central to the explanatory framework were experimental paradigms that used reinforcement and punishment. By reinforcing or punishing a certain behavior, the experimenter or educator aimed at predicting and controlling behavior, be it a laboratory animal or a

---

[1] LeDoux, "Emotion Circuits in the Brain," 155–184.

child. U.S. psychologist John B. Watson, often referred to as the "father" of behaviorism, claimed that all aspects of psychology—from language to all emotional responses—were simply patterns of stimulus and response. He believed that all differences in behavior were ultimately due to associative learning experiences. Some of the most unsettling findings in the behaviorist field came from John B. Watson's experiment on "Little Albert" performed in the winter of 1919–1920. Watson reasoned that just as Pavlov had successfully conditioned dogs a decade before him, he would be able to achieve similar results with human infants. He recruited Arvilla Merritte,[2] a wet nurse in the Harriet Lane Home for Invalid Children, and a young boy hitherto called "Little Albert. Although Little Albert's identity has not been completely clarified, there is convincing evidence that Little Albert was Merritte's son, Douglas. Being poorly paid for her work in the pediatric facility on the Johns Hopkins campus, Merritte accepted Watson's offer of one dollar per trial to have her baby boy experimented with. Little Albert was reported to be a healthy, unemotional child who rarely cried. This quality might have made the young boy just the perfect candidate for Watson's emotional conditioning experiment in which he tried to understand how phobias were generated in humans. In the now infamous experiment, Little Albert, who was about ten or eleven months at the time of testing, was exposed to a white laboratory rat. Initially, Little Albert had been interested, even attracted to the rat. During the conditioning, however, Watson would loudly strike a hammer against a steel bar out of sight of the child. This shock effect was carried out seconds after the rat was presented. The intrusive noise startled the little boy and made him burst into tears. The conditioning paradigm was performed seven times over the next seven weeks. Little Albert soon developed all signs of fear. The fear-conditioned boy immediately attempted to crawl away as soon as he saw the rat, whether the loud noise was audible or not. Watson extended the experimental setup and tested other stimuli, including a seal-skin coat, a dog, a rabbit and even a Santa Claus mask. All of these stimuli resulted in similar fear responses in the child. Through conditioning, animals and objects that once were perceived as interesting or joyful had become a trigger of fear. According to Watson, the results proved that infants can learn to fear neutral objects. Consequently, Watson and other behaviorists concluded that all human emotions could be controlled simply by providing or withholding conditioning stimuli. Spurred by these findings, Watson soon claimed that he could raise any child—irrespective of his talents, penchants, tendencies, and abilities—to become any type of specialist he wished to make the child into.[3] Little Albert unfortunately was

---

[2] Beck, et al., "Finding Little Albert," 605–614.

[3] Watson, *Behaviorism.*

never de-conditioned because Watson was dismissed by Johns Hopkins University shortly after the conditioning experiments took place.[4] It is not known whether the boy's phobia of furry objects persisted after the experiments ended. Little Albert died at the age of six of an acquired hydrocephalus, most likely a consequence of meningitis he contracted a year before his death.

Behaviorism's significant influence notwithstanding, Watson's experiments with Little Albert were soon viewed as too radical. In animal research, however, behavioristic conditioning paradigms enjoyed undiminished popularity; memory researchers in particular exploited classical conditioning trials to investigate memory processes associated with emotions.

Since then, theoretical neuroscientists have provided an explanation on how a cognitive system can learn about the world through associative learning and conditioning by means of predictive mechanisms. A central role in this learning hypothesis that is based on stimulus–stimulus associations by prediction is attributed to the neurotransmitter dopamine. For a long time, it was assumed that dopamine was released as a "pleasure chemical," or reward signal. In other words, it was believed that dopaminergic neurons become active in response to attractive and motivational stimuli that induced approach and consummatory behavior.[5] However, it also has been known for quite a while that dopaminergic neurons respond to various types of novel or unexpected stimuli in the absence of rewards, and even respond to aversive stimuli. This suggests that dopamine activity more likely encodes for signaling errors that do not necessarily occur in relation to rewards. Hence, it is more likely that dopaminergic neurons provide information about the error between what was expected (i.e., predicted) and what was really experienced. It is assumed that dopamine represents signals for three types of errors concerning outcome prediction: first, if the reward exceeds expectation (positive error); second, if the reward equals the expectation (no error); or third, if the reward undershoots the expectation (negative error). In other words, dopaminergic neurons contribute to reinforcement and punishment learning by providing information about the physiological difference between a predicted signal of what is expected to happen next and the actual signal indicating what really happened. Many organisms also use dopamine to signal errors in sensory predictions. For example, the hippocampus has been reported to encode some form of "predictive map"[6] in which hippocampal place cells alter their tuning

---

[4] The dismission was not initiated because of Watson's cruel behaviorist experiments, but because of an affair he had with his research assistant Rosalie Rayner.

[5] Schultz, "Neuronal Reward and Decision Signals," 853–951.

[6] Stachenfeld et al., "The Hippocampus as a Predictive Map," 1643–1653.

with repeated experience to fire in anticipation of future locations.[7] Also, the orbitofrontal cortex seems to encode some form of predictive representation since dopamine neurons respond to unexpected changes in sensory features of expected rewards.[8] The orbitofrontal cortex is innervated by dopaminergic pathways that can modulate sensory predictions. Accordingly, the orbitofrontal cortex has been implicated in predictive coding related to reward outcomes.[9] This seems to be particularly true for sensory-specific outcome expectations in Pavlovian conditioning.[10] Taken together, this argues for a much broader spectrum of signaling effects of dopamine. Rather than representing a simple error prediction for rewards, dopamine could be responsive to a large diversity of stimulus expectations. Consequently, the orbitofrontal cortex may exploit the dopamine system to create a "cognitive map" of state space[11] comprising a whole vector of errors. These vectors can predict changes of different features of the world, only one of which is reward.[12]

On the behavioral level, an individual will strive to minimize the error between the predicted and actual signal of each future encounter in the world and use this information to adjust neuronal connections. Put this way, it seems quite straightforward how organisms can master remarkably complex sequences of events by associative learning, such as navigating in a highly complex physical and social environment. Error signaling allows the brain to control changes of prediction values on two timescales using just one neurotransmitter, namely dopamine. On the one hand, it enables long-term changes in synaptic strength of neuronal connections. On the other hand, it also allows short-term changes based on adaptive responsivity of neurons such as changes in neurotransmission mediated by changes in receptor activity on the postsynapse. In fact, converging evidence from empirical studies has shown that dopamine and errors in predictions are intimately intertwined, both on the cell and network level. This hypothesis of error prediction mediated by dopaminergic signaling is supported by electrophysiological studies, immunochemical and optogenetics studies, and brain imaging studies. Moreover, dopaminergic modulation of cognitive functions seems to hold true for many distant species, including humans, monkeys, rats, and bees. This means that dopaminergic regulation of neuronal networks has evolved over a long time and in parallel with phylogeny. Most noteworthy, dopamine

---

[7] Mehta et al., "Experience-Dependent Asymmetric Shape," 707–715.

[8] Takahashi et al., "Dopamine Neurons Respond," 1395–1405.

[9] Wikenheiser and Schoenbaum, "Over the River, through the Woods," 513–523.

[10] Ostlund and Balleine, "Orbitofrontal Cortex," 4819–4825.

[11] Wilson et al., "Orbitofrontal Cortex as a Cognitive Map of Task Space," 267–279.

[12] Humphries, "Why Does the Brain Have a Reward Prediction Error?"

also fulfills another, extremely crucial role in many organisms that may represent an evolutionarily much older function than that of an error prediction signal. In most animals, dopamine is involved in the regulation and control of movements probably by processing signal errors of action predictions. Even invertebrates with relatively simple nervous systems use dopamine to change how neurons respond to inputs, causing altered movements. The dopamine system, which may have initially only been involved in movement control, was then later in evolution co-opted to transmit prediction error signals in sensory systems and memory processing systems. These newer findings notwithstanding, dopamine's role in memory research is still its most widely investigated function. In particular, neuroscientists continue to use classical conditioning experiments to study dopamine's role in error prediction in reward circuit.

Classical behavioristic experiments that are performed in memory research commonly draw from the theoretical foundations of fear conditioning. In fear conditioning paradigms, the neutral conditioned stimulus usually is a tone followed by an aversive unconditioned stimulus, typically a foot-shock. This experimental setup elicits emotional responses in the test animal that would normally occur in the presence of threatening stimuli (e.g., a predator) in the natural environment. In the laboratory, pairing the conditioned and the unconditioned stimuli engenders laboratory animals to react with fear in the presence of the threatening tone alone. At the same time, conditioning leads to behavioral changes (e.g., startling or freeze reactions) as well as changes in the autonomic nervous system and in hormonal activity. Fear conditioning has been used to study brain mechanisms of learning and memory in both animals and humans. This type of implicit learning and memory formation triggers responses of the autonomic nervous system through subconscious processing.

Experiments by Joseph LeDoux, a neuroscientist who has dedicated much of his scientific career to investigating fear and anxiety, has, however, challenged a too-simplistic view of fear processing. According to him, brain circuits involved in fear are not just neuronal pathways that are specifically dedicated to fear, but are essential for keeping an organism alive. Rather than merely generating fear responses, these circuits engage in detecting and responding to all kinds of threats in order to ensure survival. These survival responses are processed in the amygdala and rely on evolutionary conserved, unconscious mechanisms. The amygdala acts as a relay for incoming and outgoing sensory and motor systems and is crucial for implicit emotional memory ensuring survival responses. This type of memory responds to stimuli that have proven dangerous to our species in the evolutionary past. Implicit, emotional memory mediated by the amygdala is not consciously accessible. Conscious processes, on the other hand, interpret the implicit experiences stemming from a survival-directed pathway. In humans, conscious processing of survival responses leads to the experience of fear. Thus, following LeDoux's interpretation, it is our human consciousness that is responsible for interpreting the activation of implicit survival circuits as explicitly perceived fear.[13]

LeDoux distinguishes two brain circuits of the implicit memory system involved in classical fear conditioning. The first pathway is the one in which the conditioned stimulus (e.g., a sound) is processed and involves the (e.g., auditory) thalamus and (auditory) cortex. The second pathway is the one in which the unconditioned stimulus is processed (e.g., pain) and involves the somatosensory thalamus and the somatosensory cortex. Both pathways project to the amygdala and converge in the lateral nucleus of the amygdala and other regions. Pairing a neutral, conditioned stimulus with an aversive, unconditioned stimulus triggers associative learning. Associative learning then enables the laboratory animal to "predict" inimical events and elicit expression of fear responses. On the cellular level, the convergence of neuronal circuits in the lateral amygdala allows Hebbian learning. The consolidation of associative memory occurs via the regulation of gene expression that leads to structural changes by means of synaptic plasticity. Thus, learning to associate two stimuli is mediated by the strengthening of synapses and the synchronous firing of neuronal networks. The structural and functional changes contribute to the permanence of long-term memory formation. The enhanced, converging signals get relayed in the lateral amygdala, which communicates with the central amygdala both directly and by way of other areas within the amygdala. The central amygdala connects to the brainstem and hypothalamus, which control the expression of fear responses, including freezing behavior, hormonal responses, and activation of the autonomic nervous system. Activation of the latter results in muscle contraction as well as an increased heart rate and heightened blood pressure.

The amygdala does not function alone in fear conditioning processes but is part of a larger circuitry. This circuit comprises of sensory input systems, motor output systems, and hippocampal areas that process contextual stimuli. Interestingly, the trigger of fear responses might not only be a particular stimulus used in the experiment but also some contextual information. For example, if at a later time point, the animal encounters the same environment as in the previous experimental setting, this contextual information can activate a fear response. At the later time point, such triggers drive the retrieval of the memory content learned before in an associative manner.

---

[13] Joseph E. LeDoux, *Anxious*, 232.

Studies have revealed that mechanisms of fear conditioning in humans seem to be similar to those in laboratory animals involving the amygdala. Case studies of patients with damages to the amygdala have shown that these subjects cannot undergo fear conditioning. The probably most famous patient in fear research is patient SM, a woman in her early fifties whose brain and behavior have been studied by scientists for about thirty years.

SM first turned up at a hospital suffering from epilepsy and was referred to the Neurology Department of the University of Iowa. There, the doctors took brain scans and found calcium deposits in both of her amygdalae, causing a destruction of these brain nuclei. The calcification in the amygdalae was caused by a rare condition called Urbach-Wiethe disease. Intrigued by the brain scans of SM's severely damaged amygdalae, researchers of the University of Iowa tested whether she could recognize fear in other people's facial expressions. She was subjected to a battery of psychological tests using a series of photographs of faces. She was then asked to report on the emotions expressed in the people pictured. Surprisingly, SM utterly failed to recognize any fearful facial expressions in photographs. In fact, SM also had difficulty deciphering combinations of negative emotions, such as anger and surprise, yet she could readily identify faces that expressed positive emotions, such as happiness. SM did not only have problems recognizing fear in facial expressions; most notably, she also lacked the ability to experience fear herself. Doctors exposed her to scary animals like snakes and spiders, took her to haunted houses, and showed her renowned horror movies like *The Shining* or *Silence of the Lambs*. SM never showed signs of fear. Her intrepidity comes at a cost, however. Since her damaged amygdalae can no longer respond correctly to negative emotions expressed by other people, she fails to recognise aggression and anger in others and therefore has difficulties with social interactions. When SM was thirty years old, she walked home at night all by herself and passed by a small park. In the otherwise deserted park, a man was sitting on a bench, seemingly "drugged-out." It was approximately ten o'clock at night and it was completely dark outside. Close by was a church where she could hear voices from a local choir that was having its nightly practice. The drugged man called her to come over to him, which she did without hesitation. When she approached him, he suddenly jumped up, pulled her down by her shirt and stuck a knife to her throat. He threatened, "I'm going to cut you, bitch!" SM did not panic, or feel afraid at all. Instead, she calmly answered "If you're going to kill me, you're gonna have to go through my God's angels first." Taken aback, the man relinquished her and SM unhurriedly walk away. The event has not left any traces of fear in her memory. She continued to use the same route, passing by the same park without any trepidation.

SM is neither stupid nor unaware of what is going on around her. She performs within the normal range on standardized IQ tests. She performs well in memory, language, and perception examinations. She also has a normal concept and reaction to pain. But her sense of pain is not associated with or conditioned to another stimulus. Scientists failed to condition her, and she never managed to learn that certain things can be painful and she should thus avoid them. This is due to a lack of emotional fear labels. She cannot predict adverse situations because she does not have an emotional memory of fear attached to any previous experiences. This is clearly caused by SM's damaged amygdala, the brain region that engages in fear processing.

Interestingly, SM was not always fearless. Researchers have interviewed her about her past, scoured through her personal diaries, and talked to close family members. They could not dig up a single episode in which SM experienced fear as an adult. However, SM remembered being afraid of the dark and hiding in her older sister's bed when she was a young child. She also recollected being scared by her older brother jumping out from behind a tree when walking across a cemetery at night. She recalled running away from her brother, screaming and crying. Another time, she remembered feeling gut-wrenching fear from an incident that occurred when she was at the house of her mother's friend. SM was alone in an unfamiliar room with a large Doberman Pinscher whom she tried to pet. The dog would not have it and angrily growled at her and forced her into a corner. SM started hollering for her mother, but the dog got closer and snarled at her. Eventually, the friend came into the room and grabbed hold of the dog's chain. The friend instructed SM to slowly move toward the door and out of the room without making fast movements, otherwise, the dog may jump at her. SM remembered crying, her gut tightening up, and feeling frozen.

SM's childhood stories give testimony of her understanding what it means to feel fear. Her vivid description about how she felt when the dog menaced her particularly shows that she could normally experience fear when she was young. She reported typical fear responses like freezing behavior, a strong urge to withdraw, bodily arousal, visceral responses, emotion-congruent thoughts, and an intense feeling of dread.[14] This discrepancy between SM's fear during childhood and her apparent lack of fear as an adult is due to the progression of the Urbach-Wiethe disease. The disease usually begins in childhood and progressively develops over the course of life. There is a growing consensus among neurologists and pathologists that brain calcifications begin to emerge in childhood around the age of ten; it seems that SM's last memories of experiencing fear when she was around ten years old, concurring with this

---

[14] Feinstein et al., "The Human Amygdala," 34–38.

observation. When she was a young adult, SM's brain scans already revealed bilateral amygdala calcifications.[15] This amygdala pathology explained her apparent lack of fear.

Moreover, researchers have learned that despite her damaged amygdalae, SM clearly understands what it means to experience fear on a "cognitive" level. She can use words such as fear, terror, panic, afraid, scared, and frightened in the appropriate context in conversations. Likewise, when reading about emotional situations, she can tell with high accuracy which situations are supposed to evoke fear. Her childhood memories of frightful encounters unequivocally show that she is able to grasp what fear is supposed to feel like at an experiential level. Nonetheless, her behavior displays a severe lack of insight into her fear-related, behavioral deficits. In everyday life, she continually finds herself in precarious situations caused by her specific fear impairments.

SM's case supports the observation that we process emotional memories on an implicit as well as explicit level. While conditioning is a form of implicit learning and memory, it also has an explicit component; we can voluntarily recollect and report memories about emotional relations to experiences of classical conditioning. For explicit emotional memory, however, the hippocampus rather than the amygdala plays an essential role. The hippocampus gets activated in situations of emotional arousal and drives the formation of semantic and episodic memory about emotional situations. Interestingly, in fear condition paradigms, explicit emotional memory is not associated with obligatory fear responses, as could be seen in SM's case. Instead, explicit memory stores relational contents about emotional situations rather than consolidating emotional memories as such. Apart from emotional experiences, it is the memory about contexts and situations related to emotional experiences that activates cortical circuits and allows conscious processing. Activation of the prefrontal cortex in particular is crucial in regulating reactivity of the amygdala and in retrieval of explicit memory contents about emotional situations.

Emotional arousal increases the propensity to consolidate explicit memories of emotional situations. Even SM was able to remember in detail the frightening incident with the Doberman Pinscher and could accurately report her bodily reactions during this scary childhood event. By and large, emotionally charged situations can create powerful and vivid memories that are longer lasting and more easily recollected than those experienced in situations with little or no emotional loading. Surprisingly, this even holds true for incidents that do not affect us personally but are a concerning event of

---

[15] Tranel and Hyman, "Neuropsychological Correlates," 349–355.

public interest. This psychological phenomenon has been termed flashbulb memories and was described for the first time in an article by Roger Brown and James Kulik in 1977.[16] The authors reported that people had vivid recollections of mundane situations when they coincided with an event of high emotional significance. Two principal determinants seem to be necessary for flashbulb memories to occur: first, a high level of surprise; and second, a high level of consequentiality or emotional arousal. If these determinants attain sufficiently high levels, enhanced memory consolidation ensues. As a prototype case of flashbulb memories, the authors used the example of JFK's assassination. Almost all study participants could clearly remember where they were, what they were doing, and what they felt at the time when they heard the shocking news about JFK's death. A more recent example of flashbulb memories are the 2001 9/11 terror attacks in the United States. Flashbulb memories are considered to be one type of autobiographical memory. They refer to extraordinarily powerful and deeply engraved memories about highly newsworthy events. Of course, besides public events, private events with high personal significance[17, 18] can create very detailed and long-lasting memories, especially when repeatedly rehearsed.[19]

The effects of emotional arousal on explicit memory are due to a complex interplay between different brain areas. Generally, when experiencing fear, the amygdala gets activated and transmits information to the hypothalamus and brainstem. This occurs via neuromodulators, such as norepinephrine, dopamine, serotonin, and acetylcholine. Neuronal pathways from the amygdala to the brainstem directly activate neurons that contain neuromodulators, which then get released throughout widespread areas of the brain. On a subcellular level, the enhancement of forming and storing explicit memories occurs by stimulating synaptic plasticity. Neuromodulators have been shown to change the efficiency of neurotransmitters on synapses and thus boost synaptic transmissions and strengthen individual synapses. For instance, the sympathetic nervous system enhances cognition by indirectly arousing the hippocampus into a more alert, activated state that facilitates memory consolidation. Perception, learning, and memory formation are highly energy-demanding processes and strongly depend on glucose levels. The sympathetic nervous system mobilizes glucose into the bloodstream and increases blood flow and delivery of glucose into the brain. The glucose burst following acute stress during frightening events makes more energy available to neurons,

---

[16] Brown and Kulik, "Flashbulb Memories," 73–99.

[17] McCloskey et al., "Is There a Special Flashbulb-Memory Mechanism?," 171–181.

[18] Weaver, "Do You Need a 'Flash' to Form a Flashbulb Memory?," 39–46.

[19] Neisser, "Snapshots or Benchmarks," 43–48.

thereby fostering memory formation and retrieval. Moreover, there are some yet unexplained mechanisms by which moderate, short-term stress makes sensory receptors like taste buds, olfactory receptors, and the cochlear cells more sensitive and pass detailed information about the stressful situation to the brain. Consequently, recalling a traumatizing experience frequently concurs with a recollection of sensory details experienced during the trauma. These different mechanisms are highly adaptive as they provide the organism with vital information during threatening or dangerous situations.

In addition to the mobilization of glucose, the brainstem areas, when activated by input from the amygdala, release neuromodulators that stimulate the sympathetic autonomic nervous system, which in turn causes the adrenal medulla in the kidney to secrete epinephrine and norepinephrine into the blood circulation. Epinephrine and norepinephrine are peripheral catecholamines that do not cross the blood-brain barrier but act on peripheral nerves of the sensory component and the vagal nerve of the parasympathetic system. An excessive activation of the vagal nerve reflects a parasympathetic overcompensation for a strong sympathetic nervous system response associated with high emotional stress. The vagal nerve projects back to the brainstem, which in turn sends neuronal projections innervating the locus coeruleus. From the locus coeruleus, norepinephrine is released, stimulating the amygdala, hippocampus, and other forebrain areas. In this way, epinephrine and norepinephrine from the peripheral nervous system can enhance explicit memory. Consequently, damage to the amygdala prevents these modulatory effects on explicit memory.

It is, however, not always the case that strong emotions improve the formation of explicit memories. On the contrary, in highly intense, emotionally charged situations, a loss of explicit memory can also occur. This is due to the activity of the adrenocorticotropic hormone (ACTH) and glucocorticoids, which are produced in response to biological stress. Under normal conditions, glucocorticoids are important for brain maturation, such as for the initiation of maturation of axonal terminals and the remodeling of dendrites. But elevated glucocorticoid levels can impair brain development and function and have other adverse effects, such as higher blood pressure, cardio-metabolic disorders, and neuroendocrine dysfunction. During brain maturation, stress and elevated levels of stress hormones and neurotransmitters may lead to adverse brain development through apoptosis, delays in myelination, abnormalities in developmentally appropriate pruning, the inhibition of neurogenesis, or stress-induced decreases in brain growth factors.[20]

---

[20] Sarto-Jackson, "Wired for Social Interaction," 9–30.

Experiencing fear leads to stress response by activating the amygdala that projects to the paraventricular hypothalamus (either directly or indirectly through other areas). This stimulation causes the hypothalamus to release the corticotropin-releasing hormone (CRH) as well as the hormone arginine vasopressin (AVP) that in turn triggers the release of adrenocorticotropic hormone (ACTH) from neurons of the anterior lobe of the pituitary gland. ACTH then circulates through the bloodstream of the body to the adrenal gland in the kidneys where it stimulates the secretion of glucocorticoid hormone (CORT). CORT has ambiguous effects on memory. In mildly stressful situations, low or intermediate levels of circulating CORT get secreted and act on neuronal networks in the hippocampus, enhancing explicit memory formation. Circulating glucocorticoids such as CORT also signal back to inhibit the organism's stress reactivity and prevent excessive production of stress hormones. These negative feedback loops occur at the level of the brain and at the pituitary. In particular, inhibitory inputs from hippocampal neurons that express glucocorticoid receptors down-regulate the release of corticotropin-releasing hormone from the hypothalamus. This marks healthy stress recovery from mildly stressful situations or recovery of stressful situations of short duration.

However, when experiencing prolonged, intense stressful situations, higher levels of CORT circulate through the body and cause impairment of explicit memory. As described previously, under conditions of eustress, the activation of the stress axis results in increased production and release of corticotrophin-releasing hormone (CRH) and arginine vasopressin (AVP) from the hypothalamus. These hormones act on the anterior pituitary to stimulate adrenocorticotropic hormone (ACTH) expression and release, which in turn increases glucocorticoid production at the adrenals. Eventually, glucocorticoids exhibit negative feedback that attenuates the activation of the stress axis by reducing the level of circulating glucocorticoids. The body realizes this attenuation through the activation of hippocampal glucocorticoid receptors that inhibit neurohormone release from the hypothalamus, thereby dampening the stress reaction and causing the organism to return into a state of homeostasis

Under conditions of distress, on the other hand, prolonged exposure to glucocorticoids, impairs physiological functions of the hippocampus. In some cases, memory failure following trauma can be due to glucocorticoid-induced amnesia. This can occur in individuals exposed to distress during early development and/or excess glucocorticoids. These individuals have reduced expression of glucocorticoid receptors in the hippocampus, which leads to a loss of this feedback inhibition and an overactive stress response, both in the basal state and under conditions of stress.[21]

An important neurobiological mechanism underlying disruptions in memory and learning is the release of toxic amounts of corticosteroids from the stress response circuit when chronically high levels of stress are experienced. Cells in the hippocampus, the crucial brain area underlying memory formation and retrieval, have an unusually large number of receptors that respond to corticosteroids such as cortisol. High levels of corticosteroids attack brain cells in the developing hippocampus, initiate a process of shrinking of neuronal protrusions, lead to neuronal cell death, and ultimately result in a permanent damage to the hippocampus.[22] The hippocampus is one of the few parts of the brain that not only develops gradually, but also continues to produce new cells after birth. As demonstrated in rodents, corticosteroids inhibit neurogenesis (the generation of new neurons) in the hippocampus.[23] These phenomena—which can occur in situations of chronic maltreatment—lead to damage to the hippocampus and inhibition of the development of new hippocampal neurons, which interfere with both memory and learning. This impairment might explain why highly traumatic events often cannot be consciously recalled and lead to lacunar and situation-specific amnesia. In severe cases of neural deterioration caused by toxic exposure to corticosteroids and inhibition of neurogenesis, neither complete nor partial memory recovery may ever be achieved. This is probably due to a long-lasting hippocampal impairment.

Although the explicit memory content of a traumatic event may not be accessible, memory traces of the event may not be erased altogether. Emotional information associated with the traumatic events might be stored in the procedural memory system, which matures earlier and is less sensitive to corticosteroids. Several cases have been reported in which familiarity triggered retrieval of a traumatizing event. For example, if the victim returns to a state of arousal in a situational context similar to the one in which the memory was non-consciously stored (a process often referred to as state-dependent learning), overwhelming, traumatizing images or feelings may spontaneously arise.

Exposure to stress that causes the release of excess glucocorticoids does not only affect the physiology of individuals during postnatal development, but is particularly detrimental when it occurs prenatally. Empirical studies have

---

[21] Cottrell, "Prenatal Stress," 19.
[22] Bremner et al., "Magnetic Resonance," 23–32.
[23] Karten et al., "Stress in Early Life Inhibits Neurogenesis in Adulthood," 171–172.

shown that exposing a pregnant laboratory animal to high stressors will cause lifelong changes in the physiology of her offspring by changing glucocorticoid secretion in the fetus. In primates, high levels of maternal glucocorticoids can activate corticotrophin-releasing hormone CRH in the placenta. The CRH can spill over to the fetal circulation and stimulate the immature fetal stress axis. In this way, the fetal brain "learns" about the outside world by receiving information about the mother's environment. As a consequence, the baby of a highly stressed mother may already be born with an increased readiness in glucocorticoid secretion when expecting threatening cues. Subsequently, it grows into an adult with this physiological pre-adaptation. The long-lasting effects are changes in the levels of stress hormones, a larger stress response, and a slow recovery from the stress response. This lifelong reprogramming of stress management is—besides other components—attributable to a permanent decrease in the number of receptors for glucocorticoids in the hippocampus. Having fewer glucocorticoid receptors means that the individual is less sensitive to the hormone's signal and thus less capable of turning off the body's stress response again. These findings are not limited to animals, but it has been demonstrated that prenatal stress also programs humans for higher glucocorticoid secretion in adulthood when facing challenging situations.[24]

These altered stress levels also affect the basal levels of anxiety in an organism. If a pregnant rat encounters severe stressors, her offspring will grow up to be more anxious. As adult animals, prenatally stressed rats will show freezing behavior when exposed to minor stressors like bright lights, and they have severe difficulties with learning when exposed to novel settings. This increase in anxiety is most likely due to an increase in glucocorticoid receptors in the amygdala along with a reduced amount of inhibitory neurotransmitter receptors in the amygdala.[25, 26] The result is a lifelong tendency toward elevated levels of stress-related anxiety.

A major predictor of stress-related changes in physiology is the social status an individual attains, experiences of harassment by others (mainly by dominant individuals), and opportunities for social support. In humans, comparable findings are inevitably linked to poverty and lack of social advancements. Robert Sapolsky, professor of neurology and neurological sciences at Stanford University, has eloquently summarized this observation and cautions, "[i]f you want to see an example of chronic stress, study

---

[24] Sapolsky, *Why Zebras Don't Get Ulcers.*
[25] Stone et al., "Effects of Pre- and Postnatal Corticosterone Exposure," 492–507.
[26] Barros et al., "Prenatal Stress and Early Adoption Effects," 609–618.

poverty."[27] Being poor brings disproportionate amounts of psychological stressors because it entails a lack of control as well as a lack of predictability of one's environment. Unpredictability and helplessness trigger a physiological state of high alertness in an individual. In his bestseller *Why Zebras Don't Get Ulcers*, Sapolsky also dispels the myth that adversities make children grow strong. He argues that getting mentally stronger by overcoming hardships represents a psychological luxury for those who are socially better off and financially more affluent. Instead, children living in poverty may display a very different stress physiology in the face of social and environmental challenges. He draws from studies of school kids in Montreal that show an inverse correlation of steadily elevated glucocorticoid levels with the kids' socioeconomic status. The poorer the child, the higher the stress hormons in her organism. A tendency for elevated glucocorticoid levels was already detected in six-and eight-year-old children; by the age of ten, kids of low socioeconomic status exhibited a doubling of circulating glucocorticoids as compared to kids of a higher socioeconomic status.

However, it is important to note that more recent studies have shown that traumatization does not necessarily entail an up-regulation of glucocorticoid levels in patients. On the contrary, researchers have demonstrated that patients with post-traumatic stress disorder (PTSD) have low levels of free cortisol in urine samples tested[28] as well as lower plasma cortisol.[29] Yet much of the research studies investigating cortisol and PTSD have focused on differences in basal cortisol levels. More recent approaches have, therefore, tried to reconcile these equivocal findings by comparing stress responses during stressful versus non-stressful events in "naturalistic" settings rather than in controlled experimental situations. According to these studies, individuals with PTSD have higher cortisol levels just prior to, during, and immediately after exposure to traumatic experiences.[30, 31] At the same time, these PTSD patients who show increased cortisol responsivity during stressful events exhibit an ongoing suppression of basal cortisol levels to normal or lower cortisol levels when they are not under stress to compensate for this disproportional rise (i.e., hypercortisolism).[32]

From these examples, it is not difficult to grasp that stress does not only afflict learning, memory, and cognitive development but critically influences the way

[27] Sapolsky, *Why Zebras Don't Get Ulcers.*
[28] Shalev et al., "Post-Traumatic Stress Disorder," 2459–2469.
[29] Yehuda et al., "Minireview: Stress-Related Psychiatric Disorders," 4496–4503.
[30] Elzinga et al., "Higher Cortisol Levels," 1656–1665.
[31] Stoppelbein et al., "The Role of Cortisol in PTSD among Women," 352–358.
[32] Bremner et al., "Cortisol Response to a Cognitive Stress Challenge," 733–750.

we perceive the world and make decisions. Neurotransmitters can act as an internal guidance system that provides us with positive and negative values about the world we observe. Neurotransmitters involved in evaluating social and environmental cues convey this information to brain areas associated with decision making.[33] This is particularly relevant in situations of uncertainty when screening for predictive information about the presence of potential rewards or threats in the environment. Detected social cues inform us about the motivational significance and drive affective and behavioral responses. Researchers have shown that heightened stress reactivity causes subjects to selectively perceive ambiguous social cues as more negative[34] and disregard "safety signals." The tendency for negativity correlates with higher amygdala activity and faster reaction times. On the contrary, positive assessments correlate with the recruitment of neuronal networks of the prefrontal cortex[35] and longer reaction times. A key player in this scenario is the amygdala, which is involved in both negative valence bias and acute stress responses. This is due to the amygdala's high receptor density for glucocorticoids. The glucocorticoid receptor abundance makes this part of the brain very sensitive to cortisol release after stress exposure. Consequently, when ambiguous stimuli are encountered, appraisals are biased toward a negative or threatening valence. In addition, noradrenergic (i.e., norepinephrinergic) responses work synergistically with glucocorticoid responses to further enhance amygdala activity even after a stressor has terminated. An enhanced amygdala activity paired with a more global shift in neural processing toward threat detection and down-regulation of prefrontal circuits—the latter usually contributing to positive appraisals of ambiguous social cues—shapes subsequent emotional and behavioral responses. This is in agreement with research that demonstrates higher trait anxiety or traumatic exposure to stress convey greater sensitivity to threat perception in uncertain contexts.[36] Thus, if a child experiences prolonged stressful, traumatic experiences, not only can the levels of glucocorticoids shift over the long term, but so too can neurotransmitters, especially norepinephrine and serotonin.[37] Norepinephrine is a crucial component of the stress axis and is involved in the stress response. A shift in the serotonin system can lead to impairment in sociability and impulse control. It has been demonstrated that lack of maternal care in nonhuman primates causes a reduction in levels of serotonin. This lower neurotransmitter level correlates with greater aggression, more alcohol consumption, and more anxiety-like behaviors in adolescent

---

[33] Quartz and Sejnowski, *Liars, Lovers, and Heroes.*
[34] Brown et al., "Cortisol Responses Enhance Negative Valence Perception," 15107.
[35] Kim et al., "Inverse Amygdala and Medial Prefrontal Cortex Responses," 2317–2322.
[36] Grupe and Nitschke, "Uncertainty and Anticipation in Anxiety," 488–50.
[37] De Bellis and Zisk, "The Biological Effects of Childhood Trauma," 185–222.

animals.[38] Lower serotonin levels may, therefore, spark a cycle of aggressive behavior and social illiteracy.[39] Taken together, traumatized or people exposed to chronically stressful situations will end up living in an emotionally relabeled world in which the evaluation of social cues is biased toward the negative. This can generate a feedback loop, causing a traumatized person to readily detect threatening signals in neutral surroundings, thereby sending more threatening alarms and putting the natural defense system in a permanent state of alert.

As previously outlined, emotions are not located in a single brain area but involve several interconnected brain circuits. Antonio R. Damasio, professor of neuroscience at the University of Southern California and one of the neuroscientists of the Neurology Department of the University of Iowa who diagnosed and investigated the curious case of SM, the woman without fear (see this chapter), is one of the most renowned experts in the field of emotion research. According to Damasio, emotions are short-lived physical states that are universally similar across all humans. They have evolved as quick, physical signals of the body reacting to external or internal stimuli. For the largest part, emotional responses are processed non-consciously and subcortically. Contrarily, Damasio argues, feelings are what arise when the brain interprets emotions. Feelings are, therefore, reactions to emotions and are based on mental associations, which are influenced by personal experience, beliefs, and memories. To this end, neocortical regions are engaged in assigning meaning to emotions and make them conscious.[40] Consequently, emotions and feelings must involve different neural pathways to fulfill distinct functions. Emotional processes, on the one hand, are quick and non-conscious processes that have previously been described as the "low road" of the system.[41] Any stimulus that is perceived gets relayed via the thalamus directly to the amygdala, where it is processed automatically. Via the amygdala, the low road enables the individual to react rapidly and instinctively to putative dangers and to activate the fight-or-flight response via the stress axis if necessary. Emotions processed by the amygdala evolved as lifesavers in dangerous situations and get automatically activated when a person feels threatened by actual or presumed dangers, including ambivalent social signals. This low road normally helps humans navigate social life by constantly appraising environmental and social stimuli for positive or negative valence, safety, and danger.[42]

---

[38] Suomi, "Gene-Environment Interactions and the Neurobiology of Social Conflict," 132–139.

[39] Quartz and Sejnowski, *Liars, Lovers, and Heroes.*

[40] Damasio, *Descartes' Error: Emotion, Reason, and the Human Brain.*

[41] LeDoux, *The Emotional Brain.*

[42] Fishbane, "Wired to Connect," 395–412.

Feelings, on the other hand, have been referred to as the "high road" of the system. When experiencing feelings, the neocortex gets engaged and allows for thoughtfulness, choice, and behavioral flexibility. This happens, however, at the cost of a slower reaction time by facilitating rational interpretations of the situation. The neocortex attenuates quick responses, allowing a person to consider various options by integrating conscious information, thereby guiding "rational" decision making. A part of the prefrontal cortex, the orbitofrontal cortex acts as a regulator of the non-conscious system, particularly by dampening immediate reactions of the amygdala. The orbitofrontal cortex retains its neuroplasticity throughout life and ensures behavioral flexibility when new or additional information becomes available. The interplay between the low and the high road permits people to make behavioral choices that are in line with their long-term goals and values. This is typically the case when we go against our initial inner impulses for the benefit of distant marks.

The orbitofrontal cortex, and more generally the prefrontal cortex, have been widely recognized for being particularly important in monitoring the significance of multiple goals and switching between them. The orbitofrontal region is active when planning complex cognitive behavior and making decisions by orchestrating different thoughts and predictions in accordance with internal goals.[43] Many researchers have emphasized the role of the prefrontal cortex as the brain's "executive" center. Based on its anatomy, the prefrontal cortex synthesizes information from a wide range of other brain areas, such as sensory systems processing external information, cortical and subcortical motor systems, and limbic and midbrain structures processing internal information related to affect, memory, and reward. Accordingly, neuronal networks of the prefrontal cortex get activated by stimuli from all sensory modalities before and during various actions, as well as when recalling past events or anticipating expected events and behavioral consequences. Moreover, the prefrontal cortex also integrates modulatory information derived from motivational and attentional states,[44] thereby exerting control over behavior[45] and decision making.

It is important to mention that the neuronal pathway involved in conscious feelings is not the dominant route. Rather, connections from the amygdala to the prefrontal cortex are more abundant than connections in the opposite direction. This anatomical disparity may explain why emotions can easily

---

[43] Miller et al., "The Prefrontal Cortex," 1123–1136.
[44] Miller et al., "An Integrative Theory of Prefrontal Cortex Function," 167–202.
[45] Walle J.H. Nauta, "The Problem of the Frontal Lobe," 167–187.

become overwhelming and impair "rational" decision-making.[46] This observation is even more relevant under aversive conditions, e.g., when a child's limbic system gets frequently activated because she lives in an abusive environment, especially during the period of maturation of the amygdala shortly after birth.[47, 48] Traumatic experiences, abuse, and neglect can strongly interfere with the adaptive shaping of the functioning of the frontal cortex. As a result of adverse experiences, developing neural networks in the frontal cortex are restructured, leading to poor self-control[49] and compromised judgment involved in decision making.

Among the experiences that can constitute acute trauma are single or few events of highly negative emotional impact. These negative impacts can be serious injuries or threats to life or limb that reportedly often lead to symptoms of post-traumatic stress disorder (PTSD). PTSD was first identified in combat veterans but can also occur in survivors of natural disasters, rape, and other life-threatening or devastating incidents.[50, 51] More recently, developmental psychologists and psychiatrists have described another type of PTSD based on developmental psychological traumas. The latter refers to stressful events that occur repeatedly and cumulatively over an extended time and within specific relationships and contexts, also referred to as complex PTSD or C-PTSD.[52] Such chronic traumatization can stem from sexual, emotional, and physical childhood abuse, physical and emotional neglect, or even severe poverty. Despite some differences, people with PTSD who have suffered acute trauma show psychological reaction patterns and behaviors that are by and large similar to those of people who have experienced chronic traumatic events in childhood. The former may repeatedly re-experience the traumatic event while awake or in dreams when placed in triggering situations. The psychological reactions caused by intense emotions re-experienced during these traumatic events are manifested in visceral sensations such as heightened anxiety and panic attacks, as well as vivid visual images and other acute sensory perceptions, such as flashbacks and nightmares.[53] But research comparing PTSD and developmental psychological trauma suggests that both syndromes have overlapping mechanisms and most likely rely on similar physiological and

---

[46] LeDoux, *The Emotional Brain.*

[47] Jedd et al., "Long-Term Consequences of Childhood Maltreatment," 1577–1589.

[48] Pechtel and Pizzagalli, "Effects of Early Life Stress," 55–70.

[49] Hanson et al., "Early Stress Is Associated with Alterations," 7466–7472.

[50] van der Kolk, *The Body Keeps the Score.*

[51] Laskowitz et al., "Post-Traumatic Stress Disorder."

[52] Courtois, "Complex Trauma, Complex Reactions," 412–425.

[53] van der Kolk, *The Body Keeps the Score,* 253–265.

neurobiological processes.[54] Both people with PTSD and those with developmental psychological trauma may suffer a numbing of their responsiveness, display significantly reduced interest in daily activities, restrict the range of their emotions, and have feelings of detachment or estrangement from other people in their surroundings. Some may also suffer from heightened arousal—resulting in difficulty with falling or staying asleep—exacerbated irritability or outbursts of anger, difficulties in concentrating, hypervigilance, and an exaggerated startle response.

While psychological effects of PTSD following an acute trauma seem more pronounced (including panic attacks, flashbacks, nightmares) than those of developmental trauma, this conclusion may not fully acknowledge the complex pathology of developmental effects derived from exposure to chronic traumatization. Victims of developmental trauma usually have much more time for psychosocial adjustment and restructuring one's inner landscape to adapt to the abusive environment. But by no means does this indicate that the neuropsychological damage is smaller. Rather, the longer the duration and the developmentally earlier a traumatizing experience happens, the more dramatic and penetrative its effects with respect to neuroplastic restructuring. As a result, a chronically or developmentally traumatized person's neurophysiology will be in "emergency mode." This altered brain state is reflected in amended levels of glucocorticoids and other stress factors as wells as changes in the level of various neurotransmitter systems (see previously). In fact, it has been clearly shown the more stressful an experience and the longer its duration, the more severely memory and learning are disrupted.[55]

When survivors of domestic violence or other developmentally traumatic events re-experience similar situations at a later time point, they fall back into a reactive state of self-protection and survival behavior—very often without having episodic memory about the actual situation in their personal history. This re-experience triggers an immediate, nonconscious reaction via the low route, leading to an increase in the activation of the amygdala and the stress axis. Consequently, signals from the orbitofrontal cortex cannot get integrated due to an under-functioning of the high route. Relatively mild negative social triggers, that would normally be ignored by a person without abuse history, can activate the low route, leading to a strong overreaction. In such a case, the person re-experiences an adverse childhood situation in which a similar emotional state was aroused. This emotional state of fear and helplessness is experienced non-consciously as a threat to well-being and triggers a reactive survival behavior, i.e., a fight-or-flight response. But in contrast to the

---

[54] Ibid.
[55] Shapero et al., "Stressful Life Events and Depression Symptoms," 209–223.

traumatizing situation of the past, the affected person now probably has an extended potential for action that was not available when the traumatization occurred. As a result, the emotionally overwhelmed person may violently act upon the stress response and become abusive because the self-control via the higher cortical route is overridden. Tragically, by succumbing to developmentally non-conscious response mechanisms driven by the amygdala, situations are re-created that are emotionally similar to those experienced previously when traumatized. Hence, the traumatized person has re-generated an adaptive niche in which maltreatment continues and is socially transmitted to the next generation. This scenario can also explain secondary traumatization in professionals and other people close to a traumatized person insofar as they are exposed to a familiar niche constructed by the victim.

In contrast to the described states of trauma-induced amnesia due to hyperactive non-conscious processes, clinicians working with people suffering from PTSD have also observed hypermnesia, in which sensory experiences and visual images related to the trauma do not fade over time and remain much more vivid than other, ordinary memory traces. Hypermnesia is likely based on an interplay between several physiological processes. First, acute stress stimulates the mobilization of glucose into the bloodstream and to the brain. Second, it enhances sensory perception during the acute, stressful event. And third, it activates the secretion of epinephrine and norepinephrine into the blood circulation and triggers norepinephrine release from the locus coeruleus in the brain. These processes act together to enhance explicit memory. But most importantly, memories are usually stored in an associative manner, i.e., they get integrated into a neuronal network that has been established as a result of previous experiences. Traumatic events, however, are usually highly unexpected, acute experiences that stand isolated in one's life history. This makes it difficult for the traumatized victim to incorporate this unique but highly negative experience into an existing framework of experiences. In fact, the more unexpected and the less compatible an event is relative to a person's worldview, the more difficult it will be to integrate traumatic experiences into one's coherent and enduring sense of self and one's world. As a result, patients with severe traumatization frequently have difficultly putting the trauma behind them. They become fixated on the past, re-enact the trauma, and are unable to incorporate the event into their personal history.[56] Additionally, not only may they fail to integrate the stressful experience into their self-narrative, but they may not even be aware of this psychological incoherence. Such a psychological chasm can have devastating consequences. Since the ability to

---

[56] van der Kolk, *The Body Keeps the Score*, 253–265.

create a coherent self-image lies at the core of our capacity to generate a view of life in general, a person might be unable to link current behavior with one's future self. In other words, one's behavior and consequences ensuing this behavior (e.g., punishment) may cognitively not be connected.[57]

---

[57] Quartz and Sejnowski, *Liars, Lovers, and Heroes.*

Chapter 7

The Social Brain:

Attachment & the Effects of Emotional

and Social Neglect on Cognition

We fear violence less than our own feelings. Personal, private, solitary pain is more terrifying than what anyone else can inflict.

— Jim Morrison

In the previous chapter, I have duly referred to U.S. psychologist John B. Watson, one of the founders of behaviorism. Watson and his research assistant Rosalie Rayner—whom he later married and had children with—performed the infamous experiments on Little Albert in the winter of 1919–1920. Watson had previously claimed that every emotional response can be produced by conditioning. With his experiments on Little Albert, he aimed at demonstrating unequivocally that all differences in human behavior simply arose from associative learning experiences. The message Watson wanted to convey was that by providing a suitable environment for children to be reared, parents can create any personality trait they desired in their children. Watson's psychological school of behaviorism has strongly influenced pedagogy and educational theory. Parents and teachers have turned to the behaviorist findings that things learned by means of strong emotional incentives, such as reward or punishment, are learned fast and remembered most efficiently. Poisonous pedagogy has taken advantage of this emotional conditioning and pressured generations of children and adolescents into obedience and blind discipline. And, of course, this method also works with adults, and it works especially well if people were already primed in childhood by means of punishment and the use of triggers for negative emotions.[1] Exploiting reward and punishment methods directly addresses a person's emotions, and when conditioned in childhood and adolescence, it facilitates the generation of well-adapted adults that behave according to what they have been instructed to do

---

[1] LeDoux, "Emotional Memory," 1806.

for fitting into their "default" social niche. By the time these children have grown into adults, they have developed strategies that work best in their social environment. When observed from a different perspective, with one's own social bias, some behavior may appear maladapted for "the rest of the world." In their particular social niche, however, these strategies have proven beneficial.

Watson was a deeply committed environmentalist who rejected any assumptions about infants' instinctual nature—also unswervingly following his teaching when raising his own children. He made sure that the two sons he had with Rosalie Rayner, William and James, were raised strictly according to behaviorist principles. The couple meticulously controlled all stimuli that their children were exposed to during early infancy. Above all, they upheld the highest levels of discipline and categorically disallowed emotions. The credo was that all forms of attachment or any sign of parental emotions would interfere with their children's independence. Watson and Rayner abstained from kissing or coddling their sons. To prevent spoiling, Watson and Rayner treated their children as small adults. They believed their sons would show only acceptable forms of emotional expressions as a result of such parenting. Watson stated his behaviorist-based child-rearing practices most explicitly in his book, *Psychological Care of Infant and Child* that became an instant bestseller. In the book, he referred to motherly love as "a dangerous instrument" that "may inflict a never-healing wound, a wound which may make infancy unhappy, adolescence a nightmare, an instrument which may wreck your adult son's or daughter's vocational future and their chances for marital happiness."[2] To avoid such poisonous influence, he advised parents never to hug or kiss their children nor let them sit on their lap. Watson famously stated that by caressing a baby, "[t]he mother begins to destroy the child the moment it's born." The maximum of affection that could be tolerated without doing harm to children is to kiss them once on the forehead before sending them to bed and to shake hands with them in the morning. Only in extraordinary cases, parents were advised to give kids a pat on the head to acknowledge outstanding achievements. To retrace his strong convictions against parental affection, it may be worth mentioning that when Watson was thirteen years old, his alcoholic father abandoned the family of six children to start a new life with another woman. This experience left young Watson very angry and bitter, and he never forgave his father. At the same time, his devotedly religious mother subjected Watson to harsh religious training that left him with a lifelong reluctance against religion. Watson's mother moved the

---

[2] Watson and Watson, *Psychological Care of Infant and Child.*

family from their farm in a rural area of Greenville County, South Carolina to the city of Greenville to enable her children to get a better education. But Watson ended up loathing his new environment, suffering severe bullying at school. His subsequent teenage years were characterized by delinquency, specifically hate crimes against local Black people. One can speculate how his childhood and adolescence experiences shaped the choice of his future career and research topics.

From the vantage point of the present, it comes as little surprise that Watson's and Rayner's real-life, behaviorist experiment avoiding any emotional attachments turned into a psychological disaster for their own children. Both of their sons grew into severely disturbed adults. James claimed that their parents' emotive unresponsiveness and lack of attachment eroded his own and his brother's ability to effectively deal with everyday emotions. The parents' emotional withdrawal ultimately peaked in the boys' sheer desperation and suicide attempts. William eventually died from self-inflicted death. James blamed his father and the strictly behaviorist upbringing for his brother's death.[3]

Watson had two more children from his first marriage with Mary Ickes. These two kids, John and Mary "Polly" Ickes, also suffered severely from their father's behaviorist child-rearing principles. Like William and James, Mary "Polly" Ickes also attempted suicide multiple times. Watson's granddaughter, the actress Mariette Hartley and child of Watson's daughter Mary "Polly," recalled painful childhood memories. Following her grandfather's unswerving directives, her mother also raised young Mariette by withholding any physical affection. Mariette remembered in her autobiography[4] that her grandfather regarded children as mechanical objects without needs or feelings, who were malleable in any desirable way according to their parents' wishes. Watson expected his daughter to raise little Mariette following a strict schedule, including exact feeding times, scheduled toilet training, and precisely defined playtimes. Mary "Polly" avowed to her adult daughter, Mariette, later in life that she believed due to her father's toxic influence she could not produce any breast milk to nurse her when Mariette was a baby. To minimize undesirable behavioral patterns, Mariette was relentlessly trained not to suck her fingers or be noisy. By the age of three, she was expected to act like a young adult and abstain from dangerous social activities such as girls' pyjama parties that, according to her grandfather, would lead her straight into homosexuality.

---

[3] "Rosalie Rayner," Feminist Voices.
[4] Hartley and Commire, *Breaking the Silence.*

Eventually, Watson's utopian ideal was a physical separation of babies from their mothers, rearing them by alternating, disengaged adults in order to bar any emotional attachment between child and caregiver. These behaviorist principles—the disaffirmation of affection and attachment in order to encourage infants' autonomy and routine—were upheld for many decades in early twentieth-century America. These principles also strongly influenced European psychologists and pedagogues. From the 1930s through the 1950s, the fields of clinical and experimental psychology were dominated by behavioristic theory on the one hand and Freud's psychoanalytic theory on the other. The common denominator of both schools of thought was their highly critical view on maternal bonding. The claim was that the affectionate relationship between mother and child did not represent a form of love stemming from an instinctive behavioral pattern, but was solely due to the child's primary drive for feeding. Hence, pundits of that time—who often had little direct experience with children—warned against overly tight bonds between mother and child that were believed to do more harm than good. This view also spread across the general population, which turned toward scientific principles in the hopes of putting their child-rearing methods on solid footing. Watson and other behaviorists provided just the "right" advice for those who were looking for scientific instructions on how to raise their children. Behaviorists promised a way to rear children who later in life would be able to cope with the realities of modern life. In a behaviorist nutshell, growing into a successful adult meant learning how to stonewall and bulwark oneself with emotional habits against any putatively overwhelming adversities that one may encounter in life.

Without a doubt, Watson's influence on child pedagogues and psychologists led the field on a misguided path into a dead end. Developmental psychologist William Kessen emphasized the damage that Watson's teaching had by stating that "his impact on the field has been almost completely deleterious. His attitude toward children, his attitude toward parents in the psychological care of the child is, it seems to me, pathological."[5]

But clearly, not all scholars devoted themselves to the doctrine of how poisonous maternal bonds were. In particular, pediatricians, psychologists, and psychiatrists who worked with babies and infants on a daily basis realized the opposite: the dangers of parental emotional detachment and lack of early motherly care. One of these pundits was pediatrician Harry Bakwin, who worked at New York's Bellevue Hospital. At that time, young children treated at the hospital suffered from a significantly high mortality rate, which was

---

[5] Senn, 29.

assigned to malnutrition and infection. To counteract these health threats, health policymakers of the Bellevue Hospital replaced the then-common, open wards of the hospital by isolated, cubicled rooms. The latter were sterile rooms that could only be entered by masked and hooded nurses and physicians. All non-hospital staff, including parents or caregivers of the sick children, were excluded. Visiting the young patients was discouraged and often forbidden. It showed very quickly that these hygiene measures did not have any positive effects on children's well-being or on reducing the high mortality rate. Moreover, despite high caloric diets, the young patients did not gain any weight while in patient care. Harry Bakwin, one of the pediatricians of the Bellevue Hospital, was among the first health care professionals who voiced serious concerns about the hospital's sterile regulations. He argued that the loneliness and lack of mothering the infants endured caused "psychologic neglect" that was potentially damaging for these children.[6] Alarmed by the potential hazard, hospital policy was quickly changed back. Nurses were encouraged to pick up children and cuddle and play with them. Parents were no longer barred from visiting their sick children. Much to the surprise and relief of hospital staff and policymakers, the mortality rate for infants under one year of age fell sharply from thirty to thirty-five percent to less than ten percent after these policy changes.[7]

Another researcher who had a significant impact on health care professionals and psychologists was Jewish-Austrian psychiatrist René Spitz. Spitz had worked in sterile children's wards with Katherine Wolf in Austria, but then fled the European continent to New York. Spitz's work focused on the relationship between mother and child. He was particularly interested in Bakwin's research and also significantly contributed to infants' deprivation research.[8] Spitz coined the term "hospitalism" and described it as "a vitiated condition of the body to long confinement in a hospital, or the morbid condition of the atmosphere of a hospital."[9] In his studies, Spitz compared infants in continuous institutional care to infants in nurseries or in foundling homes and concluded based on his observations that children required affective bonds in order to undergo a healthy physical and behavioral development. In particular, the reciprocal interaction between mother (or another primary caregiver) and child seemed essential, whereas deprivation of this reciprocity proved to be critical for the child's development, including personality development.[10]

---

[6] Bakwin, "Loneliness in Infants," 30–40.
[7] van der Horst and van der Veer, "Loneliness in Infancy," 325–335.
[8] Blum, *Love at Goon Park*.
[9] Spitz, "Hospitalism," 53–74.
[10] van der Horst and van der Veer, "Loneliness in Infancy," 325–335.

Although Spitz was also vehemently criticized by some of his contemporaries, his work on the effects of hospitalization was widely cited. Many researchers were strongly influenced by his deprivation studies. Psychoanalyst Donald Winnicott overtly referred to Spitz's work when issuing the warning that "we cannot take mothers from infants without seriously increasing the psychological burdens which the next generation will have to bear."[11]

At this time, child care and developmental psychology were still strongly rooted in behaviorist teachings, as well as in Sigmund Freud's work. Despite the increasing acceptance of the importance of an affectionate relationship between mother and child, the orthodoxy held that this relational bond was solely due to the child's drive for nursing to satisfy hunger and obtain oral satisfaction. It was American psychologist Harry Harlow who shook the grounds of conventional pedagogy based on behaviorist theory that advised mothers to avoid bodily contact with their infants as well as those based on the Freudian theory that held feeding to be the crucial factor in the formation of a mother-child bond.

Harry Harlow and Robert Zimmerman's now-classic study[12] investigated the effect of maternal separation on rhesus monkeys. In their experiments, Harlow and Zimmermann demonstrated that not feeding, but contact comfort is the crucial element in the attachment process between infant and caregiver and the infant's emotional development. Having established a breeding colony of rhesus macaques in the early 1930s, Harlow had observed that infant primates that were reared in a nursery setting without mothers exhibited behavioral patterns that differed significantly from their mother-reared peers. The maternally deprived animals had apparent social deficits, were reclusive, and—most intriguingly—clung to their cloth diapers. Harlow constructed inanimate surrogate mothers made of wire and wood that rhesus infants quickly learned to recognize and socialize with. For comparison, he also built inanimate surrogate mothers that had their wire-mesh construction covered by soft terry cloth. Surprisingly, the rhesus infants would overwhelmingly more often choose the clothed mother over the wire-mesh mother, even when the latter held a bottle with food and the former did not. The infant monkeys would cling to their cloth mothers, preferred their company, and only visited the wire mother for feeding. Based on these findings, Harlow argued that the mother-infant bond was not simply based on the mother providing milk for the infant, but that physical contact is essential to the psychological development and health of infant monkeys. On the other hand, he demonstrated that lack of physical interaction proved psychologically highly stressful to the infant, as

---

[11] Winnicott, "Loneliness in Infancy," 465–465.

[12] Harlow and Zimmermann, "Affectional Response in the Infant Monkey," 421–432.

maternally deprived infants exhibited severe digestive problems that were considered a physiological manifestation of early childhood stress. Extending his studies to behavioral disorders and psychopathologies, Harlow explored the impact of prolonged social deprivation on the development of infant and juvenile rhesus macaques. In this study, he isolated young monkeys for various periods and then introduced or re-introduced them into a peer group. Disturbingly, Harlow found that monkeys placed in isolation exhibited severe social deficits, were incapable of interacting with their conspecifics, and socially withdrew themselves. These results prompted him to argue that the experimental design was a valid animal model for the study of depression. Harlow's research provoked strong criticism, mostly for ethical reasons. Critics also accused him of overestimating the importance of contact comfort while underestimating the importance of nursing.

In recent decades, neurobiological research has again brought the importance of physical contact between parents and offspring to the fore. Michael J. Meaney from McGill University in Montreal, Canada, has shown in many highly influential publications how maternal brood care in rats affects the offsprings' social behavior. Typically, female rats show an aversion to pups by withdrawing themselves unless they are in late pregnancy or lactating. In the latter cases, dams usually exhibit attentive, maternal behavior toward pups. This increased maternal responsiveness is due to the influence of ovarian hormones (especially estrogen) that affect the oxytocinergic system. It has been shown that an estrogen surge that occurs at a late stage of pregnancy has a twofold effect. First, it increases the expression of the oxytocin receptor gene in reproductive tissues as well as in multiple brain regions. Second, it drastically enhances the binding affinity of oxytocin to its respective receptor. When oxytocin is administered to nonpregnant rats, these animals show maternal behavior toward foster pups.[13] Contrarily, when female rats were treated with drugs blocking oxytocin from binding to its receptor, these animals were much more unresponsive to pups than untreated rats.[14] Researchers have found naturally occurring variations in how responsive and caring rats are with their newborns. Some mother rats lick and groom their pups freqently, while others are relatively inattentive to a level of being almost neglecting. The levels of oxytocin receptors were significantly higher in brains of dams that showed more caring behavior than in those who were less attentive.[15] The behavioral pattern of maternal care—either affectionate or neglecting—is transmitted to the next generation. Animals that have experienced neglecting maternal

---

[13] Pedersen and Prange, "Induction of Maternal Behavior," 6661–6665.
[14] Fahrbach, et al., "Possible Role for Endogenous Oxytocin," 526–532.
[15] Francis et al., "Variations in Maternal Behaviour," 1145–1148.

behavior in infancy will also behave less affectionately toward their own offspring. Despite the high familial incidence of the type of maternal brood care, this behavior is not mediated via genetic mechanisms. This has been demonstrated by exposing newborn pups of neglecting dams to more caring foster mothers. After having experienced intensive brood care from foster mothers, the female pups of neglecting mothers will eventually become more affectionate mothers as adults.

How does brood care influence the offsprings' behavior? Meaney and colleagues have collected a large body of evidence that affectionate motherly care increases the pups' resilience toward stress. Pups that receive ample licking and grooming after birth become more stress-resistant and are more open to new experiences and exploratory behavior than pups that have received little care.[16, 17] This is due to the aforementioned increased sensitivity to oxytocin that is associated with reduced levels of fearfulness.[18] Most noteworthy is that individual differences in stress reactivity are transmitted across generations: less fearful mothers beget more stress-resistant offspring. This reduction in fearfulness has been attributed to an increase in oxytocin receptor levels in the central nucleus of the amygdala found in female rats that show higher maternal brood care behavior. In addition to changes in the oxytocinergic system, maternal care in infancy also strongly impacts the development of adequate stress reactivity mechanisms by downregulating glucocorticoid and $GABA_A$ receptor systems. $GABA_A$ receptors mediate an inhibitory tone over synthesis and release of the corticotropin-releasing factor. As we may recall from Chapter 6, corticotropin-releasing factor regulates behavioral, endocrine, and autonomic responses to stress. When female rats that have previously shown affective brood care under stress-free conditions were exposed to a stressful environmental signal during subsequent gestation, the animals' pattern of maternal behavior was drastically changed. They were no longer attentive and became unresponsive and neglectful toward their pups. This negative effect persisted even with a subsequent litter in the absence of any further stress.[19] It can be concluded that chronic stress during gestation results in a sustained alteration of the neural system that causes long-term changes in maternal behavior. Meaney and co-workers have suggested that animals develop their stress response system according to the level of environmental stress that their mother encounters. Depending on external stress factors, dams change their behavioral pattern, and this triggers a

---

16 Meaney, "Maternal Care, Gene Expression," 1161–1192.

17 Weaver et al., "Maternal Care Effects on the Hippocampal Transcriptome, 3480–3485.

18 McCarthy et al., "An Anxiolytic Action of Oxytocin," 1209–1215.

19 Meek et al., "Effects of Stress during Pregnancy," 473–479.

developmental "programming" of the offspring's nervous system. In short, the quality of maternal brood care conveys information to the offspring about how stressful, threatening, or scarce the ecological niche in which they will grow into will be. The pups' nervous system is highly plastic early in life and thereby allows a response to stress that is most adaptive in a given environment. Such behavioral and neural plasticity makes sense given the large variety of ecological niches that rats can naturally inhabit and that require varied sets of responses to these different environmental demands. Since most mammals usually spend their adult life in an environment that is by and large similar to the one in which they were born, neonatal programming affords an appropriate stress response without the need for recurring periods of adaptation later in life. Fetal and neonatal programming can kick-start subsequent adaptation processes owing to neuroplasticity during infancy that can be observed in all young mammals but is particularly extensive in human children (Chapter 2). Despite neuroplastic events occurring throughout the whole life, early programming triggered by variations in maternal behavior[20] configures the basal neuroendocrine settings, endowing the individual with an idiosyncratic neurophysiological profile. These idiosyncrasies are underlain by differences in the glucocorticoid receptor system that governs stress response throughout any condition later in life and determines individual differences in vulnerability to stress.[21] As discussed earlier, the glucocorticoid receptor system is shaped by early-life events. One of the critical determinants in order to develop a well-adapted stress system is physical interaction. While maternal brood care in which pups experienced ample licking and grooming had a positive effect on their resilience, repeated periods of physical separation from the mother caused significantly increased pituitary-adrenal responses to acute stress.[22] Maternal separation resulted in decreased glucocorticoid receptor binding in the brain and an increase in corticotropin-releasing factor that regulates both norepinephrinenergic and serotonergic responses to stress. Moreover, maternal deprivation increased the death of brain cells in infant rats due to a dysregulation of stress systems. Thus, high levels of stress can not only alter neuroplasticity and change levels of neurotransmitters, both contributing to adverse brain development and cognitive impairment, but can also lead to neurodegeneration and cell death.[23] In behavioral tests, adult animals that

---

[20] Liu, "Maternal Care, Hippocampal Glucocorticoid Receptors," 1659–1662.
[21] Meaney, "Maternal Care, Gene Expression," 1161–1192.
[22] Plotsky and Meaney, "Early, Postnatal Experience," 195–200.
[23] Sapolsky, *Stress, the Aging Brain, and the Mechanisms of Neuron Death.*

were exposed to maternal separation as neonates were highly fearful[24] and exhibited increased startle responsivity.

These results from rats correspond with findings in primates. In the 1960s, psychologist Harry Harlow and coworkers demonstrated that social deprivation in infancy results in severe behavioral abnormalities as well as devastating social and emotional deficits persisting throughout adolescence and adulthood. Harlow's student, psychologist Stephen Suomi, further investigated behavior in socially challenged primates. Suomi found that in most populations of rhesus monkeys studied, there is a subgroup of high-reactive individuals that respond with expressions of fear and anxiety toward a wide range of stimuli. This trait of high reactivity in some individuals is likely based on naturally occurring genetic variants, but more importantly, this adverse trait is strongly exacerbated by low-quality maternal care. Contrarily, most other monkeys in their troop who are more laid-back find the same stimuli merely interesting and will readily explore them. In addition, the high-reactive youngsters typically cling to their mothers for a longer period, exhibit reduced exploratory behavior, and when growing up tend to be shy and withdrawn in their initial encounters with peers. In laboratory settings, these high-reactive rhesus monkeys when placed in playrooms with unfamiliar peers develop tachycardia (increased heartrates) and show significantly elevated levels of plasma corticotropin and cortisol as compared to their less reactive peers.[25] High-reactive individuals characteristically experience a significant and often prolonged activation of the hypothalamic-pituitary-adrenal axis (the stress response axis), an increase of the sympathetic nervous system arousal, and increased norepinephrinenergic turnover.[26] Most dramatically, however, are the long-term effects when environmental perturbations are extreme or continue for an extended period of time. Under such circumstances, behavioral and physiological symptoms of high-reactive rhesus monkeys often become dramatic. Upon normal maternal separations that all young monkeys experience from time to time, those infants and juveniles who show high-reactive responses lapse into behavioral depression. They become lethargic, socially withdrawn, suffer from eating and sleeping difficulties, and assume fetal-like huddling postures, which they sometimes maintain for hours.[27] In comparison, their more laid-back peers respond to normal maternal separations by adapting to their mothers' repeated departures and by extending their interactions to other members of their social group.

---

[24] Caldji, "The Effects of Early Rearing Environment," 219–229.

[25] Brauth et al., "Up-Tight and Laid-Back Monkeys," 27–56.

[26] Gittelman and Sumoi, "Anxiety-like Disorders in Young Primates," 1–23.

[27] Madden and Suomi, "Primate Separation Models of Affective Disorders," 195–214.

Importantly, these differential patterns of behavioral and physiological response to separation remain quite stable throughout development. When high-reactive females become mothers themselves, they are more likely than other mothers to provide inadequate maternal care for their first-born offspring.[28] Suomi interpreted these findings as clearly demonstrating that macaque monkeys' long-term behavioral patterns are shaped by social attachment experiences in early childhood. The behavioral consequences seem to be particularly striking in case of maternal deprivation or extended disruption of the mother-infant relationship. Giving cause for optimism, however, Suomi and coworkers have shown that high-reactive behavior and neglecting parenting style is nongenetic in nature.[29] Studies of high-reactive female neonate monkeys being foster-reared by mothers that provide a highly nurturant and caring parenting style will adapt the maternal style of their foster mothers rather than their biological mothers when having offspring themselves. Most importantly, these observations indicate that behavior is not only malleable depending on the parenting style experienced, but also that seemingly adverse behavioral responses may be highly adaptive. This is in agreement with studies from Meaney and co-workers in which they argue that a parental rearing style that favored the development of increased stress responsiveness in infants is adaptive under certain conditions.[30] Parents living in a highly demanding environment may convey "anticipatory" information about high levels of environmental adversity to their young by means of deficient maternal care. This argument is supported by mother-infant studies in macaques.[31] Here, animals were investigated under one of three different environmental conditions for several months: (1) ample food was readily available; (2) sufficient food was available but required extensive searching; and (3) food conditions were highly variable, thereby ruling out any predictability. Researchers found that living under unpredictable foraging conditions caused the most significant increase in mother-infant conflicts. Those animals showed increased levels of corticotropin-releasing factor,[32] indicating altered norepinephrinergic and serotonergic response to stress. As a consequence of suffering unpredictable conditions, those macaque infants grew into more timid, fearful, and submissive juveniles. Additionally, these

---

[28] Reite and Sumoi, "A History of Motherless Mother Monkeys," 49–77.
[29] Danieli and Suomi, "Psychobiology of Intergenerational Effects of Trauma," 623–637.
[30] Meaney, "Maternal Care, Gene Expression," 1161–1192.
[31] Rosenblum and Andrews, "Influences of Environmental Demand," 57–63.
[32] Coplan et al., "Persistent Elevations of Cerebrospinal Fluid Concentrations," 1619–1623.

animals also showed signs of depression, despite not having been separated from their mothers.

In addition to behavioral problems resulting, to a significant extent, from experiencing neglecting maternal behavior in early childhood, there is another naturally occurring subgroup of rhesus monkeys that stand out due to conduct disorders. These animals can be characterized as particularly impulsive and unable to moderate behavioral responses, often leading to escalating interactions. Highly impulsive monkeys frequently show aggressive interchanges with other group members, disproportionately often at their own expense. These behavioral features arise at an early childhood stage and remain notably stable throughout development.[33] As they grow older, impulsive males tend to be expelled from their natal troop because of their aggressive tendencies and social incompetence.[34] On the other hand, impulsive-aggressive females remain in their natal troop but typically rank at the bottom of the dominance hierarchy. As mothers, these impulsive females often provide inept maternal care for their offspring.[35] Both impulsive-aggressive males and females have unusually low serotonin levels that typically remain low as they mature.

As discussed above, social deprivation throughout infancy almost always results in extreme behavioral abnormalities and severe social and emotional deficits. However, such extreme cases are fortunately rare in nature. Nevertheless, even more "moderate" maternal deprivation during early childhood can have significant behavioral and physiological consequences. Suomi and his team have used a different rearing paradigm to mimic "moderate" maternal deprivation. They have separated rhesus monkey neonates from their mothers at birth and hand-reared them in a nursery for the first month. After this initial period, the infants were reared with same-age peers for several months and then moved into larger, mixed social groups until they reached puberty. These motherless monkey infants established strong attachment bonds to their peers. Notwithstanding the lack of maternal care, having the opportunity to emotionally and socially bond with other monkeys seemingly prevented the young from developing bizarre, idiosyncratic stereotypic patterns of behavior that are characteristic of animals reared in isolation. Nonetheless, peer-reared animals are more anxious and shyer than their mother-reared peers and typically remain at the bottom of the dominance

---

[33] Ammerman and Higley, *Handbook of Aggressive Behavior in Psychiatric Patients*, 17–32.
[34] Higley et al., "Excessive Mortality," 537–543.
[35] Higley et al., "Stability of Interindividual Differences in Serotonin Function," 67–76.

hierarchies in mixed social groups.[36] Subsequently, peer-reared monkeys develop more impulsive behavior with increasingly more frequent and severe aggressive episodes as they approach puberty, especially if they are males. These impulsive-aggressive behavioral patterns remain robust as the animals grow older and move into new social groups. In neurophysiological studies, these animals have been shown to have lower serotonin metabolites in their cerebrospinal fluid than mother-reared agemates. Moreover, when these peer-reared monkeys get separated from their peers, they exhibit quite severe behavioral reactions and have significantly stronger greater adrenocortical and norepinephrinenergic responses than their mother-reared group members. These neuroendocrinological differences with respect to separation reactions occur from infancy to adolescence.

Studies that investigate mother-child separation in primates have been criticized for overestimating the importance of bodily contact. Adversaries have claimed that physical contact as a driving factor of attachment and bonding would be of little relevance for human infants who do not show clinging behavior for survival in contrast to monkeys. However, there is more and more evidence showing that mother-child attachment is of paramount importance for healthy emotional and cognitive development in children. One of the first scholars, along with Harry Bakwin and René Spitz, who pointed this out was British psychiatrist and psychologist John Bowlby. He is amongst the most cited psychologists, famous for his work in child development, particularly for his pioneering work on mother-child attachment. His interest in social bonding and maternal separation arose on account of his own biography. Bowlby was born as one of six children and raised in a manner traditional to upper-middle-class families of the time. His mother, like many other mothers of her social class, held to teachings that considered parental attention and affection as harmful to children. Bowlby reported that he and his siblings saw their mother only one hour a day. The Bowlby children were brought up by a nanny in a separate nursery in the family house and were assisted by other nursemaids. Bowlby had a particularly close relationship with nursemaid Minnie, who acted as a mother figure. When he was around four years old, Minnie left the Bowlby family. This came as a tragic experience to him and the pain would accompany him for the rest of his life. According to his son, Sir Richard Bowlby, the loss of his primary attachment figure, Minnie, played an important part in his father's motivation for a lifetime study of the affectional bond that forms between a child and caregiver.[37] John Bowlby rarely saw his father, who was an eminent surgeon and performed military service

---

[36] Suomi and Novak, "Social Interaction in Nonhuman Primates," 308–314.
[37] Bowlby, *The Making and Breaking of Affectional Bonds*, vii-xi.

during World War I. Although his father sent letters from the front, Bowlby's mother never shared them with her children. A few years after losing his primary caregiver, nurse Minnie, Bowlby endured another separation. At the age of seven, he was sent to boarding school. He would later say in one of his books that "I wouldn't send a dog away to boarding school at age seven."[38]

As a psychiatrist and psychologist, he dedicated his career to investigating the importance of primary caregivers in development. His work was one of the first ones that strongly emphasized the importance of early environmental influences on healthy child development and outspokenly de-emphasized feeding as the crucial component in establishing a strong mother-child relationship. Bowlby became interested in the cognitive and emotional development of children who experienced separation due to wartime events. Anna Freud and Dorothy Burlingham's work on evacuees during wartime was one of the bedrocks for Bowlby's theory on mother-child attachment. In particular, he drew on Freud's studies of children at the Hampstead War Nurseries in London who had been evacuated to the countryside in comparison to children who had stayed behind in English cities and towns with their parents and witnessed bombings. Freud reported that children who stayed with their families during bomb attacks were on the whole less upset despite experiencing bombing than children who were separated from their caregivers and evacuated to the countryside. Bowlby's own work started with research on delinquent children who frequently showed affectionless behavior. He found that many of them had suffered from prolonged maternal separation experiences in early childhood.[39] Later, while working at Child Guidance Clinic in London and then at the Tavistock clinic, a specialist mental health clinic based in north London, he conducted research on the negative impact of early mother-child separation. By the late 1950s, his empirical and theoretical approaches led him to develop the theory of attachment. This theory implies the fundamental importance of mother-child attachment for healthy human development as a necessary evolutionary survival strategy. Going against the ideal of sterile, contact-less nurseries that also prevented any contact between mothers and children and prevailed at the time, Bowlby claimed that separation of young children from their mothers may even cause psychopathologies. He suggested that certain psychiatric disorders were due to a separation-triggered mental conflict so great that the normal means of cognitive and emotional regulations were shattered. According to Bowlby, this dysregulation occurs when an emotional relationship between child and primary caregiver, usually the mother, has already formed and then gets

---

[38] Schwartz, *Cassandra's Daughter*, 225.
[39] Bowlby, "Forty-Four Juvenile Thieves," 19–53.

disrupted due to separation. Prolonged separation can be damaging to the development of the infant's personality. This is due to the child's feelings of being unloved, deserted, and rejected. In his 1944 article about forty-four juvenile thieves, Bowlby cites a poem of an eleven-year-old delinquent boy whose mother had died when he was fifteen months old, and who had henceforth been looked after by several substitute mothers. The boy had written the poem during a psychotherapeutic session with one of Bowlby's colleagues. Bowlby suggested that the verses written captured the boy's sentiments concerning the reason for having been passed from one caregiver to another.

> Jumbo had a baby dressed in green,
> wrapped it up in paper and sent it to the Queen.
> The Queen did not like it because it was too fat,
> She cut it up in pieces and gave it to the cat.
> The cat did not like it because it was too thin,
> She cut it up in pieces and gave it to the King.
> The King did not like it because he was too slow,
> Threw it out the window and gave it to the crow.[40]

Bowlby relates the intense despair triggered by maternal separation to feelings of hatred. He reported that the more this delinquent boy came to care for his therapist the more prone he was to outbreaks of violent hatred. He explained the child's intense emotional ambivalence by an immature psychic regulation that was adopted in early childhood and persisted over the years, leading to pathological behavioral patterns.[41]

Although Bowlby's observations provided strong, empirical support for the importance of a loving mother-child interaction, his attachment theory was controversial in many ways. First, it broke with classical psychoanalytic theories, which postulated that an infant's inner life was determined by fantasy, not real-life events. Second, it made the assertion that maternal love was necessary for normal and healthy development. Third, it unequivocally claimed that parenting as such required the formation of a continuing relationship between parent and child.

Since his research was limited to observational studies due to ethical reasons, Bowlby turned to behavioral scientists for experimental evidence. Becoming aware of Harry Harlow's primates studies, Bowlby strongly drew from Harlow's experimental insights in formulating the attachment theory. In particular,

---

[40] Bowlby, *The Making and Breaking of Affectional Bonds,* 18.
[41] Bowlby, "Forty-Four Juvenile Thieves," 19–53.

Harlow's rhesus monkey experiments with surrogate mothers made of either mesh-wire or cloth were highly revelatory because results of the primate studies unequivocally demonstrated the importance of physical contact for the infant's normal development. Drawing from his own observations as well as animal behavioral research, Bowlby concluded that the earliest years of an infant's life are most critical for development and that the foundations of personality are laid during this period. He underscored that the development of the child's fantasy world is not merely a reflection of perceptions and activities, but has an active, creative aspect, i.e., the evolving phenomenological world is a "construction of reality" rather than a mere representation of it. Gradually, the infant gains the capacity to refashion the environment, thereby remolding reality in accordance with experience and expectations. In this remarkably insightful discourse, Bowlby emphasized the plasticity of cognition accompanied by the infants' construction of cognitive worlds, which they then inhabit and mold. From today's point of view, Bowlby's factual ingenuity anticipated findings about the pertinence of neuroplasticity for cognitive development as well as niche construction for one's social environment. As discussed in Chapter 2 (Brain Development and Plasticity) and Chapter 5 (Learning and Memory), human infant and juvenile brains are highly plastic. This plasticity is due to processes of neurogenesis, dendritic and synaptic maturation, axon overproduction and elimination, and cortical myelination. In comparison to nonhuman primates, humans have an even longer developmental phase during which extensive brain re-organization takes place.[42] While this extended developmental plasticity provides the basis for the extraordinary capacity for learning and memory in humans, this malleability also leaves the young human brain very vulnerable because of its immature neurophysiology, such as its immature stress response system.

Thus, attachment theory emphasizes the fundamental importance of mother-child bonding (or allomother-child bonding) as a necessary evolutionary survival strategy for the healthy development of a child. Over the years, attachment theory has become significantly modified due to empirical findings, but the core concepts and categories are still widely accepted today. Attachment theory divides children and adults into major categories of attachment styles that refer to impulses originally formed in early infancy in response to maternal attitudes. Developmental psychologists refer to four different attachment styles: secure; dismissive-avoidant (or anxious-avoidant); anxious-ambivalent; and disorganized. Attachment styles are developed as infants and then further strengthened or modified as children, adolescents, and adults. The four different styles describe the way people connect and form

---

[42] Geschwind and Rakic, "Cortical Evolution," 633–647.

relations with other people. The most common attachment style is secure attachment. Secure attachment develops when children experience parents who respond to their needs and readily communicate with them. On the contrary, children with a history of neglect whose needs were frequently not met by their caregivers will develop a dismissive-avoidant attachment style. This behavior is characterized by avoiding the caregiver or other resource persons in stressful or strange situations. Children who have developed a dismissive-avoidant attachment style will show a high level of independence as adults. They usually suppress their feelings, avoid forming close relationships,[43] and if they are in a relationship, they tend to distance themselves from their partners in situations of conflict. This avoidance behavior is triggered by early childhood experiences when needs remained unfulfilled. Physical and emotional neglect then lead to the internalization of a picture in which communication of emotional needs is irrelevant or even inimical in relationships. Anxious-avoidant attachment style is known to be related to high-risk environments such as experiences of severe deprivation, incestuous abuse,[44] or being raised by parents with problems of alcohol abuse.[45] In neurobiological terms, the absence of early caregiving causes a premature maturation of the amygdala, forcing infants into accelerated learning about their environment. Caregiver deprivation, for example, in orphanage environments, leads to commonly observed behavioral consequences: a decrease in the threshold for responding to sensory stimulation;[46] a hyperreactivity and sensitivity to emotional information most likely due to a hyperactive, precocious amygdala;[47, 48] and an increase in the tendency to approach unfamiliar adults. In the long term, these neurobiological changes can result in hypervigilance and an elevated risk for externalizing and internalizing problems, such as anxiety disorders and attention deficits.

Equally problematic, children who have experienced violence (against themselves or another family member) develop anxious-ambivalent attachments.[49] As adults, people with anxious-ambivalent attachment style are more likely to experience difficulties in maintaining intimate relationships. Ambivalent adults show a desire for close relationships but usually find

---

[43] Fraley and Shaver, "Adult Romantic Attachment," 132–154.
[44] Alexander, "The Differential Effects of Abuse Characteristics," 346–362.
[45] Brennan et al., "Attachment Styles, Gender and Parental Problem Drinking," 451–466.
[46] Wilbarger et al., "Sensory Processing," 1105–1114.
[47] Fries and Pollak, "Emotion Understanding," 355–369.
[48] Tottenham et al., "Prolonged Institutional Rearing," 46–61.
[49] McCarthy and Taylor, "Avoidant/Ambivalent Attachment Style as a Mediator," 465–477.

themselves in extreme forms of intimacy and low levels of autonomy as a consequence of their fear of rejection.

Alongside anxious-ambivalent and anxious-avoidant attachment, scholars have described a disorganized attachment style. This is the most extreme form of insecure attachment. It most likely is a result of inconsistent emotional support and/or abuse. This may include severe trauma from verbal, physical, sexual abuse, or experiencing extreme forms of violence by an attachment figure against another attachment figure. Most children with disorganized attachment style exhibit fear of the caregiver expressed by confused expressions, freezing, undirected movements, or contradictory (i.e., "unorganized") patterns of interaction with others. This is due to the child having become aware of the parental figure being a putative threat and someone to be feared. Typical childhood development ensures that infants exhibit potentiated preference learning and attenuated aversion learning. This means children learn to attach to their caregiver irrespective of the quality of maternal care. This paradoxical learning reflects the inability of engaging the amygdala early in life. When the mother is present, the amygdala typically remains functionally dormant.[50] When the sensitive period of stress hyporesponsiveness gradually declines, a post-sensitive period begins that is characterized by a transition to independence. At this stage, infants require both continued interactions with the mother as well as the engagement of preference/avoidance learning for independent survival.[51] Typically, the effects of maternal presence on conditioning learning ensure a positive response of the child to stimuli from the mother and, at the same time, the infant's ability to learn how to discriminate positive from aversive stimuli in the environment. Abusive mothers, however, trigger fear learning of maternal cues. Thus, when experiencing abuse at an age when amygdala-mediated preference/avoidance learning is prevalent, the child re-learns earlier cues. The child realizes that a conditioned, previously positive stimulus (e.g., seeing the mother) is now paired with an aversive stimulus (e.g., hitting). The processing of emotionally inconsistent cues may result in severe misapprehensions and erroneous assessment of the environment as the child becomes aware that she cannot rely on her own emotional responses. Adults who have developed a disorganized attachment style in their childhood often are afraid of forming intimate relationships and suffer from a negative self-image and extremely damaging self-talk. They oscillate between two behavioral extremes. On the one hand, they long for genuine relationships and feel intense loneliness due to this

---

[50] Tottenham, "Human Amygdala Development," 598–611.
[51] Moriceau and Sullivan, "Maternal Presence Serves as a Switch, 1004–1006.

desire. On the other hand, they drive away potential relationships because of their fear and need for protection from putative attachment figures.

When human attachment theory is interpreted from an evolutionary perspective, abnormal styles of attachment can be seen as adaptive in certain situations.[52] For example, if a mother is disinclined to invest in a child, secure attachment may turn out to be less beneficial for the infant than insecure attachment. The latter may function as a defense mechanism, as it helps the infant to survive a stressful situation by avoiding getting too close to the attachment figure. Thus, anxious-avoidance behavior, for example, of an infant can be adaptive when living in an abusive neglecting family. However, the same behavior may become maladaptive in other social niches, such as in an intimate relationship as an adult when closeness to the partner is desirable. In the adult's social environment, the maladaptation of anxious-avoidance behavior toward intimacy is experienced as stressful. This frequently leads to abandoning a close relationship in favor of a social environment in which partners avoid intimacy and connectedness—a situation that matches previous experiences.

Mother-child attachment can regulate behaviors that are not rigidly innate, but rather flexible, thereby providing environmental adaptivity. Such flexibility comes at a price, however, because adaptable behavioral systems can more easily be subverted from their optimal path of development. On the other hand, what is regarded as vulnerability might as well be information about the quality of environment that is transmitted from parent to offspring. For example, parents who occupy a highly demanding environment—such as scarcity of food, unpredictability of resources, or maintaining a low social rank within the dominance hierarchy—may transmit to their young an enhanced level of stress reactivity. This information about the quality of environment may pertain to environmental as well as social factors.

Consequently, high reactivity in the offspring could mediate an appropriate anticipation of a high level of environmental and/or social adversity.[53] Meaney and co-workers have found that there are potential adaptive advantages of the increased levels of stress reactivity. These higher levels of stress reactivity are mediated by an increased level of corticotropin-releasing factor in the hypothalamus and amygdala, as well as by a decrease of inhibitory neurotransmitter receptors $GABA_A$, the latter being important for dampening excitatory reactions. Additionally, anticipation of environmental adversities leads to a developmental attenuation of investment in metabolically expensive

---

[52] Chisholm, "The Evolutionary Ecology of Attachment Organization," 1–37.
[53] Meaney, "Maternal Care, Gene Expression," 1161–1192.

synaptic systems, such as hippocampal brain circuits.[54] On the other hand, growing up in environments of ecological abundance and high social status likely favors modest levels of stress reactivity and increased development neuroplasticity in the hippocampus. It is, therefore, highly likely that the behavior of the parent by means of parental care transmits information about the quality of the environment that the offspring will encounter. As Meaney concludes, there is thus no single ideal form of parenting because different environmental demands require different traits in offspring enhanced by adaptive parental care.

Infancy is then the period in which brain development due to anticipatory information transmitted via maternal care is modulated and shaped. When the child encounters novel stimuli, the sensory cortex is activated and relays the perceived information through the thalamus to the brain stem. In the brain stem, more precisely in the locus coeruleus, the neurotransmitter norepinephrine is produced. From there, neurons that secrete norepinephrine project to different brain areas such as the hypothalamus, the cerebellum, the cortex, and the amygdala. Normally, neurons in the locus coeruleus fire at a low baseline level when the child is in an unstimulated, relaxed state. When the child perceives a novel stimulus, norepinephrinergic neurons in the locus coeruleus augment their activity. This leads to an increase of norepinephrine release that in turn makes the child more alert and attentive to motivationally significant stimuli. Norepinephrinergic neurons of the locus coeruleus can trigger reactions via the hypothalamic-pituitary-adrenal axis (stress axis) in response to environmental threats (see Chapter 6: The Effects of Emotion, Stress, and Traumatic Experiences on Cognition). However, once the stressful event has passed, the system must return to a resting state; otherwise, the organism would end up in a chronic state of stress. To again reach a physiological resting state, cortisol and epinephrine/norepinephrine feedback loops downregulate the activity of the components of the stress axis. This physiological mechanism of up and downregulation as a reaction to novel stimuli, which is more pronounced to threats, has been retained throughout evolution and is already present in newborns. But as mentioned, the child's stress system is not fully matured in early infancy and thus cannot regulate stress reactions efficiently. Children are highly dependent on their social environment in order to calm their excessive bodily stress reactions by being soothed or calmed down by their primary caregivers. These soothing activities include feeding but also providing skin contact, child-directed speech, as well as rhythmic movements, such as rocking. As for the latter, Harlow and Zimmermann have demonstrated that rocking movements exert calming

---

[54] Sapolsky, Stress, *the Aging Brain, and the Mechanisms of Neuron Death*, 423.

effects in newborn monkeys.[55] Monkeys raised in the company of artificial surrogate mothers grew into socially deviant, aggressive adults, but less so if the surrogate mothers performed swinging movements. The calming effect of movements is further supported by the observation that monkeys exposed to surrogate mothers sit clutching themselves, or holding their heads and bodies in their arms and perform convulsive jerking and rocking movements. In human infants, rocking and other movements contribute to the development of the cerebellum, especially the cerebellar vermis that develops gradually and is the site of neurogenesis after birth. Interestingly, the vermis contains an extraordinarily high density of receptors for stress hormones. Thus, stimulation of the cerebellum may not only be important for the development of a healthy motor coordination, but also for the compensation and regulation of emotional instability in the face of stressful events.[56] In the event of neglect or isolation, sensorimotor interaction between the infant and primary caregiver is disrupted, and the child needs to solely rely on his/her own physiological mechanisms to regulate emotional balance and dampen the stress response. Neglected children often show kinetic automatisms or stereotypical back-and-forth rocking movements that can be understood as attempts to self-soothe, compensating for the lack of parental care. Similar rocking patterns have been observed in monkeys when they are prevented from forming bonds during the first six months of life.

In humans, skin contact and suckling during breastfeeding trigger the release of the bonding hormone oxytocin. Oxytocin is released in the baby as well as the mother, which helps to consolidate an early social connection. Interestingly, recent evidence has indicated that skin contact between fathers and their newborns also triggers oxytocin release in both baby and father.[57] Oxytocin plays a crucial role in attachment, social exploration, social recognition, and in anxiety and stress-related behaviors.[58] Experimental administration of oxytocin in combination with social support dampen neuroendocrine stress reactivity and decreases amygdala activation in response to threatening stimuli.[59] Within human populations, there are variants of the oxytocin receptor gene, a phenomenon called polymorphism (i.e., different phenotypes due to two or more variants of a particular DNA sequence). These variants are associated with differences in social behavioral, such as parenting, empathy, positive affect, and sensitivity to social support or

---

[55] Harlow and Zimmermann, "Affectional Response in the Infant Monkey," 421–432.
[56] Sarto-Jackson, "Wired for Social Interaction," 9–30.
[57] Vittner et al., "Increase in Oxytocin From Skin-to-Skin Contact," 54–62.
[58] Meyer-Lindenberg et al., "Oxytocin and Vasopressin in the Human Brain," 524–538.
[59] Kirsch et al., "Oxytocin Modulates Neural Circuitry for Social Cognition," 11489–11493.

support seeking during stress. But the polymorphism of the oxytocin receptor gene counts only for small sociobehavioral differences. Instead, interindividual differences in social cognition and behavior seem to be strongly influenced by epigenetic factors that regulate expression levels of the oxytocin receptor gene. Epigenetic changes in the regulatory sequences of the oxytocin receptor correlate with high levels of callousness, unemotionality, and differences in social perception.[60] Psychosocial stress strongly impacts epigenetic regulation. For example, prolonged deprivation in early childhood interferes with the developing oxytocin system. This has been shown for post-institutionalized children who had been reared in severely deprived conditions and later adopted. Those children had lower oxytocin levels following physical contact with their adoptive mothers than adopted children who had been reared in a typical home environment.[61] In a nutshell, traumatic experiences afflict the developing oxytocin system and cause adverse effects on attachment, bonding, anxiety, and social recognition. Yet these negative experiences may be a way to prepare children for hardship and harsh competitive environments that are expected to be encountered later in life.

Humans much more than any other animal have managed to live in highly complex and large social groups. This prosocial lifestyle has been cited as one of the crucial factors for the drastic increase in human brain volume. British anthropologist Robin Dunbar found a correlation between brain size of primates and the average size of social groups they belong to. Interestingly, the size and complexity of human brains seem to allow us to keep stable social relationships to about 150 people at the same time.[62] Although other researchers have discussed adjustments of this number and assume it may lie somewhere between 100 and 250 people, the key message remains in force. Based on human brain size and the memory capacity of the human neocortex, it seems that an individual can only track the emotional and qualitative values of inter-personal relationships to about 150 to 250 individuals. As a consequence, humans naturally limit themselves to such a number of meaningful relationships. Living in even bigger or more complex group sizes appears stressful for the human brain because it becomes increasingly more difficult to remember the hierarchical intricacies of group members. Yet over the last few centuries, humans have constructed new niches[63] in the form of villages, towns, and cities with population densities far exceeding those of any

---

[60] Kumsta et al., "Epigenetic Regulation of the Oxytocin Receptor Gene," 83.
[61] Fries et al., "From The Cover," 17237–17240.
[62] Dunbar, "Coevolution of Neocortical Size," 681–735.
[63] Laland et al., "How Culture Shaped the Human Genome," 137–148.

hunter-gatherer communities.[64] As a consequence of the overwhelming complexities of interpersonal relations within different groups (frequently accompanied by a lack of meaningful interpersonal relationships in our immediate environment due to large group sizes), maladaptive tendencies can emerge in the form of psychopathologies like social phobias, addictive behavior, and other mental disorders. Additionally, evolutionary mismatches undampened by cultural intervention (laws, religious precepts, rules of conduct, etc.) may also be causally involved in xenophobia, ethnocentrism, and racism.[65, 66]

In order to live in large social groups as humans have done over the last hundreds of thousand years, we had to evolve into a less aggressive and less competitive population. Indeed, humans evolved a higher level of cooperation than most other animals, a process necessary to form complex social environments. This can be illustrated by the fact that archaic human mothers when nursing needed about 2,300 calories a day for their own body's needs and several thousand more calories to feed their kids. These demands could only be met if a nursing mother had access to high-quality food, including meat and cooking. However, getting cooked food and meat was only possible for females with kids if they lived in a highly cooperative group, being supported by the children's father, grandparents, and others.[67]

These theoretical claims that argued how beneficial cooperation was for archaic humans' survival as well as mother and child well-being have been supported by recent experiments in rodents. Researchers from the University of Calgary have investigated how different parenting models influence the offspring's brain development. They showed that mice that were reared in different environments exhibited differences in neuronal growth and behavior.[68] Three conditions were examined: pups were raised either (1) by their biological mothers alone; (2) by their mothers and a second female; or (3) by their mothers and biological fathers together. The young were then subjected to a series of tests to measure their memory, cognitive and social skills and were also anatomically investigated to determine neuronal growth in different brain regions. Results indicated that bi-parental care (either with the offspring's father or another female) boosted neuronal growth in the dentate gyrus, a region involved in learning, storing memories, and spatial coordination. This appeared to be particularly relevant for male offspring.

[64] O'Brien and Laland, "Genes, Culture, and Agriculture," 434–470.
[65] McEvoy, "A Consideration of Human Xenophobia," 39–49.
[66] Baird et al., "Evolutionary Morality and Xenophobia," 161–166.
[67] Lieberman, *The Story of the Human Body*.
[68] Mak et al., "Bi-Parental Care Contributes to Sexually Dimorphic Neural Cell Genesis."

Similarly, female offspring that experienced bi-parental care developed twice as many neurons in the corpus callosum, a bundle of nerve fibers that connects the two brain halves, facilitates communication between the two hemispheres, and coordinates balance, attention, and arousal. Upon further behavioral observations, scientists found that the pups raised by two parents experienced more licking and grooming compared to pups that were raised by just their mothers; this enhanced brood care most likely triggered an increase in neuronal growth.

Yet the role of the father in child-rearing (or more generally, bi-parental care irrespective of gender) has hardly been studied. In fact, even Bowlby, who was among the first ones to point out how devastating the experience of separation was for an infant, barely mentioned the role of fathers. In his book *Child Care and the Growth of Love*, Bowlby wrote that "[i]n the young child's eyes father plays second fiddle and his value increases only as the child becomes more able to stand alone."[69] Also when formulating the attachment theory, Bowlby described the father as a subsidiary attachment figure rather than a principal attachment figure.[70] More recently, however, a longitudinal study found that adolescent and young adults expressed high levels of positive social behavior when they experienced bi-parental care in which their mothers and fathers combined their resources.[71] Behavioral assessments revealed that mothers' roles were crucial for infants' early attachment by providing comfort and care, whereas fathers strongly contributed to the infants' development by sensitively engaging in interactive play with children. Cognitive and emotional benefits of exciting and challenging play were found to emerge in early childhood (starting around eight to nine months of age). This prosocial avail from interactive play occurs around the same time when children start engaging in joint attention tasks (i.e., when two individuals share the focus on an object),[72] fostering infantile explorations. From the positive results of bi-parental care, researchers concluded that young children optimally do not only enjoy close relationship with a single primary caregiver but also with other adult(s). While the former offers the child an enduring secure base, the latter provides a secure base as the springboard that facilitates exploration. Generally speaking, the mother acts as primary caregiver who provides comfort when the child is in distress, whereas the father gives sensitive support during explorative play, also ensuring the child's emotional security. This is in line with Bowlby's concept of psychological

---

[69] Bowlby, *Child Care and the Growth of Love*, 15.

[70] Bowlby, *Attachment and Loss*.

[71] Grossmann et al., "The Uniqueness of the Child-Father Attachment Relationship." 301–337.

[72] Tomasello, *The Cultural Origins of Human Cognition*.

adaptation that depends on both emotional security in times of distress as well as when facing challenges.[73] Importantly, given modern advances in neonatal and infant nursing, it is reasonable to claim that the roles of mothers and fathers can also be reversed.

With increasing age, children benefit from other members of their social groups, often but not necessarily family members. Group members preferentially direct prosocial activities and altruistic behavior toward in-group members. Yet altruism is not limited to in-group members. Whether this discriminative behavior is genetically driven or not has been widely debated. U.S. neurologist and professor at Stanford University Robert Sapolsky convincingly argues that the default state in humans is to trust and exhibit altruistic behavior.[74] In experiments using an economic game (the so-called Ultimatum Game), two players negotiate how to divide a lump sum. The first player makes an offer that the second player can either accept or reject. Crucially, if the second player rejects, neither of the players gets anything. From a purely rational point of view, the second player should accept any offer no matter how small, since even a tiny amount of money is better than nothing. However, it has been shown that if the first player is too stingy with the offer, the second player usually chooses to forego his/her earnings in favor of punishing the other player, who also receives nothing as a result. Brain scans indicate that rejecting an offer is an emotional rather than purely rational decision, and the former involves the activation of the amygdala. Interestingly, people with damaged amygdalae are atypically generous in the Ultimatum Game even if receiving unfair offers. Their generosity is not caused by a lack of understanding of the rules. On the contrary, these patients seem to be "pathologically" altruistic. Sapolsky argues that this is due to the damage of the amygdala interfering with learning vigilance and distrust. He concludes that humans have an inborn sense of altruism. In subjects whose amygdala is intact, trust and altruism are unlearned through negative social experiences during development. Thus, humans' general propensity for altruism and prosocial behavior seem to have a strong inborn component that is modified during one's lifetime. Importantly, there is no prioritization of in-group members. Children show naturally altruistic behavior indiscriminately at a younger age. Only by age three do they begin to inhibit their indiscriminate behavior. They become more selective about whom they help and they share more often with those who have previously shared with them.[75] Using non-invasive imaging techniques, it has been demonstrated that the activity of neural correlates

---

[73] Bowlby, "The Making and Breaking of Affectional Bonds," 421–431.
[74] Sapolsky, *Behave: The Biology of Humans at Our Best and Worst.*
[75] Gazzaniga, *Who's in Charge?: Free Will and the Science of the Brain.*

involved in empathic and altruistic behavior was indeed different depending on whether in-group or out-group members were concerned.[76] Differing reactions to in-group versus out-group members are not innate but reflect cultural adaptations learnt during adolescence.[77] Since altruistic behavior toward in-group members relies on cultural knowledge, this behavior can be modified. For example, mere perceptual familiarity reduces prejudices against out-group members and increases cultural tolerance.[78] Thus, merely seeing a particular face or being around a certain person will make them more likely to become part of one's social group even if they were deemed out-group members without such learning experiences.

In order to form high-quality and meaningful relationships, group members need to be physically close (this was at least the case in the pre-interactive media era). As a consequence, close-knit groups are usually relatively small. Anthropologists have shown that humans interact most closely with just a handful of people to whom they devote a large chunk of their available social time. On the other hand, if humans fall significantly short of a minimal number of socially and emotionally meaningful relationships, they experience physiological stress responses. Social bonding is not only important in early childhood, as discussed above, but also during adolescence and throughout the whole life. In adolescence, social peer interactions are of paramount importance. As mentioned earlier, humans can only keep track of meaningful inter-personal relationships of about 150 to 250 individuals. In adolescence, the developing brain is constantly engaged in monitoring peer behavior and interrelationships within peer groups. Rapid changes in the quality of relationships with other group members are extremely challenging for the developing brain. Prior to the anthropocene, social relationships were probably more rigid. For example, in historical human populations, family bonds, relationships between tribe members, hierarchical status, and societal roles were often preset with little individual structuring possibilities. Contrarily, in modern societies, relationships between group members frequently vary, are broken off, or newly emerge. This volatility of relationships may contribute to psychologically stressful situations that have become increasingly prevalent in young people living in modern Western societies.

The importance of peer interactions goes beyond mere entertainment and leisure activities. Peer interactions significantly contribute to psychological development, making teenagers especially sensitive to how they fit into their

---

[76] Harada et al., "Neural Basis of Extraordinary Empathy," 1468–1475.

[77] Telzer et al., "Amygdala Sensitivity to Race," 234–244.

[78] Cloutier et al.,"The Impact of Childhood Experience," 1992–2004.

social environment.[79] This heightened sensitivity is not limited to humans but has also been observed in adolescent rodents raised in isolation. If rats are housed alone without any contact to others during their "adolescence" period (i.e., from the start of "puberty" to becoming an adult rat), the likelihood of depressive behaviors increases. These behavioral effects are associated with significant changes in the prefrontal cortex and, to a lesser extent, also in the hippocampus and amygdala.[80] Furthermore, rats show behavioral changes not only when raised in complete isolation, but also when they are exposed to periodical isolation accompanied by changes of their cage partners. This social instability (e.g., being isolated for an hour each day and housed with a different cage partner every day) has an adverse impact on adolescent rats.[81] The animals show changes in behavior, such as heightened anxiety and reduced social activity when they reach adulthood. They also have altered hormone levels, e.g., lower testosterone concentrations as adults. Researchers have pointed out that such social isolation paradigms have more severe effects concerning altered hormone production and behavioral changes in adolescent rats than in adult rats and these effects are also significantly longer-lasting in adolescent animals.

Importantly, there are some parallels to human adolescents' psychological development. Human adolescents who experience social stress suffer behavioral consequences in adulthood. Growing up in socially unstable environments, e.g., moving between foster homes and children's homes and experiencing adverse social interactions, correlates with having generally poorer physical and mental health than growing up in a relatively consistent and stable social environment.[82] It, therefore, seems evolutionarily adaptive to live in a socially stable world in childhood as well as in adolescence, the latter being particularly influenced by peer group acceptance.

Social isolation from their peer group is in fact something most mammals, including human beings, try to strongly avoid. Rhesus monkeys that have experienced neglecting maternal behavior in early childhood frequently show impulsive and aggressive behavior, as mentioned previously in this chapter. Because of their belligerent interactions with other group members, socially incompetent male monkeys tend to be expelled from their natal troop when reaching adolescence. Most of the expelled individuals become solitary. If

[79] Blakemore, *Inventing Ourselves.*
[80] Leussis and Andersen, "Is Adolescence a Sensitive Period for Depression?," 22–30.
[81] McCormick et al., "Impact of Adolescent Social Experiences on Behavior," 280–300.
[82] Blakemore, *Inventing Ourselves.*

isolated monkeys do not succeed in joining another group, they usually die within a year.[83]

It is difficult to compare such drastic findings from the animal kingdom to the effects of social isolation in humans. For ethical reasons, human adolescents can of course not be deliberately put in truly socially stressful environments to measure their reactions. To grapple with the importance of peer groups and the impact of social isolation for humans, researchers have used virtual experiments such as a computer game called Cyberball. Cyberball was originally devised by Kip Williams at Purdue University in the U.S. In this game, a test subject plays with two other players who are not present in the same room. The test person is only aware of the other players because s/he sees their icons on the screen. What the former does not know is that the other players are not human, just programmed virtual players that follow a certain experimental protocol. The game starts by throwing a ball to the participant who then virtually throws the ball to one of the other "players." The latter returns the ball to either the test person or the third "player." This virtual ball-throwing activity goes on for a few minutes. Then the pre-programmed "exclusion trials" start without the test subject being aware of the strategy behind it. The two virtual players continue throwing the ball back at each other but exclude the participant by not throwing the ball to him/her for the rest of the game. Despite it being just an online ball game with other players unknown to the test person (indeed, the other "players" are not even real persons, but this fact is unbeknownst to the test subject), being excluded causes a stress response for participants. Their mood is lowered and their anxiety is increased after exclusion trials.[84] These results are exacerbated when performing the exclusion trials of Cyberball with adolescents. Sarah-Jayne Blakemore studied groups of young adolescents, aged eleven to thirteen, and mid-adolescents, aged fourteen to sixteen, using the same experimental paradigm as described above and compared them to adults, aged twenty-two to forty-seven. The test subjects did not only believe that the other "players" were real, but also people of their own age group. What Blakemore and her coworker Catherine Sebastian found was that both adolescent groups reported significantly lower overall moods than adults after social exclusion. Moreover, young adolescents also reported higher anxiety than adults after the virtual experiment. In a nutshell, adolescents seem to be hypersensitive to social exclusion and are especially anxious about fitting into their peer environment.

If an online game can have such drastic effects on human emotions, we can only fathom how emotionally devastating it would be for anyone to be socially

---

[83] Higley et al., "Excessive Mortality," 537–543.
[84] Williams, *Ostracism: the Power of Silence.*

isolated for an extended period of time. Yet social exclusion is a reality that many adolescents face at school—a fact that should alert parents and teachers alike.

A man who experienced an extreme situation of social isolation was Robert Hillary King. King spent twenty-nine years in solitary confinement, locked into a six-by-nine-foot cell. It all started relatively idly and then gradually transitioned at full throttle into tragedy. King was born in 1942, left by his biological mother to stay with his maternal grandmother who stepped in for her oldest daughter. King lived with his sisters and several of his grandmothers' other kids in Gonzales, Louisiana in an old, shabby house just off the highway. In his biography,[85] he remembered the house being so decrepit that whenever it rained, it rained right through the roof of the old shack, sometimes flooding the house up to his knees and the water bringing in an abundance of snakes. At the age of five, King moved to New Orleans with his grandmother. There, he learned to fight, smoke, and drink alcohol, and joined a local gang when he was just over eleven years old. He soon skipped school and became involved in shoplifting and gang fights. At the age of thirteen, he met his father for the first time, who took him to live with him and his wife in Donaldsonville, a small rural town in Louisiana. It turned out that his father was a violent man who physically abused and verbally threatened and assaulted King regularly. Eventually leaving his father's draconic regime two years later, King went back to New Orleans. But things turned from bad to worse. He was charged with the robbery of a gas station, for which he claimed innocence. He was taken to juvenile court and sentenced to stay at the State Industrial School for Colored Youth. But soon, the State Industrial School was no longer responsible for King, who no longer counted as a juvenile delinquent after turning eighteen. He was released and was allowed to return to New Orleans as a free man. That said, however, at this point in his biography, King cites George Jackson, the African-American author and militant activist of the Black Panther Party, who posited that young male African-Americans were inevitably coerced into following either of the two futile life trajectories available to them: when Black men reach a certain age, they were either destined for prison or the grave. Period.

Released from the State Industrial School for Colored Youth, King struggled to find employment in New Orleans, so he left for Chicago, but his novel regular working life only gave him a short break from coming into conflict with criminal law. A few months later, when taking a short leave of absence from his job in Chicago, he met up with some old "buddies" from the State Industrial School in New Orleans. Driving around in the downtown area of New Orleans in an old jalopy, King and his mates were stopped by police cars with flashing

---

[85] King, *From the Bottom of the Heap.*

lights and wailing sirens. The Black men in the jalopy, including King, were held at gunpoint by policemen and taken into custody. Without solid evidence, a jury convicted Robert Hillary King of armed robbery, a crime he did not commit, and sentenced him to ten years in prison. At the age of eighteen, he started serving his prison sentence at Orleans Parish Prison, and was sent to Angola State Penitentiary soon after. Angola State Penitentiary—or Angola for short—also went by the nickname "Alcatraz of the South." It was and still is a maximum-security prison farm in Louisiana that housed more than four thousand convicts at the time. With a size of about eighteen thousand acres, the prison property is larger than the size of Manhattan and looked like a massive working plantation. The prison farm was in fact given the name Angola after the African country that was the origin of many slaves brought over the Atlantic ocean to Louisiana. King and other inmates there—about two-thirds of them African-Americans—were sentenced to forced labor for two and a half cents per hour. He later compared the hard lines on the sugar cane plantations of Angola as chattel slavery. In 1965, at the age of twenty-two, King was granted parole and returned to New Orleans, where he got married and started a brief semi-pro boxing career. But again, trouble caught up and a few weeks before the birth of his son, King and his acquaintance "Boogie" were arrested on charges of robbery—to be precise, they were accused of stealing a watch from a sleeping drunkard. Again, King claimed to be innocent. He insisted that the two of them were framed by a policeman who planted the alleged piece of evidence (the watch) in the course of searching the suspects' car. King was held in jail for over eleven months until his acquaintance accepted a plea bargain. This bargain, however, turned out to be quite devastating for King. Due to his plea deal, "Boogie" was now considered an admitted felon. Hence, King was deemed to be guilty of parole violation because he was arrested in the company of a felon. King was re-transferred to Angola prison, where he served another fifteen months before being released on parole again in January 1969. He once more started to engage in semi-pro bouts, fighting as "Speedy King" but soon had to give up this career path. But before getting his act together, a new conviction was looming. One day, police officers showed up at King's home. Without a warrant, the officers forced their way inside, held him at gunpoint, methodically ransacked his dwelling, and "came upon" a gun. King was later arrested on robbery charges. This time King was confident that his case would be acquitted. He had an alibi, no apparent similarities with the suspect's description, and his alleged accomplice exonerated him. His co-defendant testified that he had picked King out of a mug shot lineup only after being tortured by police into making a false statement. Nevertheless, the jury sentenced him to thirty-five years in prison despite a lack of evidence. While being held in the parish prison, he escaped, but was re-captured weeks later, brought back to court, and sentenced to an additional eight years in prison. In

Orleans Parish Prison, King met some of the Black Panther Party members who had been arrested after armed 1970 confrontations with police. King learned about the Black Panther Party's practice of "copwatching," i.e., monitoring the behavior of police officers and challenging police brutality. The party also established community social programs to address injustice concerning education, food distribution, and health care. According to the political activists of the party, they fought against oppression by providing Blacks and other oppressed peoples in America with alternative ways of resisting American-style repression politically, economically, racially, and socially.

As King put it, the Party saw revolution as the only means of altering the existing gap between the haves and the have-nots.

In 1971, King was again moved from the parish prison to Angola to serve the remainder of his sentence. Upon his arrival, he found the prison farm in an uproar. The reason was the death of a young man who had been found slain in one of the inmates' dormitories. King spoke of mass lockups and severe repression by prison officials. Although he had not been in Angola when the guard was killed, King suffered harsh torments. He was stripped of his clothing, had his head shaved, and was made to run the gauntlet past guards wielding bats and clubs. Eventually, he was locked in a cell that was about three feet wide by seven feet in length, with a slab of concrete for a bed and a naked toilet bowl. The daily food rations were so meagre that he constantly felt the threat of dying of starvation. After weeks in solitary confinement, he was brought before the prison classification board. Although King never met the slain guard, he was sent into solitary confinement for a further twenty-eight years, simply because he allied with the Black Panthers, who were accused of the guard's murder. King was locked in the Closed Correction Cell (CCR) unit of Angola prison from 1973 until 2001. He later became known as one of the "Angola Three," a trio of men kept in solitary confinement for decades. There, the convicts were kept in solitary cells for twenty-three hours a day, seven days a week. For years, King and the other two of the Angola Three were denied any time outside their six-by-nine-by-twelve-foot windowless cells, besides one hour dedicated to showering. In his biography, King remembered solitary confinement being a horrible experience that evoked a plethora of emotions in him. This experience required him to take every scrap of humanity to stay focused and sane. Those who did not cope, starved or mutilated themselves under the degrading conditions. Over all those years, he had maintained his innocence and appealed. Eventually, in 2001 he accepted a plea bargain and was released from prison, as he had already served longer than the sentence.

Since his exoneration, King became a forthright critic of the U.S. judicial system and speaks out on the need for prison reform. He dedicates his life to raising awareness about the psychological harms of solitary confinement.

Scientists agree that prolonged social isolation has severe physical, emotional, and cognitive impact, many of which may be irreversible. Isolation can cause mood swings and depression, cognitive impairment, such as impaired spatial orientation, memory, and attention abilities. Social seclusion is associated with a twenty-six percent increased risk of premature death due to an out-of-control stress response, causing higher cortisol levels, increased blood pressure, and inflammation. The activity of the amygdala is also increased in response to isolation, which indicates fear and anxiety, sometimes also triggering symptoms of psychosis. The sensory deprivation evoked by constant darkness in the cell contributes to alterations of the circadian rhythm, the internal biological clock that regulates the proper functioning of the body. This in turn can dramatically alter the activity of gene expression in the brain falling out of synchronization with one another, which affects eating, feeling, and thinking. Lastly, being socially isolated also drastically increases the risk of suicide. Thus, according to behavioral neuroscientist Stephanie Cacioppo, solitary confinement "is nothing less than the death penalty by social deprivation."[86]

Today, Robert King speaks at scientific conferences about the long-lasting effects of social isolation and sensory deprivation on the brain. Reflecting on his own cognitive experiences, he reports that his memory is significantly impaired and he can no longer navigate, not even in familiar places, making it difficult to get around. Neuroscientists attribute these symptoms to the sustained stress experienced during social isolation that has shown to lead to a loss of hippocampal plasticity, a decrease in the formation of new neurons, and hippocampal dysfunction. In addition to the damage to the hippocampus, other areas of King's neocortex also seem afflicted. Living outside prison, he quickly noticed that his conversation skills have become severely limited. Most strikingly, however, after returning to the world outside the prison walls, he was unable to recognize faces. Brain areas that are involved in facial recognition were hardly stimulated while King was locked up in the windowless cell without human contact. Neuroscientists therefore suspect that neurons of areas involved in face recognition such as the fusiform gyrus have atrophied. Luckily, King's atrophied brain areas seemed to have undergone neuroplasticity, as he slowly regained his ability to recognize faces after a while.

After being released from prison, King teamed up with scientists and lawyers who fought for the abolishment of solitary confinement. This request is not new. Pundits have convincingly argued for a long time that this form of social segregation is an extremely cruel and inhuman punishment based on centuries-old, religious corrective methods. In fact, the practice of solitary confinement was invented by Quaker reformers of the early nineteenth

---

[86] Sukel, "Understanding the Effects of Solitary Confinement on the Brain."

century. At that time, Quakers subjected wrongdoers to social isolation in correctional facilities to give them the opportunity for sober contemplation and penitence. However, already in the middle of the nineteenth century, shortly after the invention of these corrective measures, opposers strongly criticized the devastating psychological consequences for the inmates. For example, French diplomat, political scientist, and historian Alexis de Tocqueville, who traveled the U.S. to examine prisons and penitentiaries, reported in detail about his observations and reflections. After visiting New York State prison and seeing delinquents in solitary detention, de Tocqueville reported, "This absolute solitude ... is beyond the strength of man. It destroys the criminal without intermission and without pity; it does not reform, it kills."[87] More recent research has supported de Tocqueville's claims. In-depth studies of around two hundred inmates from prisons in Massachusetts and California who had experienced sustained solitary confinement revealed that most of the detainees developed syndromes of dissociation, confusion, paranoia, and chronic difficulties in social interaction.[88] Other studies of a hundred inmates kept in isolation at the supermax prison at Pelican Bay, California, demonstrated that prisoners suffered from confusion, anger, lethargy, and depression. Convicts who were kept in solitary cells exhibited clear signs of psychological stress. Seventy percent of them reported fearing an impending breakdown, forty percent experienced hallucinations, and twenty-seven percent had suicidal thoughts.[89] Furthermore, prisoners kept in socially segregated environments frequently perpetrated acts of self-mutilation, suicide attempts, and completed suicide. In 1988, suicide rates in U.S. detention centers were about nine times higher than in the general population[90] and were highest (66.9 percent) when inmates were held in isolation.

Physiological and psychological stress responses triggered by experiences of social isolation are especially severe in children and adolescents. They are particularly vulnerable due to an immature neuronal and hormonal stress response system, causing long-lasting effects on brain structure and function. Supporting the claim of the importance of age in overcoming social isolation, research on the psychological well-being of repatriated prisoners of the Vietnam war has consistently found that older age at capture strongly correlated with increased resilience to the experience of prolonged isolation

---

[87] de Beaumont and de Tocqueville, *On the Penitentiary System*, 5.
[88] Grassian, "Psychiatric Effects of Solitary Confinement," 325–383.
[89] Haney, "Mental Health Issues in Long-Term Solitary," 124–156.
[90] Hayes, "National Study of Jail Suicides," 7–29.

and torture. Thus, soldiers who were older and more experienced had a better chance of withstanding the extraordinary strains of captivity.[91]

Nonetheless, placing incarcerated juveniles into solitary confinement has remained common practice in many countries. Solitary confinement is administered for disciplinary, administrative, or personal protective reasons, and believed to be an effective measure for managing defiant behavior and maintaining discipline and safety within a detention facility. Alarmingly, out of one hundred completed suicides in juvenile detention facilities, fifty percent were found to have occurred when juveniles were confined to their rooms.[92] Also, in New York City jails, all acts of self-harm committed by adolescents under nineteen years of age most strongly correlated with the assignment to solitary confinement.[93] In these cases, self-harm may represent desperate attempts to avoid placement in the solitary unit.

Practice of solitary confinement has thus been widely condemned by health professionals, social workers, and human rights organizations. Some states in the U.S. have now passed legislation that significantly limit solitary confinement of mentally ill and juvenile offenders. The United Nations have issued Standard Minimum Rules for the Treatment of Prisoners that were revised in 2015 as the Nelson Mandela Rules.[94] These rules prohibit solitary confinement for children and for individuals with mental disabilities that will be exacerbated by measures of social isolation. The United Nations Special Rapporteur on Torture has labeled prolonged solitary confinement (more than fifteen days) as well as solitary confinement for juveniles and for adults with mental illness as cruel, inhuman, degrading, and possibly torturous.[95]

One of the most important lessons learned from Robert King's tragic case was that despite decades of sensory deprivation due to near-complete isolation, King's physiological and psychological symptoms were not as severe as would have been expected. King attributes this to the fact that he became part of a larger social group, the Black Panther Party, thereby seeing beyond his personal fate and fighting for a greater cause. Since he had supporters who believed that the "Angola Three" were falsely convicted for political reasons, he felt that surviving the ordeal would serve a larger purpose. Thus, King's connection to a larger social group and their shared goal most likely increased his resilience.

---

[91] Park et al., "Does Wartime Captivity Affect Late-Life Mental Health?," 191–209.
[92] Hayes, "Juvenile Suicide in Confinement," 353–363.
[93] Kaba et al., "Solitary Confinement and Risk of Self-Harm," 442–447.
[94] "Nelson Mandela Rules."
[95] "Report of the Special Rapporteur on Torture."

Behavioral neuroscientist Stephanie Cacioppo summed up that "collective identity is protective against individual loneliness."

Chapter 8

The Devastating Impact of Violence

When a child hits a child, we call it aggression. When a child hits an adult, we call it hostility. When an adult hits an adult, we call it assault. When an adult hits a child, we call it discipline.

— Haim G. Ginott

It was the time of Le Grande Noirceur (i.e., The Great Darkness) when poverty was widespread in Canada. The conservative Premier Maurice Duplessis of Quebec only meagerly invested in social services. Many families in Quebec who lived in extreme poverty and could not afford to raise their children sent them to orphanages. Other Quebecer "orphans" who were abandoned by their mothers were those children who were born out of wedlock and considered "children of sin." The orphaned children of that time gained sad fame as "Duplessis orphans."

In Canada, abandoned children were usually first placed in a crèche (i.e., a home for foundlings) until they were about six years old. In the crèche, children were cared for by nuns who looked over shared dormitories that housed up to twelve children. At the age of six, children were transferred to a single-sex orphanage. There, they lived in dormitories that housed around fifty children. Life was scarce in these institutions and kids received very limited education. Conditions in orphanages were quite bad all over the world at that time; however, during the period of Le Grande Noirceur, orphanages in Quebec became tied to a particularly horrid history. During the 1940s and 1950s, a sizable number of orphans in Quebec were wrongly diagnosed and labeled as mentally retarded. In fact, the Quebec government and the Roman Catholic Church falsely certified thousands of Quebec orphans as mentally ill. The reason for these children being declared mentally disabled was pure profit making. At that time, the federal government granted subsidies to the Quebec government for building hospitals, but it hardly supported orphanages. While orphanages received only 1.25 dollars a day per child, psychiatric clinics received 2.75 dollars a day per patient.[1] The fact that federal subsidies were

---

[1] Kimette, "The Duplessis Orphans."

much higher for hospitals than for orphanages provided a strong financial incentive for the reclassification of the Quebec orphans. As a result of these false diagnoses, orphans labeled mentally ill underwent psychiatric treatment, spent their childhood in confinement, and suffered from a lack of schooling and integration into any social community. Most shockingly, a lot of these children were covertly exploited for unauthorized human medical experimentation, from which many of them died. Orphaned children and adolescents who were lucky enough not to be subjected to psychiatric treatment were rented out to farms or village homes for hard labor, which the children described as exploitive. Those who survived finally left the institutions in their late teens or twenties, frequently with severe psychopathologies and psychosocial disorders.

It was 1946, during the time of Le Grande Noirceur, when Mary was born. From birth until she was six years old, she lived in a crèche. She could not remember whether any of the nuns took any interest in her. But she remembered how she often felt humiliated when "she had to go without shoes, because she was considered too tough on them, or when she had to walk around with her underwear on her head for a reason she could not remember."[2] When she asked the nuns why nobody ever came to pay a visit to her or the other orphans, she was slapped and told that she did not deserve to be visited. She recalled that she was sometimes locked in the bathtub or the laundry room where she would stare through the frosted windows and daydream. She also reported that she never spent Christmas with other kids. At the age of six, Mary was transferred to a hospital orphanage. There, she lived in a dormitory with a nun and a monitor to whom she developed a trusting relationship. Those were the happiest memories she had because she felt like she could confide in the nun, who taught her how to sew and would sometimes encourage her to study for a better future. But when Mary turned ten, the nun was sent away from the orphanage, and the nuns who took charge of the dormitory were much more severe and drastic in their punishments. The children were punished often without given any reason. Mary recalled a particularly sad event in her life when she and other kids received Christmas presents from well-meaning benefactors. Mary was extraordinarily happy to have received a doll, but the nuns took away the toys and never gave them back. Mary remembered how hard she cried after having the doll taken away. When Mary turned eleven, she was transferred to a room for mentally retarded children although the diagnosis was not specified. When she realized how badly the patients were treated there, she began to despair and cried frequently. At that time, she also worked at the cafeteria six days a week. Once, she lied about being sick, and when her lie was

---

[2] Perry et al., "Seven Institutionalized Children," 283–301.

discovered, she was severely punished. She was hit and locked in a cell. Because she reported the bad treatment, the nuns took even harsher measures to counteract her disobedience. Mary was tied to her bed with a straight jacket and hit with a chair for fifteen minutes. She lost consciousness and only remembered waking up the following morning. For the next eight years, Mary was mostly kept in this cell. Sometimes, when another patient or orphan was confined to the cells, Mary had to stay in the corridor. She remembered spending two weeks in the corridor at least once. The nuns had her tied to a pipe in the corridor with her straight jacket on and a pillowcase on her head. She was not allowed to talk to anyone, but she sometimes cried and screamed in desperation. The nuns would not have any of these emotional outbursts. To calm her down, she was given chlorpromazine at very high doses that caused cardiac palpitations. At the age of eighteen, she was diagnosed with severe cardiac problems. Mary remembered that when she was released from the cell, she had lost the ability to speak properly. It took her years to catch up linguistically. As a young adult, when she worked in a hospital, she was still derided because of her speech problem. During her adult life, she was sexually abused, physically exploited, and developed agoraphobic symptoms and social anxieties. Eventually, Mary re-learned how to speak, learned to write, and became involved in a romantic relationship that gave her hope and strength. She never wanted to have contact with other "Duplessis orphans," as she felt this would remind her of the degrading and abusive experiences of her childhood.

Mary's story as reported by Perry and co-workers[3] serves as a tragic example of a child who was raised almost exclusively by neglecting and abusive caregivers. Due to the lack of support by alloparents (i.e., adults other than parents who are involved in the upbringing of a child) who could compensate for the maltreatment, children like Mary who suffer from severe abuse usually develop a life-long disposition of fear and sadness. These social responses are actually adaptive, because not only do they help kids cope with severely adverse situations but also prepare them for survival in a highly stressful, violent social niche later in life.

Following this line of argument, human attachment theory (see Chapter 7) can be interpreted from an evolutionary perspective. Fear and depression expressed by children are considered adaptive social reactions. But what about abusive parents? It seems hardly adaptive from the parents' perspective to harm their biological offspring. Clearly, Darwinian fitness is diametrically opposed to violence against one's children. In other words, it is adaptive to increase the number of healthy offspring and maladaptive to reduce it. It thus

---

[3] Ibid.

stands to reason that evolution has selected against violent parental behavior. But this reasoning probably only pertains to parent-child relations who are genetically akin. In contrast, according to Darwinian fitness, violence can be adaptive if exerted toward non-kin descendants under certain circumstances. Probably the best-known examples of extreme violence committed by unrelated adults come from studies of lions. If a contending male lion takes over a pride, the intruder ousts the alpha lion and aims at killing all cubs of the pride. The infanticide causes the lionesses—that no longer have cubs to nurse—to go into estrous again and mate with the new alpha male. This behavior seems to make perfect sense in terms of Darwinian fitness. A new alpha lion does not gain fitness by investing resources into raising the other male's cubs. On the contrary, those cubs are most likely unrelated to the new alpha male and don't carry his genes. Hence, rather than raising unrelated young, a male lion will sire as many of his own young as possible to pass on his genes. Thus, infanticide by unrelated adult animals is not considered pathological in the animal kingdom, but recognized as part of a reproductive strategy. To counteract the evolutionary risk of infanticide by unrelated adults, some species have evolved effective counter-strategies. For example, females may be highly promiscuous (as is the case for Bonobos) thereby confusing males about which offspring they have fathered. By keeping males in the dark about whether an offspring is related to the male or not, females protect their offspring from putative infanticide.

Infanticide by unrelated adults has also been observed in other mammals, such as dolphins and almost every primate species, including chimpanzees, gorillas, and sadly, also humans. Evolutionary psychologists Martin Daly and Margo Wilson have shown that human infanticide is predominantly committed by unrelated males (e.g., stepfathers or "the new boyfriend" of the mother) rather than a child's genetic parent.[4] Drawing from statistical information from Canada, Daly and Wilson found that infants under three years of age are particularly at risk when living with one or two non-genetic parent(s). The authors claim that the risk of being killed is seventy times higher for children living in the same household with non-genetic parent(s) than for children living with two genetic parents. Supporting Daly and Wilson's findings, anthropologists have postulated that the risk of infants being killed by unrelated males was the key driver of evolution switching from a multi-male mating system to monogamy in humans and other primates.[5]

Infanticide is not limited to males, but females also kill infants. For example, infant survival of Norway rats correlates with the social rank of the mother. A

---

[4] Daly and Wilson, *Homicide.*

[5] Opie et al., "Male Infanticide Leads to Social Monogamy in Primates," 13328–13332.

study showed that while pups of high-ranking, unscarred rats were basically left unharmed, sixty percent of pups of low-ranking, scarred female rats were killed.[6] Also, in other species like suricates, dominant females commonly kill pups that are born to subordinates. One study reported that of the litters born to dominant females, most survived (eighty-five percent) and grew into pups, whereas only fifty-one percent of litters born to subordinate females grew into pups.[7] The newborns of subordinate mothers died usually within twenty-four hours, most likely due to infanticide. Infanticide by females is not limited to catlike and rodents, but also occurs in many primate species.[8] Sadly, humans are no exception to these findings.

Prima facie, violent behavior toward infants and infanticide seems to be plausibly explainable in terms of Darwinian fitness if the victim is unrelated. The death of non-genetic infants can benefit the perpetrator, representing a reproductive strategy. On the contrary, maltreatment and filicide (i.e., infanticide committed by biological parents) clearly contradict Darwinian fitness and seem non-adaptive. Harming or killing one's offspring jeopardizes the number of one's own healthy progeny and reduces fitness. Despite being seemingly maladaptive, filicide does occur. It is well-known that animals kept in confinement quite frequently kill, even devour, their young. Filicide has also been reported in the wild. For example, bird clutch sizes exhibit regional variations that strongly depend on environmental conditions, especially food supply[9] and availability of safe nesting sites. In plentiful environments, there is less competition for resources and therefore clutch size is at a maximum in many bird species. On the other hand, in relatively poor environments, competition is fierce and parents invest only in the largest and strongest nestlings. The smaller nestlings are neglected, left for starvation, siblicide, or filicide.[10] These extreme forms of violence toward the offspring seem irreconcilable with Darwinian fitness. To explain this conundrum, Robert Trivers suggested that filicide can be a result of parent-offspring conflict.[11] According to Trivers, this conflict has its biological foundation in the fact that parents and progeny are genetically non-identical, as they only share fifty percent of their genes. At the same time, parents as well as progeny are driven by natural selection to spread their genes. Hence, in extremely scarce or life-threatening conditions, parents and progeny display opposing interests. This

---

[6] Fox, "Cannibalism in Natural Populations," 87–106.
[7] Clutton-Brock et al., "Infanticide and Expulsion of Females," 2291–2295.
[8] Hrdy, "Infanticide among Animals," 13–40.
[9] Lack, "The Significance of Clutch-Size," 302–352.
[10] Lack, *The Natural Regulation of Animal Numbers.*
[11] Campbell and Trivers, "Parental Investment and Sexual Selection," 136–179.

can lead to dreadful incidents when parents trade their offspring's survival for their own. In cases of opposing interests between parents and offspring, parents trade reproductive success for their own survival. In many species, a mother facing poor or dangerous conditions for child rearing may abort or, where physiologically possible, reabsorb the fetus prior to birth.[12, 13, 14] A quite extreme strategy is adopted by female kangaroos. A mother kangaroo when under pursuit from a predator will sacrifice her baby by reaching into the pouch and throwing her joey into the predator's path to rescue herself.[15]

Importantly, the aforementioned examples of filicide in animals—whether explained in terms of parent-offspring conflict or not—occur in situations of extreme, often life-threatening stress. It may, therefore, be particularly instructive to consider stress and severely adverse life conditions when investigating infanticide in humans. Filicide has been reported throughout human history and can be found in every human culture. According to anthropologist Laila Williamson "[i]nfanticide has been practiced on every continent and by people on every level of cultural complexity, from hunter-gatherers to high civilizations, including our own ancestors. Rather than being an exception then, it has been the rule."[16] Liubov Ben-Noun, Professor Emeritus at Ben Gurion University of the Negev in Israel, claims that filicide, and in particular neonaticide, is and has always been a predominant phenomenon of socioeconomy. Ben-Noun has collected a devastating amount of historical and cross-cultural examples of infanticide, and has summarized the findings by stating that "infanticide victims are usually "superfluous" children whose mother is very poor or without rights; such children are often girls. Infanticide is epidemic in times of a famine or great increases in population."[17] Human mothers are most at risk of committing filicide if they detect a lack of social support, especially within the first few hours after birth. Italian psychologists Andrea Ciani and Lilybeth Fontanesi investigated 110 cases of mothers who killed their newborns.[18] They concluded that mothers who killed their babies had "no psychopathologies." Rather, their acts could be seen as reproductive disinvestment. By killing children born at times of hardship, parents aim at saving resources for future offspring born into better socioeconomic conditions. Phrased in this callous and brutish way, infanticide seems even more appalling to us. But taking a stroll through history, dead

---

[12] Baird, "The Influence of Social and Economic Factors on Stillbirths," 339–366.
[13] Bruce, "A Block To Pregnancy in the Mouse," 96–103.
[14] Fraser-Smith, "Male-Induced Pregnancy Termination in the Prairie Vole," 1211–1213.
[15] Low, "Environmental Uncertainty and the Parental Strategies," 197–213.
[16] Kohl, "Infanticide: An Anthropological Analysis," 61–75.
[17] Ben-Noun, *NEONATICIDE, INFANTICIDE AND FILICIDE.*
[18] Ciani and Fontanesi, "Mothers Who Kill Their Offspring," 519–527.

children were a familiar sight not so long ago. About 150 years ago, William Burke Ryan painted a picture of England that was stricken by widespread infanticide triggered by economic deprivation. In Ryan's words, nineteenth-century England was marked by the

> feeble wail of murdered childhood in its agony… at every turn: Turn where we may, still are we met by the evidence of a widespread crime. In the quiet of the bed room we raise the box-lid, and the skeletons are there. In the calm evening walk we see in the distance the suspicious looking bundle, and the mangled infant is within. By the canal-side, or in the water, we find the dead child. In the solitude of the wood we are horrified by the ghastly sight; and if we betake ourselves to the rapid rail in order to escape the pollution, we find at our journey's end that the mouldering remains of a murdered innocent have been our travelling companion.[19]

Over the last century, infanticide rates have dropped, especially in the Western world. Neonaticide rates decreased significantly in several countries due to the legalization of abortion.[20, 21] But infanticides continue at a much higher rate in areas of extreme poverty and overpopulation where female infants are much more at risk to get killed.[22] Besides sex-selective infanticide, infanticide in this day and age is a complicated and multi-factorial act, yet there are certain trends that can be identified that allow a tentative categorization of child murder.[23] Phillip Resnick created an influential classification of filicide that drew from psychiatric literature from 1751 to 1967. This classification has been further enhanced in more detail.[24] Resnik found five different motives that drove parents to kill their children: (1) Altruistic filicide that is committed by a parent who believes that the murder is in the child's "best interest." Those parents usually suffer from psychopathologies and often commit suicide or attempt suicide after killing their children. According to Resnik, this type of filicide can be seen as extended suicide. (2) Acute psychotic filicide committed by a psychotic parent with no rational motive. This concerns mothers or fathers who suffer from a mental disorder, struggle with many acute stressors in their lives, and lack personal resources or systemic support. (3) Unwanted child filicide committed by a parent who regards the child as a hindrance. Parents

---

[19] Ryan, "Infanticide: Its Law, Prevalence, Prevention and History," 1–27.
[20] Paul et al., "Clinical Assessment and Ultrasound in Early Pregnancy," 63–77.
[21] Brown and Eisenberg, *The Best Intentions.*
[22] "Gendercide Watch."
[23] Resnick, "Child Murder by Parents," 325–334.
[24] Guileyardo et al., "Familial Filicide and Filicide Classification," 286–292.

who kill their children to get "rid" of them because they are an "inconvenience" are usually not in difficult socioeconomic situations. Rather, the offenders benefit from their children's death in a cruelly "hedonistic" way, e.g., by inheriting insurance money, or being free to marry a partner who does not approve of step-children. (4) Spouse revenge filicide committed by a parent in order to hurt the spouse. In these cases, the act of violence is actually intended against the partner. The murder of the child is perceived by the perpetrator as "collateral damage." (5) Accidental filicide is committed when a parent unintentionally kills the child as a result of abuse.

Taken together, there is no single, simple explanation for infanticide. It, therefore, makes sense to turn to evolutionary theory as the first line of explanation of infanticide. Multiple reasons can contribute to infanticide, including psychopathologies, severely disturbed feelings, or highly anxious thoughts and beliefs about the child, and the relationship between parent and child. Many of the causal explanations of infanticide mentioned above are not primarily associated with child abuse, with the clear exception of the last category of Resnick's classification. This category, accidental filicide, is caused by parental aggression and violence. In the subsequent discussion, I will focus on this last category.

Importantly, a large body of research revealed that escalating violence leading to infanticide is often linked to the socioeconomic hardship of the perpetrator. This explanation, however, cannot fully capture the phenomenon. Deprivation—with respect to food, sleep, or social interactions—occurs quite frequently in the animal kingdom. Yet extreme violence leading to the offspring's death is relatively rare. Drawing from comparative ethology, researchers found that maternal infanticide is more prevalent in species that exhibit "cooperative breeding," i.e. when an infant is cared for by other group members in addition to the biological mother. In cooperative breeders, mother and offspring largely depend on their social support system rather than relying solely on their own resources. This is clearly the case for humans, which have essentially been termed a cooperative breeding species.[25] As described in Chapter 3 (Normalcy in the Light of Plasticity), the onset of agriculture in human populations and the increase in community size offered females access to extended kin and non-kin social support by means of prosocial child rearing practices as well as high caloric diet. These evolutionary incidents causally contributed to reduced intervals between births and to higher overall birth rates in humans.[26] Following a positive feedback loop, short inter-birth

---

[25] Hrdy, "Infanticide among Animals," 13–40.
[26] Bocquet-Appel and Bar-Yosef, "Xplaining the Neolithic Demographic Transition," 35–55.

intervals and the high investment in a child drove young mothers to even more strongly depend on social support systems. Yet social support can be a two-edged sword. If social support from group members is lacking, young mothers will consequentially struggle with fulfilling their maternal roles. Biologically speaking, high reproduction rates do not unequivocally correlate with well-being, but frequently run counter to it. While having more children is equated with success in terms of Darwinian fitness, it can be quite bad for the mother's well-being. Therefore, experiencing a lack of social support is experienced as an evolutionary tocsin to signal the mother that her own survival is at risk. This risk is exacerbated when the mother is not only isolated from her family but also when economic circumstances are dire. A lack of economic and capital assets limits access to non-kin childcare as well as parental empowerment. In the postpartum period, maternal responsiveness is highly sensitive to cues of social support. In this sensitive period, an endurable social network makes sure that a young mother quickly recovers from the strains of giving birth, remains healthy, and can provide enough milk for the baby. If on the other hand, a mother feels that her support system is not viable, she may recoil from raising the child alone and stop investing in her child. Primatologist Sarah Blaffer Hrdy argues that in previous times, nature acted as a pacesetter for the timing of primipara (i.e., giving birth to the first child). Young women's health and nutritional status would set the time for ovulation and conception. A young woman in the Pleistocene who experienced a lack of support by her group would suffer from malnutrition and would thus likely face physiological difficulties for getting pregnant. In modern times, in large parts of the Western world, severe undernourishment is no longer an issue. Due to the availability of high caloric nutrition, nowadays women ovulate at a very young age. But being well-fed and healthy does not necessarily correlate with having stable social support for raising a child. As concluded by Ciani and Fontanesi, neonaticide is almost always committed by relatively young, poor women, usually with no partners and little social support. Hence, neonaticide and filicide should be looked at as problems of a given society rather than viewing them as inscrutable, individual cases. This alternative perspective that emphasizes socioeconomic stress as a main factor contributing to infanticide highlights the necessity of well-functioning support systems for socially isolated, economically burdened mothers.

This line of argument is supported by the findings of a Swedish research team. The team surveyed all child homicides that occurred in Sweden between 1975 and 1995. The researchers found that in contrast to data from Canada analyzed by Daly and Wilson (see previously in this chapter) children in Sweden who lived in families with a step-parent were not at higher risk of getting killed than children living with both their genetic parents.[27] There were actually no indications that step-parents are more likely to become offenders. Moreover, while Daly and Wilson's work revealed that the risk of infanticide was particularly high for very young children, the Swedish study also did not confirm the Canadian findings. The Canadian study reported that the estimated risk per million children per year when living with one non-genetic and one genetic parent declined with the increase of children's age: for kids up to three years of age, the risk of being murdered was 0.064 percent (i.e., 640 infanticides per million children per year), for kids up to six years of age, it was 0.0135 percent, and for kids older than six years of age, it fell to less than 0.001 percent. In the Swedish study, however, there was no indication that very young children were at a higher risk of being killed than older children when living in families with one step-parent. The average rate of infanticide was 0.00034 percent (i.e., 3.4 infanticides per million children per year when living with one genetic and one non-genetic parent) with no significant differences between children's age from zero to fifteen years. The differences between the data from Canada and Sweden are striking, especially when taking into consideration that about four times more young children (aged zero to four years old) live with a step-parent in Sweden than in Canada (1.7 percent in Sweden versus 0.4 percent in Canada). Thus, the Swedish study seriously questions oversimplified Neo-Darwinian interpretations (i.e., a purely gene-centric view of natural selection, ignoring processes like niche construction, social selection, and others) of human filicide (as it showed that there was no prevalence of infanticide by unrelated perpetrators). The claim that killing non-kin offspring and spreading one's genetic legacy are the main drivers of infanticide seems to fall short as an explanation when including cultural and social factors. The Swedish study authors argue that one major reason that Swedish children living with non-genetic parents are *not* at a higher risk of becoming murder victims is due to sociocultural differences. Sweden has a long history of legal abortions. As a consequence, the occurrence of unwanted births is relatively low in Sweden.[28] On the contrary, countries that have stricter abortion laws have much higher rates of unwanted births. As a consequence, so the study authors speculate, children who are born from unwanted pregnancies are entangled in cascades of emotionally destructive processes of their parents. This may be especially true for young mothers who find themselves in unstable social situations, sometimes at the mercy of a violent partner (irrespective of the partner being the child's biological father). Economic and social instability can

---

[27] Temrin et al., "Step–Parents and Infanticide," 943–945.

[28] *Sharing Responsibility: Women, Society and Abortion Worldwide.*

trigger emotional outbursts, violence, maltreatment, in the worst case leading to infanticide. This interpretation emphasizes the importance of social support for raising a child. This collaborative effort in child rearing is memorably captured by the African proverb "[i]t takes a village to raise a child."

What stands out in the debate about violent intergenerational conflicts leading to infanticide is that fatally violent behavior almost always occurs in situations of extreme stress, often culminating in existential threat. It is crucial to elucidate what parents may perceive as threats in a given environment. Threatening factors can vary in different social and cultural niches, though neurophysiological parameters for maternal filicide will be comparable across cultures and social niches and are a result of increased individual vulnerability and overwhelming environmental stress. Investigating this assumption, an Italian research team studied hormone levels of criminally insane, filicidal women.[29] For testing, the researchers selected filicidal inpatients from a high-security psychiatric hospital for the criminally insane and matched them with psychiatric, non-filicidal, criminal mothers with comparable traumatic abuse records. Filicidal mothers had higher cortisol levels and significantly higher adrenocorticotropin hormone (ACTH) levels than both the normative values and those of non-filicidal inpatients. Under stressful conditions, the human body typically responds with alterations of the stress axis (HPA axis). This leads to an increased release of corticosteroids like cortisol into the blood. The increased corticosteroid level can either occur in a transient manner as in healthy subjects under temporary stress or in a chronic manner, such as in patients with major depression. Importantly, it can be expected that there is a positive correlation between cortisol and ACTH levels. This means higher levels of cortisol in the plasma ensure increased ACTH production. This correlation between cortisol and ACTH was shown in the aforementioned study of psychiatric, non-filicidal, criminal mothers. While cortisol levels of homicidal mothers were twenty percent higher than normal adult ranges, the levels were not significantly higher than that found in non-filicidal, convicted perpetrators. The same study showed that mothers who killed their own children exhibited little correlation between the two hormones, ACTH and cortisol. In homicidal mothers, ACTH plasma levels were on average fifty percent higher than ACTH levels in all other control groups, including non-filicidal criminals. This divergence happened despite the fact that the study was performed about four years after the filicides and convicted perpetrators received pharmacological treatment, which should have rebalanced the women's hormone levels. This pattern of untypical physiological parameters points to a link between filicidal behavior, severe depression, and altered HPA function. Enhanced and long-

---

[29] Spironelli et al., "Cortisol and ACTH Plasma Levels," 622–627.

lasting release of cortisol and ACTH marks a severely altered functioning of the HPA axis with reduced sensitivity of adrenal glands and pituitary glands to the negative feedback of cortisol.[30, 31] The negative feedback mechanism is the most important homeostatic control of stress modulation. The feedback loop prevents an uncontrolled hypersecretion of glucocorticoids that would be harmful to the body. However, in cases of chronic stress and major depression, the stress axis is dysregulated, which is physiologically associated with high stable levels of cortisol, ACTH, and corticotropin-releasing factor (CRF).[32, 33, 34] Also, depressed patients who suffer from violent suicidal behavior show HPA dysregulation and altered cortisol homeostasis.[35] The imbalance of cortisol and ACTH indicates a reduced secretion efficiency of the adrenal glands and concomitant chronic hyper-cortisolism. This disturbance of the stress axis is most likely due to long-term affective stress from which the filicidal women suffered and which preceded child homicide. Psychosocial stressors that could have worsened psycho-biological stress-sensitivity and contributed to the precipitation of violent behavior leading to filicide are lack of family support, severe family conflicts, unemployment, and unwanted pregnancies. In fact, clinical records of homicidal mothers supported these assumptions. Before admission to the psychiatric hospital for the criminally insane, the convicted women had reportedly suffered from various adverse and traumatic events, such as loss and grievance, serious problems in their family of origin (e.g., growing up with a depressed mother and/or an alcoholic father, and/or sexual abuse in childhood or adolescence), complicated pregnancies, and typically faced a lack of support and help from partners. Despite the observation that environmental stressors and traumatic experiences of both groups—filicidal mothers and psychiatrically matched controls—were similar, the main factor that differentiates the two groups is the dispositional vulnerability to externalized violent behavior. Biological vulnerability causes women to react to the same hostile environment through antisocial behavior, psychotic depression, drug abuse, or, in most extreme cases, with filicide.[36] Typically, biologically young women seem to display greater psychobiological sensitivity to stressful and adverse stimuli, manifesting itself in an overall larger startle reflex and startle-aversive modulation. Typically, biologically more vulnerable

---

[30] Barden et al., "Do Antidepressants Stabilize Mood through Actions," 6–11.

[31] Stokes, "The Potential Role of Excessive Cortisol," 77–82.

[32] Carroll et al., "Urinary Free Cortisol Excretion in Depression," 43–50.

[33] Dedovic et al., "The Brain and the Stress Axis," 864–871.

[34] Heit et al., "Corticotropin-Releasing Factor, Stress, and Depression," 186–194.

[35] Roy, "Hypothalamic-Pituitary-Adrenal Axis Function," 812–816.

[36] Spironelli et al., "Cortisol and ACTH Plasma Levels," 622–627.

women with higher sensitivity to stress have hyperactive amygdalae.[37] The amygdala controls the HPA axis (as discussed in Chapter 5), thereby influencing stress-dependent cortisol production. Cortisol appears to act as a biological marker of vulnerability to major depression and comorbid anxiety.[38] This in turn can drive the development of a severe mood disorder associated with filicidal behavior. Accordingly, environmental stress may trigger extreme behavioral patterns if an individual has the misfortune of being genetically predisposed to high vulnerability.

As discussed in Chapter 4, scientists have found genetic predispositions that are associated with increased violent behavior, although genetic variants alone do not pose a determinant for developing violent or antisocial behavior. These genetic/allelic variants seem to take effect only when environmental risk factors are also present. Psychologists Avshalom Caspi and Terrie Moffitt tried to disentangle the classic nature versus nurture question with respect to violent behavior and looked at individual vulnerability to maltreatment. They drew from data material of the Dunedin Multidisciplinary Health and Development Study, one of the most comprehensive and probing investigations of human development. The Dunedin Study was launched in 1972 and provided a meticulous and detailed observations of the life courses of about one thousand New Zealanders. Using the Dunedin Study, Caspi and Moffitt searched for genetic and epigenetic risk factors for antisocial behavior of people who experienced childhood violence and abuse. They found that about half of the boys with abusive childhoods grew into men who committed violent crimes.[39] Caspi and Moffitt analyzed the DNA of the Dunedin Study members for the MAO-A gene and MAO-A enzyme activity (a gene we have already encountered in Chapter 4 when we took a closer look at Bradley Waldroup's case of capital offense). They found that those men who were maltreated as children were far more likely to become violent adults if they had low levels of MAO-A activity. They concluded that the MAO-A gene influenced criminal behavior. This effect was only detectable when perpetrators suffered childhood abuse. Those study participants who did not experience maltreatment in their childhood did not show any correlation between MAO-A activity and violence.

Besides the gender-specific vulnerability linked to MAO-A gene activity in males, other genetic variabilities that underlie stress-triggered vulnerability have been found more frequently in women. Compared to men, women have been shown to generally exhibit a greater psychobiological sensitivity to

---

[37] Frodl et al., "Larger Amygdala Volumes in First Depressive Episode," 338–344.
[38] Vreeburg et al., "Major Depressive Disorder," 617–626.
[39] Caspi, "Influence of Life Stress on Depression," 386–389.

stressful situations and adverse stimuli[40] as measured by an overall larger startle reflex and stronger startle-aversive modulation. This gender-specific difference in vulnerability toward stress correlates with the observation that women have a greater disposition for major depression and comorbid anxiety.[41] Patients with first-episode depression showed enlarged amygdala volumes[42] that seem to correlate with enhanced cerebral blood flow, increased metabolism in the amygdala of depressed patients,[43] and overactivation of the amygdala,[44] indicating higher neural activity. As discussed previously, the amygdala is a paired brain region of the limbic system that is involved in aggression as well as in fear generation and processing. Hyperactivation of the amygdalae most likely co-occurs with an increase in stress response via hypothalamic-pituitary-adrenal (HPA) axis and a subsequent increase in the production of stress-dependent cortisol for a prolonged time. Hypercortisolism, in turn, has been implicated in the pathophysiology of major depression and comorbid anxiety. Caspi and Moffitt, the psychologists who identified genetic variants of the MAO-A gene that exacerbated children's sensitivity to maltreatment, looked into genetic factors that influenced vulnerability to depression. The patient samples were again taken from the members of the Dunedin Multidisciplinary Health and Development Study. In their prospective-longitudinal study, Caspi and Moffitt found variations (so-called functional polymorphisms) in the regulatory sequence of a serotonin transporter (5-HTT) gene that predicted genetic vulnerability to adult depression in those patients who were previously exposed to childhood maltreatment.[45] In other words, childhood abuse significantly enhanced the risk of suffering from major depression in adulthood when paired with a vulnerable genetic makeup. Individuals with one or two copies of one genetic variant (i.e., the short allele of the 5-HTT promoter polymorphism) exhibited more depressive symptoms, diagnosable depression, and suicidality when previously encountering stressful life events than individuals with two copies of the other variant who encountered equally stressful life events. Stressful life events that were taken into consideration by the researchers involved threat, loss, humiliation, or defeat, which all have been reported to influence the onset

[40] Bianchin and Angrilli, "Gender Differences in Emotional Responses," 925–932.
[41] Vreeburg et al., "Major Depressive Disorder," 617–626.
[42] Frodl et al., "Larger Amygdala Volumes in First Depressive Episode," 338–344.
[43] Abercrombie et al., "Metabolic Rate in the Right Amygdala," 3301–3307.
[44] Sheline et al., "Increased Amygdala Response to Masked Emotional Faces," 651–658.
[45] Caspi, "Influence of Life Stress on Depression," 386–389.

and course of depression.[46, 47, 48, 49] Caspi and Moffitt's epidemiological study provided clear evidence of a gene–environment interaction, in which an individual's psychopathology is influenced by a crosstalk between his or her genetic makeup and childhood experiences.

At the same time, it is particularly noteworthy that individuals with other genetic variants were not as susceptible to environmental risks as those more vulnerable individuals. Not all people who encounter equally stressful life experiences succumb to depressogenic effects or become violent as adults. Some people have a high genetic risk for developing certain psychopathologies after a stressful event, while others have a low genetic risk for those psychopathologies under the same circumstances.[50] By implication, some people are better protected against environmental insults. This means certain genetic variants provide resilience against adversities. To which extent genes exacerbate or buffer the effects of stressful life events is a matter of debate. Critics of this gene-centric approach have pointed out that genetic effects only show in people who have been exposed to severely stressful events during childhood and that the effects that are found are so small and variable as to be dwarfed by the effects of childhood abuse itself.

Physical, sexual, and emotional abuse as well as other stressful life events (death of a caregiver, neglect, bullying, etc.) in childhood cause excessive and prolonged activation of stress response systems in the body and brain. Experiencing maltreatment in childhood is comparable to a traumatic event or series of chronic traumatic events (see also Chapter 6). It activates the body's biological stress response systems and has behavioral and emotional effects that are similar to symptoms arising after PTSD. The physiological response protects the individual against environmental life threats by shifting metabolic resources away from "routine operation" toward a "fight or flight" (and/or freezing) reaction. Abusive stressors cause information from the sensory systems to get processed via the thalamus and activate the amygdala, priming the body for fear detection. Cortisol levels become elevated through the transmission of fear signals to the prefrontal cortex, hypothalamus, and hippocampus, and activity increases in the sympathetic nervous system. The intense and/or lasting activation of the stress response systems can derail healthy brain development and damage other organ systems—a noxious process that is frequently referred to as toxic stress. Often, toxic stress response

46 Brown, "Genetic and Population Perspectives," 363–372.
47 Kendler et al. "Causal Relationship Between," 837–842.
48 Kessler, "The Effects of Stressful Life Events on Depression," 191–214.
49 Pine et al., "Adolescent Life Events as Predictors of Adult Depression," 49–57.
50 Kendler et al., "Stressful Life Events," 833–842.

is triggered by multiple sources, for example, when physical or emotional abuse co-occur with chronic neglect, substance abuse by caregivers, or mental illness of attachment figures, or the accumulated burdens of economic hardship without adequate adult support. Such toxic stress has damaging effects on cognitive functions, behavior, and health in general across one's lifespan.

Studies of long-term consequence of early childhood trauma experiences have shown that cortisol does not remain constantly elevated throughout life, whereas corticotropin-releasing factor (CRF) elevation seems to persist into adulthood. It came as a surprising observation that adult victims of childhood trauma often showed significantly lower cortisol levels[51, 52] than non-abused controls. In fact, the longer the time that passed between trauma and testing for physiological markers, the lower the cortisol and ACTH levels were measured. As discussed in detail in Chapter 6, at the onset of trauma, ACTH and cortisol levels are significantly elevated. Prolonged stress exposure and elevated levels of CRF, however, cause a rebalancing of the stress system by downregulating psychobiological responses. This attenuation process of components of the stress axis has been demonstrated in a longitudinal psychobiological study of sexually abused girls. In this study, researchers assessed cortisol levels of sexually abused girls at six time points from childhood to young adulthood. Cortisol levels were always measured under non-stress conditions. Initially, shortly after the abused girls reported the sexual assaults, non-stress cortisol was significantly higher than in non-abused girls. But as more and more time passed, cortisol levels in the abused girls were attenuated. Eventually, when tested as young adults, those women who were abused had significantly lower cortisol levels compared to non-abused females.[53] Similar results have been found in adults suffering from PTSD derived from past trauma.[54, 55] Thus, (complex) trauma experiences reset the HPA axis, leading to a paradoxically low baseline of ACTH and cortisol secretions during "normal," everyday conditions. In this way, organisms adapt to perpetual, challenging conditions by down-regulating potentially harmful components of the stress response to prevent physical harm of the body. Yet these physiological countermeasures come at the expense of an adequate stress response—a psychophysiological phenomenon that is referred to as allostatic load.[56] Without the adequate response system in place, new stressors

---

[51] Miller et al., "If It Goes up, Must It Come down?," 25–45.
[52] Yehuda et al., "Low Urinary Cortisol Excretion in Holocaust Survivors," 982–986.
[53] Trickett et al., "Attenuation of Cortisol," 165–175.
[54] Martin et al., "Endocrine Aspects of PTSD," 245–206.
[55] Yehuda et al., "Low Urinary Cortisol Excretion in Holocaust Survivors," 982–986.
[56] McEwen, "Physiology and Neurobiology of Stress and Adaptation: 873–904.

trigger increasingly intense stress responses. This sensitization (also called priming) to even minor traumatic reminders exacerbate vulnerability to stress, thereby increasing the allostatic load throughout lifetime.

Particularly strong effects of sensitization were found in post-institutionalized children from Romanian or Russian orphanages who suffered from severe neglect during early infancy and were later adopted by parents in the U.S. At the time of testing, the children had spent at least three years with their adoptive parents. When the post-institutionalized children interacted with their adoptive mothers, their basal cortisol levels increased in response to parental interactions during playtime.[57] Thus, traumatized children generalize caregiver interactions as reminders of the emotional trauma when they were previously exposed to severe neglect from institutional rearing. Paradoxically, due to the disruption of the normal regulation of the HPA axis, post-institutionalized children experience close physical contact with a caregiver as particularly challenging (i.e., "priming") rather than as a buffer against sociobiological stress. The take-home message for caregivers and foster parents, therefore, is that severely traumatized, post-institutionalized children remain in an "alarm state" at their new homes for several years, despite being provided with a safe and loving environment. Toxic stress effects in traumatized children are more pronounced the more severe the experiences of socioemotional neglect were, the worse the overall quality of care (starvation, freezing, lack of physical contact, etc.) was, and the more sources of traumatization (e.g., neglect in addition to poverty and physical, sexual, or emotional abuse) were endured. Stress responses caused by multiple sources have a cumulative toll on an individual's physical and mental health (i.e., allostatic load). As a rule of thumb, the more frequent adverse experiences a child encountered, the greater the likelihood of developmental and cognitive delays and health problems, such as heart disease, diabetes, substance abuse, and depression. It is important to recall that cortisol and glucocorticoids in general are not commonly harmful but exert vital bodily functions during conditions of eustress (i.e., positive stress). Short-term increase in cortisol levels enhance learning and memory (via preferential stimulation of a certain type of high-affinity receptors in the hippocampus). Only during distress does cortisol interfere with learning and memory formation. Because cortisol levels are sustained, they are high enough to saturate another receptor type, namely low-affinity glucocorticoid receptors[58] that are also abundant in the hippocampus. Stress-mediated cognitive impairment correlates with hippocampal-related deficits in spatial

---

[57] Fries et al., "Neuroendocrine Dysregulation," 588–599.
[58] McEwen and Sapolsky, "Stress and Cognitive Function," 205–216.

navigation, episodic memory[59, 60] and verbal memory.[61] In the long run, traumatic stressors cause morphological changes in the hippocampus, reducing the number of dendritic spines and branches of neurons in a subregion of the hippocampus[62] and suppressing the production of new neurons in another hippocampal subregion.[63] Interestingly, while stress impairs hippocampal memory tasks, it enhances competing non-hippocampal (e.g., amygdala-related) memory tasks in rats and humans.[64, 65] The amygdala, which enhances cortisol secretion in response to stress itself undergoes stress-induced changes in the cytoarchitecture. In the amygdala, stress increases dendritic arborizations and spines of neurons. These morphological changes are regarded as mechanisms that underlie stress-associated anxiety disorders. [66]

A team of researchers from NYU School of Medicine led by developmental behavioral neuroscientist Regina Sullivan used animal studies to disentangle the effects of abusive parenting from the related stress that follows it and the involvement of the amygdala and the hippocampus. The scientists prompted abusive behavior in rodent mothers during the pivotal first weeks of life of the pups when mother–infant bonds are formed by withholding sufficient nesting materials. Shortage of nesting materials induces rough handling of pups by the mother. Just after one week of abuse by the mother, the young rats suffered sinistral (i.e., left) hippocampal damage due to stress from abuse. The same was true if the rat pups were injected with stress-inducing drugs irrespective of maternal abuse. Thus, during the critical first weeks after birth, elevated stress hormones alone—regardless of social context—are sufficient for shrinkage of the infants' hippocampi.[67] The results found in rats replicate extensive work in humans that shows enhanced effects of maltreatment on the volume of the left hippocampus.[68, 69] This effect of toxic stress is most likely due to an indirect mediation of glucocorticoid via glutamate.[70] Since newborns and infants cannot yet regulate stress responses themselves due to an immature

---

[59] Kim and Diamond, "The Stressed Hippocampus," 453–462.

[60] Ajai Vyas et al., "Chronic Stress Induces Contrasting Patterns," 6810–6818.

[61] Bremner et al., "MRI-Based Measurement of Hippocampa," 973–981.

[62] Conrad et al., "Repeated Restraint Stress," 902–913.

[63] Schoenfeld and Gould, "Stress, Stress Hormones, and Adult Neurogenesis," 12–21.

[64] Kim et al., "Amygdala Is Critical for Stress-Induced Modulation" 5222–5228.

[65] L. Schwabe and O. T. Wolf, "Stress Modulates," 11042–11049.

[66] Vyas et al., "Chronic Stress Induces Contrasting Patterns," 6810–6818.

[67] Raineki et al., "During Infant Maltreatment," 22821–22832.

[68] Teicher et al., "Childhood Maltreatment Is Associated," E563–E572.

[69] Stein et al., "Hippocampal Volume in Women," 951–959.

[70] Armanini et al., "Glucocorticoid Endangerment," 7–12.

physiology, they rely on their mother or primary caregiver to soothe them in order to attenuate stress hormone release in the young bodies. This process of maternal stress regulation in the child is termed social buffering; however, abusive caregivers compromise the default process of social buffering. Rather than buffering stress hormones, they become elevated because of maltreatment. Moreover, the infant learns that stress always occurs when the mother is present. The combined physiological and social effects (i.e., the increment of stress hormones and the simultaneously perceived cues like smell, sound, and sight of the mother) caused hyperactivity of the amygdala in the pups and triggered infant social behavior deficits. The maltreated pups showed aberrant social behavior with the mother, such as reduced nursing time and more time behind the mother's back instead of nursing. This effect was not due to high levels of stress hormones alone; it required a social context (the mother's presence even if she was anesthetized) for infants to learn to associate social features (e.g., the abusive mother's smell or visual appearance) with negative cues. Elevated stress hormones without the mother's presence neither caused amygdala impairment nor aberrant social behavioral in pups. In other words, infant rodents learn to pair stress with the caregiver's presence, which then leads to an impaired attachment and initiates developmental perturbations in the infant. This perturbation is due to the precocious activation of the amygdala that increases anxiety and disrupts social behavior toward the mother.

Regina Sullivan's findings are highly instructive for understanding psychological and neurobiological development in humans. In most mammals, some features of infant ontogeny like species-typical amygdala maturation are crucially dependent upon maternal presence during stress. This interplay of maternal care and environmental factors illustrates the importance of social figures in guiding brain development. Paradoxically, other animal experiments confirmed that pups continue to respond to the mother as an attachment figure despite her abusive behavior, but they reduce prosocial interactions with her. It is known from animal experiments that abusive caregiving, including administration of physical pain (e.g., electroshocks) in the presence of a caregiver elicits an approach response to the caregiver (i.e., fostering attachment) rather than an aversion.[71] Neonates have shown to form memories of odors associated with both pleasant or aversive stimuli. This paradoxical response relies on the neural circuitry of the infant brain that is probably specialized to optimize the learning necessary for mother-infant attachment, irrespective of the actual maternal behavior. From a neurobiological point of view, attachment learning of aversive stimuli by the

---

[71] Bolhuis and Honey, "Imprinting, Learning and Development," 306–311.

caregiver is enabled by the attenuation of fear and avoidance, which is typically mediated by the amygdala. It has been shown in rodents that attenuated aversion learning relies not only on the hypofunctioning of the amygdala but also on the hyperfunctioning of the norepinephrinenergic locus coeruleus. The locus coeruleus stimulates reward by releasing high levels of norepinephrine, which prevents habituation to repeated stimuli presentations by the caregiver. This circuitry is only hyperactive during the early attachment period.[72] Yet, there is little neuroplasticity of the amygdala during attachment learning.[73, 74] Consequently, fear responses such as cued fear conditioning, inhibitory conditioning, and passive avoidance do not functionally emerge in infants until after the sensitive period of attachment learning has terminated.[75] Synaptic plasticity of the amygdala starts only at the end of the sensitive period of attachment learning. At that time point, infants begin to discriminate between preferences and aversions. Preference as well as aversion learning rely on processes of classical conditioning.[76] It is most noteworthy that the amygdala is not part of the neural network that is involved in the social behavior of typically developing infants. Only if the quality of parental care is bad, does the amygdala gets hyperactivated at an early childhood age (as in the aforementioned case of maltreated pups). Importantly, the sensitive period of attachment learning can be altered depending on the level of stress hormones; the higher the levels the quicker fear learning mediated by the amygdala is initiated. Thus, stress hormones have a direct impact on infant conditioning by switching from attachment to avoidance learning. The child's precocious amygdala activation then disrupts social behavior with the mother, as also shown in non-human primates.[77, 78] Consequently, if the quality of maternal care is low, infants typically exhibit heightened anxiety mediated by amygdala hyperactivity and show disrupted social behavior of mother-infant interactions.[79] This is in good agreement with behavioral deficits detected in children with insecure attachment styles when they are exposed to stressful situations.[80] Most of the neurobiological data concerning attachment versus preference/avoidance learning come from animal data. Despite the high homology between mammals (including humans) concerning neuronal

---

[72] Moriceau and Sullivan, "Unique Neural Circuitry," 1182–1189.

[73] Barr et al., "Transitions in Infant Learning," 1367–1369.

[74] Sullivan et al., "Good Memories of Bad Events in Infancy," 38–39.

[75] Moriceau and Sullivan, "Maternal Presence Serves as a Switch, 1004–1006.

[76] Roth and Sullivan, "Memory of Early Maltreatmen," 823–831.

[77] Bachevalier et al., "Effects of Selective Neonatal Temporal Lobe," 545–559.

[78] Amaral, "The Amygdala, Social Behavior, and Danger Detection," 337–347.

[79] Raineki et al., "Developing a Neurobehavioral Animal Model," 1137–1145.

[80] Ainsworth and Bell, "Attachment, Exploration, and Separation," 4967.

circuitries as well as underlying neuromolecular processes, it is difficult to transfer results about developmental time frames from animal studies to humans. Most noteworthy is the Bucharest Early Intervention Project,[81, 82] which has provided evidence that the sensitive period for attachment learning in human infants ranges from the first to third year of life, depending on the behavioral neural system being studied.

The Bucharest Early Intervention Project as well as many other studies have clearly demonstrated that child maltreatment is a potent risk factor for psychopathologies. It is important to point out that when maltreatment is terminated after an extended episode of abuse, stress hormone levels return to the baseline and social behavior appears normal. However, latent maltreatment effects reappear at a later time point and neurobehavioral deficits again emerge.[83] In abused children, reduced amygdala and hippocampal volume have been observed[84] that probably contribute to alterations in fear conditioning following maltreatment. Furthermore, experiencing stress in early childhood is associated with changes in the ventromedial prefrontal cortex's thickness and volume,[85, 86] indicating impaired extinction learning.[87] Extinction learning refers to the observation that response to a conditioned stimulus (e.g., fear response) gradually decreases when the stimulus is presented without reinforcement. Childhood abuse interferes with the extinction of conditioned fear and this in turn can contribute to trauma-related psychopathologies.[88, 89] Both, people who experienced childhood abuse and patients suffering from posttraumatic stress disorder (PTSD) fail to maintain extinction learning.[90] Crucial for normal fear extinction learning is the ventromedial prefrontal cortex that projects to both, the amygdala and hippocampus thereby exerting inhibitory action during stress. PTSD patients' fear response as well as abused children's fear response do not gradually decrease despite the respective conditioned stimulus being presented again and again without reinforcement. They simply cannot inhibit their fear memory, even in the presence of safety cues.[91]

---

[81] Nelson et al., "Cognitive Recovery in Socially Deprived Young Children," 1937–1940.

[82] Smyke et al., "A New Model of Foster Care for Young Children,". 721–734.

[83] Raineki et al., "Developing a Neurobehavioral Animal Model," 1137–1145.

[84] Hanson et al., "Behavioral Problems After Early Life Stress," 314–323.

[85] Hanson et al., "Early Stress Is Associated with Alterations," 7466–7472.

[86] Milad et al., "Thickness of Ventromedial Prefrontal Cortex," 10706–10711.

[87] Hartley et al., "Brain Structure Correlates of Individual Differences," 1954–1962.

[88] Jovanovic and Ressler, "How the Neurocircuitry and Genetics of Fear," 648–662.

[89] Lissek and van Meurs, "Learning Models of PTSD," 594–605.

[90] Milad et al., "Neurobiological Basis of Failure," 1075–1082.

[91] Jovanovic and Seth Norrholm, "Neural Mechanisms of Impaired Fear."

The impaired maturation of the prefrontal cortex as a consequence of childhood maltreatment is particularly noteworthy. The prefrontal cortex undergoes the most striking and protracted change during adolescence and early adulthood. The functional deficits that result from damage to the human frontal lobe are diverse and devastating, particularly if both hemispheres are involved. The broad range of clinical effects stems from the fact that the frontal cortex has a wider repertoire of functions than any other neocortical region. It is involved in a wide variety of high-level cognitive and executive functions, including decision making, planning, inhibition of inappropriate or risk-taking behavior, social interactions (e.g., understanding other people), and self-awareness. The frontal cortex integrates complex perceptual information from sensory and motor cortices, as well as from the parietal and temporal association cortices. The result is an appreciation of self in relation to the world that allows behaviors to be planned and executed normally. When this ability is compromised, the afflicted individual often has difficulty carrying out complex behaviors that are appropriate to the circumstances. This effect is exacerbated in stressful situations, even when the trigger is only minor, because the inhibitory regulation of the stress response is spectacularly failing. For example, anxiety disorders and externalizing psychopathology have been associated with childhood abuse. General anxiety disorders have been demonstrated to be associated with an exaggerated fear response during conditioning and extinction learning.[92, 93] People with anxiety disorders will suffer from uncontrollable and persistent worries, fears, and an inability to deal with uncertainties. They have trouble concentrating, as well as relaxing, and are often haunted by intrusive thoughts. Children with anxiety disorders may refuse to go on school field trips, participate in new activities, or even go to school altogether. They have trouble joining in, making friends, and experience difficulties in going to sleep or staying asleep. Externalizing psychopathology, on the other hand, is associated with blunted fear conditioning and an impaired capability of discriminating between threat and safety cues.[94] Maltreated children exhibit blunted physiological responses to threat cues during fear conditioning. This pattern of altered fear conditioning is most likely due to a reduced production of cortisol, causing a blunted sympathetic nervous system reactivity in response to potential threats.[95, 96] As discussed, stress causes infants to activate the sympathetic nervous system by releasing excessive amounts of corticotropin-releasing factor, ACTH, and cortisol. As infants' autonomous nervous system is not yet mature enough, they

[92] Craske et al., "Is Aversive Learning a Marker of Risk," 954–967.
[93] Lau et al., "Fear Conditioning in Adolescents With Anxiety Disorders," 94–102.
[94] Fairchild et al., "Fear Conditioning and Affective Modulation," 279–285.
[95] MacMillan et al., "Cortisol Response to Stress in Female Youths," 62–68.
[96] McLaughlin et al., "Child Maltreatment," 538–546,

rely on their mothers' soothing presence in regulating infant stress responses. If the mother is absent or the child is exposed to prolonged traumatic experiences without adequate maternal support, the production of cortisol is downregulated, and the sympathetic nervous system reactivity gets blunted in response to potential threats. Exposure to severe abuse or extended episodes of maltreatment affect the maturation of the ventromedial prefrontal cortex that typically occurs later in childhood and continues until early adulthood. Impairment of prefrontal cortex development worsens the pathological outcome, as behavioral inhibition cannot be mastered. This neurophysiological pattern is frequently observed in people with externalizing psychopathology, a mental disorder characterized by maladaptive behaviors directed toward the environment, which lead to an inability to "function normally" in daily life. People suffering from externalizing psychopathology act out their feelings and thoughts, which often results in disruptive behavior disorders or conduct problems. In adulthood, these patients may turn to alcohol, drug abuse, or exhibit antisocial behavior.

Returning to the beginning of this chapter, some of the Duplessis orphans who survived physical and sexual abuse, emotional neglect, and hardship were able to live a self-determined life as adults. But despite their best efforts, their childhood experiences caught up with them later in life.[97] The developmental trajectories available to them were severely constrained, often leading to troubled personalities and the expression of psychopathological symptoms, like depression or generalized anxiety. Furthermore, most of the severely neglected and abused children never formed meaningful relationships later in life.

Alarmingly, parents who have also been victims of domestic violence are at a higher risk of exerting violence against their own children and severely interfering with their children's development of a secure attachment style. Abusive mothers are themselves particularly vulnerable to stress because they have severe difficulty with emotion regulation.[98] They frequently exhibit high anxiety caused by neurophysiological alterations of their stress hormones and serotonin metabolites[99] as a result of their own early adverse experiences.[100] The risk of becoming an abusive parent is significantly exacerbated when living socially isolated and enduring serious emotional and/or economic stress. Childhood experiences shape internal mental structures and simultaneously form a sort of template of how social relationships with spouses, friends, and other people in general are expected to be. Thus, adult relationships usually

---

[97] "A New Look at The Duplessis Orphan Scandal."
[98] Parmigiani et al., "Mechanisms of Primate Infant Abuse," 199–210.
[99] Maestripieri et al., "Neurobiological Characteristics of Rhesus Macaque," 51–57.
[100] Troisi et al., "Severity of Early Separation," 277–284.

reflect early social experiences and the attachment style developed in childhood. These expectations are carried over to other niches such as workplaces, professional associations, political affiliations, and various interest groups.

Alarmingly, if external environments that are available do not match internal, mental, and emotional structures, individuals will act to manipulate their environment. This process has been described as "niche construction" (Chapter 1). In doing so, humans generate niches to match their internal structures rather than trying to modify their internal structures,[101] even if the social environment created is to their families ' and their own detriment. The concept of niche construction can help explain why when abused or neglected children become parents, they themselves frequently create abusive or neglecting familial environments. When becoming parents, they transfer their adverse childhood experiences—which were adaptations to their family environment—to their adult lives and new niches. As adults, they then either pick or create an abusive environment. Intergenerational violence is a highly complex phenomenon[102] that is strongly entangled with human niche construction; the vantage point of different niches is particularly relevant for human behavior concerning parental care and child-rearing practices. Clearly, human parental care is strongly influenced by culture. Cultural niches play an important role in how parents mold children's behavior, thinking patterns, and reasoning by exposing them to their culture-specific languages and beliefs, yet children are not only born into a particular cultural niche, but also into a social niche. Scholars understand a social niche as the sum of all social selection pressures, the latter being the result of a social negotiation process on expectations about behaviors of role holders in hierarchically organized role structures.[103] The role structures in a social niche may be entrenched, but they are not fixed. They can be subject to change due to economic development. Most eminently, with the advent and rise of agriculture and trade in the last millennia, societies became more and more inegalitarian.[104] Owing to the emergence of private property, inheritance, and larger trade networks that perpetuated and compounded economic advantages, increasing inequality took hold and social role structures became institutionalized. In order to maintain hierarchies of wealth, social status, and power, certain subgroups within a population rigorously enforced norms that prevented others from acquiring more status, authority, or resources, ensuring the former to take even

---

[101] Wexler, *Brain and Culture: Neurobiology, Ideology, and Social Change*.
[102] Hrdy, "Infanticide among Animals," 13–40.
[103] Lipatov et al., "The Influence of Social Niche," 901–917.
[104] Power, *The Egalitarians, Human and Chimpanzee*.

greater advantage of the latter.[105] These man-made rules that guaranteed the order of a society were manifested in a series of hierarchical, sometimes overlapping role structures.[106] Role structures of a social niche also determine how children are raised and cared for. Social niches, in conjunction with economic conditions usually tied to it, determine material resources, wider social interactions, and parental investment. Typically, access to social support strongly depends on the social niche in which a child grows up. Thus, socioeconomic betterment represents one of the most important leverage points for preventing child maltreatment.

---

[105] Rogers, "Inequality: Why Egalitarian Societies Died Out."
[106] *The Foundations of Social Anthropology.*

Chapter 9

Resilience & Nurture Put into Practice

Every child needs at least one adult who is irrationally crazy about him or her.

— Urie Bronfenbrenner. Ecological Systems Theory of Development

At the age of nine, the young girl became the frequent object of sexual abuse. After being raped first by a cousin at an uncle's house, she was repeatedly sexually abused until she was fourteen. She remembered these traumatic events as unending and persistent. The perpetrators were numerous—some of them relatives, others boyfriends of her mother. Initially, she did not talk about the rapes, as she did not understand what had happened to her. The cousin who abused her first told her after the rape that the incident was a secret between the two of them. He bribed her with ice cream and a trip to the local zoo. Even years later, when she knew that these abusive incidents were deeply wrong, she remained quiet. Like many rape victims and abused children, she blamed herself for the terrible things that had happened to her. For more than twelve years, she kept this "big, looming, dark secret." Eventually, she confided in her mother, whom she believed had known about the abuse all the time and had failed to protect her. But her mother categorically refused to talk about the incidents and did not believe her daughter. Consequently, the young woman never again brought the topic up with her mother. She also confided in other members of her family, but none of them was supportive. Her father strongly denied the allegations that one of his brothers had been one of the perpetrators. Only when she reached her thirties did she dare speak up. And eventually, she did so in public, on television, at a time when she was already famous. This time, people did not doubt her allegations.

The girl who had been molested, abused, left unprotected, and with nobody believing her was Oprah Winfrey.[1] Today, Oprah Winfrey is a world-renowned media executive, television producer, and philanthropist. She is best known for her talk show that became one of the highest-rated television programs of its kind in history and brought her the title "Queen of All Media." By 2007, she was

---

[1] Garson, *Oprah Winfrey: a Biography*.

ranked several times as the most influential woman in the world. Beside becoming world-famous, she also became the richest African American of the twentieth century and North America's first Black multi-billionaire. Despite her traumatizing experiences, she overcame her adversities and developed into a highly successful woman who made her way right to the top.

How is it possible that some people thrive and become highly successful and happy with their lives despite having experienced unspeakable horror and abuse? Why do some people overcome traumatizing events while others crash on the rocky shores of life? The initial answers about what makes children strong in the face of adversities came from research performed by American developmental psychologist Emmy Werner. Werner studied 698 infants on the Hawaiian island of Kauai, an entire birth cohort of one year of the island. She followed these children for forty years, from birth to adulthood. At that time, Kauai and its inhabitants were economically very poor. Most of the children studied in the longitudinal study grew up with alcoholic or mentally ill parents in households shaken by poverty and parental unemployment. Unsurprisingly, many children who grew up in these detrimental situations developed destructive behaviors in their later teen years, such as chronic unemployment, substance abuse, and unwanted pregnancies. As adults, these children experienced problems with delinquency, mental and physical health, and suffered from family instability and lack of social relationships. Unexpectedly, Werner's study revealed that not all children of Kauai shared this destiny; one-third of the children of this very cohort did not exhibit destructive behaviors as teenagers or later in life. They grew into caring, competent, and confident adults despite experiencing similar risk factors as the others. Werner termed these children who thrived despite their high-risk developmental histories as "resilient."[2] Thus, psychological resilience research was born. Werner subsequently pioneered decades of work that aimed at uncovering protective factors for balancing out risk factors at critical periods in infant and childhood development, protective factors that help children withstand adversity and bounce back from setbacks and, ultimately, allow them to become more successful. Among the protective factors identified, one that stood out was a strong bond between child and caretaker. The resilient children of Kauai were lucky enough to have adult relatives or teachers—at least one caring person— who counterbalanced the missing parental bonds.

Neurobiological research of the last two decades has confirmed that supportive, responsive relationships with caring adults can prevent or reverse the damaging effects of toxic stress triggered by abusive or neglectful parents. For example, high-quality maternal brood care in rats bucks negative

---

[2] Werner and Smith, *Vulnerable, but Invincible.*

experiences in infancy. As adults, the offspring of mothers that exhibit high-quality maternal care are substantially less fearful, more stress-resistant, shown higher exploratory behavior, and in general, are socially more competent than the offspring of mothers that provide low-quality care.[3] Thus, affectionate, physical contact is an important factor in enhancing resilience.

Behavioral changes in the more resilient rats can also be seen on the molecular level. The less fearful infants of more caring mothers show increased numbers of inhibitory neurotransmitter receptors (i.e., benzodiazepine receptors) in the amygdala and the locus coeruleus as well as a decrease in corticotropin-releasing hormone receptor density in the locus coeruleus.[4] These alterations are highly relevant for fear and anxiety that is mediated by both brain regions, the amygdala, and locus coeruleus. A decrement of receptor density for corticotropin-releasing hormone in the locus coeruleus mitigates the effect of stress hormones. As the locus coeruleus is a central component of the stress axis and an area of norepinephrine synthesis, the stress reaction is bound to be relatively weakened in resilient individuals. Additionally, the increase of inhibitory neurotransmitter receptors in the amygdala and locus coeruleus conveys an anxiolytic effect, entailing an increase in natural curiosity and exploratory behavior. As discussed in more detail in Chapter 4 (Gene Expression: Nurture Fueling Nature), these changes in behavioral patterns are due to transient processes. This means regulation of gene expression is under environmental control and can be subject to positive interventions by others. Hence, resilience and emotional well-being can be "learned" on a molecular level when experiencing high-quality care.

These findings underscore that mothers and other close caregivers have special access to the infant brain. In other words, mothers or their surrogates have the ability to mitigate genetic predispositions or social and environmental risk factors by means of good parenting. This observation is highly relevant for humans where alloparenting is particularly common. In some human populations (e.g., in Efé, a hunter-gatherer group of Central Africa), infants spend more than half a day with caregivers other than their mothers by eighteen weeks of age.[5] On average, this refers to about fourteen different caretakers, including both related and unrelated individuals. Many children in Western nations also spend a significant amount of their infancy being cared for by alloparents (e.g., grandparents, crèches, nurseries, or babysitters). This extensive form of alloparenting—also found to a lesser extent in chimpanzees and macaques— seems to be characteristic for collaborative breeding species, such as humans.

---

[3] Meaney, "Maternal Care, Gene Expression," 1161–1192.
[4] Caldji et al., "Maternal Care during Infancy Regulates," 5335–5340.
[5] MacDonald et al,. "On Why It Takes a Village," 167–189.

The observation that human infants show a delayed development of "stranger distress" as compared to other primates (i.e., appearing at approximately seven months in humans, four months in chimpanzees, and three months in macaques) accentuates the adaptive advantages of human alloparenting. The delayed fear response related to "stranger distress" in primates is mediated by aforementioned attenuation in the development of the amygdala during the first year of life (see also Chapter 8).

From a neurophysiological perspective, the caregivers' positive effect on the infant's brain is tied to the hormone oxytocin. Oxytocin acts in complementary ways to cortisol. When oxytocin is experimentally administered in combination with social support, it dampens neuroendocrine stress reactivity and decreases amygdala activation in response to threatening stimuli.[6] The neurophysiological changes attenuate anxiety, stress-related behaviors, and depression. Oxytocin mediates its activity through receptors distributed in several brain regions, in particular, the hypothalamus and the amygdala. On the other hand, reduced oxytocin levels correlate with increased stress vulnerability and cortisol increment.

Due to its effects on social attachment and trust, oxytocin has been hailed as the "love" and bonding hormone. For it to be released and exert its effects, it is pivotal that parents (fathers included!) and children have physical contact and affectionate relations.[7, 8, 9, 10]

Oxytocin levels depend on a variety of factors. Healthy individuals can possess different gene variants of the oxytocin receptor gene, i.e., the receptor that oxytocin hormones bind to. This individual variation makes some people more responsive to oxytocin than others. Depending on the gene variants, different persons exhibit differences in social behavior. These behavioral differences include different parenting styles, empathy, positive affect, and sensitivity to social support or support-seeking during stress.[11] More importantly, however, oxytocin expression is strongly influenced by environmental factors. It can be dynamically regulated by exposure to psychosocial stress. For example, women with a history of childhood abuse exhibit lower oxytocin concentrations in their cerebrospinal fluid than other women.[12] Thus, traumatic experiences have a negative impact on the developing oxytocin system and interfere with social

---

[6] Kirsch et al., "Oxytocin Modulates Neural Circuitry for Social Cognition," 11489–11493.

[7] Brauer et al., "Frequency of Maternal Touch," 3544–3552.

[8] McLaughlin et al., "Neglect as a Violation," 462–471.

[9] Moore et al., "Epigenetic Correlates of Neonatal Contact in Humans," 1517–1538.

[10] Vittner et al., "Increase in Oxytocin From Skin-to-Skin Contact," 54–62.

[11] Kumsta and Heinrichs, "Oxytocin, Stress and Social Behavior," 11–16.

[12] Heim et al., "Lower CSF Oxytocin Concentrations," 954–958.

bonding abilities later in life. Human connectivity and physical touch activate the parasympathetic nervous system via the vagus nerve. The parasympathetic nervous system is the counterpart of the sympathetic nervous system that we have discussed in length in Chapters 6 and 8. The parasympathetic nervous system's "tend-and-befriend" response functions antagonistically to the sympathetic nervous system's "fight-or-flight" response. Activation of the parasympathetic nervous system increases oxytocin and reduces cortisol. Mice that experience "bullying" by other mice have increased cortisol levels and causes social aversion to all other mice. But when cortisol receptors are blocked and their brain no longer responds to cortisol, the "bullied" mice become more resilient and no longer avoid other mice. Thus, early positive interventions, affectionate child care, and loving support by alloparents are of paramount importance for enhancing resilience.

What measurements can be taken to enhance resilience and provide children with protective resources against challenges in life? The first line of support is clearly to provide a secure environment. In order to get out of the vicious circle of distress, children and adolescents who experience severe adversities need a safe place. Ideally, this secure place would be provided by a trusted family member. Alternatively, it can be enabled by a trained social worker who offers temporary relief from the emotional and physiological effects of stressful situations and ensures that the biological needs (food, shelter) are met. The importance of safety was first recognized by American psychologist Abraham Maslow, who proposed a hierarchy of human needs,[13] placing physiological and safety needs at the base of the pyramid. On the levels above these survival needs are needs for individual growth, including belonging, esteem, and self-actualization. Almost eighty years later, Maslow's well-known hierarchy of needs[14] is still the most-cited model of human motivation[15] and remains one of the most enduring contributions to psychology. It has also become an inspiration for many other theories and applied research models in contemporary personality and social psychology. According to Maslow, most emotional and behavioral problems in children, adolescents, as well as adults are rooted in unmet needs.[16] Thus, in order to help children thrive, providing safety comes first, followed by an endeavor to meet their needs for individual growth.

As a society, we frequently miss the goal to help children grow and find their place in the world. This is particularly true for children who have faced multiple

---

[13] Maslow, "A Theory of Human Motivation," 370–396.
[14] Maslow, "The Farther Reaches of Human Nature," 1–9.
[15] Cory, *Toward Consilience.*
[16] Maslow, "Psychological Data and Value Theory," 119–136.

adversities during their development, ranging from poverty to maltreatment, and repudiation by society. As a result, we are increasingly confronted with disconnected young (or not so young) people who provide their communities with enormous challenges. We can witness this disconnection in children who constantly break rules, disengage from learning and their social community, and exhibit non-compliance and aggressive behavior.

Martin Brokenleg, a professor of Native American Studies, and Larry Brendtro, a professor in children's behavior disorders, developed the "Circle of Courage," a holistic approach for working with children and adolescents at risk. The circle draws on Native American culture, nourishing children while completely abstaining from using punitive discipline. It is rooted in an alternative viewpoint that links well-being, behavior, and learning by moving the focus from deficits to strengths, thereby building up resilience in young people. The Circle of Courage is strongly linked to Maslow's hierarchy of needs and portrays four growth needs of all children: Belonging, Mastery (Esteem), Independence (Self-Actualization), and Generosity (Self-Transcendence).[17] The latter element of the circle, generosity, has also been identified by Maslow, who corrected his earlier oversight and placed self-transcendence, the commitment beyond self, at the top of his hierarchical model.[18] In their very successful work with children and adolescents, Brokenleg, Brendtro, and co-workers put the focus on establishing a respectful relationship with their young clients by engaging the four elements of the circle in order to meet the children's biosocial needs:

(1) form a close emotional bond (to ensure belonging)

(2) expose the child to increasingly complex tasks (to enable self-esteem)

(3) shift the power to the learner (to provide room for self-actualization)

(4) build a relationship of reciprocity (to pave the path to self-transcendence)

The Circle of Courage can function as a compass to navigate toward a healthier and more respectful community.

According to indigenous wisdom underlying the Circle of Courage, a broken circle can be mended by helping children meet their need to belong without making them dependent upon the immediate caregiver. Throughout history, it was the group rather than the nuclear family that ensured the survival of those belonging to them. In agreement with this observation, the social group has a responsibility in supporting growth of the next generation. This is even more relevant if parents cannot provide enough resources for their child's biological,

---

[17] Brendtro, "Pathways From Pain to Resilience," 5–24.
[18] Koltko-Rivera, "Rediscovering the Later Version," 302–317.

emotional, and psychological needs. In a society in which more and more children grow up without extended family members, increasingly more teachers, coaches, and social workers will inevitably have this task assigned to them.

Following the Circle of Courage, let us start with the element of "Belonging." Attachment, which is the basis of belonging, is a fundamental need of infants and children. In traditional kinship systems, many adults can act as alloparents, as belonging is based on behavior, not genetics. Belonging creates powerful bonds that establish a ramified network of relationships based on mutual respect. Today, opportunities for forming bonds are drastically pruned as children grow up in micro-nuclear families with little contact with neighbors and are only loosely integrated into other communities. As a consequence, children may feel alienated, rejected, and emotionally disconnected. When children feel rejected by others, they either internalize or externalize this rejection. Internalized rejection is characterized by children becoming resentful, withdrawn, and reluctant to do anything. If their sense of belonging is not re-established, they will resist efforts of gaining their trust. In the worst case, they turn against themselves, become self-defeating, self-destructive, and might blunder into substance abuse. Externalized rejection is characterized by children becoming rebellious, aggressive, destructive, and refusing to cooperate. In the worst case, they might become revengeful and turn to mobbing and violence. On the contrary, when a child can attach to a trusted adult, there won't be the need for avoidance behavior. Close-knit human bonds are vital for physical and mental health. Children who feel socially connected, safe, and self-reliant have reduced cortisol levels and increased oxytocin levels. Caregivers must make sure to provide an environment in which children believe they are welcome. Time is an issue, because the quantity of encounters matters in order to build a relationship. Also, active listening is a skill that should be honed by all adults. Almost right from birth onwards, babies will attempt to interact with their mother. Infants try to babble, reach out, cry, or chatter to get the caregiver's attention. This need for interaction remains throughout our whole life. To reach a child and enable bonding, it is crucial to hold eye contact, perform active listening, and respond by rephrasing and providing respectful feedback. Treating children as partners in the process of attachment requires appropriate self-disclosure as a way of showing trust and creating alliances. To reduce stress, efforts of bonding can be optimally supported by touching, laughing[19] and listening to music.[20] Touching, like deliberate hugs and incidental, safe touches as well as laughing together are

---

[19] Savage et al., "Humor, Laughter, Learning, and Health!," 341–347.
[20] Thoma et al., "The Effect of Music on the Human Stress Response."

ways to connect, reassure, and create trust. Of course, it is also important to be guided by a child's body language. If she flinches or shies away from being touched, caregivers must respect that.

The next element of the Circle of Courage is "Mastery." Fostered by cultural evolution, humans are embedded in an environment that enables cooperative learning. The two most important tools for passing on knowledge are using narratives and creating opportunities for shared experiences (adventures). Both methods leave ample room for personal creativity and forgo competition based on adversarial spirit. The mindset of indigenous cultures that underlie the Circle of Courage emphasizes cooperativity rather than individual competition. However, in our everyday life, we usually encounter highly competitive environments that generate a few "winners" and many "losers." This is not only toxic to individuals who start with a disadvantage due to their socioeconomic status, but it is also harmful to the whole society, as it causes the loss of intellectual and societal potential of those who don't receive adequate support to reach their full capabilities. Moreover, the spirit of high competitiveness limits our society to promote a set of virtues that mirror only a few successful leaders, enforcing conformity instead of diversity. Contrarily, in indigenous cultures, children and adolescents develop mastery under the stewardship of different mentors. Mentors may be elders or skilled peers from whom they can gain competence in social, physical, intellectual, emotional, and spiritual domains. Importantly, mastery is tied to becoming a mentor, not a rival, in a particular area. That said, it is important to bear in mind that children will only learn from somebody with whom they have a positive relationship. Children who are alienated from adults have severe problems developing competence and achievement. The frustration of ongoing failure can cause anger, avoidance, and the feeling of being inadequate or stupid. To regain self-respect, children counteract the negative feelings by exhibiting hostile behavior and oppose adults and community rules. It takes about five to seven positive interactions to make up for one negative interaction, because brains are evolutionarily conditioned to remember negative incidents better than positive ones. Thus, to create a stimulating environment for achievement, it is necessary to build kids up by giving them meaningful praise and opportunities to succeed and gain a sense of mastery. Eventually, mastery facilitates feelings of belonging, self-worth, and well-being.

The third element of the Circle of Courage is "Independence." In Western culture, children are raised following obedience-based models of discipline. In order to foster obedience in children, adults employ methods of classical conditioning using rewards and punishments. Reward/punishment learning is still a frequently used method, despite modern pedagogy having moved past behaviorism a long time ago (see also Chapter 6). Obedience, however, can be more correctly equated with dressage or drill. It works against the development of independent minds. Indigenous cultures, on the other hand, teach children to make decisions, solve problems, and show personal responsibility, an idea that resonates with teachings from Maria Montessori, who centered her work around infant and child development by encouraging them to become independent in every aspect of their life. Children are encouraged to experience freedom of movement, freedom of choice, freedom of activities, and spontaneous engagements with the environment and others that pave the path for further mental independence during adolescence.[21] At the same time, children learn that freedom of choice is based on social rules, thereby linking freedom with responsibility, social awareness, and taking initiative. Native American teachings that inform the Circle of Courage are designed to build respect and teach inner discipline by modeling adults who nurture, exemplify values, and give feedback. Parents and teachers who respect children and youth carefully discipline them by providing abundant opportunities to make choices without coercion and to take responsibility for these choices. In this vein, independence is not self-sufficiency but rather the responsibility to set actions for a successful and valuable life. Children who have been raised by parents and alloparents who are devoted to appreciation and respect grow into adolescents and adults who show a deep respect for themselves, their own path of life, for others, and for the environment. Respect teaches respect, responsibility teaches responsibility, while requesting discipline without creating a space of mutual respect will culminate in a lack of agreement between both sides. Ultimately, a situation of disrespect will elicit responses ranging from feigned acceptance to passive aggression to outright rebellion. The Circle of Courage emphasizes the importance of empowerment in children. Empowerment comprises of striving for consensus, handing over responsibilities to children, and believing in children's capacity to solve problems. For children to gain a sense of personal power, they must master self-regulation. Having a sense of power over one's own life is a major contributor to pride and self-worth, while a person who feels powerless and unable to govern himself and his own life can easily plunge into depression and hopelessness. Powerlessness can be triggered by traumatic experiences. Trauma involves a combination of perceiving a life-threatening situation and at the same time being incapable of escaping this situation. This emotional combination of experiencing helplessness has life-long effects on health and well-being.[22] Animal studies have corroborated these observations; when laboratory animals are exposed to inescapable threats (like electroshocks), they subsequently exhibited severely

---

[21] Montessori, *The Absorbent Mind.*
[22] Keltner, *The Power Paradox: How We Gain and Lose Influence.*

impaired responses in avoidance learning. Maltreated animals do not learn to avoid a successive negative situation, because they have previously been conditioned to believe that there was no escape. This is what American psychologist Martin Seligman dubbed "learned helplessness."[23] Similarly, humans who have internalized the perception that their actions have no bearing on the aversive outcome struggle with severely impeded learning. Moreover, perceived absence of control over the outcome of a situation frequently leads to clinical depression[24] and social anxiety. In recent decades, a large body of research has shown that traumatic experiences that lead to depression alter hippocampal memory functioning in animals and humans,[25] which expunges readiness to learn and obliterates resilience.

In humans, learned helplessness is the opposite of self-efficacy, which is intimately tied to independence and denotes an individual's belief in her ability to achieve goals. To foster children's beliefs in their ability to achieve goals on their own, they need to have opportunities to take some responsibility for what they learn, how they learn it, and how they can demonstrate their growing competence.

Finally, let us proceed to the fourth element of the Circle of Courage, "Generosity." Generosity and unselfishness are the highest virtues in Native American culture. In contrast to a strongly self-centered Western culture, indigenous cultures teach children how altruism creates and sustains a community in which each member of the group has the responsibility to consider the welfare of everyone in the community.

Generosity relies on respect. This means exemplifying that everybody has the same rights concerning individual freedom and social resources. In helping others, children learn not only how to contribute to others' well-being, thereby demonstrating respect for their social environment, but also enrich their own sense of self-worth and positive identity. Generosity enhances feelings of belonging in the recipient while giving a sense of purpose to the benefactor. From a perspective of biological evolution, the ultimate sacrifice is to give up one's own reproductive success in helping others. In the animal realm, such behavior is only seen in hypersocial insect societies, such as ants or bees in which all individuals share the same genes. Though humans also exhibit extraordinary eusocial behavior, our species is indeed one of the most altruistic species, as discussed in Chapter 7. In fact, humans unselfishly help others, often at the expense of their own reproduction. This seems paradoxical when

---

[23] Seligman, "Learned Helplessness," 407–412.

[24] Seligman, *Helplessness: on Depression, Development, and Death.*

[25] Bremner et al., "Hippocampal Volume Reduction in Major Depression," 115–118.

we have subscribed to the Neodarwinian idea of "survival of the fittest," because giving up one's reproductive success clearly reduces one's fitness. But unselfishness fits well with the tenets of cultural evolution, cooperative breeding, and alloparenting that were discussed in previous chapters. All these issues were of pivotal importance in human evolution. In contrast to females from almost any other species, human females live well past their reproductive age. This longevity without reproduction is an evolutionary conundrum that cannot be explained by a narrow, biological-evolutionary interpretation, because this process does not benefit a population's fitness. Yet, when looking at it in terms of cultural evolution, it makes perfect sense that older individuals who are no longer fertile still contribute largely to the community by supporting others. The benefits of having postmenopausal females in a population that support younger, fertile group members was first contemplated by evolutionary biologist George C. Williams, who formulated the so-called grandmother hypothesis.[26] The hypothesis claims that it is more advantageous for women to redirect their efforts from their own reproduction toward supporting the existing offspring in their reproductive efforts. In so doing, they avoid the age-related risks associated with reproduction and ensure the survival of their genes through younger generations. Coincidently, non-reproductive elders who act as alloparents can share the wisdom of a long life, enhance their group's social network, and, most importantly, enable better resource acquisition through teaching and mentoring. These effects extend past kin into larger community networks and benefit wider group fitness. Humans, as paradigmatic examples for cultural evolution, have clearly benefitted from having individuals in their communities who do not (or no longer) reproduce but nurture others' children. It seems evident that the same cultural evolutionary arguments also count for altruistic behavior in males.

Altruism is the highest form of social needs that is required for personal fulfillment. If altruism (i.e., generosity in terms of the Circle of Courage) is impaired, children display highly selfish behaviours, such as ignoring others, teasing, putting others down, harassing, and bullying others, or exhibiting greed, vandalism, and stealing. If children have hardly experienced altruism, they have difficulties in acting altruistically themselves. Parents and alloparents should, therefore, aim at counteracting the emptiness of growing up in a de-personalized, materialistic, and self-serving culture by providing opportunities for children to contribute to others' well-being. This can be done by encouraging young people to get involved in community activities, service projects, or peer-coaching programs, to name a few examples. By providing an adequate social environment that stimulates cooperation, children can prove

---

[26] Williams, "Pleiotropy," 398–411.

their sense of worth by being of value to others and thereby seeing meaning in their lives. Altruism can heal children who feel disconnected and lack a sense of belonging. We can start by fostering altruism in our families, schools, and communities and employing it as an antidote to pain-based behavior. Meeting children's universal needs and values for belonging and generosity will enable them to thrive and heal "broken minds."

Since children learn by emulating and imitating adults, it is essential that opportunities are provided where they can observe and learn from adults on a consistent basis how to collaborate, help and care for others. This is particularly important in today's world of highly individualistic culture where young people are often socially remote from one another. Without sufficient belonging, kids suffer from emotional emptiness that can only be overcome by making genuine contact with others. Rather than falling prey to self-centred thinking, selfishness, and excessive materialism, altruism and empathy guide the way to achieving a sense of purpose in life. The latter is the crux of the matter of a fulfilled life. According to Austrian neurologist and psychiatrist Viktor Frankl, the need for finding purpose in life by far surpasses the desire to gain pleasure or avoid pain. Frankl's psychotherapeutic approach (logotherapy) is based on the concept that striving to find purpose in life is the strongest and most motivating driving force in human existence. By finding purpose in life despite being trapped in a difficult, painful situation that causes suffering, humans can overcome conflicts and grow. Purpose can be achieved by creating work or doing a deed; by developing and experiencing relationships; and by finding meaning in unavoidable suffering. When putting Frankl's teachings in relation to the Circle of Courage based on indigenous wisdom, significant parallels can be seen. Frankl's approach of creating meaningful work is closely related to the indigenous idea of "Mastery," while Frankl's approach of forming relationships is captured by the indigenous ideas of "Belonging" and "Generosity." Finally and most importantly, Frankl's approach of finding purpose in unavoidable suffering is well represented in the indigenous idea of "Independence" and owning up to one's personal responsibility. Put simply, the latter accepts that injustice will happen because life is not fair. This stance allows a detachment to situations by choosing self-efficacy toward these situations, even if they are appalling. By taking responsibility yet accepting limitations as factors that are clearly beyond one's control, both Frankl's school of thought and the "Circle of Courage" reject surrendering to victimhood, thereby breaking up the shame-guilt-anxiety cycle.

There is cross-cultural accordance about how personal growth in the face of adversity (through finding a purpose) goes hand-in-hand with developing resilience. Choosing creativity, altruism, and embeddedness in a rewarding social community will pave the way for a purposeful existence; in other words, it will contribute to making a resilient mind. There is no better example of an unbreakable, resilient mind than the one of Viktor Frankl. His teachings are so highly authentic and life-affirming because his ideas spawned from his harrowing experiences of being brutally coerced into forced labor in Nazi concentration camps. Losing his pregnant wife, parents, and his brother to the Nazis' atrocities, Frankl survived the Holocaust and dedicated the rest of his life to helping others. His teachings and writings have guided countless people in finding meaning in life, taking responsibility in the face of adversity, and developing resilience, even under the most difficult circumstances. Frankl's teachings do not only speak to adults, but also young people, especially adolescents. This is due to the fact that the transition from childhood to adulthood is marked by an increasing comprehension of life's purpose and directedness. Developing an increasing self-responsibility on how to conduct one's life coincides with neuroplastic, restructuring processes during adolescence. The neural restructuring of the adolescent brain offers an opportunity for working through conflicts that belong to the past (encountered in infancy and childhood) while at the same time responding and integrating age-specific demands. In this vein, adolescents do not only mentally deal with happenings in the external world, but also with repercussions of past events. These repercussions correlate with reorganisation processes of cortical neuronal networks from more diffuse proto-network toward more focused and specialized neuronal subnetworks. [27] As a result of these rearrangements in brain anatomy and physiology, the precision of cognitive processes, such as working memory and executive processes, are increased, which marks brain maturation in early adulthood. On a psychological level, this phase is inextricably linked with finding one's place in society and the world at large. For children who suffered abuse, adolescence and the ensuing neuroplastic processes can respresent a "second chance" when appropriate guidance is available.

How can neuroscience contribute to guiding people who have suffered or are suffering from experiences of abuse, neglect, poverty, and social isolation or work with people at risk? One of the main objectives of this book is to help adolecents, parents, caregivers as well as health care and welfare workers learn about the effects of abusive and neglecting social environments on brain development. One very successful way to teach this is by means of psychoeducation. Psychoeducation, how it is presently practiced, is based on the work of American psychiatrist and researcher Carol M. Anderson, who first used this approach for the treatment of schizophrenic patients. The approach

---

[27] Uhlhaas and Singer, "Oscillations and Neuronal Dynamics in Schizophrenia," 1001–1009.

of psychoeducational intervention was highly successful and diminished relapse rates of schizophrenic patients. Based on years of empirical work, Anderson argues that psychoeducation counteracts the patients' knowledge deficit that leads to psychological impairment, which in turn increases vulnerability to external stimuli.[28] In keeping with this explanation, it seems evident to implement psychoeducation also in psychotherapy and mental health care for children and youth.

In psychoeducation, interventions employ systematic and didactic knowledge transfer about somatic or mental illnesses, suffering, and treatments. The approach integrates emotional and motivational aspects that enable clients to cope with the mental assessment of their situation and improve treatment adherence and efficacy. In psychoeducational sessions, persons directly or secondarily afflicted by adverse experiences obtain information about the neurophysiological and putative neuropathological effects of negative experiences and get the opportunity to explore their thoughts and feelings related to the information.

This book aims at providing state-of-the-art knowledge at the interface of neuroscience, biological psychology, and social pedagogy that experts from neighboring disciplines can use for psychoeducation. Importantly, as discussed in Chapter 3, there is good reason for avoiding the use of "pathologizing language" that is usually focused on deficiencies. Pathologizing language undergirds power imbalance in the therapist-client relationship and reinforces positions in the power hierarchy. Pathologizing developmental effects triggered by abuse, neglect, and traumas may not only cause feelings of helplessness but also of shame or guilt. The latter is especially true if interventions do not bring the desired improvements. Failures of the interventions may then be interpreted by the client as being due to one's individual shortcomings and thus unchangeable. Instead, in a psychoeducational approach, it is important to create a therapeutic environment in which one voice is no longer privileged over another. Therapists offer knowledge, but clients are strongly encouraged to trust their own voice and interpret the information obtained through their personal lens of past experiences. In doing so, clients are enabled to identify resilience factors rooted in their idiosyncratic life journey and mobilize skills associated with them to effectively confront current and future problems.

Providing a tool for psychoeducation, I highlighted multifaceted aspects of the nature–nurture interplay in this book that allow for a re-evaluation of biological preeminence while stressing the importance of psychosocial factors for development. As argued throughout the book, developmental trajectories

---

[28] Anderson et al., "Family Treatment of Adult Schizophrenic Patients," 490–505.

are shaped by multiple biological, social, environmental, and economic factors. This makes the narrative about one's personal history much more nuanced, more accessible, and open to being retold. However, the more severe a person's suffering, the more difficult it will be to reframe one's personal history. This is the challenge that experts face who work with abused children and adolescents, as well as their support networks. Having access to neuroscientific knowledge can help experts mobilize skills and abilities in their clients for the purpose of the healing process. It is the therapist's, social worker's or psychologist's task to translate the scientific knowledge about the effects of abuse, trauma, neglect, and poverty into a story that resonates with the client's own life story. This book hopes to pave the way for handing back options for life-affirming actions to the person afflicted, thereby fostering a commitment to long-term involvement and self-efficacy.

Bibliography

Abercrombie, Heather C., Stacey M. Schaefer, Christine L. Larson, Terrence R. Oakes, Kristen A. Lindgren, James E. Holden, Scott B. Perlman, et al. "Metabolic Rate in the Right Amygdala Predicts Negative Affect in Depressed Patients." *NeuroReport* 9, no. 14 (1998): 3301–7. https://doi.org/10.1097/00001756-199810050-00028.

Ábrahám, Hajnalka, Tamás Tornóczky, György Kosztolányi, and László Seress. "Cell Formation in the Cortical Layers of the Developing Human Cerebellum." *International Journal of Developmental Neuroscience* 19, no. 1 (2001): 53–62. https://doi.org/10.1016/s0736-5748(00)00065-4.

Agnihotri, N. T., R. D. Hawkins, E. R. Kandel, and C. Kentros. "The Long-Term Stability of New Hippocampal Place Fields Requires New Protein Synthesis." *Proceedings of the National Academy of Sciences* 101, no. 10 (2004): 3656–61. https://doi.org/10.1073/pnas.0400385101.

Ainsworth, Mary D., and Silvia M. Bell. "Attachment, Exploration, and Separation: Illustrated by the Behavior of One-Year-Olds in a Strange Situation." *Child Development* 41, no. 1 (1970): 49–67. https://doi.org/10.2307/1127388.

Akers, K. G., A. Martinez-Canabal, L. Restivo, A. P. Yiu, A. De Cristofaro, H.-L. Hsiang, A. L. Wheeler, et al. "Hippocampal Neurogenesis Regulates Forgetting During Adulthood and Infancy." *Science* 344, no. 6184 (May 9, 2014): 598–602. https://doi.org/10.1126/science.1248903.

Alexander, Pamela C. "The Differential Effects of Abuse Characteristics and Attachment in the Prediction of Long-Term Effects of Sexual Abuse." *Journal of Interpersonal Violence* 8, no. 3 (September 1, 1993): 346–62. https://doi.org/10.1177/088626093008003004.

Amaral, David G. "The Amygdala, Social Behavior, and Danger Detection." *Annals of the New York Academy of Sciences* 1000, no. 1 (December 24, 2006): 337–47. https://doi.org/10.1196/annals.1280.015.

Ammerman, R. T., J. D. Higley, M. Linnoilia, and S. J. Suomi. "Ethological Contributions." Essay. In *Handbook of Aggressive Behavior in Psychiatric Patients*, 17–32. New York, NY: Raven, 1994.

Anderson, C. M., G. E. Hogarty, and D. J. Reiss. "Family Treatment of Adult Schizophrenic Patients: A Psycho-Educational Approach." *Schizophrenia Bulletin* 6, no. 3 (January 15, 1980): 490–505. https://doi.org/10.1093/schbul/6.3.490.

Armanini, Mark P., Chris Hutchins, Becky A. Stein, and Robert M. Sapolsky. "Glucocorticoid Endangerment of Hippocampal Neurons Is NMDA-Receptor Dependent." *Brain Research* 532, no. 1-2 (November 5, 1990): 7–12. https://doi.org/10.1016/0006-8993(90)91734-x.

Armstrong, T. "The Myth of the Normal Brain: Embracing Neurodiversity." *AMA Journal of Ethics* 17, no. 4 (April 1, 2015): 348–52. https://doi.org/10.1001/journalofethics.2015.17.4.msoc1-1504.

"Article XIV: Sixty Phreonological Speciment, Approved and Described by Dr. Spurzheim." Essay. In *Phrenological Journal and Miscellany Vol VII*, 285–88. Edinburgh, 1823.

Bachevalier, Jocelyne, Ludise Málková, and Mortimer Mishkin. "Effects of Selective Neonatal Temporal Lobe Lesions on Socioemotional Behavior in Infant Rhesus Monkeys (Macaca Mulatta)." *Behavioral Neuroscience* 115, no. 3 (June 2001): 545–59. https://doi.org/10.1037/0735-7044.115.3.545.

Bacskai, B., B Hochner, M Mahaut-Smith, Adams, B. Kaang, E. Kandel, and R. Tsien. "Spatially Resolved Dynamics of CAMP and Protein Kinase A Subunits in Aplysia Sensory Neurons." *Science* 260, no. 5105 (1993): 222–26. https://doi.org/10.1126/science.7682336.

Baird, Dugald. "The Influence of Social and Economic Factors on Stillbirths and Neonatal Deaths*." *BJOG: An International Journal of Obstetrics and Gynaecology* 52, no. 4 (1945): 339–66. https://doi.org/10.1111/j.1471-0528.1945.tb07636.x.

Baird, Robert M., Stuart E. Rosenbaum, and E. O. Wilson. "Evolutionary Morality and Xenophobia." Essay. In *Hatred, Bigotry, and Prejudice: Definitions, Causes & Solutions*, 161–66. Amherst, NY: Prometheus Books, 1999.

Bakwin, Harry. "Loneliness in Infants." *Archives of Pediatrics & Adolescent Medicine* 63, no. 1 (1942): 30–40. https://doi.org/10.1001/archpedi.1942.02010010031003.

Barden, N., J.M.H.M. Reul, and F. Holsboer. "Do Antidepressants Stabilize Mood through Actions on the Hypothalamic-Pituitary-Adrenocortical System?" *Trends in Neurosciences* 18, no. 1 (1995): 6–11. https://doi.org/10.1016/0166-2236(95)93942-q.

Barker, D J. "Fetal Origins of Coronary Heart Disease." *BMJ* 311, no. 6998 (1995): 171–74. https://doi.org/10.1136/bmj.311.6998.171.

Barr, Gordon A, Stephanie Moriceau, Kiseko Shionoya, Kyle Muzny, Puhong Gao, Shaoning Wang, and Regina M Sullivan. "Transitions in Infant Learning Are Modulated by Dopamine in the Amygdala." *Nature Neuroscience* 12, no. 11 (September 27, 2009): 1367–69. https://doi.org/10.1038/nn.2403.

Barros, Virginia G., Pablo Rodríguez, Irene D. Martijena, Adriana Pérez, Victor A. Molina, and Marta C. Antonelli. "Prenatal Stress and Early Adoption Effects on Benzodiazepine Receptors and Anxiogenic Behavior in the Adult Rat Brain." *Synapse* 60, no. 8 (December 15, 2006): 609–18. https://doi.org/10.1002/syn.20336.

Barry, Ann Marie. "Perception and Visual Communication Theory." *Journal of Visual Literacy* 22, no. 1 (2002): 91–106. https://doi.org/10.1080/23796529.2002.11674583.

Beaumont, Gustave de, and Alexis de Tocqueville. *On the Penitentiary System in the United States, and Its Application in France: with an Appendix on Penal Colonies, and Also, Statistical Notes*. Translated by Francis Lieber. Philadelphia, PA: Carey, Lea & Blanchard, 1833.

Beck, Hall P., Sharman Levinson, and Gary Irons. "Finding Little Albert: A Journey to John B. Watson's Infant Laboratory." *American Psychologist* 64, no. 7 (2009): 605–14. https://doi.org/10.1037/a0017234.

Ben-Noun, Liubov. *NEONATICIDE, INFANTICIDE AND FILICIDE: Unique Medical Research in Biblical Times from the Viewpoint of Contemporary Perspective.* Israel: B.N. Publication House, 2017.

Bianchin, Marta, and Alessandro Angrilli. "Gender Differences in Emotional Responses: A Psychophysiological Study." *Physiology & Behavior* 105, no. 4 (February 28, 2012): 925–32. https://doi.org/10.1016/j.physbeh.2011.10.031.

Blakemore, Sarah-Jayne. *Inventing Ourselves: the Secret Life of the Teenage Brain.* New York, NY: PublicAffairs, 2018.

Blos, Peter. *The Adolescent Passage: Developmental Issues.* New York, NY: International Universities Press, 1979.

Blum, Deborah. *Love at Goon Park.* New York, NY: Berkley Books, 2004.

Blume, Harvey. "Autistics, Freed from Face-to-Face Encounters, Are Communicating in Cyberspace." *New York Times.* June 30, 1997.

Boccella, Kathy. "20 Years after Surgery, a Full Life with Half a Brain." *The Philadelphia Inquirer.* February 14, 2016.

Bocquet-Appel, Jean-Pierre, and Ofer Bar-Yosef. *The Neolithic Demographic Transition and Its Consequences.* Milton Keynes: Springer + Business Media, 2010.

Bocquet-Appel, Jean-Pierre, and Ofer Bar-Yosef. "Xplaining the Neolithic Demographic Transition." Essay. In *The Neolithic Demographic Transition and Its Consequences,* 35–55. Milton Keynes: Springer + Business Media, 2010.

Bolhuis, Johan J., and Robert C. Honey. "Imprinting, Learning and Development: from Behaviour to Brain and Back." *Trends in Neurosciences* 21, no. 7 (1998): 306–11. https://doi.org/10.1016/s0166-2236(98)01258-2.

Boorse, Christopher. "Health as a Theoretical Concept." *Philosophy of Science* 44, no. 4 (December 1977): 542–73. https://doi.org/10.1086/288768.

Bowlby, J. *Child Care and the Growth of Love: Based by Permission of the World Health Organization on the Report Maternal Care and Mental Health.* Harmondsworth: Penguin, 1957.

Bowlby, J. "Forty-Four Juvenile Thieves: Their Characters and Home-Life." *The International Journal of Psychoanalysis* 25 (1994): 19–53.

Bowlby, John. *Attachment and Loss.* New York, NY: Basic Books, 1982.

Bowlby, John. "Introduction." Essay. In *The Making and Breaking of Affectional Bonds: with a New Introduction by Richard Bowlby,* vii-xi. London: Routledge, 2005.

Bowlby, John. "SEPARATION ANXIETY: A CRITICAL REVIEW OF THE LITERATURE." *Journal of Child Psychology and Psychiatry* 1, no. 4 (1960): 251–69. https://doi.org/10.1111/j.1469-7610.1960.tb01999.x.

Bowlby, John. "The Making and Breaking of Affectional Bonds." *British Journal of Psychiatry* 130, no. 5 (1977): 421–31. https://doi.org/10.1192/bjp.130.5.421.

Bowles, S., and J.-K. Choi. "Coevolution of Farming and Private Property during the Early Holocene." *Proceedings of the National Academy of Sciences* 110, no. 22 (2013): 8830–35. https://doi.org/10.1073/pnas.1212149110.

Boyce, W. Thomas. *The Orchid and the Dandelion: Why Some Children Struggle and How All Can Thrive.* New York, NY: Knopf, 2019.

Brauer, Jens, Yaqiong Xiao, Tanja Poulain, Angela D. Friederici, and Annett Schirmer. "Frequency of Maternal Touch Predicts Resting Activity and

Connectivity of the Developing Social Brain." *Cerebral Cortex* 26, no. 8 (August 26, 2016): 3544–52. https://doi.org/10.1093/cercor/bhw137.

Brauth, Steven E., William S. Hall, Robert J. Dooling, and S. J. Suomi. "Up-Tight and Laid-Back Monkeys: Individual Differences in the Response to Social Challenges." Essay. In *Plasticity of Development*, 27–56. Cambridge, MA: MIT Press, 1991.

Bremner, J. D., P. Randall, T. M. Scott, R. A. Bronen, J. P. Seibyl, S. M. Southwick, R. C. Delaney, G. McCarthy, D. S. Charney, and R. B. Innis. "MRI-Based Measurement of Hippocampal Volume in Patients with Combat- Related Posttraumatic Stress Disorder." *American Journal of Psychiatry* 152, no. 7 (1995): 973–81. https://doi.org/10.1176/ajp.152.7.973.

Bremner, J. Douglas, Meena Narayan, Eric R. Anderson, Lawrence H. Staib, Helen L. Miller, and Dennis S. Charney. "Hippocampal Volume Reduction in Major Depression." *American Journal of Psychiatry* 157, no. 1 (2000): 115–18. https://doi.org/10.1176/ajp.157.1.115.

Bremner, J. Douglas, Penny Randall, Eric Vermetten, Lawrence Staib, Richard A. Bronen, Carolyn Mazure, Sandi Capelli, Gregory McCarthy, Robert B. Innis, and Dennis S. Charney. "Magnetic Resonance Imaging-Based Measurement of Hippocampal Volume in Posttraumatic Stress Disorder Related to Childhood Physical and Sexual Abuse—a Preliminary Report." *Biological Psychiatry* 41, no. 1 (January 1, 1997): 23–32. https://doi.org/10.1016/s0006-3223(96)00162-x.

Bremner, J.D, M Vythilingam, E Vermetten, J Adil, S Khan, A Nazeer, N Afzal, et al. "Cortisol Response to a Cognitive Stress Challenge in Posttraumatic Stress Disorder (PTSD) Related to Childhood Abuse." *Psychoneuroendocrinology* 28, no. 6 (August 28, 2003): 733–50. https://doi.org/10.1016/s0306-4530(02)00067-7.

Brendtro, Larry K. "Pathways From Pain to Resilience." *International Journal of Child, Youth and Family Studies* 10, no. 2-3 (April 8, 2019): 5–24. https://doi.org/10.18357/ijcyfs102-3201918850.

Brennan, Kelly A., Phillip R. Shaver, and Ann E. Tobey. "Attachment Styles, Gender and Parental Problem Drinking." *Journal of Social and Personal Relationships* 8, no. 4 (1991): 451–66. https://doi.org/10.1177/02654075918 4001.

Brown, Catherine C., Candace M. Raio, and Maital Neta. "Cortisol Responses Enhance Negative Valence Perception for Ambiguous Facial Expressions." *Scientific Reports* 7, no. 1 (November 8, 2017): 15107. https://doi.org/10.1038/s41598-017-14846-3.

Brown, G. W. "Genetic and Population Perspectives on Life Events and Depression." *Social Psychiatry and Psychiatric Epidemiology* 33, no. 8 (August 13, 1998): 363–72. https://doi.org/10.1007/s001270050067.

Brown, Roger, and James Kulik. "Flashbulb Memories." *Cognition* 5, no. 1 (1977): 73–99. https://doi.org/10.1016/0010-0277(77)90018-x.

Brown, Sarah S., and Leon Eisenberg. *The Best Intentions: Unintended Pregnancy and the Well-Being of Children and Families*. Washington, D.C., VA: National Academy Press, 1995.

Bruce, H. M. "A Block To Pregnancy in the Mouse Caused by Proximity of Strange Males." *Reproduction* 1, no. 1 (February 1960): 96–103. https://doi.org/10.1530/jrf.0.0010096.

Brunner, H., M Nelen, X. Breakefield, H. Ropers, and B. van Oost. "Abnormal Behavior Associated with a Point Mutation in the Structural Gene for Monoamine Oxidase A." *Science* 262, no. 5133 (1993): 578–80. https://doi.org/10.1126/science.8211186.

Buaer, Patricia J. "Oh Where, Oh Where Have Those Early Memories Gone? A Developmental Perspective on Childhood Amnesia." American Psychological Association. American Psychological Association, December 2004. https://www.apa.org/science/about/psa/2004/12/bauer.

Burnham, John B. *Family Therapy: First Steps towards a Systemic Approach.* London: Tavistock Publications Ltd, 1986.

Caldji, C. "The Effects of Early Rearing Environment on the Development of GABAA and Central Benzodiazepine Receptor Levels and Novelty-Induced Fearfulness in the Rat." *Neuropsychopharmacology* 22, no. 3 (2000): 219–29. https://doi.org/10.1016/s0893-133x(99)00110-4.

Caldji, C., B. Tannenbaum, S. Sharma, D. Francis, P. M. Plotsky, and M. J. Meaney. "Maternal Care during Infancy Regulates the Development of Neural Systems Mediating the Expression of Fearfulness in the Rat." *Proceedings of the National Academy of Sciences* 95, no. 9 (April 28, 1998): 5335–40. https://doi.org/10.1073/pnas.95.9.5335.

Campbell, Bernard Grant. "Parental Investment and Sexual Selection." Essay. In *Sexual Selection and the Descent of Man, 1871-1971*, 136–79. Chicago, Il: Aldine Pub. Co, 1972.

Campbell, Bernard, and R. L. Trivers. "Parental Investment and Sexual Selection." Essay. In *Sexual Selection and the Descent of Man: 1871-1971*, 136–79. Chicago, IL: Aldine, 1977.

Camperio Ciani, Andrea S., and Lilybeth Fontanesi. "Mothers Who Kill Their Offspring: Testing Evolutionary Hypothesis in a 110-Case Italian Sample." *Child Abuse & Neglect* 36, no. 6 (2012): 519–27. https://doi.org/10.1016/j.chiabu.2012.05.001.

Carroll, Bernard J., George C. Curtis, B. M. Davies, J. Mendels, and A. Arthur Sugerman. "Urinary Free Cortisol Excretion in Depression." *Psychological Medicine* 6, no. 1 (1976): 43–50. https://doi.org/10.1017/s0033291700007480.

Cartwright, Samuel A. "Diseases and Peculiarities of the Negro Race." PBS. Public Broadcasting Service, 1851. https://www.pbs.org/wgbh/aia/part4/4h3106t.html.

Caspi, A. "Influence of Life Stress on Depression: Moderation by a Polymorphism in the 5-HTT Gene." *Science* 301, no. 5631 (July 18, 2003): 386–89. https://doi.org/10.1126/science.1083968.

Caspi, A. "Role of Genotype in the Cycle of Violence in Maltreated Children." *Science* 297, no. 5582 (2002): 851–54. https://doi.org/10.1126/science.1072290.

Chi, J. G., E. C. Dooling, and F. H. Gilles. "Left-Right Asymmetries of the Temporal Speech Areas of the Human Fetus." *Archives of Neurology* 34, no. 6 (1977): 346–48. https://doi.org/10.1001/archneur.1977.00500180040008.

Chisholm, J S. "The Evolutionary Ecology of Attachment Organization." *Human Nature*, March 7, 1996, 1–37.

"Closing the Gap in a Generation: Health Equity through Action on the Social Determinants of Health - Final Report of the Commission on Social Determinants of Health." World Health Organization. World Health Organization, August 27, 2008. https://www.who.int/publications/i/item/WHO-IER-CSDH-08.1.

Cloutier, Jasmin, Tianyi Li, and Joshua Correll. "The Impact of Childhood Experience on Amygdala Response to Perceptually Familiar Black and White Faces." *Journal of Cognitive Neuroscience* 26, no. 9 (September 26, 2014): 1992–2004. https://doi.org/10.1162/jocn_a_00605.

Clutton-Brock, T. H., P. N. Brotherton, R. Smith, G. M. McIlrath, R. Kansky, D. Gaynor, M. J. O'Riain, and J. D. Skinner. "Infanticide and Expulsion of Females in a Cooperative Mammal." *Proceedings of the Royal Society of London. Series B: Biological Sciences* 265, no. 1412 (December 7, 1998): 2291–95. https://doi.org/10.1098/rspb.1998.0573.

Colman, Andrew M. "Race Differences in IQ: Hans Eysenck's Contribution to the Debate in the Light of Subsequent Research." *Personality and Individual Differences* 103 (2016): 182–89. https://doi.org/10.1016/j.paid.2016.04.050.

Colucci-D'Amato, L., V. Bonavita, and U. di Porzio. "The End of the Central Dogma of Neurobiology: Stem Cells and Neurogenesis in Adult CNS." *Neurological Sciences* 27, no. 4 (2006): 266–70. https://doi.org/10.1007/s10072-006-0682-z.

Conrad, Cheryl D., Ana María Magariños, Joseph E. LeDoux, and Bruce S. McEwen. "Repeated Restraint Stress Facilitates Fear Conditioning Independently of Causing Hippocampal CA3 Dendritic Atrophy." *Behavioral Neuroscience* 113, no. 5 (1999): 902–13. https://doi.org/10.1037/0735-7044.113.5.902.

Coplan, J. D., M. W. Andrews, L. A. Rosenblum, M. J. Owens, S. Friedman, J. M. Gorman, and C. B. Nemeroff. "Persistent Elevations of Cerebrospinal Fluid Concentrations of Corticotropin-Releasing Factor in Adult Nonhuman Primates Exposed to Early-Life Stressors: Implications for the Pathophysiology of Mood and Anxiety Disorders." *Proceedings of the National Academy of Sciences* 93, no. 4 (February 20, 1996): 1619–23. https://doi.org/10.1073/pnas.93.4.1619.

Cory, Gerald A. *Toward Consilience: the Bioneurological Basis of Behavior, Thought, Experience, and Language*. New York, NY: Kluwer Academic/Plenum Publishers, 2000.

Cosmides, Leda, and John Tooby. "Origins of Domain Specificity: The Evolution of Functional Organization." *Mapping the Mind*, 1994, 85–116. https://doi.org/10.1017/cbo9780511752902.005.

Cottrell, Elizabeth C. "Prenatal Stress, Glucocorticoids and the Programming of Adult Disease." *Frontiers in Behavioral Neuroscience* 3 (September 7, 2009): 19. https://doi.org/10.3389/neuro.08.019.2009.

Courtois, Christine A. "Complex Trauma, Complex Reactions: Assessment and Treatment." *Psychotherapy: Theory, Research, Practice, Training* 41, no. 4 (2004): 412–25. https://doi.org/10.1037/0033-3204.41.4.412.

Craske, Michelle G., Allison M. Waters, R. Lindsey Bergman, Bruce Naliboff, Ottmar V. Lipp, Hideki Negoro, and Edward M. Ornitz. "Is Aversive Learning a Marker of Risk for Anxiety Disorders in Children?" *Behaviour Research and Therapy* 46, no. 8 (2008): 954–67. https://doi.org/10.1016/j.brat.2008.04.011.

Cunningham, Daniel John, and Victor Horsley. *Contribution to the Surface Anatomy of the Cerebral Hemispheres.* Dublin, 1892.

Daly, Martin, and Margo Wilson. *Homicide.* New York, NY: De Gruyter, 1988.

Damasio, Antonio R. *Descartes' Error: Emotion, Reason, and the Human Brain.* London: Penguin, 2005.

Danieli, Yael, and Stephen Suomi. "Psychobiology of Intergenerational Effects of Trauma: Evidence from Animal Studies." Essay. In *International Handbook of Multigenerational Legacies of Trauma*, 623–37. New York, NY: Springer, 2011.

Darwin, Charles. *On the Origin of Species by Means of Natural Selection, or the Preservation of Favoured Races in the Struggle for Life.* London: John Murray, 1859.

De Bellis, Michael D., and Abigail Zisk. "The Biological Effects of Childhood Trauma." *Child and Adolescent Psychiatric Clinics of North America* 23, no. 2 (February 16, 2014): 185–222. https://doi.org/10.1016/j.chc.2014.01.002.

DeBaun, Michael R., Emily L. Niemitz, D. Elizabeth McNeil, Sheri A. Brandenburg, Maxwell P. Lee, and Andrew P. Feinberg. "Epigenetic Alterations of H19 and LIT1 Distinguish Patients with Beckwith-Wiedemann Syndrome with Cancer and Birth Defects." *The American Journal of Human Genetics* 70, no. 3 (2002): 604–11. https://doi.org/10.1086/338934.

Dedovic, Katarina, Annie Duchesne, Julie Andrews, Veronika Engert, and Jens C. Pruessner. "The Brain and the Stress Axis: The Neural Correlates of Cortisol Regulation in Response to Stress." *NeuroImage* 47, no. 3 (September 4, 2009): 864–71. https://doi.org/10.1016/j.neuroimage.2009.05.074.

Dehaene, S., E. Spelkel, P. Pinel, R. Stanescu, and S. Tsivkin. "Sources of Mathematical Thinking: Behavioral and Brain-Imaging Evidence." *Science* 284, no. 5416 (1999): 970–74. https://doi.org/10.1126/science.284.5416.970.

Dehaene, Stanislas, and Laurent Cohen. "Cerebral Pathways for Calculation: Double Dissociation between Rote Verbal and Quantitative Knowledge of Arithmetic." *Cortex* 33, no. 2 (1997): 219–50. https://doi.org/10.1016/s0010-9452(08)70002-9.

Dennert, James Walter. "The Embryo Project Encyclopedia." Henry Herbert Goddard (1866–1957) | The Embryo Project Encyclopedia, May 6, 2021. https://embryo.asu.edu/pages/henry-herbert-goddard-1866-1957.

Diagnostic and Statistical Manual of Mental Disorders: DSM-5. Arlington, VA: American Psychiatric Association, 2017.

Diggs, George M. "Evolutionary Mismatch: Implications Far Beyond Diet and Exercise." *Journal of Evolution and Health* 2, no. 1 (2017). https://doi.org/10.15310/2334-3591.1057.

Dittrich, Luke. *Patient H.M. a Story of Memory, Madness and Family Secrets.* London: Vintage, 2017.

Dorra, Janina. "Noah Wurde Praktisch Ohne Gehirn Geboren - so Ergeht Es Ihm Heute." NetMoms.de, January 19, 2018. https://www.netmoms.de/nachri

chten/dieses-baby-wurde-praktisch-ohne-gehirn-geboren-so-ergeht-es-ih m-heute/?obref=outbrain-www-fol.

Duhl, David M., Harry Vrieling, Kimberly A. Miller, George L. Wolff, and Gregory S. Barsh. "Neomorphic Agouti Mutations in Obese Yellow Mice." *Nature Genetics* 8, no. 1 (1994): 59–65. https://doi.org/10.1038/ng0994-59.

Dully, Howard, and Charles Fleming. *My Lobotomy: a Memoir.* London: Vermilion, 2008.

Dunbar, R. I. "Coevolution of Neocortical Size, Group Size and Language in Humans." *Behavioral and Brain Sciences* 16, no. 4 (1993): 681–94. https://doi.org/10.1017/s0140525x00032325.

E., Martin, and P. Seligman. *Helplessness: on Depression, Development, and Death.* New York, NY: Freeman, 1975.

Eberstaller, Oscar. "Das Stirnhirn. Ein Beitrag Zur Anatomie Der Oberflache Des Grosshirns." *The American Journal of Psychology* 3, no. 3 (1890): 371. https://doi.org/10.2307/1411701.

Eichenbaum, H., A.P. Yonelinas, and C. Ranganath. "The Medial Temporal Lobe and Recognition Memory." *Annual Review of Neuroscience* 30, no. 1 (2007): 123–52. https://doi.org/10.1146/annurev.neuro.30.051606.094328.

Eichenbaum, Howard. "Memory on Time." *Trends in Cognitive Sciences* 17, no. 2 (2013): 81–88. https://doi.org/10.1016/j.tics.2012.12.007.

Eissler, K. R. "Notes on Problems of Technique in the Psychoanalytic Treatment of Adolescents." *The Psychoanalytic Study of the Child* 13, no. 1 (1958): 223–54. https://doi.org/10.1080/00797308.1958.11823181.

Elzinga, Bernet M, Christian G Schmahl, Eric Vermetten, Richard van Dyck, and J Douglas Bremner. "Higher Cortisol Levels Following Exposure to Traumatic Reminders in Abuse-Related PTSD." *Neuropsychopharmacology* 28, no. 9 (September 28, 2003): 1656–65. https://doi.org/10.1038/sj.npp.1300226.

"The Encyclopedia of DNA Elements (ENCODE)." Genome.gov, n.d. https://www.genome.gov/Funded-Programs-Projects/ENCODE-Project-ENCyclopedia-Of-DNA-Elements.

Engelhardt, H Tristram. "John Hughlings Jackson and the Mind-Body Relation." *Bulletin of the History of Medicine* 49, no. 2 (1975): 137–51. https://doi.org/https://www.jstor.org/stable/44450214.

Eriksson, Peter S., Ekaterina Perfilieva, Thomas Björk-Eriksson, Ann-Marie Alborn, Claes Nordborg, Daniel A. Peterson, and Fred H. Gage. "Neurogenesis in the Adult Human Hippocampus." *Nature Medicine* 4, no. 11 (1998): 1313–17. https://doi.org/10.1038/3305.

Fahrbach, Susan E., Joan I. Morrell, and Donald W. Pfaff. "Possible Role for Endogenous Oxytocin in Estrogen-Facilitated Maternal Behavior in Rats." *Neuroendocrinology* 40, no. 6 (June 1985): 526–32. https://doi.org/10.1159/000124125.

Fairchild, Graeme, Stephanie H. Van Goozen, Sarah J. Stollery, and Ian M. Goodyer. "Fear Conditioning and Affective Modulation of the Startle Reflex in Male Adolescents with Early-Onset or Adolescence-Onset Conduct Disorder and Healthy Control Subjects." *Biological Psychiatry* 63, no. 3 (2008): 279–85. https://doi.org/10.1016/j.biopsych.2007.06.019.

Feinstein, Justin S., Ralph Adolphs, Antonio Damasio, and Daniel Tranel. "The Human Amygdala and the Induction and Experience of Fear." *Current Biology* 21, no. 1 (January 11, 2011): 34–38. https://doi.org/10.1016/j.cub.2010.11. 042.

Fishbane, Mona Dekoven. "Wired to Connect: Neuroscience, Relationships, and Therapy." *Family Process* 46, no. 3 (2007): 395–412. https://doi.org/ 10.1111/j.1545-5300.2007.00219.x.

Flynn, James R. *Are We Getting Smarter?: Rising IQ in the Twenty-First Century.* Cambridge: Cambridge University Press, 2012.

Forder, Anthony. "Social Work and System Theory." *The British Journal of Social Work* 6, no. 1 (January 1, 1976): 23–42. https://doi.org/10.1093/oxford journals.bjsw.a056695.

Fox, L R. "Cannibalism in Natural Populations." *Annual Review of Ecology and Systematics* 6, no. 1 (1975): 87–106. https://doi.org/10.1146/annurev.es. 06.110175.000511.

Fraley, R. Chris, and Phillip R. Shaver. "Adult Romantic Attachment: Theoretical Developments, Emerging Controversies, and Unanswered Questions." *Review of General Psychology* 4, no. 2 (June 1, 2000): 132–54. https:// doi.org/10.1037/1089-2680.4.2.132.

Francis, D. D., F. C. Champagne, and M. J. Meaney. "Variations in Maternal Behaviour Are Associated with Differences in Oxytocin Receptor Levels in the Rat." *Journal of Neuroendocrinology* 12, no. 12 (December 12, 2001): 1145–48. https://doi.org/10.1046/j.1365-2826.2000.00599.x.

Fraser-Smith, A. "Male-Induced Pregnancy Termination in the Prairie Vole, Microtus Ochrogaster." *Science* 187, no. 4182 (March 28, 1975): 1211–13. https://doi.org/10.1126/science.1114340.

Fries, A. B., T. E. Ziegler, J. R. Kurian, S. Jacoris, and S. D. Pollak. "From The Cover: Early Experience in Humans Is Associated with Changes in Neuropeptides Critical for Regulating Social Behavior." *Proceedings of the National Academy of Sciences* 102, no. 47 (November 22, 2005): 17237–40. https://doi.org/10.1073/pnas.0504767102.

Fries, Alison B., and Seth D. Pollak. "Emotion Understanding in Postinstitutionalized Eastern European Children." *Development and Psychopathology* 16, no. 02 (2004): 355–69. https://doi.org/10.1017/s09545 79404044554.

Fries, Alison B., Elizabeth A. Shirtcliff, and Seth D. Pollak. "Neuroendocrine Dysregulation Following Early Social Deprivation in Children." *Developmental Psychobiology* 50, no. 6 (2008): 588–99. https://doi.org/ 10.1002/dev.20319.

Frodl, Thomas, Eva Maria Meisenzahl, Thomas Zetzsche, Christine Born, Markus Jäger, Constanze Groll, Ronald Bottlender, Gerda Leinsinger, and Hans-Jürgen Möller. "Larger Amygdala Volumes in First Depressive Episode as Compared to Recurrent Major Depression and Healthy Control Subjects." *Biological Psychiatry* 53, no. 4 (2003): 338–44. https://doi.org/10.1016/s0006-3223(02)01474-9.

Gailer, Juan Pablo, Ivan Calandra, Ellen Schulz-Kornas, and Thomas M. Kaiser. "Morphology Is Not Destiny: Discrepancy between Form, Function and

Dietary Adaptation in Bovid Cheek Teeth." *Journal of Mammalian Evolution* 23, no. 4 (2016): 369–83. https://doi.org/10.1007/s10914-016-9325-1.

Galaburda, Albert M., Joan Corsiglia, Glenn D. Rosen, and Gordon F. Sherman. "Planum Temporale Asymmetry, Reappraisal since Geschwind and Levitsky." *Neuropsychologia* 25, no. 6 (1987): 853–68. https://doi.org/10.1016/0028-3932(87)90091-1.

Garson, Helen S. *Oprah Winfrey: a Biography*. Santa Barbara, CA: Greenwood, 2011.

Gaylin, Willard M., Joel S. Meister, Robert C. Neville, and H G Vaughan. "Psychosurgery and Brain Stimulation in Historical Perspective." Essay. In *Operating on the Mind the Psychosurgery Conflict*, 24–72. New York: Basic Books, 1975.

Gazzaniga, Michael S. *Who's in Charge?: Free Will and the Science of the Brain*. London: Hachette, 2012.

"Gendercide Watch." IALS, February 8, 2019. https://ials.sas.ac.uk/eagle-i/gendercide-watch.

Geschwind, Daniel H., and Pasko Rakic. "Cortical Evolution: Judge the Brain by Its Cover." *Neuron* 80, no. 3 (October 30, 2013): 633–47. https://doi.org/10.1016/j.neuron.2013.10.045.

Gittelman, Rachel, and Stephen Sumoi. "Anxiety-like Disorders in Young Primates." Essay. In *Anxiety Disorders of Childhood*, 1–23. New York, NY: Guilford Press, 1986.

Goldberg, Susan, Roy Muir, John Kerr, and Stephen Suomi. "Influence of Bowlby's Attachment Theory on Research on Nonhuman Primate Biobehavioural Development." Essay. In *Attachment Theory: Social, Developmental, and Clinical Perspectives*, 185–201. Hillsdale, NJ: Routledge, 1995.

Gould, Jay, and Richard Lewontin. "The Spandrels of San Marco and the Panglossian Paradigm: a Critique of the Adaptationist Programme." *Proceedings of the Royal Society of London. Series B. Biological Sciences* 205, no. 1161 (1979): 581–98. https://doi.org/10.1098/rspb.1979.0086.

Gould, Stephen Jay, and Elisabeth S. Vrba. "Exaptation—a Missing Term in the Science of Form." *Paleobiology* 8, no. 1 (1982): 4–15. https://doi.org/10.1017/s0094837300004310.

Grassian, Stuart. "Psychiatric Effects of Solitary Confinement." *Washington University Journal of Law and Policy* 22 (January 2006): 325–83.

Grossmann, Karin, Klaus E. Grossmann, Elisabeth Fremmer-Bombik, Heinz Kindler, Hermann Scheuerer-Englisch, and and Peter Zimmermann. "The Uniqueness of the Child-Father Attachment Relationship: Fathers' Sensitive and Challenging Play as a Pivotal Variable in a 16-Year Longitudinal Study." *Social Development* 11, no. 3 (2002): 301–37. https://doi.org/10.1111/1467-9507.00202.

Grupe, Dan W., and Jack B. Nitschke. "Uncertainty and Anticipation in Anxiety: an Integrated Neurobiological and Psychological Perspective." *Nature Reviews Neuroscience* 14, no. 7 (June 20, 2013): 488–501. https://doi.org/10.1038/nrn3524.

Guileyardo, Joseph M., Joseph A. Prahlow, and Jeffrey J. Barnard. "Familial Filicide and Filicide Classification." *The American Journal of Forensic*

Medicine and Pathology 20, no. 3 (1999): 286–92. https://doi.org/10.1097/00000433-199909000-00014.

Hacking, Ian. *Mad Travelers: Reflections on the Reality of Transient Mental Illnesses.* Harvard, Il: Harvard Univ. Press, 2006.

Hacking, Jan. *The Social Construction of What.* Cambridge: Harvard University Press, 1999.

Hagerty, Barbara Bradley. "Can Your Genes Make You Murder?" NPR. NPR, July 1, 2010. https://www.npr.org/templates/story/story.php?storyId=128043329.

Haney, Craig. "Mental Health Issues in Long-Term Solitary and 'Supermax' Confinement." *Crime & Delinquency* 49, no. 1 (2003): 124–56. https://doi.org/10.1177/0011128702239239.

Hanson, J. L., M. K. Chung, B. B. Avants, E. A. Shirtcliff, J. C. Gee, R. J. Davidson, and S. D. Pollak. "Early Stress Is Associated with Alterations in the Orbitofrontal Cortex: A Tensor-Based Morphometry Investigation of Brain Structure and Behavioral Risk." *Journal of Neuroscience* 30, no. 22 (June 2, 2010): 7466–72. https://doi.org/10.1523/jneurosci.0859-10.2010.

Hanson, Jamie L., Brendon M. Nacewicz, Matthew J. Sutterer, Amelia A. Cayo, Stacey M. Schaefer, Karen D. Rudolph, Elizabeth A. Shirtcliff, Seth D. Pollak, and Richard J. Davidson. "Behavioral Problems After Early Life Stress: Contributions of the Hippocampus and Amygdala." *Biological Psychiatry* 77, no. 4 (February 15, 2015): 314–23. https://doi.org/10.1016/j.biopsych.2014.04.020.

Harada, Tokiko, Trixie Lipke, and Joan Y. Chiao. "Neural Basis of Extraordinary Empathy and Altruistic Motivation." *NeuroImage* 51, no. 4 (July 15, 2010): 1468–75. https://doi.org/10.1016/j.neuroimage.2010.03.025.

Harlow, H. F., and R. R. Zimmermann. "Affectional Response in the Infant Monkey: Orphaned Baby Monkeys Develop a Strong and Persistent Attachment to Inanimate Surrogate Mothers." *Science* 130, no. 3373 (August 21, 1959): 421–32. https://doi.org/10.1126/science.130.3373.421.

Hartley, C. A., B. Fischl, and E. A. Phelps. "Brain Structure Correlates of Individual Differences in the Acquisition and Inhibition of Conditioned Fear." *Cerebral Cortex* 21, no. 9 (September 24, 2011): 1954–62. https://doi.org/10.1093/cercor/bhq253.

Hartley, Mariette, and Anne Commire. *Breaking the Silence.* New York, NY: Penguin Books, 1991.

Hayes, Lindsay M. "Juvenile Suicide in Confinement—Findings from the First National Survey." *Suicide and Life-Threatening Behavior* 39, no. 4 (2009): 353–63. https://doi.org/10.1521/suli.2009.39.4.353.

Hayes, Lindsay M. "National Study of Jail Suicides: Seven Years Later." *Psychiatric Quarterly* 60, no. 1 (1989): 7–29. https://doi.org/10.1007/bf01064362.

Hebb, D. O. *The Organization of Behavior; a Neuropsychological Theory, (by) D.O. Hebb. Science Editions.* New York, NY: John Wiley and Sons, 1967.

Heijmans, B. T., E. W. Tobi, A. D. Stein, H. Putter, G. J. Blauw, E. S. Susser, P. E. Slagboom, and L. H. Lumey. "Persistent Epigenetic Differences Associated with Prenatal Exposure to Famine in Humans." *Proceedings of the National*

Academy of Sciences 105, no. 44 (2008): 17046–49. https://doi.org/10.1073/pnas.0806560105.

Heim, C, L J Young, D J Newport, T Mletzko, A H Miller, and C B Nemeroff. "Lower CSF Oxytocin Concentrations in Women with a History of Childhood Abuse." *Molecular Psychiatry* 14, no. 10 (October 28, 2008): 954–58. https://doi.org/10.1038/mp.2008.112.

Heit, Stacey, Michael J. Owens, Paul Plotsky, and Charles B. Nemeroff. "Corticotropin-Releasing Factor, Stress, and Depression." *The Neuroscientist* 3, no. 3 (1997): 186–94. https://doi.org/10.1177/107385849700300312.

Helige, Barbara, Michael John, Helge Schmucker, Gabriele Wörgötter, Marion Wisinger, and Hemma Mayrhofer. *Endbericht Der Kommission Wilhelminenberg.* Wien: Institut für Rechts- und Kriminalsoziologie, 2013.

Herrnstein, Richard J., and Charles A. Murray. *The Bell Curve: Intelligence and Class Structure in American Life.* New York, NY: Free Press, 1997.

Higley, J. Dee, M. Linnoila, S. J. Suomi, D. M. Taub, S. G. Lindell, J. Vickers, B. Fernald, S. B. Higley, and P. T. Mehlman. "Excessive Mortality in Young Free-Ranging Male Nonhuman Primates With Low Cerebrospinal Fluid 5-Hydroxyindoleacetic Acid Concentrations." *Archives of General Psychiatry* 53, no. 6 (June 5, 1996): 537–43. https://doi.org/10.1001/archpsyc.1996.0183 0060083011.

Higley, J., S. King, M. Hasert, M. Champoux, S. Suomi, and M. Linnoila. "Stability of Interindividual Differences in Serotonin Function and Its Relationship to Severe Aggression and Competent Social Behavior in Rhesus Macaque Females." *Neuropsychopharmacology* 14, no. 1 (January 14, 1996): 67–76. https://doi.org/10.1016/s0893-133x(96)80060-1.

Hobbes, Thomas, and William Molesworth. *The English Works of Thomas Hobbes of Malmesbury.* Aalen: Scientia, 1962.

Hobbes, Thomas. *De Homine.* Roma: Centro internazionale di studi umanistici, 1961.

Holtmaat, Anthony, Linda Wilbrecht, Graham W. Knott, Egbert Welker, and Karel Svoboda. "Experience-Dependent and Cell-Type-Specific Spine Growth in the Neocortex." *Nature* 441, no. 7096 (June 22, 2006): 979–83. https://doi.org/10.1038/nature04783.

Homburger, August. *Vorlesungen Über Psychopathologie Des Kindesalters.* Berlin Heidelberg: Springer-Verlag, 1926.

Hrdy, Sarah Blaffer. "Infanticide among Animals: A Review, Classification, and Examination of the Implications for the Reproductive Strategies of Females." *Ethology and Sociobiology* 1, no. 1 (1979): 13–40. https://doi.org/10.1016/0162-3095(79)90004-9.

Humphrey, T. "The Development of the Human Hippocampal Fissure." *Journal of Anatomy*, September 10, 1967, 655–76.

Humphries, Mark. "Why Does the Brain Have a Reward Prediction Error?" Medium. The Spike, December 30, 2019. https://medium.com/the-spike/why-does-the-brain-have-a-reward-prediction-error-6d52773bd9e7.

"Incredible Man-Machine Analogies." Top Design Magazine. TDM S.R.L, n.d. http://www.topdesignmag.com/incredible-man-machine-analogies/.

Jablensky, Assen. "The Diagnostic Concept of Schizophrenia: Its History, Evolution, and Future Prospects." Dialogues in clinical neuroscience. Les Laboratoires Servier, September 12, 2010. https://www.ncbi.nlm.nih.gov/pmc/articles/PMC3181977/.

Jacobs, Harriet. *Incidents in the Life of a Slave Girl: Seven Years Concealed.* Auckland, New Zealand: The Floating Press, 1861.

James, William. *The Principles of Psychology.* New York, NY: Henry Holt and Company, 1890.

Jedd, Kelly, Ruskin H. Hunt, Dante Cicchetti, Emily Hunt, Raquel A. Cowell, Fred A. Rogosch, Sheree L. Toth, and Kathleen M. Thomas. "Long-Term Consequences of Childhood Maltreatment: Altered Amygdala Functional Connectivity." *Development and Psychopathology* 27, no. 4pt2 (November 27, 2015): 1577–89. https://doi.org/10.1017/s0954579415000954.

Josselyn, S. A., and P. W. Frankland. "Infantile Amnesia: A Neurogenic Hypothesis." *Learning & Memory* 19, no. 9 (2012): 423–33. https://doi.org/10.1101/lm.021311.110.

Jovanovic, Tanja, and Kerry J. Ressler. "How the Neurocircuitry and Genetics of Fear Inhibition May Inform Our Understanding of PTSD." *American Journal of Psychiatry* 167, no. 6 (2010): 648–62. https://doi.org/10.1176/appi.ajp.2009.09071074.

Jovanovic, Tanja, and Seth Davin Norrholm. "Neural Mechanisms of Impaired Fear Inhibition in Posttraumatic Stress Disorder." *Frontiers in Behavioral Neuroscience* 5 (2011). https://doi.org/10.3389/fnbeh.2011.00044.

Ju, Harang, Costa M. Colbert, and William B. Levy. "Limited Synapse Overproduction Can Speed Development but Sometimes with Long-Term Energy and Discrimination Penalties." *PLOS Computational Biology* 13, no. 9 (2017). https://doi.org/10.1371/journal.pcbi.1005750.

Kühne, Ulrich. "Der Mensch Als Industriepalast." Telepolis, February 4, 2010. https://www.heise.de/tp/features/Der-Mensch-als-Industriepalast-3384323.html.

Kaba, Fatos, Andrea Lewis, Sarah Glowa-Kollisch, James Hadler, David Lee, Howard Alper, Daniel Selling, et al. "Solitary Confinement and Risk of Self-Harm Among Jail Inmates." *American Journal of Public Health* 104, no. 3 (March 2014): 442–47. https://doi.org/10.2105/ajph.2013.301742.

Kandel, Eric R. "The Molecular Biology of Memory: CAMP, PKA, CRE, CREB-1, CREB-2, and CPEB." *Molecular Brain* 5, no. 1 (2012): 14. https://doi.org/10.1186/1756-6606-5-14.

Karmiloff-Smith, Annette. "Ontogeny, Genetics, and Evolution: A Perspective from Developmental Cognitive Neuroscience." *Biological Theory* 1, no. 1 (2006): 44–51. https://doi.org/10.1162/biot.2006.1.1.44.

Karten, Yashmin J.G., Ana Olariu, and Heather A. Cameron. "Stress in Early Life Inhibits Neurogenesis in Adulthood." *Trends in Neurosciences* 28, no. 4 (April 2005): 171–72. https://doi.org/10.1016/j.tins.2005.01.009.

Keltner, Dacher. *The Power Paradox: How We Gain and Lose Influence.* New York, NY: Penguin Books, 2017.

Kendler, K. S., R. C. Kessler, E. E. Walters, C. MacLean, M. C. Neale, A. C. Heath, and L. J. Eaves. "Stressful Life Events, Genetic Liability, and Onset of an

Episode of Major Depression in Women." *American Journal of Psychiatry* 152, no. 6 (1995): 833–42. https://doi.org/10.1176/ajp.152.6.833.

Kendler, Kenneth S., Laura M. Karkowski, and Carol A. Prescott. "Causal Relationship Between Stressful Life Events and the Onset of Major Depression." *American Journal of Psychiatry* 156, no. 6 (1999): 837–41. https://doi.org/10.1176/ajp.156.6.837.

Kessler, Ronald C. "The Effects of Stressful Life Events on Depression." *Annual Review of Psychology* 48, no. 1 (1997): 191–214. https://doi.org/10.1146/annurev.psych.48.1.191.

Kim, Hackjin, Leah H. Somerville, Tom Johnstone, Andrew L. Alexander, and Paul J. Whalen. "Inverse Amygdala and Medial Prefrontal Cortex Responses to Surprised Faces." *NeuroReport* 14, no. 18 (December 19, 2003): 2317–22. https://doi.org/10.1097/00001756-200312190-00006.

Kim, Jeansok J., and David M. Diamond. "The Stressed Hippocampus, Synaptic Plasticity and Lost Memories." *Nature Reviews Neuroscience* 3, no. 6 (2002): 453–62. https://doi.org/10.1038/nrn849.

Kim, Jeansok J., Hongjoo J. Lee, Jung-Soo Han, and Mark G. Packard. "Amygdala Is Critical for Stress-Induced Modulation of Hippocampal Long-Term Potentiation and Learning." *The Journal of Neuroscience* 21, no. 14 (July 15, 2001): 5222–28. https://doi.org/10.1523/jneurosci.21-14-05222.2001.

Kimette. "The Duplessis Orphans." Pound Pup Legacy, July 29, 2008. http://poundpuplegacy.org/node/20814.

King, Robert Hillary. *From the Bottom of the Heap: the Autobiography of Black Panther Robert Hillary King.* Oakland, CA: PM, 2012.

Kirsch, Peter, Andreas Meyer-Lindenberg, Bernd Gallhofer, Venkata S Mattay, Harald Gruppe, Sarina Siddhanti, Stefanie Lis, Daniela Mier, Qiang Chen, and Christine Esslinger. "Oxytocin Modulates Neural Circuitry for Social Cognition and Fear in Humans." *Journal of Neuroscience* 25, no. 49 (December 7, 2005): 11489–93. https://doi.org/10.1523/jneurosci.3984-05.2005.

Knoth, Rolf, Ilyas Singec, Margarethe Ditter, Georgios Pantazis, Philipp Capetian, Ralf P. Meyer, Volker Horvat, Benedikt Volk, and Gerd Kempermann. "Murine Features of Neurogenesis in the Human Hippocampus across the Lifespan from 0 to 100 Years." *PLoS ONE* 5, no. 1 (January 29, 2010). https://doi.org/10.1371/journal.pone.0008809.

Knott, Graham W, Anthony Holtmaat, Linda Wilbrecht, Egbert Welker, and Karel Svoboda. "Spine Growth Precedes Synapse Formation in the Adult Neocortex in Vivo." *Nature Neuroscience* 9, no. 9 (September 9, 2006): 1117–24. https://doi.org/10.1038/nn1747.

Kohl, Marvin, and L. Williamson. "Infanticide: An Anthropological Analysis." Essay. In *Infanticide and the Value of Life*, 61–75. Buffalo, NY: Prometheus Books, 1978.

Koltko-Rivera, Mark E. "Rediscovering the Later Version of Maslow's Hierarchy of Needs: Self-Transcendence and Opportunities for Theory, Research, and Unification." *Review of General Psychology* 10, no. 4 (2006): 302–17. https://doi.org/10.1037/1089-2680.10.4.302.

Komorowski, R. W., J. R. Manns, and H. Eichenbaum. "Robust Conjunctive Item-Place Coding by Hippocampal Neurons Parallels Learning What

Happens Where." *Journal of Neuroscience* 29, no. 31 (2009): 9918–29. https://doi.org/10.1523/jneurosci.1378-09.2009.

Konnikova, Maria. "The Man Who Couldn t Speak and How He Revolutionized Psychology." Scientific American. Scientific American, February 8, 2013. https://blogs.scientificamerican.com/literally-psyched/the-man-who-couldnt-speakand-how-he-revolutionized-psychology/.

Kumsta, Robert, and Markus Heinrichs. "Oxytocin, Stress and Social Behavior: Neurogenetics of the Human Oxytocin System." *Current Opinion in Neurobiology* 23, no. 1 (2013): 11–16. https://doi.org/10.1016/j.conb.2012.09.004.

Kumsta, Robert, Elisabeth Hummel, Frances S. Chen, and Markus Heinrichs. "Epigenetic Regulation of the Oxytocin Receptor Gene: Implications for Behavioral Neuroscience." *Frontiers in Neuroscience* 7 (2013): 83. https://doi.org/10.3389/fnins.2013.00083.

Lack, D. "The Significance of Clutch-Size." *Ibis* 89, no. 2 (April 1947): 302–52. https://doi.org/10.1111/j.1474-919x.1947.tb04155.x.

Lack, David. *The Natural Regulation of Animal Numbers*. Oxford: Calrendon Press, 1954.

Laland, K N, F J Odling-Smee, and M W Feldman. "Evolutionary Consequences of Niche Construction and Their Implications for Ecology." Proceedings of the National Academy of Sciences of the United States of America. The National Academy of Sciences, August 31, 1999. https://www.ncbi.nlm.nih.gov/pmc/articles/PMC17873/.

Laland, K. N., J. Odling-Smee, and M. W. Feldman. "Cultural Niche Construction and Human Evolution." *Journal of Evolutionary Biology* 14, no. 1 (2001): 22–33. https://doi.org/10.1046/j.1420-9101.2001.00262.x.

Laland, Kevin N., John Odling-Smee, and Sean Myles. "How Culture Shaped the Human Genome: Bringing Genetics and the Human Sciences Together." *Nature Reviews Genetics* 11, no. 2 (February 2010): 137–48. https://doi.org/10.1038/nrg2734.

Laland, Kevin, Blake Matthews, and Marcus W. Feldman. "An Introduction to Niche Construction Theory." *Evolutionary Ecology* 30, no. 2 (2016): 191–202. https://doi.org/10.1007/s10682-016-9821-z.

Laskowitz, Daniel, Gerald Grant, J R Howlett, and M B Stein. "Post-Traumatic Stress Disorder: Relationship to Traumatic Brain Injury and Approach to Treatment." Essay. In *Translational Research in Traumatic Brain Injury*. Boca Raton: CRC Press, 2016.

Lau, Jennifer Y.F., Shmuel Lissek, Eric E. Nelson, Yoon Lee, Roxann Roberson-Nay, Kaitlin Poeth, Jessica Jenness, Monique Ernst, Christian Grillon, and Daniel S. Pine. "Fear Conditioning in Adolescents With Anxiety Disorders: Results From a Novel Experimental Paradigm." *Journal of the American Academy of Child & Adolescent Psychiatry* 47, no. 1 (2008): 94–102. https://doi.org/10.1097/chi.0b01e31815a5f01.

Lawrence, Cera R. "Hartsoeker's Homunculus Sketch from Essai De Dioptrique." The Embryo Project Encyclopedia, August 14, 2008. https://embryo.asu.edu/pages/hartsoekers-homunculus-sketch-essai-de-dioptrique.

LeDoux, Joseph E. *Anxious*. Richmond, VA: Oneworld, 2015.

LeDoux, Joseph E. "Emotion Circuits in the Brain." *Annual Review of Neuroscience* 23, no. 1 (2000): 155–84. https://doi.org/10.1146/annurev.ne uro.23.1.155.

LeDoux, Joseph E. *The Emotional Brain: the Mysterious Underpinnings of Emotional Life.* New York, NY: Simon & Schuster, 1996.

LeDoux, Joseph. "Emotional Memory." *Scholarpedia* 2, no. 7 (2007): 1806. https://doi.org/10.4249/scholarpedia.1806.

Leussis, Melanie P., and Susan L. Andersen. "Is Adolescence a Sensitive Period for Depression? Behavioral and Neuroanatomical Findings from a Social Stress Model." *Synapse* 62, no. 1 (January 6, 2008): 22–30. https://doi.org/ 10.1002/syn.20462.

Lewontin, Richard L. *Dialectical Biologist.* Cambridge, MA: Harvard University Press, 1985.

Lieberman, Daniel E. *The Story of the Human Body: Evolution, Health, and Disease.* New York, NY: Pantheon Books, 2013.

Lieberman, David. *The Story of the Human Body: Evolution, Health and Disease.* London: Penguin Books Ltd, 2013.

Lipatov, Mikhail, Melissa J. Brown, and Marcus W. Feldman. "The Influence of Social Niche on Cultural Niche Construction: Modelling Changes in Belief about Marriage Form in Taiwan." *Philosophical Transactions of the Royal Society B: Biological Sciences* 366, no. 1566 (March 27, 2011): 901–17. https:// doi.org/10.1098/rstb.2010.0303.

Lissek, Shmuel, and Brian van Meurs. "Learning Models of PTSD: Theoretical Accounts and Psychobiological Evidence." *International Journal of Psychophysiology* 98, no. 3 (2015): 594–605. https://doi.org/10.1016/j.ijpsy cho.2014.11.006.

Liu, D. "Maternal Care, Hippocampal Glucocorticoid Receptors, and Hypothalamic-Pituitary-Adrenal Responses to Stress." *Science* 277, no. 5332 (September 12, 1997): 1659–62. https://doi.org/10.1126/science.277.5332.1659.

Lloyd, Elisabeth, David Sloan Wilson, and Elliott Sober. "Evolutionary Mismatch And What To Do About It: A Basic Tutorial." *Evolutionary Applications*, September 25, 2011. https://evolution-institute.org/wp-content/uploads/2015/08/Mismatch-Sept-24-2011.pdf.

Locke, John. *An Abridgment of Mr. Locke's Essay Concerning Human Understanding.* Boston, MA: Cummings & Hilliard, 1822.

Lokhorst, Gert-Jan. "Descartes and the Pineal Gland." Stanford Encyclopedia of Philosophy. Stanford University, September 18, 2013. https://plato.stanford. edu/entries/pineal-gland/.

Low, Bobbi S. "Environmental Uncertainty and the Parental Strategies of Marsupials and Placentals." *The American Naturalist* 112, no. 983 (1978): 197–213. https://doi.org/10.1086/283260.

MacDonald, Christopher J., Kyle Q. Lepage, Uri T. Eden, and Howard Eichenbaum. "Hippocampal 'Time Cells' Bridge the Gap in Memory for Discontiguous Events." *Neuron* 71, no. 4 (2011): 737–49. https://doi.org/ 10.1016/j.neuron.2011.07.012.

MacDonald, Kevin B., Robert G. Burgess, and S. B. Hrdy. "On Why It Takes a Village: Cooperative Breeders, Infant Needs and the Future." Essay. In

Evolutionary Perspectives on Human Development, 167–89. Thousand Oaks, CA: Sage Publications, 2005.

MacMillan, Harriet L., Katholiki Georgiades, Eric K. Duku, Alison Shea, Meir Steiner, Anne Niec, Masako Tanaka, et al. "Cortisol Response to Stress in Female Youths Exposed to Childhood Maltreatment: Results of the Youth Mood Project." *Biological Psychiatry* 66, no. 1 (2009): 62–68. https://doi.org/10.1016/j.biopsych.2008.12.014.

Madden, John, and Stephen Suomi. "Primate Separation Models of Affective Disorders." Essay. In *Neurobiology of Learning, Emotion, and Affect,* 195–214. New York, NY: Raven Press, 1998.

Maestripieri, Dario, Stephen G. Lindell, Alejandro Ayala, Philip W. Gold, and J. Dee Higley. "Neurobiological Characteristics of Rhesus Macaque Abusive Mothers and Their Relation to Social and Maternal Behavior." *Neuroscience & Biobehavioral Reviews* 29, no. 1 (February 2005): 51–57. https://doi.org/10.1016/j.neubiorev.2004.05.004.

Maillard, Kevin Noble. "Rethinking Children as Property." Syracuse University, July 26, 2012. https://surface.syr.edu/lawpub/75/.

Mak, Gloria K., Michael C. Antle, Richard H. Dyck, and Samuel Weiss. "Bi-Parental Care Contributes to Sexually Dimorphic Neural Cell Genesis in the Adult Mammalian Brain." *PLoS ONE* 8, no. 5 (May 1, 2013). https://doi.org/10.1371/journal.pone.0062701.

Martin, Colin R., Vinood B. Patel, Victor R. Preedy, N. P. Daskalakis, M. A. McGill, A. Lehrner, and R. Yehuda. "Endocrine Aspects of PTSD: Hypothalamic-Pituitary-Adrenal (HPA) Axis and Beyond." Essay. In *Comprehensive Guide to Post-Traumatic Stress Disorders,* 245–06. Cham: Springer International Publishing, 2016.

Maslow, A. "A Theory of Human Motivation." *Psychological Review* 50, no. 4 (1943): 370–96. https://doi.org/10.1037/h0054346.

Maslow, A. H. "The Farther Reaches of Human Nature." *Journal of Transpersonal Psychology* 1 (1969): 1–9.

Maslow, Abraham Harold, and A. Maslow. "Psychological Data and Value Theory." Essay. In *New Knowledge in Human Values,* 119–36. New York, NY: Harper, 1959.

Mason, Mary Ann. *From Father's Property to Children's Rights: the History of Child Custody in the United States.* New York, NY: Columbia University Press, 1994.

McCarthy, Gerard, and Alan Taylor. "Avoidant/Ambivalent Attachment Style as a Mediator between Abusive Childhood Experiences and Adult Relationship Difficulties." *Journal of Child Psychology and Psychiatry* 40, no. 3 (1999): 465–77. https://doi.org/10.1111/1469-7610.00463.

McCarthy, Margaret M, Christelle H McDonald, Phillip J Brooks, and David Goldman. "An Anxiolytic Action of Oxytocin Is Enhanced by Estrogen in the Mouse." *Physiology & Behavior* 60, no. 5 (1996): 1209–15. https://doi.org/10.1016/s0031-9384(96)00212-0.

McCloskey, Michael, Alfonso Caramazza, and Annamaria Basili. "Cognitive Mechanisms in Number Processing and Calculation: Evidence from Dyscalculia." *Brain and Cognition* 4, no. 2 (1985): 171–96. https://doi.org/10.1016/0278-2626(85)90069-7.

McCloskey, Michael, Cynthia G. Wible, and Neal J. Cohen. "Is There a Special Flashbulb-Memory Mechanism?" *Journal of Experimental Psychology: General* 117, no. 2 (1988): 171–81. https://doi.org/10.1037/0096-3445.117.2.171.

McCormick, Cheryl M., Sergio M. Pellis, and Jodi L. Lukkes. "Impact of Adolescent Social Experiences on Behavior and Neural Circuits Implicated in Mental Illnesses." *Neuroscience & Biobehavioral Reviews* 76 (May 7, 2017): 280–300. https://doi.org/10.1016/j.neubiorev.2017.01.018.

McDermott, R., D. Tingley, J. Cowden, G. Frazzetto, and D. D. Johnson. "Monoamine Oxidase A Gene (MAOA) Predicts Behavioral Aggression Following Provocation." *Proceedings of the National Academy of Sciences* 106, no. 7 (2009): 2118–23. https://doi.org/10.1073/pnas.0808376106.

McEvoy, Chad Joseph. "A Consideration of Human Xenophobia and Ethnocentrism from a Sociobiological Perspective." *Human Rights Review* 3, no. 3 (April 2002): 39–49. https://doi.org/10.1007/s12142-002-1018-x.

McEwen, Bruce S, and Robert M Sapolsky. "Stress and Cognitive Function." *Current Opinion in Neurobiology* 5, no. 2 (1995): 205–16. https://doi.org/10.1016/0959-4388(95)80028-x.

McEwen, Bruce S. "Physiology and Neurobiology of Stress and Adaptation: Central Role of the Brain." *Physiological Reviews* 87, no. 3 (2007): 873–904. https://doi.org/10.1152/physrev.00041.2006.

McLaughlin, Katie A., Margaret A. Sheridan, and Charles A. Nelson. "Neglect as a Violation of Species-Expectant Experience: Neurodevelopmental Consequences." *Biological Psychiatry* 82, no. 7 (2017): 462–71. https://doi.org/10.1016/j.biopsych.2017.02.1096.

McLaughlin, Katie A., Margaret A. Sheridan, Sonia Alves, and Wendy Berry Mendes. "Child Maltreatment and Autonomic Nervous System Reactivity." *Psychosomatic Medicine* 76, no. 7 (2014): 538–46. https://doi.org/10.1097/psy.0000000000000098.

Meaney, Michael J. "Maternal Care, Gene Expression, and the Transmission of Individual Differences in Stress Reactivity Across Generations." *Annual Review of Neuroscience* 24, no. 1 (2001): 1161–92. https://doi.org/10.1146/annurev.neuro.24.1.1161.

Meek, Leslie R, Patricia L Dittel, Maureen C Sheehan, Jing Y Chan, and Sarah R Kjolhaug. "Effects of Stress during Pregnancy on Maternal Behavior in Mice." *Physiology & Behavior* 72, no. 4 (March 2001): 473–79. https://doi.org/10.1016/s0031-9384(00)00431-5.

Mehta, Mayank R., Michael C. Quirk, and Matthew A. Wilson. "Experience-Dependent Asymmetric Shape of Hippocampal Receptive Fields." *Neuron* 25, no. 3 (March 25, 2000): 707–15. https://doi.org/10.1016/s0896-6273(00)81072-7.

Meyer-Lindenberg, Andreas, Gregor Domes, Peter Kirsch, and Markus Heinrichs. "Oxytocin and Vasopressin in the Human Brain: Social Neuropeptides for Translational Medicine." *Nature Reviews Neuroscience* 12, no. 9 (August 19, 2011): 524–38. https://doi.org/10.1038/nrn3044.

Milad, M. R., B. T. Quinn, R. K. Pitman, S. P. Orr, B. Fischl, and S. L. Rauch. "Thickness of Ventromedial Prefrontal Cortex in Humans Is Correlated with

Extinction Memory." *Proceedings of the National Academy of Sciences* 102, no. 30 (July 15, 2005): 10706–11. https://doi.org/10.1073/pnas.0502441102.

Milad, Mohammed R., Roger K. Pitman, Cameron B. Ellis, Andrea L. Gold, Lisa M. Shin, Natasha B. Lasko, Mohamed A. Zeidan, Kathryn Handwerger, Scott P. Orr, and Scott L. Rauch. "Neurobiological Basis of Failure to Recall Extinction Memory in Posttraumatic Stress Disorder." *Biological Psychiatry* 66, no. 12 (2009): 1075–82. https://doi.org/10.1016/j.biopsych.2009.06.026.

Miller, Earl K., and Jonathan D. Cohen. "An Integrative Theory of Prefrontal Cortex Function." *Annual Review of Neuroscience* 24, no. 1 (2001): 167–202. https://doi.org/10.1146/annurev.neuro.24.1.167.

Miller, Earl K., David J. Freedman, and Jonathan D. Wallis. "The Prefrontal Cortex: Categories, Concepts and Cognition." *Philosophical Transactions of the Royal Society of London. Series B: Biological Sciences* 357, no. 1424 (August 29, 2002): 1123–36. https://doi.org/10.1098/rstb.2002.1099.

Miller, Gregory E., Edith Chen, and Eric S. Zhou. "If It Goes up, Must It Come down? Chronic Stress and the Hypothalamic-Pituitary-Adrenocortical Axis in Humans." *Psychological Bulletin* 133, no. 1 (2007): 25–45. https://doi.org/10.1037/0033-2909.133.1.25.

Ming, Guo-li, and Hongjun Song. "ADULT NEUROGENESIS IN THE MAMMALIAN CENTRAL NERVOUS SYSTEM." *Annual Review of Neuroscience* 28, no. 1 (2005): 223–50. https://doi.org/10.1146/annurev. neuro.28.051804.101459.

Mitchell, Denis, A.S Koleszar, and Robert A Scopatz. "Arousal and T-Maze Choice Behavior in Mice: A Convergent Paradigm for Neophobia Constructs and Optimal Arousal Theory." *Learning and Motivation* 15, no. 3 (August 1984): 287–301. https://doi.org/10.1016/0023-9690(84)90024-9.

Montessori, Maria. *The Absorbent Mind.* Adyar: The Theosophical Publishing House, 1949.

Moore, Sarah R., Lisa M. McEwen, Jill Quirt, Alex Morin, Sarah M. Mah, Ronald G. Barr, Thomas W. Boyce, and Michael S. Kobor. "Epigenetic Correlates of Neonatal Contact in Humans." *Development and Psychopathology* 29, no. 5 (December 22, 2017): 1517–38. https://doi.org/10.1017/s0954579417001213.

Moriceau, Stephanie, and Regina M Sullivan. "Maternal Presence Serves as a Switch between Learning Fear and Attraction in Infancy." *Nature Neuroscience* 9, no. 8 (August 9, 2006): 1004–6. https://doi.org/10.1038/nn1733.

Moriceau, Stephanie, and Regina M. Sullivan. "Unique Neural Circuitry for Neonatal Olfactory Learning." *Journal of Neuroscience* 24, no. 5 (February 4, 2004): 1182–89. https://doi.org/10.1523/jneurosci.4578-03.2004.

Nadel, Siegfried Frederick. *The Foundations of Social Anthropology.* New York, NY: Free Press, 1951.

Nauta, Walle J.H. "THE PROBLEM OF THE FRONTAL LOBE: A REINTERPRETATION." *Principles, Practices, and Positions in Neuropsychiatric Research,* 1972, 167–87. https://doi.org/10.1016/b978-0-08-017007-7.50007-0.

Navawongse, R., and H. Eichenbaum. "Distinct Pathways for Rule-Based Retrieval and Spatial Mapping of Memory Representations in Hippocampal Neurons." *Journal of Neuroscience* 33, no. 3 (2013): 1002–13. https://doi.org/10.1523/jneurosci.3891-12.2013.

Naya, Y., and W. A. Suzuki. "Integrating What and When Across the Primate Medial Temporal Lobe." *Science* 333, no. 6043 (2011): 773–76. https://doi.org/10.1126/science.1206773.

Neisser, Ulric. "Snapshots or Benchmarks." Essay. In *Memory Observed: Remembering in Natural Contexts*, 43–48. San Francisco, CA: W.H. Freeman and Co., 1982.

"Nelson Mandela Rules." United Nations. United Nations, n.d. https://www.un.org/en/events/mandeladay/mandela_rules.shtml.

Nelson, C. A., C. H. Zeanah, N. A. Fox, P. J. Marshall, A. T. Smyke, and D. Guthrie. "Cognitive Recovery in Socially Deprived Young Children: The Bucharest Early Intervention Project." *Science* 318, no. 5858 (December 21, 2007): 1937–40. https://doi.org/10.1126/science.1143921.

Nelson, Katherine. "Quantitative and Qualitative Research in Psychological Science." *Biological Theory* 10, no. 3 (2015): 263–72. https://doi.org/10.1007/s13752-015-0216-0.

Nelson, Katherine. "Sociocultural Theories of Memory Development." *The Wiley Handbook on the Development of Children's Memory*, 2013, 87–108. https://doi.org/10.1002/9781118597705.ch5.

"A New Look at The Duplessis Orphan Scandal." The McClaughry's Blog, March 18, 2020. https://mikemcclaughry.wordpress.com/virginias-research/a-new-look-at-the-duplessis-orphan-scandal/.

Noël, Françoise, and Amy Bennett. *The Dionne Quintuplets and Their Entourage: Student Papers on Media Representation.* North Bay, Ont.: Nipissing University, 2010.

Odling-Smee, F. John, Kevin N. Laland, and Marcus W. Feldman. *Niche Construction the Neglected Process in Evolution.* Princeton, N.J: Princeton University Press, 2003.

Opie, C., Q. D. Atkinson, R. I. Dunbar, and S. Shultz. "Male Infanticide Leads to Social Monogamy in Primates." *Proceedings of the National Academy of Sciences* 110, no. 33 (June 29, 2013): 13328–32. https://doi.org/10.1073/pnas.1307903110.

Ostlund, S. B., and B. W. Balleine. "Orbitofrontal Cortex Mediates Outcome Encoding in Pavlovian But Not Instrumental Conditioning." *Journal of Neuroscience* 27, no. 18 (May 2, 2007): 4819–25. https://doi.org/10.1523/jneurosci.5443-06.2007.

O'Brien, Michael J., and Kevin N. Laland. "Genes, Culture, and Agriculture." *Current Anthropology* 53, no. 4 (2012): 434–70. https://doi.org/10.1086/666585.

Paracelsus. *De Natura Rerum, IX Bücher. Ph. Theophrasti Von Hohenheim, Genant Paracelsi.* Straßburg: Jobin, 1584.

Park, Crystal L., Anica Pless Kaiser, Avron Spiro, Daniel W. King, and Lynda A. King. "Does Wartime Captivity Affect Late-Life Mental Health? A Study of Vietnam-Era Repatriated Prisoners of War." *Research in Human Development* 9, no. 3 (2012): 191–209. https://doi.org/10.1080/15427609.2012.705554.

Pastalkova, E., V. Itskov, A. Amarasingham, and G. Buzsaki. "Internally Generated Cell Assembly Sequences in the Rat Hippocampus." *Science* 321, no. 5894 (2008): 1322–27. https://doi.org/10.1126/science.1159775.

Paul, Maureen, Steve Lichtenberg, Lynn Borgatta, David A. Grimes, Stubblefield PhillipÂ G., Mitchell D. Creinin, and S. R. Goldstein. "Clinical Assessment and Ultrasound in Early Pregnancy." Essay. In *Management of Unintended and Abnormal Pregnancy: Comprehensive Abortion Care*. Somerset: Wiley, 2011.

Pawar, Komal Ramchandra. Transgenic Animals: A Short Review, February 28, 2017. https://www.biotecharticles.com/Biotech-Research-Article/Transgenic-Animals-A-Short-Review-3806.html.

Pechtel, Pia, and Diego A. Pizzagalli. "Effects of Early Life Stress on Cognitive and Affective Function: an Integrated Review of Human Literature." *Psychopharmacology* 214, no. 1 (March 24, 2010): 55–70. https://doi.org/10.1007/s00213-010-2009-2.

Pedersen, C. A., and A. J. Prange. "Induction of Maternal Behavior in Virgin Rats after Intracerebroventricular Administration of Oxytocin." *Proceedings of the National Academy of Sciences* 76, no. 12 (December 1979): 6661–65. https://doi.org/10.1073/pnas.76.12.6661.

Penfield, W, and J Evans. "The Frontal Lobe in Man: a Clinical Study of Maximum Removals." *Brain* 58 (March 1935): 115–33.

Penfield, Wilder, and Lamar Roberts. *Speech and Brain Mechanisms*. Princeton, NJ: Princeton University Pres, 1959.

Perreault, Charles. "The Pace of Cultural Evolution." *PLoS ONE* 7, no. 9 (2012). https://doi.org/10.1371/journal.pone.0045150.

Perry, J. Christopher, John J. Sigal, Sophie Boucher, and Nikolas Paré. "Seven Institutionalized Children and Their Adaptation in Late Adulthood: The Children of Duplessis (Les Enfants De Duplessis)." *Psychiatry: Interpersonal and Biological Processes* 69, no. 4 (2006): 283–301. https://doi.org/10.1521/psyc.2006.69.4.283.

Pine, Daniel S, Patricia Cohen, Jeffrey G Johnson, and Judith S Brook. "Adolescent Life Events as Predictors of Adult Depression." *Journal of Affective Disorders* 68, no. 1 (February 2002): 49–57. https://doi.org/10.1016/s0165-0327(00)00331-1.

Plotsky, Paul M., and Michael J. Meaney. "Early, Postnatal Experience Alters Hypothalamic Corticotropin-Releasing Factor (CRF) MRNA, Median Eminence CRF Content and Stress-Induced Release in Adult Rats." *Molecular Brain Research* 18, no. 3 (1993): 195–200. https://doi.org/10.1016/0169-328x(93)90189-v.

Power, Margaret. *The Egalitarians, Human and Chimpanzee: an Anthropological View of Social Organization*. Cambridge, UK: Cambridge University Press, 2005.

Preston, Alison R., and Howard Eichenbaum. "Interplay of Hippocampus and Prefrontal Cortex in Memory." *Current Biology* 23, no. 17 (2013). https://doi.org/10.1016/j.cub.2013.05.041.

Quartz, Steven R., and Terrence Joseph Sejnowski. *Liars, Lovers, and Heroes: What the New Brain Science Reveals about How We Become Who We Are*. New York, NY: Harper Collins, 2002.

Quiroga, R. Q., R. Mukamel, E. A. Isham, R. Malach, and I. Fried. "Human Single-Neuron Responses at the Threshold of Conscious Recognition." *Proceedings of the National Academy of Sciences* 105, no. 9 (2008): 3599–3604. https://doi.org/10.1073/pnas.0707043105.

Quiroga, R. Quian, G. Kreiman, C. Koch, and I. Fried. "Sparse but Not 'Grandmother-Cell' Coding in the Medial Temporal Lobe." *Trends in Cognitive Sciences* 12, no. 3 (2008): 87–91. https://doi.org/10.1016/j.tics. 2007.12.003.

Raineki, Charlis, Maya Opendak, Emma Sarro, Ashleigh Showler, Kevin Bui, Bruce S. McEwen, Donald A. Wilson, and Regina M. Sullivan. "During Infant Maltreatment, Stress Targets Hippocampus, but Stress with Mother Present Targets Amygdala and Social Behavior." *Proceedings of the National Academy of Sciences* 116, no. 45 (October 21, 2019): 22821–32. https://doi.org/10.1073/pnas.1907170116.

Raineki, Charlis, Stephanie Moriceau, and Regina M. Sullivan. "Developing a Neurobehavioral Animal Model of Infant Attachment to an Abusive Caregiver." *Biological Psychiatry* 67, no. 12 (2010): 1137–45. https://doi.org/10.1016/j.biopsych.2009.12.019.

Ramachandran, V. S. "Consciousness and Body Image: Lessons from Phantom Limbs, Capgras Syndrome and Pain Asymbolia." *Philosophical Transactions of the Royal Society of London. Series B: Biological Sciences* 353, no. 1377 (November 29, 1998): 1851–59. https://doi.org/10.1098/rstb.1998.0337.

Ramón y Cajal Santiago, Raoul M. May, Javier DeFelipe, and Edward G. Jones. *Cajal's Degeneration and Regeneration of the Nervous System.* New York, NY: Oxford University Press, 1928.

Ramón y Cajal, Santiago. "The Croonian Lecture.—La Fine Structure Des Centres Nerveux." *Proceedings of the Royal Society of London* 55, no. 331-335 (1894): 444–68. https://doi.org/10.1098/rspl.1894.0063.

Reblin, Maija, and Bert N Uchino. "Social and Emotional Support and Its Implication for Health." *Current Opinion in Psychiatry* 21, no. 2 (August 20, 2008): 201–5. https://doi.org/10.1097/yco.0b013e3282f3ad89.

Reid, James Martin. Excess mortality in the Glasgow conurbation: exploring the existence of a Glasgow effect, January 1, 1970. http://theses.gla.ac.uk/846/.

Reiss, John O. *Not by Design: Retiring Darwin's Watchmaker.* Berkeley, CA: University of California Press, 2011.

Reite, Martin, and Stephen Sumoi. "A History of Motherless Mother Monkeys Mothering at the University of Wisconsin Primate Laboratory." Essay. In *Child Abuse: the Nonhuman Primate Data,* 49–77. New York, NY: Liss, 1983.

"Report of the Special Rapporteur on Torture and Other Cruel, Inhuman or Degrading Treatment or Punishment." Refworld, March 5, 2015. https://www.refworld.org/docid/550824454.html.

Resnick, Phillip J. "Child Murder by Parents: A Psychiatric Review of Filicide." *American Journal of Psychiatry* 126, no. 3 (1969): 325–34. https://doi.org/10.1176/ajp.126.3.325.

Retzius, Gust. *Das Menschenhirn: Studien in Der Makroskopischen Morphologie.* Stockholm: Norstedt, 1896.

Richardson, Sarah. "A Violence in the Blood." Discover Magazine. Discover Magazine, October 15, 2019. https://www.discovermagazine.com/the-sciences/a-violence-in-the-blood.

Rogers, Deborah. "Inequality: Why Egalitarian Societies Died Out." New Scientist, July 25, 2012. https://www.newscientist.com/article/dn22071-inequality-why-egalitarian-societies-died-out/.

Rosack, Margaret Lynn. "The Dionne Quintuplets: Perinatal Care à La 1930s Style." *AWHONN Lifelines* 8, no. 4 (2004): 348–55. https://doi.org/10.1177/1091592304269634.

"Rosalie Rayner." Feminist Voices, n.d. https://feministvoices.com/profiles/rosalie-rayner.

Rosenblum, Leonard A, and Michael W Andrews. "Influences of Environmental Demand on Maternal Behavior and Infant Development." *Acta Paediatrica* 83, no. s397 (1994): 57–63. https://doi.org/10.1111/j.1651-2227.1994.tb13266.x.

Rosenzweig, Mark R. "Aspects of the Search for Neural Mechanisms of Memory." *Annual Review of Psychology* 47, no. 1 (1996): 1–32. https://doi.org/10.1146/annurev.psych.47.1.1.

Roth, Tania L., and Regina M. Sullivan. "Memory of Early Maltreatment: Neonatal Behavioral and Neural Correlates of Maternal Maltreatment within the Context of Classical Conditioning." *Biological Psychiatry* 57, no. 8 (April 15, 2005): 823–31. https://doi.org/10.1016/j.biopsych.2005.01.032.

Roy, Alec. "Hypothalamic-Pituitary-Adrenal Axis Function and Suicidal Behavior in Depression." *Biological Psychiatry* 32, no. 9 (1992): 812–16. https://doi.org/10.1016/0006-3223(92)90084-d.

Rubin, David C. *Autobiographical Memory*. Cambridge, MA: Cambridge University Press, 1988.

Rutten, Geert-Jan. *BROCA-WERNICKE DOCTRINE: a Historical and Clinical Perspective on Localization of Language Functions*. SPRINGER INTERNATIONAL PU, 2017.

Ryan, W. B. "Infanticide: Its Law, Prevalence, Prevention and History." *The British and Foreign Medico-Chirurgical Review* 31, no. 61 (January 31, 1863): 1–27.

Sapolsky, Robert M. *Behave: The Biology of Humans at Our Best and Worst*. London: Penguin Press, 2017.

Sapolsky, Robert M. *Stress, the Aging Brain, and the Mechanisms of Neuron Death*. Cambridge, MA: MIT Press, 1992.

Sapolsky, Robert M. *Why Zebras Don't Get Ulcers: the Acclaimed Guide to Stress, Stress-Related Diseases, and Coping*. New York, NY: Henry Holt and Co., 2004.

Sarason, Seymour Bernard, and John Doris. *Educational Handicap, Public Policy, and Social History: a Broadened Perspective on Mental Retardation*. New York, NY: Free Press, 1979.

Sarrazin, Thilo. *Deutschland Schafft Sich Ab Wie Wir Unser Land Aufs Spiel Setzen*. München: Deutsche Verlags-Anstalt, 2010.

Sarto-Jackson, Isabella. "Wired for Social Interaction: What an Interdisciplinary Approach From Neurobiology, Evolutionary Biology, and Social Education Work Can Teach Us About Psychological Truama." *International Journal of Child, Youth and Family Studies* 9, no. 1 (March 19, 2018): 9–30. https://doi.org/10.18357/ijcyfs91201818117.

Savage, Brandon M., Heidi L. Lujan, Raghavendar R. Thipparthi, and Stephen E. DiCarlo. "Humor, Laughter, Learning, and Health! A Brief Review."

Advances in Physiology Education 41, no. 3 (July 5, 2017): 341–47. https://doi.org/10.1152/advan.00030.2017.

Scarr, Sandra, and Kathleen McCartney. "How People Make Their Own Environments: A Theory of Genotype Environment Effects." *Child Development* 54, no. 2 (1983): 424–35. https://doi.org/10.1111/j.1467-8624.1983.tb03884.x.

Schoenfeld, Timothy J., and Elizabeth Gould. "Stress, Stress Hormones, and Adult Neurogenesis." *Experimental Neurology* 233, no. 1 (2012): 12–21. https://doi.org/10.1016/j.expneurol.2011.01.008.

Schultz, Wolfram. "Neuronal Reward and Decision Signals: From Theories to Data." *Physiological Reviews* 95, no. 3 (July 2015): 853–951. https://doi.org/10.1152/physrev.00023.2014.

Schwabe, L., and O. T. Wolf. "Stress Modulates the Engagement of Multiple Memory Systems in Classification Learning." *Journal of Neuroscience* 32 (2012): 11042–49.

Schwartz, Eric L., and John G Daugman. "Brain Metaphor and Brain Theory." Essay. In *Computational Neuroscience*, 9–18. Cambridge, MA: MIT Press, 1990.

Schwartz, Joseph. *Cassandra's Daughter: a History of Psychoanalysis.* Oxfordshire: Routledge, 2019.

Scott, Anna L., Marco Bortolato, Kevin Chen, and Jean C. Shih. "Novel Monoamine Oxidase A Knock out Mice with Human-like Spontaneous Mutation." *NeuroReport* 19, no. 7 (2008): 739–43. https://doi.org/10.1097/wnr.0b013e3282fd6e88.

Scoville, W. B. "The Limbic Lobe in Man." *Journal of Neurosurgery* 11, no. 1 (1954): 64–66. https://doi.org/10.3171/jns.1954.11.1.0064.

Seligman, M E. "Learned Helplessness." *Annual Review of Medicine* 23, no. 1 (1972): 407–12. https://doi.org/10.1146/annurev.me.23.020172.002203.

Senn, MJE. Unpublished transcript of an interview with Dr. John Bowlby in London, England. Other, 1977.

Seress, L, H Ábrahám, T Tornóczky, and Gy Kosztolányi. "Cell Formation in the Human Hippocampal Formation from Mid-Gestation to the Late Postnatal Period." *Neuroscience* 105, no. 4 (2001): 831–43. https://doi.org/10.1016/s0306-4522(01)00156-7.

Shalev, Arieh, Israel Liberzon, and Charles Marmar. "Post-Traumatic Stress Disorder." *New England Journal of Medicine* 376, no. 25 (2017): 2459–69. https://doi.org/10.1056/nejmra1612499.

Shapero, Benjamin G., Shimrit K. Black, Richard T. Liu, Joshua Klugman, Rachel E. Bender, Lyn Y. Abramson, and Lauren B. Alloy. "Stressful Life Events and Depression Symptoms: The Effect of Childhood Emotional Abuse on Stress Reactivity." *Journal of Clinical Psychology* 70, no. 3 (2013): 209–23. https://doi.org/10.1002/jclp.22011.

Shapleske, J, S.L Rossell, P.W.R Woodruff, and A.S David. "The Planum Temporale: a Systematic, Quantitative Review of Its Structural, Functional and Clinical Significance." *Brain Research Reviews* 29, no. 1 (1999): 26–49. https://doi.org/10.1016/s0165-0173(98)00047-2.

Sharing Responsibility: Women, Society and Abortion Worldwide. New York, NY: Alan Guttmacher Institute, 1999.

Sheline, Yvette I., Deanna M. Barch, Julie M. Donnelly, John M. Ollinger, Abraham Z. Snyder, and Mark A. Mintun. "Increased Amygdala Response to Masked Emotional Faces in Depressed Subjects Resolves with Antidepressant Treatment: an FMRI Study." *Biological Psychiatry* 50, no. 9 (2001): 651–58. https://doi.org/10.1016/s0006-3223(01)01263-x.

Shutts, David. *Lobotomy: Resort to the Knife*. New York, NY: Van Nostrand Reinhold, 1982.

Siegler, Robert S., and Katherine Nelson. "How Young Children Represent Knowledge of Their World in and out of Language." Essay. In *Children's Thinking: What Develops?: 13th Annual Carnegie Cognition Symposium*, 255–73. Hillsdale, NJ: Erlbaum, 1978.

Sierra, Amanda, Juan M. Encinas, and Mirjana Maletic-Savatic. "Adult Human Neurogenesis: From Microscopy to Magnetic Resonance Imaging." *Frontiers in Neuroscience* 5 (April 4, 2011): 47. https://doi.org/10.3389/fnins.2011.00047.

Slaughter of the Innocents: Child Abuse through the Ages and Today. New York, NY: Plenum Press, 1990.

Smith, C. N., and L. R. Squire. "Medial Temporal Lobe Activity during Retrieval of Semantic Memory Is Related to the Age of the Memory." *Journal of Neuroscience* 29, no. 4 (2009): 930–38. https://doi.org/10.1523/jneurosci.4545-08.2009.

Smyke, Anna T., Charles H. Zeanah, Nathan A. Fox, and Charles A. Nelson. "A New Model of Foster Care for Young Children: The Bucharest Early Intervention Project." *Child and Adolescent Psychiatric Clinics of North America* 18, no. 3 (July 18, 2009): 721–34. https://doi.org/10.1016/j.chc.2009.03.003.

Spironelli, Chiara, Federica Gradante, Giuseppe Gradante, and Alessandro Angrilli. "Cortisol and ACTH Plasma Levels in Maternal Filicides and Violent Psychiatric Women." *Journal of Psychiatric Research* 47, no. 5 (May 4, 2013): 622–27. https://doi.org/10.1016/j.jpsychires.2013.01.001.

Spitz, Rene A. "Hospitalism." *The Psychoanalytic Study of the Child* 1, no. 1 (1945): 53–74. https://doi.org/10.1080/00797308.1945.11823126.

Squire, Larry R., John T. Wixted, and Robert E. Clark. "Recognition Memory and the Medial Temporal Lobe: a New Perspective." *Nature Reviews Neuroscience* 8, no. 11 (2007): 872–83. https://doi.org/10.1038/nrn2154.

Stachenfeld, Kimberly L, Matthew M Botvinick, and Samuel J Gershman. "The Hippocampus as a Predictive Map." *Nature Neuroscience* 20, no. 11 (October 2, 2017): 1643–53. https://doi.org/10.1038/nn.4650.

Stedman, Thoma Lathrop. "A Practical Medical Dictionary." HathiTrust, n.d. https://babel.hathitrust.org/cgi/pt?id=ien.35558005332206&view=page&seq=286&q1=drapetomania.

Stein, M. B., C. Koverola, C. Hanna, M. G. Torchia, and B. McClarty. "Hippocampal Volume in Women Victimized by Childhood Sexual Abuse." *Psychological Medicine* 27, no. 4 (1997): 951–59. https://doi.org/10.1017/s0033291797005242.

Stettler, Dan D., Homare Yamahachi, Wu Li, Winfried Denk, and Charles D. Gilbert. "Axons and Synaptic Boutons Are Highly Dynamic in Adult Visual Cortex." *Neuron* 49, no. 6 (2006): 877–87. https://doi.org/10.1016/j.neuron.2006.02.018.

Stevens, Anthony, and John Price. *Evolutionary Psychiatry: a New Beginning.* London: Routledge, 2016.

Stokes, Peter E. "The Potential Role of Excessive Cortisol Induced by HPA Hyperfunction in the Pathogenesis of Depression." *European Neuropsychopharmacology* 5 (1995): 77–82. https://doi.org/10.1016/0924-977x(95)00039-r.

Stone, David J., John P. Walsh, Ronnie Sebro, Renna Stevens, Harry Pantazopolous, and Francine M. Benes. "Effects of Pre- and Postnatal Corticosterone Exposure on the Rat Hippocampal GABA System." *Hippocampus* 11, no. 5 (2001): 492–507. https://doi.org/10.1002/hipo.1066.

Stoppelbein, L., L. Greening, and Paula Fite. "The Role of Cortisol in PTSD among Women Exposed to a Trauma-Related Stressor." *Journal of Anxiety Disorders* 26, no. 2 (June 1, 2012): 352–58. https://doi.org/10.1016/j.janxdis.2011.12.004.

Sukel, Kayt. "Understanding the Effects of Solitary Confinement on the Brain." BrainFacts.org, March 21, 2019. https://www.brainfacts.org/neuroscience-in-society/law-economics-and-ethics/2019/understanding-the-effects-of-solitary-confinement-on-the-brain-032119.

Sullivan, Regina M., Margo Landers, Brian Yeaman, and Donald A. Wilson. "Good Memories of Bad Events in Infancy." *Nature* 407, no. 6800 (September 7, 2000): 38–39. https://doi.org/10.1038/35024156.

Sun, T. "Early Asymmetry of Gene Transcription in Embryonic Human Left and Right Cerebral Cortex." *Science* 308, no. 5729 (2005): 1794–98. https://doi.org/10.1126/science.1110324.

Suomi, S. J., and M. A. Novak. "Social Interaction in Nonhuman Primates: An Underlying Theme for Primate Research." *Laboratory Animal Science* 41 (1991): 308–14.

Suomi, Stephen J. "Gene-Environment Interactions and the Neurobiology of Social Conflict." *Annals of the New York Academy of Sciences* 1008, no. 1 (December 10, 2003): 132–39. https://doi.org/10.1196/annals.1301.014.

Suthana, Nanthia, and Itzhak Fried. "Percepts to Recollections: Insights from Single Neuron Recordings in the Human Brain." *Trends in Cognitive Sciences* 16, no. 8 (2012): 427–36. https://doi.org/10.1016/j.tics.2012.06.006.

Takahashi, Yuji K., Hannah M. Batchelor, Bing Liu, Akash Khanna, Marisela Morales, and Geoffrey Schoenbaum. "Dopamine Neurons Respond to Errors in the Prediction of Sensory Features of Expected Rewards." *Neuron* 95, no. 6 (September 13, 2017): 1395–1405. https://doi.org/10.1016/j.neuron.2017.08.025.

Teicher, M. H., C. M. Anderson, and A. Polcari. "Childhood Maltreatment Is Associated with Reduced Volume in the Hippocampal Subfields CA3, Dentate Gyrus, and Subiculum." *Proceedings of the National Academy of Sciences* 109, no. 9 (2012): E563–E572. https://doi.org/10.1073/pnas.1115396109.

Telzer, Eva H., Kathryn L. Humphreys, Mor Shapiro, and Nim Tottenham. "Amygdala Sensitivity to Race Is Not Present in Childhood but Emerges over Adolescence." *Journal of Cognitive Neuroscience* 25, no. 2 (April 17, 2013): 234–44. https://doi.org/10.1162/jocn_a_00311.

Temrin, Hans, Susanne Buchmayer, and Magnus Enquist. "Step–Parents and Infanticide: New Data Contradict Evolutionary Predictions." *Proceedings of the Royal Society of London. Series B: Biological Sciences* 267, no. 1446 (May 7, 2000): 943–45. https://doi.org/10.1098/rspb.2000.1094.

Thoma, Myriam V., Roberto La Marca, Rebecca Brönnimann, Linda Finkel, Ulrike Ehlert, and Urs M. Nater. "The Effect of Music on the Human Stress Response." *PLoS ONE* 8, no. 8 (August 5, 2013). https://doi.org/10.1371/journal.pone.0070156.

Tomasello, Michael. *The Cultural Origins of Human Cognition.* Cambridge, MA: Harvard University Press, 2003.

Tottenham, Nim, Todd A. Hare, Brian T. Quinn, Thomas W. McCarry, Marcella Nurse, Tara Gilhooly, Alexander Millner, et al. "Prolonged Institutional Rearing Is Associated with Atypically Large Amygdala Volume and Difficulties in Emotion Regulation." *Developmental Science* 13, no. 1 (January 1, 2010): 46–61. https://doi.org/10.1111/j.1467-7687.2009.00852.x.

Tottenham, Nim. "Human Amygdala Development in the Absence of Species-Expected Caregiving." *Developmental Psychobiology* 54, no. 6 (September 19, 2012): 598–611. https://doi.org/10.1002/dev.20531.

Tranel, D., and B. T. Hyman. "Neuropsychological Correlates of Bilateral Amygdala Damage." *Archives of Neurology* 47, no. 3 (March 1, 1990): 349–55. https://doi.org/10.1001/archneur.1990.00530030131029.

Trevathan, Wenda, Euclid O. Smith, and James J. McKenna. *Evolutionary Medicine.* New York, NY: Oxford University Press, 1999.

Trickett, Penelope K., Jennie G. Noll, Elizabeth J. Susman, Chad E. Shenk, and Frank W. Putnam. "Attenuation of Cortisol across Development for Victims of Sexual Abuse." *Development and Psychopathology* 22, no. 1 (2010): 165–75. https://doi.org/10.1017/s0954579409990332.

Troisi, A., F. R. D'Amato, S. Parmigiani, and F. Vom Saal. "Mechanisms of Primate Infant Abuse: the Maternal Anxiety Hypothesis." Essay. In *Infanticide and Parental Care*, 199–210. London: Harwood, 1994.

Troisi, Alfonso, Filippo Aureli, Paola Piovesan, and Francesca R. D'Amato. "Severity of Early Separation and Later Abusive Mothering in Monkeys: What Is the Pathogenic Threshold?" *Journal of Child Psychology and Psychiatry* 30, no. 2 (1989): 277–84. https://doi.org/10.1111/j.1469-7610.1989.tb00240.x.

Trott, Sarah von. *"Und Dann Bin Ich Abgehauen": Traumatische Familienerfahrungen Als Ursache für Straßenkarrieren Jugendlicher.* Marburg: Tectum-Verl, 2011.

Uchino, Bert N. "Social Support and Health: A Review of Physiological Processes Potentially Underlying Links to Disease Outcomes." *Journal of Behavioral Medicine* 29, no. 4 (June 7, 2006): 377–87. https://doi.org/10.1007/s10865-006-9056-5.

Uhlhaas, Peter J., and Wolf Singer. "Oscillations and Neuronal Dynamics in Schizophrenia: The Search for Basic Symptoms and Translational Opportunities." *Biological Psychiatry* 77, no. 12 (2015): 1001–9. https://doi.org/10.1016/j.biopsych.2014.11.019.

van der Horst, Frank C., and René van der Veer. "Loneliness in Infancy: Harry Harlow, John Bowlby and Issues of Separation." *Integrative Psychological and Behavioral Science* 42, no. 4 (December 13, 2008): 325–35. https://doi.org/10.1007/s12124-008-9071-x.

van der Kolk, Bessel. *The Body Keeps the Score: Brain, Mind, and Body in the Transformation of Trauma.* New York, NY: Viking, 2014.

Vittner, Dorothy, Jacqueline McGrath, JoAnn Robinson, Gretchen Lawhon, Regina Cusson, Leonard Eisenfeld, Stephen Walsh, Erin Young, and Xiaomei Cong. "Increase in Oxytocin From Skin-to-Skin Contact Enhances Development of Parent–Infant Relationship." *Biological Research For Nursing* 20, no. 1 (January 11, 2017): 54–62. https://doi.org/10.1177/1099800417735633.

Vreeburg, Sophie A., Witte J. Hoogendijk, Johannes van Pelt, Roel H. DeRijk, Jolanda C. Verhagen, Richard van Dyck, Johannes H. Smit, Frans G. Zitman, and Brenda W. Penninx. "Major Depressive Disorder and Hypothalamic-Pituitary-Adrenal Axis Activity." *Archives of General Psychiatry* 66, no. 6 (2009): 617–26. https://doi.org/10.1001/archgenpsychiatry.2009.50.

Vyas, Ajai, Rupshi Mitra, B. S. Shankaranarayana Rao, and Sumantra Chattarji. "Chronic Stress Induces Contrasting Patterns of Dendritic Remodeling in Hippocampal and Amygdaloid Neurons." *The Journal of Neuroscience* 22, no. 15 (August 1, 2002): 6810–18. https://doi.org/10.1523/jneurosci.22-15-06810.2002.

Waddington, C. H. *The Strategy of the Genes: A Discussion of Some Aspects of Theoretical Biology.* London: George Allen & Unwin, 1957.

Wade, Nicholas. "Genetic Code of Human Life Is Cracked by Scientists." The New York Times. The New York Times, June 22, 2000. https://partners.nytimes.com/library/national/science/062700sci-genome.html.

Walker, A Earl. "The Development of the Concept of Cerebral Localization in the Nineteenth Century." *Bulletin of the History of Medicine* 31, no. 2 (1957): 99–121.

Walsh, D., N. Bendel, R. Jones, and P. Hanlon. "It's Not 'Just Deprivation': Why Do Equally Deprived UK Cities Experience Different Health Outcomes?" *Public Health* 124, no. 9 (2010): 487–95. https://doi.org/10.1016/j.puhe.2010.02.006.

Waterland, Robert A., and Randy L. Jirtle. "Transposable Elements: Targets for Early Nutritional Effects on Epigenetic Gene Regulation." *Molecular and Cellular Biology* 23, no. 15 (2003): 5293–5300. https://doi.org/10.1128/mcb.23.15.5293-5300.2003.

Watson, J B. *Behaviorism.* New York, NY: People's Institute Pub. Co., 1925.

Watson, John Broadus, and Rosalie Rayner Watson. *Psychological Care of Infant and Child.* New York, NY: Arno Press & the New York times, 1972.

Weaver, Charles A. "Do You Need a 'Flash' to Form a Flashbulb Memory?" *Journal of Experimental Psychology: General* 122, no. 1 (1993): 39–46. https://doi.org/10.1037/0096-3445.122.1.39.

Weaver, I. C., M. J. Meaney, and M. Szyf. "Maternal Care Effects on the Hippocampal Transcriptome and Anxiety-Mediated Behaviors in the Offspring That Are Reversible in Adulthood." *Proceedings of the National Academy of Sciences* 103, no. 9 (2006): 3480–85. https://doi.org/10.1073/pnas.0507526103.

Werner, Emmy E., and Ruth S. Smith. *Vulnerable, but Invincible: a Longitudinal Study of Resilient Children and Youth.* New York, NY: Adams, Bannister, Cox, 1998.

West-Eberhard, Mary Jane. "Sexual Selection, Social Competition, and Speciation." *The Quarterly Review of Biology* 58, no. 2 (1983): 155–83. https://doi.org/10.1086/413215.

Wexler, Bruce E. *Brain and Culture Neurobiology, Ideology, and Social Change.* Cambridge, MA: The MIT Press, 2008.

Wexler, Bruce E. *Brain and Culture: Neurobiology, Ideology, and Social Change.* Cambridge, MA: MIT Press, 2008.

White, William A. "The Geographical Distribution of Insanity in the United States." *The Journal of Nervous and Mental Disease* 30, no. 5 (1903): 257–79. https://doi.org/10.1097/00005053-190305000-00001.

Wikenheiser, Andrew M., and Geoffrey Schoenbaum. "Over the River, through the Woods: Cognitive Maps in the Hippocampus and Orbitofrontal Cortex." *Nature Reviews Neuroscience* 17, no. 8 (August 3, 2016): 513–23. https://doi.org/10.1038/nrn.2016.56.

Wilbarger, Julia, Megan Gunnar, Mary Schneider, and Seth Pollak. "Sensory Processing in Internationally Adopted, Post-Institutionalized Children." *Journal of Child Psychology and Psychiatry* 51, no. 10 (October 25, 2010): 1105–14. https://doi.org/10.1111/j.1469-7610.2010.02255.x.

Williams, George C. "Pleiotropy, Natural Selection, and the Evolution of Senescence." *Evolution* 11, no. 4 (1957): 398–411. https://doi.org/10.2307/2406060.

Williams, Kipling D. *Ostracism: the Power of Silence.* New York, NY: Guilford, 2002.

Wilson, Robert C., Yuji K. Takahashi, Geoffrey Schoenbaum, and Yael Niv. "Orbitofrontal Cortex as a Cognitive Map of Task Space." *Neuron* 81, no. 2 (January 22, 2014): 267–79. https://doi.org/10.1016/j.neuron.2013.11.005.

Wimber, Maria, Arjen Alink, Ian Charest, Nikolaus Kriegeskorte, and Michael C Anderson. "Retrieval Induces Adaptive Forgetting of Competing Memories via Cortical Pattern Suppression." *Nature Neuroscience* 18, no. 4 (2015): 582–89. https://doi.org/10.1038/nn.3973.

Winnicott, D. W. "Loneliness in Infancy." *BMJ* 2, no. 4267 (1942): 465–65. https://doi.org/10.1136/bmj.2.4267.465-c.

Winocur, Gordon, and Morris Moscovitch. "Memory Transformation and Systems Consolidation." *Journal of the International Neuropsychological Society* 17, no. 05 (2011): 766–80. https://doi.org/10.1017/s1355617711000683.

Yehuda, R., B. Kahana, K. Binder-Brynes, S. M. Southwick, J. W. Mason, and E. L. Giller. "Low Urinary Cortisol Excretion in Holocaust Survivors with Posttraumatic Stress Disorder." *American Journal of Psychiatry* 152, no. 7 (1995): 982–86. https://doi.org/10.1176/ajp.152.7.982.

Yehuda, Rachel, and Jonathan Seckl. "Minireview: Stress-Related Psychiatric Disorders with Low Cortisol Levels: A Metabolic Hypothesis." *Endocrinology* 152, no. 12 (October 4, 2011): 4496–4503. https://doi.org/10.1210/en.2011-1218.

Index